LET'S TALK CRIMINAL JUSTICE

SECOND EDITION

PETER JOHNSTONE

University of North Texas

Cover image © Shutterstock, Inc.

Kendall Hunt
publishing company

www.kendallhunt.com
Send all inquiries to:
4050 Westmark Drive
Dubuque, IA 52004-1840

Copyright © 2013, 2014 by Peter Johnstone

ISBN 978-1-4652-4847-3

Kendall Hunt Publishing Company has the exclusive rights to reproduce this work, to prepare derivative works from this work, to publicly distribute this work, to publicly perform this work and to publicly display this work.

All rights reserved. No part of this publication may be reproduced, stored in a retrieval system, or transmitted, in any form or by any means, electronic, mechanical, photocopying, recording, or otherwise, without the prior written permission of the copyright owner.

Printed in the United States of America
10 9 8 7 6 5 4 3 2 1

CONTENTS

PREFACE vii

CHAPTER 1 A BRIEF HISTORY OF POLICING CRIME 1
  Hammurabi 2
  Biblical Law 3
  The Hittites 4
  Greek Law 4
  Roman Law 5
  Crime as a Legal Construct 7
  Criminal Justice in Early England 7
  The Influence of William I 9
  Spilling of Blood and Benefit of Clergy 11
  Circuit Courts and Juries 12
  Torture and Pressing 14
  Rogues, Vagabonds and Crime Waves: The Late Middle Ages 16
  Criminal Justice Arrives in America 20
  The Birth of Policing 23
  The Enlightenment Movement 24
  Contemporary Criminal Justice 25
  Summary 28
  Questions 29

CHAPTER 2 THE RAW MATERIALS OF CRIMINAL JUSTICE 35
  Introduction 35
  Counting Crime 36
  National Incident-Based Reporting System (NIBRS) 42
  National Crime Victimization Survey (NCVS) 44
  Do Official and Victimization Data Match? 48
  Criminal Justice Structure and the Magnitude of the Crime Problem 49
  Summary: Balancing Crime Control and Due Process 52
  Web Links 52
  Questions 54

CHAPTER 3 — ORIGINS OF MODERN POLICING ... 59
Early Days: Sheriffs, Constables and Night Watchmen ... 60
Introducing the Word 'Police' ... 63
Sir Robert Peel ... 65
French Detectives ... 67
Colonial Policing in America ... 67
Private Policing and the Emergence of State Troopers ... 69
City Policing in America ... 70
Summary ... 71
Questions ... 72

CHAPTER 4 — POLICE RECRUITMENT ... 85
Basic Requirements ... 87
Arlington, Texas ... 88
Four-Year Degree Requirement ... 88
Deputy Sheriffs ... 90
State Police ... 91
Summary ... 92
Questions ... 93

CHAPTER 5 — FEDERAL AGENCIES ... 97
The Big Four ... 98
Department of Homeland Security ... 99
ATF ... 99
The Secret Service ... 101
US Marshals ... 103
FBI Special Units ... 104
Summary ... 105
Questions ... 106

CHAPTER 6 — POLICE AND THE RULE OF LAW ... 113
Introduction ... 113
Warrants ... 114
The Exclusionary Rule ... 115
Exceptions to the Exclusionary Rule and Warrantless
    Searches and Seizures ... 117
Police Custody, Interrogation, and *Miranda* ... 121

The Costs of *Miranda?* 125
Summary: Balancing Crime Control and Due Process 129
Web Links 129
Questions 130

CHAPTER 7 BAIL, JAIL, AND THE PRETRIAL PERIOD 135
Introduction 135
Bail/Bond 137
Pretrial Services Today 142
Bond Decision-Making and Determinants of Release/Detention 145
The Effects of Pretrial Detention 148
Jails 151
Summary: Balancing Crime Control and Due Process 155
Web Links 156
Questions 157

CHAPTER 8 TRIALS, PLEA BARGAINS, AND THE PHILOSOPHY OF PUNISHMENT 163
Introduction 163
Court Appearances and Procedures 165
Plea-Bargaining 168
Trials and Trial Procedures 173
Motions 185
Summary: Balancing Crime Control and Due Process 188
Web Links 188
Questions 189

CHAPTER 9 PRISON 195
Introduction 195
History of American Prisons 197
Statistical Profile of Prisoners and Prisons 203
Prisoner Criminality 208
Summary: Balancing Crime Control and Due Process 212
Web Links 213
Questions 213

CHAPTER 10 — PROBATION AND PAROLE 219
Introduction 219
Probation 220
Qualification for Probation 221
Types of Probation 222
Origin of Parole 224
Executive Privilege 227
Summary 228
Questions 229

CHAPTER 11 — HOW THE SYSTEM WORKS 233
Introduction 233
The Police 234
Crime Scene Investigation 235
The Court 239
Summary 247

CHAPTER 12 — GLOBAL CRIMINAL JUSTICE 249
South Korea 251
The Kingdom of Saudi Arabia 253
Finland 255
Sweden 257
Norway 258
Canada 259
The RCMP 262
International Police Responses 263
Summary 267

ANSWERS TO CHAPTER QUESTIONS 271

GLOSSARY 275

PREFACE

The second edition of *Let's Talk Criminal Justice* reflects the growing trend towards making books available in electronic format. In addition, this edition provides students with study aids, a bank of questions drawn from the material in each chapter. These questions are a mixture of multiple choice and true and false and are representative of the range of questions that might be selected for use in weekly or chapter conclusion quizzes.

CHAPTER 1: A BRIEF HISTORY OF POLICING CRIME

To commit a crime implies that the offender has participated in an act that is more than offensive or damaging to one individual person, the victim; it is an action that offends all of a given society. Consequently over time various societies have recorded those actions that offend individual and group members and these transgressions have formed the basis of modern criminal legislation and legal systems. Initially there was little distinction between an act that was a private wrong and one that is now considered a public wrong. For many years in England a person who was the victim of theft was responsible for bringing the matter to court. In many ways this merged the idea of a private and a public action so much so that numerous offences were never prosecuted, as the victims were not in a position to pay for a trial and private arrangements were made to compensate the victim. Eventually it was recognized that the feelings of the community were important and that sophisticated society needed

a means of holding criminals accountable regardless of whether or not the aggrieved party could afford a prosecution. Once the distinction between a private action and a public action was firmly established the role of the state was clearly apparent as crimes were then, as they are today, prosecuted in the name of the crown or the state, e.g. R v Smith[1] or The People v Smith or Commonwealth v Smith.

Just as the responsibility for prosecuting a criminal act has now been transferred to the state so too are the

From *Crime and Policing Crime* by Peter Johnstone. Copyright © 2013 by Kendall Hunt Publishing Company. Reprinted by permission.

subsequent sentence and application of punishment. It is often considered that the defining difference between criminal law and all other forms of law is that criminal law attracts punishment. In some respects this is true but it is not an absolute. For example if you fail to pay your taxes and a penalty is imposed on you, is this a criminal fine or a civil fine?[2] Contemporary discussions often raise the question as to whether it is possible to apply the criminal law to corporate entities and if this is not possible then why have criminal laws that make certain corporate actions criminal. This discussion is beyond the scope of the introduction but it should be immediately clear that for all of the clarity the law seeks to bring to our lives the actions of real, corporate and virtual criminals will always challenge our understanding of what it is to act criminally. For this book, crimes are the actions are those that are brought by the state against an individual(s) in response to a formal disapproval of the individual's action or inaction, the remedy for which is punitive—a fine, imprisonment or loss of life. In addition crime also embraces a degree of seriousness that may be minimal—a misdemeanor or very serious, a felony. Also, crimes capture acts that may offend against the community's sense of morality.[3]

Crime is organic. No society has developed a code of conduct from its origin and retained that code without amendments and additions. The nature of human action is such that we alter our behavior over time and create new and often inventive ways of circumventing the law. In response, laws are modified and matured to accommodate societal development. For example, killing another human being may be murder or manslaughter; it may be done intentionally or through carelessness; by accident or due to the insane actions of a deranged person who does not know they are participating in the death of another person. The variables of human killing are almost infinite. The role of the criminal law is to establish those killings that are unacceptable to society at that point in time in the development of that society. As we all know crimes change over time and an action that was criminal in the past may not be a crime today and a criminal offense today may not have been such in the past.[4] That said, it is generally accepted that taking another person's life is an evil act that all societies find repugnant.

Hammurabi

The Code of Hammurabi was created about 2200 BC.[5] It comprises engravings on a piece of black diorite stone about seven feet tall. The codes show a significant level of sophistication in terms of the rights of individual citizens. They also give us a reference point for future trial methods. For example, code 132 states that "plunge into the sacred river" is used as a test of innocence or guilt. Three thousand years later, this method of testing innocence was widely used across Europe and the US as a means of establishing innocence and punishment as the 'ducking stool'. The contemporary manifestation, water boarding, is still in contentious use today.

The great achievement of Hammurabi was that in creating the Code he brought together customs and judicial decisions into one body of law. This is a model that has been copied numerous times since then by leaders such as Roman emperor Justinian and French emperor Napoleon Bonaparte. Vestiges of the code remained apparent for many centuries after the death of Hammurabi and can be seen in practice in mode of trial and punishment during the formation of the Common Law and the Civil Law with use of ordeals and purgation oaths and communal liability for criminal offences conducted within the borough.[6] Further evidence of incorporation of the code is found in early medieval distinctions between the value of the aristocracy and serfs in terms of compensation tariffs for the loss of life or limb.[7]

The influence of Hammurabi upon the biblical laws of Israel continues to be debated today. Sin is a concept that pervades biblical laws and is believed by some to be an inherent part of any discussion about crime. Contemporary Western thought frequently excludes sin from inclusion in a meaning of 'crime'. Yet it was the case that the two were intertwined because many rulers, such as Hammurabi, believed that they had a divine right to rule and therefore the laws promulgated were a fusion of god given authority alongside a secular means to control the people. Over time the religious aspects of a criminal action were transferred into a moral issue so that now we view offences such as pornography as a moral crime whereas in the past this would have been a crime against god and a sin. The transition from ecclesiastical dominance to secular is clearly seen in the evolution of the Common Law in England during the Middle and late Middle Ages.

Biblical Law

Biblical Israel's legal system is recorded in the books of Exodus, Leviticus, Numbers and Deuteronomy. The much quoted 'eye for an eye' concept embraced in the lex talionis[8] moved away from the hierarchical principles of Hammurabi in that all people were treated equally under God's law. Under Israelite law all crimes were an offense against god as recorded in the Mosaic codes drawn from the Ten Commandments delivered to Moses by god. Although the Ten Commandments placed an outright ban on all killing of humans, killing during war or unintentional killing was excusable. In cases of homicide though, the idea of compensation for a life, as apparent in the Hammurabic code, was not an option under Mosaic Law, and a culpable death required the shedding of the blood of the offender to redress the harm caused. In cases where an offender was not traced the village was liable to shed the blood of an animal in lieu of a culprit.[9] In instances where bloodletting was not a suitable means of redress, for example in cases of theft of property, the thief was fined to the amount of the value of the stolen items.

Under Mosaic and Hammurabic law, prosecutions were brought by individuals, and the instances of state intervention were largely restricted to matters involving warfare claims. The importance of the individual claim was expressed in the rule that in cases where the death penalty was imposed the individual bringing the prosecution was liable to throw the first stone at the condemned person.[10] Four centuries after Moses, King Solomon introduced a number of legal provisions that are still evident today. Two witnesses were required to find a defendant guilty. This was subsequently followed by the Romans, who required two eyewitnesses to a crime, and in lieu of two one witness and torture could be utilized, a theme that became commonplace in France during the establishment of the Civil Law system of that country. In cases where there were not two eyewitnesses the defendant could opt for taking an exculpatory oath. This too was an option across Europe for more than 1,500 years following Solomon. Punishment fashion also followed Solomon in cases of capital crimes where the offense was deemed particularly heinous the body of the offender was displayed at the scene of the crime to deter future offenders. This translated into use of the gibbet across Europe as well as the displaying of the head and limbs of offenders in strategic locations around the city in which the offence took place.

The Hittites

The Hittites established a kingdom around current northwest Syria and Lebanon between the 18th and 11th centuries, BC. They used cuneiform script, one of the earliest known forms of written expression. Due to the prevalence of recording the written word, the Hittites have provided us with a comprehensive body of treaties and legal documents. The society was highly stratified and legal rules reflected the status of slaves, serfs and an aristocracy. The Hittites were a conquering people and therefore many of the legal materials relate to the rights and status of conquered countries and their populations with specific references to 'vassals' and 'runaway slaves'. Apparently the death penalty was not favored and an elaborate system of monetary compensation existed rather than the later lex talionis direct physical exchange. In lieu of a death penalty, serious crimes were punished by way of slavery and hard labor.

Greek Law

The best-known legal system from ancient Greece is the Laws of Athens. However, for many centuries Greece was not one unified nation or legal system but a cluster of city-states separated by harsh terrain and mountains. Some states, such as Corinth, were run by a group of leaders, whereas one or even two kings ruled others, such as Sparta. Athens is the city that today we associate with the birthplace of democracy largely due to the leaders of Athens involving its citizens in some level of decision-making—the Assembly, the Council of 500 and the People's Court.

Before the classical period of Athenian history the laws resembled those of ancient Israel and protection by the state was considered the most valuable asset available to a citizen. Consequently, many criminal offences attracted the sentence of deprivation of citizenship, banishment. Homicide, intentional or negligent, was punishable with exile from both Athens and the surrounding countryside. Notwithstanding these provisions under Athenian law some homicides were justifiable such as execution of an exile that returned to the kingdom (also available as a sentence in England up until the 19th century for those who returned form America and Australia, having been banished). So too was killing in the height of passion or '*crime passionelle*' in instances where a male found his wife or his lover in the embrace of another.

Laws in relation to theft offences bear greater similarity to the Israelite legal system. Housebreaking at night was subject to the death penalty and also contained a 'Make my day' provision whereby the house owner was exempt from prosecution if he killed a nighttime intruder. Kidnapping was also a capital offense as were counterfeiting and forgery. The influence of the Greeks upon the Roman legal system is apparent in a number of ways. One lasting impact was the creation and use of magistrates. In ancient Greece, an aggrieved party was not solely responsible for bringing a prosecution. He could utilize the services of a city magistrate who would assist in making an arrest and completing forms and court paperwork. It was the magistrate who would hold a preliminary hearing and hold the matter over for trial.

The fundamental feature of a state official taking control of the prosecution remained a mainstay of the Civil Law system. It took the Common Law until the mid-18th century to catch up and bring cases on behalf of the state or the crown. Once the Athenian period became the dominant force in the legal system, oath taking became a normal feature of establishing guilt or innocence. This era also saw the introduction of juries; sometimes up to 50 citizens sat as a jury. Each member cast a secret ballot to determine guilt or innocence. If a defendant could muster more 'oath-helpers' than the prosecution, the case was dismissed. Under Athenian law, premeditated murder was always considered a special crime subject to trial before a specially appointed tribunal of magistrates, *archons,* and at a special location. Premeditated murder attracted the death penalty, which if delivered was conducted immediately after the trial. The mode of sentence varied from drinking hemlock to burial alive in an open pit to impalement.

Roman Law

The influence of Roman law remains apparent today, most notably within the Civil Law system of continental Europe and those countries influenced by the colonizing continental European nations. A significant association stems from the use of the term justice taken from Emperor Justinian who established a *Corpus Iuris Civilis* during the 6th century; 12 books of the Codex, 50 books of the Digest, the best-known Institutes and the Novels. However, it should be remembered that by this time the Western Roman empire had collapsed and therefore the influence of Justinian's collective works would have been largely limited to the eastern empire.

In the west marauding bands of Visigoths, Burgundians and Franks were establishing themselves as the dominant groups across a fragmented Europe. Nevertheless, the impact of Justinian did reach the West, initially in Italy and then throughout most of southern Europe. Prior to the collapse of the empire, Rome was the most influential and powerful democracy on earth. Its government, known as a republic, was based upon elected officials representing the people. The Greeks, via the Etruscans, naturally influenced the early era legal system, and from the basis of the Greek legal system the Romans refined and grew legislation to make many of the laws ultimately uniquely Roman.[11] Society was highly stratified and this was reflected in the legal system. Upper, protected classes consisted of those who should be treated differently by the laws than the commoners. For example, after the Christianization of Rome by Constantine, priests and clerics were included in the elite group of citizens who were not subject to the ordinary rules of trial. Those in holy orders, alongside senators, equestrians and teachers, were exempt from the requirement to appear before an ordinary tribunal when answering a criminal charge. This anomaly developed into the famous, and infamous, practice of Benefit of Clergy that allowed criminous clerks to avoid prosecution in secular courts for 1,200 years and to seek the protection and sanctity of the bishop.[12]

In Rome, criminal offenses were classified in terms of severity; intentional homicide attracted the death penalty, unintentional homicide resulted in the payment of financial compensation to the aggrieved family. Sex offenses were clearly articulated in the early years of the Roman Empire, but as the status of Rome grew and it paid greater attention to the rights of citizens, so too did the law expand to capture a range of criminality that exposed the victim to abuse of a slanderous as well as of a sexual nature. Compensation was utilized far more extensively in Rome than had been the case in the biblical or the Greek legal systems. Nevertheless, the victim could kill burglars caught in the act, in flagrante delicto, if the intruder was in the premises at nighttime or if he had a weapon with him during the daytime. Slaves caught breaking into a house, regardless of the time of day or whether they had a weapon or not were flogged and then thrown from the Tarpeian Rock.[13] In criminal cases, if the defendant was a Roman citizen, he was entitled to an appeal. Originally this was to a body of citizens. Julius Caesar changed this to be an appeal directly to the emperor. Intentional homicide, perjury, treason and accepting bribes (as a public official) were all subject to beheading. Arson was subject to death by burning.

Crime as a Legal Construct

As we look back at the early era of defining actions as criminal, certain common themes are apparent. All the civilizations discussed viewed the intentional killing of a human being as the most serious level of crime. All of the societies implemented sanctions against those found guilty of killing a superior, equal or inferior citizen, and all of the societies started to incorporate alternative sanctions so that the death penalty might be transmuted to exile or banishment for certain classes of society. Killing rulers and leaders was, and remains today, viewed as a particularly heinous crime, and punishments increased in savagery and calculated pain infliction over the next millennia as rulers continued to view themselves as divinely appointed.

That said, crime cannot be viewed as an absolute in any of the early era civilization groups as a number of factors come to bear upon why certain laws were implemented and what impact those laws had upon individual societies. Essentially, crime may be a legal construct, an act punishable by law, or it may be a social construct that is variable depending upon the norms or moral values of a given group of people. Reconciling these two positions is complex and features as a major factor in the division between the approaches the Common Law took when compared and contrasted with the Roman law based Civil Law.[14] As Professor of Roman Law Frank Wieacker commented, "The substantial reception of Justinian's law and the unrestricted dominance of the academically-trained jurist appointed by a sovereign did not, with certain exceptions, occur in the Anglo-American system."[15] Where we do see a resounding influence of Roman law upon the legal systems of continental Europe and the Common Law countries of England and Wales and, to some extent the United States, is in the development and impact of canon law.

Criminal Justice in Early England

Our discussion so far has centered upon the influence of major civilizations upon the meaning of crime and how various groups treated it. By the time that the Roman Empire had collapsed, the legal influence of the Babylonians, Hittites, Greeks and Romans was such that parts of their systems would inevitably feature in the new order that would be established across Europe over the next 1,000 years. England developed a system of dealing with crimes that became distinctly different from the rest of Europe. Today we call this English origin family of law, the Common Law.

In France, Germany and the rest of Europe there remained closer ties with the Roman tradition and the system of law that developed included more references to the Roman legal tradition than to the Common Law. We call the codified legal system of Europe the Civil Law.[16] Through colonization and empire building England, exported the Common Law and The Netherlands, Spain, Germany, Italy, Portugal and France exported the Civil Law. During the last 200 years, some countries that operated an individual legal system have modified their provision to now be a codified system that resembles that of the Civil Law. Examples of this include Russia and Japan.

During the Dark Ages Britain was subject to numerous attacks and invasions from tribes based in Germany, Denmark, Norway and France. Throughout Europe many regions were tribal and autonomous, with local kings and tribal leaders attempting to gain territory and power through the process of marauding warfare. Medieval Europe experienced a period of social chaos after the Romans and brute force was the ruling factor. The only unifying feature was the Christian church and to a lesser extent the Latin language.

It was from the church that literacy, learning and teaching emanated. But even the church could not withstand the forces of tribalism and it too became fragmented and regionalized with power being vested in local bishops rather than one unified Holy See. Out of this patchwork of social order the definition of a crime reverted back to customary interpretation with a spattering of Roman law. Crime control was based upon local group support and a system of compensation based upon the loss of a life or a limb became the standard way of resolving criminal actions. Expulsion from the protection of the group, as we saw in ancient Greece, was viewed as one of the more serious sanctions, as exile or banishment could literally mean death. Without the protection of the group and family members, an individual was unlikely to survive long in the forests and wastelands of Europe.

Although it may be hard to imagine today, what was occurring across Europe was the foundation of nation states and formal legal order. Because it was poorly recorded due to the lack of literacy, much of what was happening across Europe perpetuated the social order constructed in Babylonia, Israel, Syria, Athens and Rome. A new social order was definitely in the making, however, and with this came the need for a structured legal system that could effectively deal with criminal conduct. But the basis for the new order was a fusion of established societies, the burgeoning influence of the Christian church and a basic instinct for survival in the midst of rampaging tribes. Europe was experiencing a period of weak and unreliable government and it was individual rights and associated avenues for redress that would inevitably come to the forefront of the criminal justice system.

By the early Middle Ages, the European Frankish kingdom was divided into three regions that today represent the nations of France, Germany and Italy. Due to geography and a longer Roman presence in these countries, Roman law is more strongly evident in the burgeoning legal systems here than in Britain. Also, there was the beginning of a divide between matters that were viewed private and those that were public, particularly with respect to criminal matters.

The Roman system of appointing a magistrate to conduct criminal trials was to become a standard feature in Europe and the use of torture also became necessary and prevalent for six hundred years. With some degree of legal snobbery, the English will claim they do not mar their criminal justice system with the use of torture, but this is stretching the imagination rather far unless you are prepared to ignore one hundred years of torture inflicted by the Tudor monarchs. The reality is that the use of torture is not commonplace in the English Common Law and it is not a fundamental and necessary element in the laws of proof.

In Europe, reliance upon the Roman law means that two eyewitnesses are needed to secure a conviction. Without such, then one eyewitness and persuasive accompanying evidence may suffice. In lieu of any witnesses, then torture was used in Rome and was taken up across Europe as the only alternative means to gathering sufficient evidence to hold a trial. As history has demonstrated, the lack of correlation between inflicted pain upon a person and their propensity to tell any truth whatsoever has been tragically clear for decades. Nevertheless, the developing Civil Law system of Europe bound itself to a Roman tradition that had little alternative other than to torture suspects. It has been alleged that the Enlightenment was the driving force of change, but this too is open to debate as in reality there is a considerable body of evidence to the effect that it was the adoption of a jury system under the Civil Law that collapsed the reliance upon torture and not enlightened philosophical rhetoric in an age of plenty.

Alongside the development of a separate and different legal system in Europe and England ran the church and its laws. For much of the early period, the monarchs of Europe were heavily reliant upon the church to provide scribes and lawyers. Latin was the language of the aristocracy and the courts, and training in reading and writing was the preserve of the church. Church scholars were themselves influenced by the Romans, and over time a body of canon, ecclesiastical, law developed. By the late Middle Ages, canon law and Civil Law were the main subjects of study at the universities of Europe, and together the two laws formed a united body of laws applicable throughout continental Europe.

The difference between England and the rest of Europe, however, was that church law in England was increasingly becoming a separate body of law, whereas in continental Europe canon law informed the development of the main body of laws. Eventually the two families of law, Common and Civil, took on distinctly different features. Ultimately both were to influence the establishment of law in the US, particularly in some individual states, notably Louisiana and a number of the Southwestern states. California is an interesting example as it has a state civil code that is a fusion of Roman law influences and Common Law.

◆ The Influence of William I

With the arrival of the Frenchman William the Conqueror in England in 1066, a new legal landscape was about to unfurl. William subsumed existing English customs and vestiges of Romano-canon law into what was to become the Common Law. Revenge and blood feud had been commonplace in England for the four hundred years preceding William's arrival. A system of involuntary compensation existed for families that suffered loss of a family member through unlawful killing. In lieu of compensation, slavery by the culprit for the aggrieved family was an option. The Church also managed to retain a prominent position in the compensation stakes; stealing from the church was compensatible at a higher rate than stealing from a commoner, and if the life of a cleric was taken, this too was valued at a considerably higher rate than if you killed a serf or a peasant. Society was highly stratified generally, so that a serf's life was valued at two hundred shillings and a nobleman's at twelve hundred shillings. Under Alfred the Great an ear was valued at thirty shillings and a nose at sixty.[17] During the Dark Ages and the early Middle Ages there was no distinction between a felony and a misdemeanor.

William I was keen to see an end to blood feuds as they deprived the king of control over the legal system, and a loss of life was viewed as a waste when that person might be needed subsequently to serve the king in peacetime or in battle. From 668 onwards, English kings had made extensive use of clerics to assist in trials. Truth finding was achieved through use of the 'compurgatory oath'. If the exchange of oaths did not result in a conviction or acquittal then the parties moved onto the next stage, a cessation of the case or ordeal. Hot water was one common form of ordeal; water boarding, ducking, poisoning and hot oil and coals were approved variations. Remaining unscathed from the ordeal denoted God's intervention on behalf of the innocent. Death by drowning or visible injuries sustained from burning the flesh indicated guilt at which point if you could still live long enough you would be put to death for the crime. The ordeal process was lengthy and calculated and was run by the clergy. In time this was to prove fatally problematic as the church disassociated itself with trial procedures that resulted in the letting of blood. Well, let's agree that in principle they did. In reality if your crime was against the church, heresy for example, then the clerics became masters of torture and non-blood-letting means until proven guilty. At that point, when it was proven you were a heretic, you were excommunicated and handed over to the secular authorities for a positively bloody death.

William I introduced a new form of trial, the Trial by Battle.[18] He extended the use of the death penalty in lieu of numerous mutilation sentences, and he precluded bishops from significant involvement in secular trials. William also created a new court system, the king's court, the *curia regis,* at which, like his forefathers in France, he periodically sat personally to administer justice. It has been suggested that William also introduced the first office of 'Constable' to England. There existed at the time a *Comte de Stable* in France who was a person with responsibility for the king's stables. It has been mooted that this term was employed in England and derivated in use to become a person with responsibility for maintaining the king's peace.

William most definitely extended the role and function of the shire-reeve to become an integral part of the entire justice system. His influence upon this role is still apparent today in the sheriff in the US who can probably claim the longest direct heritage of any law enforcement official in the country. As stated, William did not create the office of shire-reeve, sheriff or *scirgerefa*;[19] this was achieved by King Ine, King of Wessex, 688–726. What William did was to seize the opportunity to use a well-known law enforcement official and extend his authority beyond that of tax collector and prison keeper to the chief law officer for a county. In his role as the chief law officer for a shire, the sheriff held the authority to demand assistance from local village people. The 'Hue and Cry'. Additionally, over time various appointments were made to provide a level of local rudimentary protective services that from modest beginnings as watchmen and vigilantes[20] would eventually form the basis of a professional police force for England.

Overall, however, one of the most decisive moves that William made during his reign was to divide church and state through the establishment of church courts with separate jurisdiction from the secular courts. His ability to dilute the power of the church in legal matters was a decisive blow to the power of the church—one, which in England, it never recovered from. This was most certainly not the case in continental Europe where the influence of the church upon the establishment of the new legal order was paramount.

Spilling of Blood and Benefit of Clergy

Perhaps stimulated by the separation of church and state started by William the Conqueror or perhaps due to a genuine concern over clerical involvement in legal procedures that resulted in the spilling of blood, by the 13th century the church removed itself entirely from any legal procedures that required a cleric to participate in bloodletting. Determined to reform clerical abuses that had grown over centuries, Pope Innocent III instigated the meeting of the Fourth Lateran Council in 1215, the result of which was to effectively abolish trial by ordeal from the legal calendar.

The quandary for England and the Continental European justice systems was how would they replace divine intervention, the ordeal, with a man-made judicial process?

Who would believe that a human judge could or should sit in judgment of another person when for the past thousand years everybody knew that it was God who sat in judgment?

For England, the substitution was to be the jury. It would henceforth be your peers that judged you, much in reality as they had done for hundreds of years anyway since the involvement of William the Conqueror.

For Europe, the question was more challenging, as they had no jury system. Continental Europe had relied upon the Roman law principles of proof, which might or might not include torture. For the time being at least, Europe had no choice; it would have to formalize the use of torture and embed it into its legal culture. Serious crimes, felonies, would be subject to torture and lesser offences, misdemeanors, would not.

In addition to taking the religious high ground on involvement in the secular legal system, Pope Innocent III also wanted to extend the privileges associated with being a member of the clergy, so that they were afforded even greater protection from the expanding arms of the secular law. Clearly, if the church was not to be a part of the secular law then its members, the clergy, should not be subject to this new legal system.

Benefit of Clergy had been established with the conversion of Emperor Constantine to Christianity when he pronounced that clerics should join the list of protected persons who should not be subject to the ordinary courts in Rome. This privileged status was reinforced periodically throughout the next millennium so that by the close of the 12th century the term cleric captured a broad range of males that were associated with working for the church. The problem was that many of these 'clergymen' were common criminals who managed to escape justice by claiming their privilege. Via the vehicle of the Fourth Lateran Council, Innocent III was able to disrupt the English legal system's reliance upon trials by battle, wager and ordeal, especially ordeal, by imposing an absolute ban upon clerical involvement. He was then able to reinforce this abstention by demanding, and achieving, greater protections for the clergy through the use of the clerical privilege, Benefit of Clergy.

By a circuitous route, however, the extension of Benefit of Clergy actually helped many more people than the large number of alleged 'criminal clerics'. Over time the process for establishing that a defendant in the secular courts was exempt from trial or sentence was by asking the 'cleric' to recite a psalm from the Bible. With the passage of time and familiarity of use the cited psalm was always the same, Psalm 51, the misère.[21] It now became possible for genuine members of the clergy to school commoners and non-clerics in the required Bible verse so that innocent citizens could avoid the increasingly draconian English criminal law by falsely claiming they were clerics.

It became so commonplace for non-clerics to claim 'their benefit' that judges routinely asked defendants if they wished to claim the privilege. After hundreds of years of use and abuse many serious crimes that attracted the death penalty were downscaled to be 'clergyable', so much so that eventually the requirement to cite the psalm was abolished and first time offenders were routinely branded rather than executed under the fiction that they were clerics. The high point of the system was when women too were allowed to claim they were clerics in an era when it was only men who could join the tonsured ranks of the cloth. Benefit of Clergy became such an established method of downgrading the severity of a crime and its sentence, that it was transported to America and existed in this country too until the mid-19th century.[22] Perhaps not unsurprisingly, Psalm 51 became known as the 'neck verse' as it saved the neck of the person reciting it.

◆ Circuit Courts and Juries

Henry II had taken the lead from his great-grandfather William the Conqueror and extended the role of the secular courts. He created the circuit court system, increased the role of royal judges and formalized the twelve-member jury system. He expanded the writ system as a means for the king to send sealed massages to the sheriffs, and he established a Court of Chancery that would evolve into the Court of Equity where inequities or wrongs could be addressed. Overall, Henry II can be credited with having an influential and positive role in the formation of the Common Law—a legal system that would become the most widely adopted in the world.

In continental Europe, the criminal justice system was developing in a different direction where judges played a more active role in gathering evidence and speaking to defendants and witnesses. Over time these inquisitorial methods became the established mode of trial across Europe. A dominant feature of the Inquisition was that defendants were required to answer questions put to them not by a lay accuser but by a judge. Under the English model, the judge was relegated to being an impartial referee who ensured that the parties adhered to the rules of play. In Europe, the judge conducted the game of play and asked whatever questions he liked. In Europe, the accuser was the church or the state. In England, it was, and remained for many years, an individual. In England, evidence was obtained through a process of questioning witnesses and confronting the accused. Under the English model, it was assumed that there are two sides to every story and these should be tested. Under the Civil Law model, one truth is attainable and that truth is achieved by drawing together all of the available evidence, and it may be necessary through torturing the accused to obtain that evidence.

It is easy to see why over time it became a mainstay of the legal system that the state prosecution would need to have a confession from the defendant as this proved guilt and was a part of the evidence. Consequently, obtaining a confession became an art form via the implementation of torture. Initially France was not disposed towards using torture in 'ordinary' procedures, that is, in cases that were not unusual or extraordinary. However, by the 14th century the use of torture had spread to most hearings and secret hearings, and trials were becoming normal practice. "By 1400, torture became a fundamental part of French criminal procedure and torture times were directly related to the time it took to recite a prayer such as the Pater Noster."[23] By the middle of the 16th century France had formalized use of the extraordinary method of investigation into a two-stage process, examination before one judge followed by a trial before an entire bench. There was no right to representation, nor was there in England either at this time, and the accused was not permitted to confront witnesses. Largely due to the manic belief that heresy was rampant throughout the civilized world and that Satan was manifest in numerous aberrations, criminal trials were not restricted to humans and the inquisitorial process prosecuted animals as well as humans during this time. Animals, however, were not subject to torture but they could, and did, receive the death sentence.

An important distinction between the Civil Law and the Common Law has now started to develop. Under the Civil Law the decisions of the judge are individual to each case. This is not viewed as potentially confrontational as a qualified judge runs each investigation and then another bench of judges hears the trial; there is no need to record the trial proceedings or outcomes as the process is run and administered by professional judges.

Under the Common Law the trial was essentially run by lay people who did not have expert legal training; therefore, it would be prudent to record the events and the outcome so that good practice may be replicated in the future and similar trials have similar outcomes. The very basis for the Common Law is that it is commonly applied to all participants and the decisions of trials; nowadays the decisions of judges are similar and will bind future cases.

The basis of the Civil Law is that professional judges do not need to bind each other or have an unerring need to follow previous cases in succession. These two distinctly different features will be commented upon further at a later stage in the discussion, but it is worth noting now that the lasting differences between the two legal systems and the manner in which criminal trials are conducted have a history that started in the fundamentally different approach taken towards who should bring forth a prosecution and whether or not the proceedings should be recorded or not.

As we shall subsequently establish, these differences have a significant impact upon the nature and form of police investigations into serious crime, particularly those offences that transcend national borders.

Torture and Pressing

With such a variety of sophisticated levels of redress being developed in Europe and England it would perhaps seem unnecessary to submit citizens to torture. However, as we have established, with the removal of supernatural ordeals a means was needed to test the veracity of the parties to an alleged crime.

In Europe, torture was employed wholesale. In England, this was not the case, generally due to the countrywide use of juries by 1240.

However, the English legislators did create their own dilemma. In the initial period of jury use defendants could elect to have the matter heard before the jury or accept banishment. Banishment was for life, but it had some advantages, principally, if you accepted banishment then you were not subject to forfeiture of your goods and property; they could be transferred to your family. The great advantage was that although you would no longer be with your family (you were dead), they would not be destitute. The applicable law of England at the time stated that if you elected to stand trial and lost, then the crown took all your belongings and your family would be turned out onto the streets. If you were never found guilty, the crown could not confiscate your chattels.

Once this legal lacuna was recognized, the legislators decided to apply pressure upon defendants to accept trial. The pressure was a literal pressure; it was torture by means of pressing your body with weights until you either gave in and accepted a trial or you died under the weights placed upon your chest.

This torture—as it clearly was torture—was known as *peine forte et dure,* a French term meaning pain, hard and long. During the process the accused was stripped naked and starved and then weights were then placed upon the defendant's chest, usually blocks of iron. The number of weights was then increased until such a time as the defendant elected to stand trial or the person responsible for conducting the pressing formed the opinion that the person must be innocent and released him. The third likely outcome was that the defendant died under the pressure or, if he was lucky, a few friends would bribe the gaoler and they would be allowed into the torture room and stand on the defendant's chest to help bring about an early death.

Now at this point you may be questioning how it is possible to differentiate the application of torture across Europe with the isolated instance of the application of torture in England, particularly as the English would claim, vehemently, that they did not engage in the practice of torture. This is how the argument was put. England did not use torture. Pressing was used as a means to compel the accused to accept a rational form of trial. It was not used a means to secure evidence or a confession. The continental reason for using torture was to force an accused to admit guilt and in doing so to eliminate the need for further evidential proof. These are very different positions to take, and the English were convinced that pressing was not torture. You may wish to decide for yourselves whether or not a contemporary interpretation would be quite so flexible.

By 1361, England had a comprehensive system of trial courts that were visited by travelling judges on a circuit. Sheriffs were charged with holding suspects in a secure gaol before arrival of the judge and his court entourage. The travelling court would then set up in a local hostelry or meeting rooms and the sheriff would present the 12 local men he had selected for jury service. The jurors were responsible for ensuring they were familiar with the case, and so the court proceeded to try the defendant. If the accused refused to stand trial, he was encouraged to do so by a visit to the press. This ordinarily resulted in the defendant then returning to court the same day, and so the trial would proceed. Juries were active participants in the trial process, and they were expected to ask questions of the defendant and witnesses. The case was brought by the aggrieved party, who would be required to attend court alongside witnesses; failure to do so resulted in the aggrieved and witnesses being liable to a fine.

The trial process was very quick by today's standards. Even murder trials only lasted minutes or perhaps an hour. All of the evidence for one trial was heard without recess and then the jury would proceed to hear other cases. It was rare for a jury to retire between cases, and ordinarily the jury would hear a number of cases in the morning, retire for lunch and come back in the afternoon to deliver verdicts. In capital cases, the defendant, who had no right of appeal, would be sentenced immediately and the death sentence would be carried out the following day unless it was a Sunday or a Holy Day.

Hanging was the most common form of execution. Burning was used in cases of heresy, sometimes for traitors and also for women who committed petty treasons, such as killing their husbands. Sometimes a special punishment would be created if the offence was particularly unpleasant or if it caught the attention of the monarch. Attempts on the life of the king or his favorites normally attracted a gruesome death: beheading for aristocrats and hanging then quartering for commoners. Drowning was not a sentence except in cases of murder committed on board a royal vessel; the accused and the deceased victim were tied together and tossed overboard to a united watery grave. Also, women who committed murder in the royal dockyard city of Portsmouth were subjected to drowning; they were tied to a stake on the shoreline and drowned on the incoming tide.

Rogues, Vagabonds and Crime Waves: The Late Middle Ages

During the Middle and Late Middle Ages, Europe underwent massive social changes and a number of natural disasters also, such as the Black Death in 1348. Many of these events caused the criminal law to respond. This was also a time of expansion and changing frontiers with monarchs and the church vying for power and land. Territories changed hands and citizens were repeatedly subject to new leaders and new laws. War has always been the cause of significant domestic social change, and crime tends to increase locally at the cessation of war when thousands of displaced military return from periods of employment to vagrancy and petty crime. Despite the tragedy of war, it is an effective way to produce wealth and employment, and certainly England suffered enormously with the problem of millions of men returning from years of active service in Europe to long-term unemployment at home. Inevitably many of these men resorted to crime as a source of income.

For more than 500 years the collective response to crime was principally one of increasing the severity of punishment as a perceived deterrent. The use of the death penalty increased exponentially across Europe throughout the late Middle Ages and the early modern era. Prisons were rarely used other than for debtors with the irony that once sentenced to prison the unfortunate criminal was then required to pay for this room and lodging inside the prison, thereby exacerbating the very problem that caused him to be in prison in the first place.

The first prison to open in England was located in Fleet Street, London. It is believed it was established during the twelfth century.[24] Over time the distinction between those who could work and those who would not work divided the prison system into poor houses and houses of detainment. Regardless of the distinction, neither establishment was a pleasant experience for the inmates, as was made clear to women and children upon arrival at the Bridewell, London; they were whipped on arrival day to remind them that they had arrived at a correctional institution.

In Europe, the concept of a dungeon was developing and the windowless pit in the ground or in the basement of a castle became synonymous with a secret and miserable place of confinement where many entered but few ever left alive.

Eventually all of these factors combined. The establishment of defined countries, the nervousness of the Catholic Church (the Protestant Reformation was looming), the frequency of wars, local natural disasters, the growth of a merchant class and a massive growth in the overall population were leading all of the countries of Europe towards the need for a modern and effective criminal justice system with established and effective police, courts and corrections provisions.

The monarchs and noble classes of Europe were rightly nervous; new crimes were occurring almost daily and social unrest was growing. The immediate solution was to increase the nature and scope of criminal offences; use the death penalty more frequently and across a broader range of crimes. This would suffice for a brief period of time. What was really needed was a complete overhaul of the systems that had grown organically in two separate directions, the Civil and Common Law. If change was not to be introduced by the legislators then the citizens of Europe would seize the responsibility themselves and force a new a legal order, one that reflected equality of treatment for all, regardless of rank or birth.

Henry VIII is viewed as one of the great characters of the British monarchy, in part due to his marrying so many times, but also because he was a strong and often rigid monarch who took his position as king to be an absolute endorsement of his ability to write and re-write the laws of England as he deemed necessary. Henry VIII was responsible for early editions of codification of English law when he caused the writing of the Act of Supremacy in 1534. In creating a new religion for England, the Church of England, Henry sent shockwaves through the established Catholic Church and its local representatives, the bishops and lower orders of the clergy. How could it now be possible to employ the protections of Benefit of Clergy to those in holy orders and to the unfortunates who hid behind the protections but were not clerics, if the church itself was now an alternative creation? In effect, who were the clergy? Alongside this confusion was a distinct nervousness created by Henry that caused him to extend the reaches of the laws of treason, and for the first time we see the introduction of torture as a means of extracting a confession being used under the Common Law. It was, however, always deemed to be an extraordinary measure and required the personal signature of the king or his direct representative, the Privy Council.

The Stuarts succeeded the Tudors and James I started his reign by repealing legislation that had provided the security of being able to plead the Benefit of Clergy for the offence of witchcraft. Under his reign numerous heresy trials were held and England embarked upon a mini-Inquisition type era with witches apparently appearing almost daily to create havoc and devilry across the nation; or at least that's how it seemed if the number of witches found to be operating were actually a reflection of anything other than a perverse male sexual repression or abject madness.²⁵ Guy Fawkes was also soon to make the king even more nervous with his attempt at blowing up of the king and his parliament.

Most importantly, it was the time that introduced the beginnings of constitutional government and direct involvement of the people in the affairs of the people. When attempting to trace the most influential events that shaped the development of the US and its legal system, we must consider this period in English history the most closely.

Much of the distinctiveness of the Common Law can be tracked back directly to this time of political and actual civil war. Revolution seemed inevitable as the kings of England embarked upon increasingly negative and exclusory legislative provisions. Parliament was *de facto* excluded from attempting to influence the development of the legal system and the great divide between the 'haves and have-nots' of society was soon to be resolved on the battlefield. Since the time of Henry VIII, the crown of England had used the criminal law as a weapon to force conformity with the practices of the new Church of England. Any degradation of the sacrament of the host was punishable by death and any personal religious belief that did not conform to state doctrine was a crime. Never before had the English criminal law seen such a fusion of religion and criminal actions; even the courts had a level of overlapping jurisdiction, and the strenuous efforts of William I and his immediate offspring to separate church and state had been undone over a period of a few years by Henry VIII.

The people of England were both confused and frightened. James I was mistrusted and his interference in the criminal law confirmed that he was intent upon seizing regal power at the expense of meaningful legislation that would improve the lives of the citizenry. James even weakened the protections of the jury trial as more and more authority went to the king's courts of the Star Chamber and the Privy Council. And yet, despite these flaws and his questionable personal life, James was mourned when he died and left the crown to Charles I.

Like his predecessor Charles believed in the Divine Right of Kings. He paid the ultimate price and was executed after a disastrous civil war forced him to be tried for treason. He was found guilty and beheaded on Tuesday 30 January 1649.²⁶ However, not all of Charles' reign was negative and he promulgated legal provisions that ensured citizens would not be subject to taxation without parliamentary approval and that there would be no imprisonment without cause. The demise of Charles I was followed by an unsuccessful interregnum period and then the British public invited Charles's son to assume the English throne. Charles II took the English crown on his 39th birthday, 29 May 1658, and so entered the period of the 'Merry Monarch', who undoubtedly had a penchant for the hedonistic life.²⁷ Charles II treated the interregnum period as though it had never happened, and after 1660 all legal documents were dated as though Charles II had immediately succeeded his father in 1649. During the interregnum period the custodian of the English republic was Oliver Cromwell. He was a dour and sober character, and soon after the regicide of Charles I legislation was enacted that made adultery and incest a capital offence. This pattern of sexual control legislation was a hallmark of the Cromwellian period and it is perhaps fortunate that Charles II abolished all of the interregnum legislative provisions as otherwise he would have been personally caught by many of them. During the Restoration Charles II reintroduced theatre and plays to London as well as relaxing the laws relating to the consumption of alcohol and gaming; he also legalized brothels for England.

Restoration of the monarchy heralded a new social order and a retrenchment from Puritanism generally. It was also a time of renewal due to the destruction of London in the Great Fire of 1666. The flamboyant, boisterous and expensive lifestyle of Charles II was inevitably going to put him at odds with parliament, as he had incurred massive debts throughout his lifetime and his detractors gained political mileage out of his failure to produce a legitimate heir even though he had fathered numerous bastards.

The legal environment that Charles II inherited was severe and oppressive. Judges held their office at the pleasure of the crown, which had the adverse effect of making them far too likely to find in favor of the crown; and juries were equally hampered in their objectivity, as they were subject to personal fines if they failed to return a verdict directed to them by the presiding judge. What this amounted to was a situation where the crown or parliament could adversely influence the outcome of a trial. Given that during this time many of the most contentious actions appearing before the courts involved the right to free speech, spoken and written, the law was in retrenchment rather than development. Alongside this curtailment of freedom of speech, religious prosecutions were alive and well under Charles II and his successor James II. At the forefront of this religious suppression was 'Hanging Judge Jeffreys' who took a personal delight in characterizing defendants as worthless plagues upon society. This was rather rich given that Jeffreys himself often came into court drunk and fined people for swearing when he himself swore openly in the courtroom. During his most notorious trial, of the Monmouth Rebels believed to be attempting a monarchical coup, he informed the defendants that a "not guilty plea would mean the death sentence."[28] One wonders what sentence a guilty plea would result in.

The reign of James II was unsuccessful. Somehow he managed to annoy the British public to the extent that they were prepared to have a second overthrow of the monarchy in the space of less than one hundred years. His involvement in the legislative process was often petty and self-serving and his attempt to substitute Catholicism, yet again, for the Church of England was a step too far. The matter of the monarch being the head of the Church of England needed to be settled once and for all. William of Orange and his Protestant wife Mary were invited to take the English throne and James II imposed abdication upon himself by fleeing to France. William and Mary jointly held the throne from 1689. They both imposed conditions upon acceptance and had a number of conditions imposed upon them. The authority of parliament was enshrined in legislation and royal authority was restricted through the process of royal prerogative. A Bill of Rights[29] was enacted, which significantly improved the human rights and conditions of life for all British subjects. The Bill of Rights also established religious tolerance throughout the realm so that finally the jostling for religious supremacy started on the path to becoming a moment of history—well, almost. The Bill did, however, retain the provision that Roman Catholics were to be excluded from political life. Importantly, the Bill of Rights also prevented the monarch from holding a standing army and it guaranteed all Protestants the right to bear arms. Debates in parliament were now afforded exemptions so that freedom of political speech was no longer subject to criminal sanctions. Also under the criminal section it was now illegal to impose arbitrary and excessive fines or make excessive demands for bail sureties. Cruel punishments were also prohibited and blanket immunity from prosecution for the king and queen was restricted so that they were, and would always be, answerable for certain criminal actions. Importantly, judges were to be appointed and remain in office on the basis of ability and good standing and not at the pleasure of the king. In treason cases, the defendants were now entitled to know the content of the indictment and they would be assigned legal counsel to assist them in the preparation of their defense and at trial. Evidentiary laws were also improved and two witnesses were required in all treason cases. This could be waived if a confession, without violence, was freely given by the accused. What is often considered a fundamental part of the Common Law, the right to silence, more accurately the right not to self-incriminate, was also now enshrined in the English legal system under the Bill of Rights.

Part of the period of sovereignty of William and Mary coincided with that of Louis XIV in France, 1643–1715. Louis was active in bringing about legislative reform and modernization of the criminal law. On March 15, 1667, he authorized the appointment of the first Lieutenant of Police for Paris. To a student of the Common Law, this police force would not resemble contemporary policing, or at least only in part, as the sphere of responsibilities assigned to the Paris police was extensive and captured a number of activities normally associated with alternative occupations. In addition to arresting thieves and burglars, the Lieutenant was to manage a force required to: control begging, issue licenses for markets, wine shops and butchers; ensure adherence to the rules of no citizen eating meat on a Friday (France was a resolutely Catholic country); and have oversight of the public drainage system, the sewers and the jails. It was also the responsibility of the police to light and extinguish the street lamps of Paris, a feature that was believed, rightly so, to deter crime. It took London another 150 years to recognize the importance of environmental crime prevention. It also took England another 150 years to establish a permanent police presence in its capital city, London.

◆ Criminal Justice Arrives in America

The 16th and 17th centuries were periods of monumental legislative change in England and across Europe. They were also a time of global expansion and the establishment of permanent, often disputed, settlements around the world. In America, the

British and French both sought to gain control and ownership of the new world; and for many years the burgeoning legal system was subject to influences from the old world, as well as to local interpretation and application. In the Southern colonies, a spirit of entrepreneurship pervaded. In the more religious communities of the north, biblical law was the mainstay of the new legal order. Perhaps obviously, the new world inhabitants brought with them practices and customs from the countries they were leaving behind.

A complex fusion of contemporary European laws and rights and customs that resembled those from feudal England was put into use.

Benefit of Clergy travelled with the colonists and came into use almost immediately. Why? Because the vast majority of permanent residents in the new world's Southern states had been transported to America as slaves to serve a minimum seven-year sentence in lieu of the death penalty. It was Benefit of Clergy that had spared them the hangman's noose, and so virtually all of the new workforce had some direct experience of the mitigatory plea and were comfortable subsuming it into the American legal culture.

The adoption of the feudal protection system of 'Hue and Cry', and appointing local watchmen to secure the perimeter of the village at night, was also a practical solution to security in a land where individual and remote villages were commonplace and vulnerable.

It followed that those who transgressed the village laws would be subject to feudal, village style, sanctions, in particular banishment from the village, which in the remote and dangerous new world would effectively be a death sentence anyway.

Over time, English criminal law became more useful to the colonies and it was subsumed in entirety in some states such as Virginia. This is apparent in the law pertaining to treason where in keeping with the English statute a convicted treasonist was stretched on a rack until his back was broken, then disemboweled while still alive, hanged until dead and then exhibited around the perimeter of the village to warn potential future transgressors.

Eventually though, it was recognized that depleting the workforce of labor was not viable and many death sentences were commuted to extended periods of slavery. Public humiliation and denouncement by the community were also a carry-over from England and the stocks and pillory found full employment in northern and southern states.

Women, in common with England and continental Europe, always received special treatment in law—treatment that invariably involved humiliation and had sexual connotations. If a wife was too liberal with her speech, she was placed in a device that literally held her tongue in place, making conversation impossible. The device, a Bride's Scold, was a direct implant from England and Scotland where it had been favored as a humiliation tool for centuries. The 'ducking stool' was also reserved for women.

Religious intolerance ran alongside sexual intolerance in the Northern states and homosexuality attracted the death penalty for centuries. It had been outlawed in England by specific statute in 1533 whereby it was a capital felony to "commit the detestable and abominable vice of buggery with mankind or beast," and this provision remained largely unchanged in English law until 1861. The new world colonies readily accepted these provisions intact.

The Southern states adopted the English model of county courts where the majority of criminal cases were tried. Capital cases were tried before the superior, general courts. The Northern states present a sharp contrast to the 'business focused' South. Early settlers were attempting to escape religious suppression and the church featured in the lives of all citizens. The Quakers were absolutely opposed to the death penalty. Other English dissenters also incorporated religious orthodoxy into their legal frameworks so that religious compliance, regardless of the flavor of religion concerned, became the dominant feature in the application of the law. Leaving behind a history of religious confusion and multiple changes in required religious practice, the Northern new world colonists sought to achieve a level of equity alongside adherence to biblical principles.

In time, particularly after the American Revolution, the Common Law was dressed into a modified English format to suit the social and political climate of the US. It may seem curious that a new nation so intent upon breaking away from the restrictions and oppression of Europe would embrace with such vigor the familiar legal system of England, and yet the US had so integrated the customs of the English law before the Revolution that it was impossible for it to forge ahead without reliance upon the now established ways.

Even those who may have wanted to reject the English law found it impossible to ignore the recent and applicable English legal system. Within 50 years of the Revolution, America produced its own version of Blackstone, *Commentaries on American Law* by James Kent. He quoted, "We live in the midst of the Common Law, we inhale it at every breath, imbibe it at every pore; we meet it when we wake, and when we lie down to sleep, when we travel and when we stay at home; it is interwoven with the very idiom that we speak; and we cannot learn another system of laws, without learning, at the same time, another language."[30]

Amazingly, or at least so it appeared to users of the Civil Law, this system that the US was familiar with and embraced for its future was not written down; it was so common, so well known, so understood, that it was not necessary for the English to ever write it down in a codified fashion and presumably it would also not be necessary for the US do so either.

It was William Penn, an Englishman who came to the US, who famously challenged the familiarity of the Common Law and was rebuked for his audacity in doing so. In 1670, William Penn stood trial for illegally preaching in the streets of London. The jury ardently refused to find him guilty and they were held in contempt of court without food or water until they returned the verdict the judge requested. They refused twice and set a precedent for judges no longer to have the power to control juries. William Penn himself was confused about the actual charge he was answering to and asked the trial judge for clarity on what was the Common Law. An enraged judge retorted, "You are an impertinent fellow, will you teach the court what it is? It is *lex non scripta* that many have studied thirty or forty more years to know, and you would have me tell you what it is in a moment?" Penn replied, "Certainly, if the Common Law be so hard to understand it is far from being common."

The Birth of Policing

As the US firmly adopted the Common Law, France was undergoing a revision of its legal provision under the intense oversight of Napoleon Bonaparte. In 1800, Napoleon assigned four senior jurists to write a comprehensive legal code. The commission held 102 sessions and Napoleon himself attended 57 meetings. The *Code Civil des Français* was issued in 1804. It contained 2,281 articles. To the world, this work became known as the *Code Napoleon*. The blueprint for the new code had been the work of Justinian and his *Corpus Juris Civilis*. The Napoleonic Code has been replicated in varying degrees of mirror image throughout all the countries of the world that use the Civil Law. Revision of the criminal law soon followed so that by 1808 a new *Code Penal* was issued by Napoleon. Combined, the new codes totally revised the legal system and offences across France. In addition to revising the entire legal system and rewriting the criminal code, Napoleon also significantly strengthened the role of the police in France. As a military leader, he took particular interest in the civilian policing function of the military police, the *Gendarmerie*. He also strengthened and grew the second police force of France, the civilian police force of Paris, to provide a uniformed police presence in all the major cities of France. This force was the genesis of the modern-day *Police Nationale*.

Napoleon took over in France at a time of unrest and confusion. The dreams of the Revolution had become clouded by despotism and a reign of terror. Napoleon recognized the need for a strong police force for two primary reasons: The nation needed stability and he needed an efficient police force if much of his time was to be spent abroad conducting military campaigns. The result was a period of overkill and much criticism of Napoleon as his police forces were viewed domestically as a team of spies running a police state.

It was the intense fear of a police state that caused the British to wait so long for a police force in London as, frankly, for the British parliament anything was better than what was happening in France. The delicate route to the establishment of a non-French police force for London is the subject of later discussion.

At this point it is worth remembering though that with Britain at war with France, and the French suffering from internal unrest, criticism of the French police was easy from the comfort of an English armchair. In reality, the model of the French *Gendarmerie* was highly successful and was utilized extensively in colonial Common Law, as well as Civil Law, jurisdictions across the world.

Louis Napoleon, Napoleon III, continued his uncle's legacy and extended the extraordinary powers of the civil police, the *Surete,* to the continuing chagrin of the French people. Although the detective limb of this force was undoubtedly highly successful and provided a model for the establishment of the Pinkerton private detectives in the US, dislike and mistrust of the French police was so strong in England that London's Metropolitan Police mimicked the *Surete* and then became their nemesis. The world remembers the famous Scotland Yard detectives, but for the English speaking world the Surete have been relegated to musical hall songs and a few lines in a history of policing book.

The Enlightenment Movement

The monumental impact of the commercial revolution of the 13th century was finally eclipsed by the revolution of thought, the Enlightenment. During the 18th century the modern world was overtaken by social reform and the advancement of knowledge. Not only was scientific discovery and social change promoted, intellectuality was too.

The salons of Europe and the New World were alive with debate and the political order was about to be recast through the Declaration of Independence, the US Bill of Rights, the Declaration of the Rights of Man and of the Citizen and the French Revolution.

The build-up to these events started in the mid-1600s. Descartes' *Discourse on Methods* was published in 1637; Britain had had another bloodless revolution in 1688; and John Locke published *Concerning Human Understanding* and the *Second Treatise on Government* in 1690. By its conclusion, the Enlightenment had reshaped Europe and changed the relationship between the rulers and the ruled, forever.

In due course, the Enlightenment led towards Romanticism as the philosophical thinkers of the modern world embraced former Athenian and Roman ideologies. Religion was relegated to a minor role in life and the last remains of a powerful church were either swept away or more damagingly totally ignored; Montesquieu's *The Spirit of the Laws* was placed on the list of banned books by the Catholic Church in 1751.

The Age of Reason was most adamantly the age of man's reason not god's. Inevitably the movements across the modern world would result in significant changes to the way citizens were treated by the law. Napoleon was soon to undertake a total revision of the criminal law in France and the power of the French police courts was to be reined in also. Louis XVI had agreed to the concept of a presumption of innocence, but he signed the law into effect far too late to save himself. His 1788 proclamation in Versailles also banned the wearing of prison uniforms, even for those on death row, and the right of appeal was strengthened for criminal defendants.

Many of the philosophical commentators of the time looked to England as a model, for after all there was no torture there. And the jury system appeared to protect the rights of innocent individuals, particularly after judges were banned from intimidating and coercing juries after the outrageous behavior of the trial judge in the William Penn case. What the voices of the day wanted were clear and unambiguous laws that would be applied equally to all citizens regardless of rank or status. Given the exchange between William Penn and his trial judge over the Common Law, it may seem incredible that England was heralded as an example.

But what the *philosophes* were attempting to achieve was a sense of rightness and balance and, in the case of Beccaria particularly, a sense of legal certainty. Central to the list of objections was the use of torture, and there was general agreement, spearheaded by Voltaire, that torture could not, and would not, be tolerated in a civilized society. There was, therefore, some logical flow to the idea of looking at the Common Law as it could, allegedly, show that torture did not exist. If in the future punishment was to serve as a deterrent to crime then torture as part of the criminal process punished a person not for guilt but for simply having been accused. It was an inevitable concomitant of the Enlightenment movement that penology would emerge as the viable alternative to corporal and capital punishment. Europe was on the cusp of accepting this idea and had a mechanism in place—rewriting all the criminal codes—to accommodate these ideas. For England this would be decidedly problematic.

William Blackstone[31] undertook the task of attempting to make the Common Law appear as a cogent body of definable rules that could be written into a format that had some resemblance to a code. He published his findings as part of series of lectures at Oxford University commencing in 1765. They were titled *Commentaries on the Laws of England*. They were, and remain, a resounding success and form the bedrock of all Common Law study. He is famous for the quote "Better that ten guilty persons escape than one innocent man be wrongly convicted." Blackstone was also responsible for finally bringing the study of law into English universities.

The period of the Enlightenment was the catalyst for a revision of all the criminal laws across the modern world. Parliaments responded with varying degrees of enthusiasm, and this period marked the beginning of the end for the wholesale use of capital punishment. The divisions between the Common Law and Civil Law were now firmly established and procedural developments began to take on increasingly diverse and complex rules that pertained exclusively to the two different legal systems.

Contemporary Criminal Justice

In England, what had once been a system of redress driven by the willingness of an individual party to pay for a trial process that might result in further personal loss, financially or bodily, had matured into a complex system of legal measures driven by the state on behalf of all the citizens of that country so that collective social values became available for scrutiny and testing. The protections and privileges once afforded by the church had been substituted for a different protective covering born out of the feudal monarchs of Europe, who in turn were themselves forced to give greater status and recognition to the common people due to the pressure and ability of the courts to modify and interpret legislative intention.

What the courts achieved in a typically solemn and quasi-religious environment, the intellects of Europe professed from the written and oracular platform to collectively cause permanent changes to the legal culture, a legal culture that convincingly confirmed the establishment of two distinctly separate but workable legal families: the Common Law and the Civil Law.

By the 20th century, the public face of retribution was already a large government machine constructed around policing, the courts and corrections, where the professionals employed within the three divisions each have separate levels of training, development and spheres of responsibility in assisting citizens to understand the parameters of acceptable behavior.

We no longer rely on local citizens to provide nighttime security services, and we no longer are guaranteed that the members of the jury will know us personally and have a comprehensive knowledge of the case they are hearing.

Under the Common Law, the role and function of the jury has changed forever; so too has that of the judge. Now relegated to a passive role, the jury and judiciary sit back and have the facts told to them, the arguments manicured for them by lawyers and the investigation of witnesses conducted on their behalf.

The judge, ever conscious of an appeal, is now a near silent umpire whose activity is limited to controlling the over-zealous lawyer and ensuring each warfaring party is adhering to the multitude of complex rules of play. Long gone are the days of jury questioning and judicial interruptions.

What gains the jury and judge achieved to protect the innocent in the formative years of the Common Law have been traded out and handed over to the all-powerful lawyers. Today under the Common Law it is the lawyers who have real control of the proceedings. It is the lawyers who have an absolute right of audience when once they had none, and it is the lawyers who manipulate and test the law to bring about legal reform in lieu of the church and the knights of battle by wager. Without the lawyer our courtrooms may well not be so busy, for it is thanks to the lawyer that we have such an endless supply of litigants.

But this path may not continue to be woven unabated, for the 21st century has already seen an increase in the nature and form of global crime—international drugs trafficking, terrorism and trafficking in humans, a return of piracy on the high seas and criminality never envisaged in the time of Blackstone: computer crime and software piracy.

All of these new faces of crime are causing the criminal justice system to undergo significant changes again. Nation-bound criminal laws are no longer capable of making sense of terrorism, and the societal norms that domestic criminal justice efforts seek to protect and enforce are frequently irrelevant.

Local law enforcement agencies are now being tasked with ensuring they have effective anti-terrorism measures in place and yet these same agencies of the criminal justice system have little training or experience in international terrorism. It may be the case that the system that has been devised, piecemeal and with planning, over the past thousand years will itself now undergo another period of radical reform as the Common Law and Civil Law combine to provide an effective measure of redress for all citizens regardless of their legal culture.

As seen in this chapter, legal systems come and go and they are highly adaptable. The dominance of cannon law has dissipated; Roman law is influential still but is no longer the primary legal system in the modern world; and although biblical law is no longer significant in the daily operation of the Civil or Common Law, religious based legal systems are still a major force in some parts of the world. These too may become a greater feature in a collective response to international criminality over the course of the next century.

Over the course of the last three thousand years mankind has sought to define and record certain actions as so offensive, not just to the injured individual but also to all of society that these actions should be subject to collective condemnation. The timeframes under which individual countries have delineated the action as public rather than private have varied hugely. However, in today's world those actions deemed as criminal are now prosecuted on behalf of the individual by the state. On occasion, the individual may not support a prosecution. On some occasions the victim is the offender and most certainly does not support a prosecution. An example of this might be where a person consents to a level of physical harm that is so severe society deems that the individual cannot give consent even though he or she might wish to.

To commit a crime is to engage in some action for which a governing entity can impose a penalty. That penalty may be a fine, a reduction in liberty or the removal of life. No individual can impose these sanctions upon another individual, and it is the collectivity and ability of a group to impose a sanction that makes crime a unique feature of any body of laws. Due to the public nature of bringing a prosecution and imposing a sentence, criminal law is considered to be Public Law. Actions brought by an individual to seek redress for a harm or a wrong are viewed as Private Law. It is perfectly possible for a person to break a law and in doing so to commit an offence that is not part of the criminal law. The concern of the criminal justice system is those actions that citizens commit that impact individuals and all of society as a whole, which in today's society we call a crime.

The classic interpretation of liability in criminal law is that there are two requisites, an action and a state of mind. The action may be doing an act or failing to do an act; the state of mind is the ability of the jury to open up the mind of the defendant and to see into his brain so that the jury can be convinced that it knows what it was the defendant was thinking at the time of the criminal act. Now this may sound like a piece of cerebral dexterity beyond the ability of the average jury member, as none of us can literally implant ourselves into the mind of another, and even if we could it would be the mind the defendant today in court, not when the criminal act was done. What the state of mind, the *mens rea,* is attempting to achieve is the exculpation of defendants who did not mean to do what they did. In other words, it is trying to protect the innocent and convict the guilty. As Judge Oliver Wendell Holmes so eloquently put it, "Even a dog distinguishes between being stumbled over and being kicked."[32]

The criminal law is seeking to establish that the defendant intended to do what happened; he kicked the dog. By comparison, the private law of tort does not seek to achieve this to the same standard. It is reasonable to say that if the ultimate sanction for committing a crime is that the community imposes the death sentence, then the society imposing that sanction should be absolutely certain, or as certain as it can possibly be, that it is convicting the right person. Consequently, the standard of proof required to prove a person committed a crime is significantly higher than the standard we would expect for proving that a person did not deliver goods to my market stall or house as agreed.

Consequently the criminal law seeks to prove that the defendant was guilty of an inaction or inaction, *actus reus,* and guilty of intentionally causing the harm that resulted from the action, *mens rea.*

Summary

This chapter has established that certain actions are so offensive that all of a community suffers and, consequently, laws have been written, divinely or by man, to control the behavior of citizens. We call these actions and the law that controls them criminal.

Regardless of when in history or where on Earth it has taken place, all societies punish those who transgress the criminal law; there has been a lack of agreement though on the level of punishment that should be applied. This dilemma has not been resolved. Over time the leading civilizations of the Western world developed written bodies of law that had varying degrees of impact upon future generations. In Europe, the Roman laws played a significant role in shaping the ecclesiastical laws, canon law, as well as the secular laws that became known as the Civil Law.

In England, the impact of the Romans was less and the influence of the Catholic Church was also less strong. Consequently, strong British monarchs, many of French origin, asserted their authority in place of canon laws so that over the course of five centuries the impact of canon law was minimal and England developed its own legal system known as the Common Law.

Together the Civil Law and the Common Law form the two largest bodies of law in use in the world today. Canon Law and another religion-based law, sharia law, are also important and both impact the lives of many millions of people as well.

The Common Law was for many centuries handed down through the decisions of judges, and it took many hundreds of years before users of this system recognized a need for any level of codification. By contrast, the French Civil Law was a fusion of custom and Roman and church law, and it became codified at an early stage in its history. Napoleon Bonaparte was instrumental in having the codes of France rewritten and modernized and his work is still considered a leading example of clarity and order.

Alongside the development of legal families or systems of law, the developing nations of the world need to have state officials with the authority to implement the public parts of the law, especially the criminal actions of citizens. Taking the lead from the Roman example, the villages and towns of Europe started a vigilante and night watch system of protection. This grew into a county-wide system of protection that was under the direction of a royal appointee, the sheriff.

Eventually the growth of the merchant classes and the desire to explore our world meant that trade, industry and the migration of people would need more sophisticated responses to control than local watchmen could provide. The communities of the new nations of Europe and America needed police, courts and corrections officers to service a complex society.

The evolution of these authorities is discussed in greater detail later in this book.

By the 16th century, the role of judges and the criminal law under the two legal families was clearly established. America not unsurprisingly followed Britain's lead and followed the Common Law with varying degrees of exactness depending upon the need for the laws, whether commercially based Southern needs or biblically based Northern. Throughout the journey, the legal systems so familiar to users of the criminal justice system today can be traced back time and again to the Greeks and Romans. Between them was instigated a comprehensive system of proofs, judges and juries, defined sentences, justifiable homicide, a written body of laws that would inform future generations and many more important influences that will feature throughout our discussion.

Questions

1. To commit a crime implies that the offender has participated in an act that is more than offensive or damaging to one individual person.

    a. True
    b. False

2. It is often considered that the defining difference between criminal law and all other forms of law is that criminal law attracts punishment. This is true but it is not an absolute.

    a. True
    b. False

3. Crime embraces a degree of seriousness; minor crime and major crime are often referred to as:

   a. Misdemeanors and Serious
   b. Misdemeanors and Indictable
   c. Non-serious and Felonies
   d. Misdemeanors and Felonies

4. Most societies have developed a code of conduct from their origin and retained that code without amendments and additions.

   a. True
   b. False

5. The Code of Hammurabi was created about:

   a. 2200 BC
   b. 3200 BC
   c. 2700 BC
   d. 4200 BC

6. From 668 onwards English kings had made extensive use of clerics to assist in trials. Truth-finding was achieved through the use of

   a. Consolatory oaths
   b. Compurgatory oaths
   c. Conditional oaths
   d. Clerical oaths

7. In continental Europe the _____ laws played a significant role in shaping ecclesiastical laws and canon law, as well as secular laws.

   a. Roman
   b. Greek
   c. Etruscan
   d. French

8. The Common Law was for many centuries handed down through the decisions of judges. These decisions are known as:

   a. res judica
   b. ratio decendi
   c. lex tallionis
   d. res ipsa loquitor

9. _____ was instrumental in having the codes of France rewritten and modernized and his work is still considered a leading example of clarity and order.

   a. Jean Paul Gaultier
   b. Napoleon Bonaparte
   c. Louis IVX
   d. Jean Jacque Rousseau

10. Taking the lead from the Roman example, the villages and towns of Europe started a _____ system of protection.

    a. Vigilante and night watch
    b. Constable and Sheriff
    c. Gladiator and servile
    d. Neighborhood watch

11. America not unsurprisingly followed the lead from _____ and followed the _____ law with varying degrees of exactness:

    a. France and the Civil law
    b. Britain and the Civil Law
    c. France and the Common Law
    d. Britain and the Common Law

Endnotes

1. R v Smith would indicate an action brought on behalf of the crown, Regina v Smith or, in the case of a king, Rex v Smith.
2. Some jurisdictions have struggled with the delineation of a fine as either a punitive action or a civil action that is outside of the scope of the criminal law, e.g. corporate liability.
3. See Jones, M. and Johnstone, P. 2011. *History of criminal justice.* 5th ed. New York: Elsevier, p. 5.
4. There are numerous examples to consider, particularly in the area of sexual conduct and offences governed by the church. Also consider that contemporary society has computer-based crimes that were not even thought of as potential crimes as recently as the 1970s.
5. There is some measure of disagreement over the actual date, with opinion varying between around 2250 BC and 1750 BC.
6. See Vincent, supra, who cites Pollock and Maitland at p. 748 and note 2.
7. Vincent, supra. p. 749
8. Talion, meaning a punishment identical to the offense and taken from the law of talion. Although often viewed as a literal translation wherein the punishment is identical to the offense, contemporary understanding captures the concept of the punishment 'fitting' the crime.
9. Jones and Johnstone, supra. p. 18
10. Jones and Johnstone, supra. p. 24
11. E.g. the creation of the office of *praetor* who headed up the uniquely Roman invention of private law courts. Many aspects of the *praetor's* role are apparent today in the Prefect of France. Another important addition to legal history was the establishment of professional jurists. A public official who was not a judge or an advocate, the jurist held high social status in Rome and was available by appointment to members of the ruling classes, the *nobilitas,* exclusively. As we shall see, infra, the exclusivity of appointment as a Justice of the Peace in England bears close resemblance to the Roman 'jurist'.
12. Although formally ended in America in the mid-19th century and soon after in England, the concept of a privileged status for priests remains and was seen in practice during the 1990s when the Pope refused to allow Archbishop Paul Marcinkus to stand trial in Italy on charges of money laundering. Marcinkus was given diplomatic immunity by the Pope under the protection of the papal city of the Vatican.
13. See Jones and Johnstone, supra. p. 23
14. See Frank Wieacker, 1981, The importance of Roman law for Western civilization and Western legal thought. *Boston College International and Comparative Law Review,* 4(2), pp. 257–281.
15. Wieacker, supra. p. 259
16. The term comes from the Roman law, *ius civile,* the law that all citizens, *cives,* were subject to.
17. See Jones and Johnstone, supra. p. 44
18. Battle was strictly controlled with a specific time and date set, as well as initially a field and then a marked arena being used for the event. The accuser brought an appeal of felony, *fello* (Latin), and combatants or their champions fought to the death. Mutilation resulted

in being unable to continue or continuing until sunset. By a curious oversight of the English lawmakers, trial by battle remained an option under English law until 1819 when embarrassingly a man claimed his right and the legislators had to admit they had forgotten to remove it from legal options. See further: Jones and Johnstone, supra. p. 48

19. Late O.E. scirgerefa "representative of royal authority in a shire," from scir (see shire) + gerefa "chief, official, reeve" (see reeve). In Anglo-Saxon England, the representative of royal authority in a shire. As an American county official, attested from 1662; sheriff's sale first recorded 1798. http://www.etymonline.com/index.php?term=sheriff
20. We take the term from the 3rd century Roman firewatchers, Vigiles. The term has commonly come to mean legal, or extra-legal, citizen participation in law enforcement.
21. "Have mercy on me, O God, according to your unfailing love, according to your great compassion blot out my transgression."
22. Privilegium Fori was abolished in 1823.
23. Jones and Johnstone, supra. p. 65
24. At one time Fleet Prison housed William Penn before his departure to America. It was known as the 'Largest brothel in England' as it housed male and female prisoners together and drunkenness and sexual debauchery were commonplace.
25. The self-appointed 'Witch-finder General' Matthew Hopkins, who sold his services for payment for villages across the south of England, managed to find 200 witches over a two year period. He eventually suffered the same fate as his victims and was drowned trying to prove his own innocence.
26. His son, Charles II, canonized his father for his preservation of Apostolic Succession. He is the only saint, Charles the Martyr, to be canonized by the Anglican Church.
27. Charles II acknowledged at least 12 illegitimate children from a number of mistresses.
28. Jones and Johnstone, supra. p. 102
29. This was also known as the Declaration of Rights and served as the blueprint for the US Bill of Rights.
30. Kent, J. 1826. *Commentaries on American law*. New York: O. Halstead. Vol. 1. Lecture XVI, p. 322. Kent was himself quoting Du Ponceau On jurisdiction, p. 19.
31. 1723–1780. A professor at Oxford University, a judge and a member of Parliament, William Blackstone is revered as one of the great jurists of the Common Law.
32. Oliver Wendell Holmes Jr. 1881. *The common law*. Boston: Little Brown, p. 3. Available at www.gutenberg.org

CHAPTER 2
THE RAW MATERIALS OF CRIMINAL JUSTICE

◆ Introduction

According to the most recent data collection, 13,636 people were the victims of murder or non-negligent manslaughter in 2009, for which 12,418 people were arrested.[1] Unless you were a criminologist or otherwise an avid reader of governmental publications on crime, it is unlikely that you would know this. Indeed, most people do not accurately quantify the crime problem. Consider the following example: Criminologists Margaret Vandiver and David Giacopassi administered questionnaires to 323 introductory students and 45 seniors majoring in criminal justice to determine how well they grasped the magnitude of the crime problem relative to other mortality conditions. They found that almost 50% of the introductory students estimated that 250,000 murders were committed annually in the United States. Fifteen percent of the students estimated that more than one million people were murdered each year.[2] For many reasons, perhaps most notably the extensive media focus on crime, students overestimated the likelihood of being murdered, but underestimated the prevalence of other causes of death that were less sensationalistic.

© 2012 by pixbox77. Used under license of Shutterstock, Inc.

The purpose of the current chapter is to provide basic information about the "which, who, what, where, and how" of crime. Which behaviors constitute the most serious crimes? Who counts all of the crimes

From *Criminal Justice: Balancing Crime Control and Due Process*, 3/e, by Matt Delisi. Copyright © 2011 by Kendall Hunt Publishing Company. Reprinted by permission.

that occur in the United States? What are the assorted ways that crime is quantified? Where can you find crime-related statistics? How are crimes processed through the criminal justice system? Answers to these and other basic questions are provided.

To adequately understand criminal justice, it is crucial to understand the three essential players or components of the criminal justice process: criminals or offenders, crime victims, and the various agents of the criminal justice system, such as police. More dramatically, the sheer quantitative magnitude of the crime problem means that the criminal justice system cannot handle all criminal cases. The state simply does not have the capacity or resources to process *all* crimes. Instead, cases are diverted or funneled through the criminal justice system for a variety of reasons that this book explores. In a way, the criminal justice system responds to crime similarly to the medical triage model: the most serious crimes get the most attention.

The imbalance between the volume of crime and the capacity of the criminal justice system to respond to crime necessitates that criminal justice personnel use their discretion in determining which crimes are most deserving of system resources. In other words, at all points of the criminal justice system, personnel such as police, prosecutors, and detention staff must balance the objectives of crime control and due process in completing the course of their duties.

Counting Crime

Uniform Crime Reports (UCR)

History and Scope of the UCR Program

For the first three decades of the 20th Century, the United States did not have a systematic, nationwide policy on counting crime. Instead, crimes were recorded by individual police agencies across the country. In 1927, the International Association of Chiefs of Police (IACP) led efforts to create a national crime statistics initiative and formed the Committee on Uniform Crime Records. The Committee determined that the number of offenses known to law enforcement, whether or not there was an arrest, would be the most appropriate measure of the nation's criminality. From the beginning, the Committee realized that differences between state criminal codes precluded the mere aggregation of state statistics to arrive at a national total. Differences in state statutes also precluded accurate distinguishing between felony and misdemeanor crimes. To avoid these problems and to provide nationwide uniformity in crime reporting, the Committee formulated standardized offense definitions in which law enforcement agencies were to submit data without regard to local statutes.[3]

The Committee identified seven main offense classifications variously known as Part I crimes. Seven crimes were originally selected—murder and non-negligent manslaughter, forcible rape, robbery, aggravated assault, burglary, larceny-theft, and motor vehicle theft. In 1978, Congress mandated the collection of arson data and in 1982 directed the FBI to permanently count arson as a Part I offense. Part II offenses were less serious crimes and included 21 offenses, other assaults, forgery and counterfeiting, fraud, embezzlement, buying/receiving/possessing stolen property, vandalism, weapons carrying, prostitution and commercialized vice, sex offenses (other than forcible rape and prostitution), drug abuse violations, gambling, offenses against family and children, driving under the influence, liquor laws, drunkenness, disorderly conduct, vagrancy, "other" offenses, suspicion, curfew and loitering (applies to persons under age 18), and runaways (applies to persons under age 18).

Law enforcement agencies that participated in the UCR Program (it is voluntary) performed two important functions: classifying and scoring. Classifying is determining the proper crime category in which to report an offense to the UCR Program. Scoring is counting the number of offenses after they have been classified and entering the total count on the appropriate reporting form. The UCR Program relies on the hierarchy rule whereby only the highest offense in a multiple-offense situation is counted. The clearance rate refers to crimes known to the police that have been solved in the sense that a defendant has been arrested for the crime. Crimes cleared by exceptional means refer to cases where arrest is impossible, such as the death of the suspect, but police knew who had committed the crime.[4]

Congress enacted Title 28, Section 534, of the United States Code authorizing the Attorney General to gather crime information. The Attorney General charged the Federal Bureau of Investigation (FBI) with collecting the crime data from police departments, serving as the national crime data clearinghouse, and disseminating the crime information nationally. In September 1930, the UCR program began with 400 cities from 43 states participating in the data collection effort. By 2011, the UCR encompassed more than 17,000 law enforcement agencies that represented about 95% of the U. S. population. This data collection effort results in three annual publications, *Crime in the United States, Hate Crime Statistics,* and *Law Enforcement Officers Killed and Assaulted.* Additionally, the FBI publishes the *Preliminary Semiannual Uniform Crime Reports and Preliminary Annual Uniform Crime Reports.* The UCR data provide our basis for understanding the incidence of crime in the United States.

Over the years, the UCR Program has been revisited and improved to include more detailed information about the extent of the crime problem. There are several examples of the refinement of UCR data. In 1952, agencies began collecting data on the age, sex, and race of arrestees. In 1958, the FBI incorporated the concept of a national Crime Index, the total of six Part I offenses (excluding arson) and larceny over $50 to serve as the general indicator of criminality. The UCR was expanded in 1960 to collect statistics on law enforcement officers killed and again in 1962 to collect detailed information on homicide which constituted the Supplementary Homicide Report (SHR). In 1966, the National Sheriffs' Association (NSA) established a Committee on Uniform Crime Reporting to serve in an advisory capacity and to encourage county-level sheriffs throughout the country to fully participate in the program. The UCR program would continue to be revised in the 1980s, ultimately culminating in the National Incident-Based Reporting System (NIBRS) data collection program (described later in this chapter).

Definitions and Rates of UCR Index Offenses

Violent Part I Offenses

Murder and non-negligent manslaughter is the willful killing of one human being by another. As a general rule, any death caused as the result of an interpersonal fight, argument, quarrel, assault, or other crime is classified as murder and non-negligent manslaughter. Suicides, fetal deaths, traffic fatalities, accidental deaths, assaults to murder, and attempted murder are not classified as criminal homicides. Certain willful killings must be classified as justifiable or excusable. According to the UCR, justifiable homicide is the killing of a felon by a peace officer in the line of duty or the killing of a felon, during the commission of a felony, by a private citizen.

In legal parlance, first-degree murder refers to a homicide committed with premeditation, malice aforethought, intention, or one that is otherwise planned. It is the most serious crime. Second-degree murder typifies intentional but unplanned killings, such as a domestic killing during an intense argument (or "heat of passion"). Thankfully, murder is the rarest violent Index crime. The national murder rate is 5 murders per 100,000 in the population.[5]

Forcible rape is the carnal knowledge of a female forcibly and against her will. According to the UCR Handbook, carnal knowledge is the act of a man having sexual bodily connections with a woman or sexual intercourse involving penile penetration of the vagina. Other sexual-based offenses such as statutory rape, incest, rape by instrumentation, sodomy, or forcible fondling are not classified as forcible rape. Instead they are classified as assaults or other sex offenses. Because of its strict definition, males cannot be raped according to the UCR.[6] Forcible rape is about six times more prevalent than murder. According to the most recent data, the forcible rape rate was 28.7 per 100,000 females in the population.

Robbery is the taking or attempting to take anything of value from the care, custody, or control of a person or persons by force or threat of force or violence and/or by putting the victim in fear. Robbery is a vicious theft committed in the presence of the victim. Unlike thefts, robbery is aggravated by the element of force or threat of force. Because of the element or actual presence of force, robbery should always be considered a violent crime. The UCR delineates robbery in four ways depending on the means that the robbery was committed. In descending order of seriousness, robbery can be perpetrated with a firearm, knife or cutting instrument, other dangerous weapon, and strong-arm via hands or feet. Colloquialisms such as stickups, holdups, heists, muggings and related terms are robberies. The robbery rate is 133 per 100,000 in the population making it nearly 27 times more prevalent than murder.

Aggravated assault is an unlawful attack by one person upon another for the purpose of inflicting severe or aggravated bodily injury. This type of assault usually is accompanied by the use of a weapon or by means likely to produce death or serious bodily harm. Aggravated assault encompasses a variety of charges such as assault with intent to kill, assault with intent to murder, assault with a dangerous or deadly weapon, mayhem, maiming, and others. Reporting agencies must consider the seriousness of the injury incurred as the primary factor in establishing whether an assault is aggravated or simple. Generally speaking, injuries that require immediate medical care or hospitalization, such as broken bones or internal injuries, qualify an assault as aggravated. The aggravated assault rate is 263 per 100,000 rendering it nearly twice as prevalent as robbery.

Property Part I Offenses

Burglary is the unlawful entry into a structure to commit a felony or theft. The UCR Program classifies offenses locally known as burglary (any degree), unlawful entry, breaking and entering, housebreaking, safecracking, and attempts of these offenses as burglary. Persons who conceal themselves inside a building to commit felonies or theft and then exit the structure should also be described as burglars. Burglary is further classified by the means that entry occurs, such as forcible entry, unlawful entry without force, or attempted forcible entry. According to conventional wisdom, residential burglary is viewed as a more grievous offense than commercial or business burglary because of the potential that victims are home and could confront the burglar. In fact, about one third of burglaries target residences or dwellings during the day. The national burglary rate is 716 per 100,000 in the population.

Larceny-theft is the unlawful taking, carrying, leading, or riding away of property from the possession or constructive possession of another. Constructive possession is to exercise dominion or control over a thing. Larceny and theft have the same meaning and are used interchangeably. Larceny-theft encompasses many offenses such as stealing, pocket-picking, purse-snatching, shoplifting, and the like. Larceny-theft is the most prevalent crime in the United States, with a rate of 2,061 per 100,000 inhabitants. The theft rate is 412 times greater than the murder rate!

Motor vehicle theft, defined as the theft or attempted theft of a motor vehicle (e.g., auto, truck, bus, or other vehicle), is a separate property Index offense. According to the most recent UCR, the motor vehicle theft rate is 259 per 100,000 in the population.

Arson is any willful or malicious burning or attempt to burn, with or without intent to fraud, a dwelling house, public building, motor vehicle or aircraft, personal property of another, etc. Arson is classified according to what was burned, such as structures, mobile units, or other property. Reporting agencies can only report arson or attempts to burn after an investigation has determined that the fire was willfully set. Fires of suspicious or unknown origin should not be reported as arsons. Arson is a unique crime. It is by far the least prevalent property crime. With a rate of 21.3 per

100,000, arson has approximately the same incidence as forcible rape. Additionally, arson is committed disproportionately by juvenile offenders. More than 47% of arsons are cleared by the arrest of a person under age eighteen.[7]

Part II Offenses

The UCR Program also collects data on 21 additional crimes. Part II offenses are considered less serious than Index crimes and are defined below.

Other assaults described as interpersonal attacks in which weapons are not used and the injuries incurred or minor. The following types of crimes should be classified as other assaults: simple or minor assault, assault and battery, stalking, intimidation, coercion, resisting or obstructing an officer, or hazing.

Forgery and counterfeiting is the altering, copying, or imitating of something without authority or right with the intent to deceive or defraud by passing the copy as an original. Forgery and counterfeiting are treated as allied offenses and include forging of public records, forging wills or other financial documents, and signing the name of another person or fictitious person with the intent to defraud.

Fraud is the intentional perversion of the truth for the purpose of inducing another person or other entity in reliance upon it to part with something of value or to surrender a legal right. According to the UCR Handbook, fraud involves either the offender receiving a benefit or the victim incurring a detriment. Both benefits and detriments can be tangible or intangible. Agencies should classify various acts such as passing bad checks (except forgeries), false pretenses, swindling, credit card/ATM/welfare/wire fraud, and impersonation as fraud.

Embezzlement is the unlawful misappropriation or misapplication by an offender to his or her own use or purpose of money, property, or some other thing of value entrusted to his or her control. Generally, the victims of embezzlement are businesses. Most people recognize embezzlement as "stealing from one's work or place of employment."

Buying, receiving, possessing, selling, concealing, or transporting any property with the knowledge that it has been unlawfully taken is classified as a stolen property violation. Many jurisdictions use the letters RSP as a catch-all for this violation, meaning receiving stolen property.

Vandalism is the willful or malicious destruction of property without the consent of the owner. Vandalism covers a wide range of malicious acts such as cutting tires, drawing obscene images on public restrooms, destroying school property, or defacing books.

The violations of laws prohibiting the manufacture, sale, purchase, transportation, possession, concealment, or use of firearms, cutting instruments, explosives, incendiary devices, or other deadly weapons is a weapons violation. One of the most common weapons violations is carrying a concealed weapon (or CCW).

Prostitution and commercialized vice is the unlawful promotion of or participation in sexual activities for profit. To solicit customers or to transport persons for prostitution purposes; to own, manage, or operate a dwelling or other establishment for the purpose of prostitution; or to assist or otherwise promote prostitution is also illegal.

The generic sex offenses classification includes offenses against chastity, common decency, morals, and the like. Unlike forcible rape, which is defined as a male against female crime, sex offenses can include cases where males are the victim of sexual assault or abuse. The types of crimes that are viewed as sex offenses include adultery and fornication, buggery, seduction, sodomy or crime against nature, incest, indecent exposure, indecent liberties, and statutory rape.

Drug abuse violations include the unlawful possession, sale, use, growing, manufacturing, or making of any controlled drug or narcotic substance, such as marijuana, cocaine, heroin, morphine, methamphetamine, barbiturates, etc. The UCR specifies that agencies differentiate between drug violations involving mere possession or use and those involving manufacturing or sale. In this sense, a distinction is made between drug dealers and drug users.

Gambling violations include unlawfully betting or wagering money on something else of value; assisting, promoting, or operating a game of chance for money; possessing or transmitting wager information; or tampering with the outcome of a sporting event or contest to gain a gambling advantage. Reporting agencies divide gambling arrests into three categories: bookmaking (horse and sport book), numbers and lottery, and all other.

Offenses against the family and children are unlawful non-violent acts by a family member or legal guardian that threaten the physical, mental, or economic well-being or morals of another family member and that are not classifiable as other offenses, such as assault or sex offenses. These include non-violent cruelty or abuse; desertion, abandonment, or nonsupport of spouse or child; neglect; non-payments of alimony; or attempts to commit any of these acts.

Driving under the influence is operating a motor vehicle while mentally or physically impaired as the result of consuming an alcoholic beverage or using drugs/narcotics. Depending on jurisdiction, this offense is described as drunk driving (DUI, DWI, OWI, or OUI).

Four Part II offenses are commonly known as public-order or nuisance crimes that involve the public use of alcohol. These crimes frequently but not always are committed by transients. Liquor laws entail the violation of ordinances prohibiting the manufacture, sale, purchase, transportation, possession, or use of alcoholic beverages. Variants of liquor laws include bootlegging and the underage possession of alcohol. Drunkenness is to drink alcoholic beverages to the extent that one's mental faculties and physical coordination are substantially impaired. Disorderly conduct is any behavior that tends to disturb the peace or decorum, scandalize the community, or shock the public sense of morality. Vagrancy is the violation of a court order, regulation, ordinance, or law requiring the withdrawal of persons from the streets or other specified areas; prohibiting persons from remaining in an area of place in an idle or aimless manner; or prohibiting persons from going from place to place with visible means or support. Offenses included as vagrancy are begging, loitering, and vagabondage.

All violations of state or local laws that are not specifically identified as Part I or II offenses, except traffic violations, are termed other offenses. Some miscellaneous crimes in this category include blackmail and extortion, bribery, kidnapping, bigamy, trespassing, and the like.

Suspicion is an interesting thing. It is not a criminal offense; instead it is the grounds for many arrests in jurisdictions where the law permits. After law enforcement officers conduct an investigation, they either formally charge the prisoner with a crime or release him or her. Suspicion essentially facilitates law enforcement as they gather information to formally charge.

Finally, two Part II offenses pertain to juveniles or persons under the age of eighteen. Curfew and loitering laws are violations of specific ordinances that limit the times of night when youth should not be on the streets. Runaway is limited to juveniles taken into protective custody under local statutes. It is also known as "running away from home."[8]

Weaknesses of UCR Data

Over the years, a variety of criticisms of the UCR Program and official crime data generally have been levied. Some of these are that the UCR is voluntary and incomplete, omits many types of crime, and underestimates crimes because of its use of the hierarchy rule. In June 2004, it was recommended that the FBI discontinue the Crime Index and instead publish a violent crime total and property crime total. Over time, it was recognized that the Crime Index was not an accurate measure of the degree of criminality in a locality because larceny-theft comprised 60% of all crimes reported. Consequently, the volume of thefts overshadows more serious but less frequently committed crimes, such as murder or robbery.[9] For more information on the prevalence of crime, the arrest totals for all UCR offenses appear in Box 2-1.

National Incident-Based Reporting System (NIBRS)

In the 1980s, the Bureau of Justice Statistics, the Department of Justice agency responsible for funding criminal justice information projects, initiated efforts to overhaul the UCR Program because of the limitations of its data. The Federal Bureau of Investigation awarded a contract to develop new offense definitions and data elements for the redesigned system. The goals were to revise the definitions of Index offenses, to identify additional significant offenses, to refine definitions of offenses, and to develop incident details for all UCR offenses. In short, the Department of

BOX 2-1

ARRESTS IN THE UNITED STATES

OFFENSE	NUMBER OF ARRESTS
Total	13,687,241
Murder and Non-negligent manslaughter	12,418
Forcible rape	21,407
Robbery	126,725
Aggravated assault	421,215
Burglary	299,351
Larceny-theft	1,334,933
Motor vehicle theft	81,797
Arson	12,204
Other assaults	1,319,458
Forgery and counterfeiting	85,844
Fraud	210,255
Embezzlement	17,920
Stolen property	105,303
Vandalism	270,439
Weapons	166,334
Prostitution and commercialized vice	71,355
Sex offenses	77,326
Drug abuse violations	1,663,582
Gambling	10,360
Offenses against family and children	114,564
Driving under the influence	1,440,409
Liquor laws	570,333
Drunkenness	594,300
Disorderly conduct	655,322
Vagrancy	33,388
All other offenses	3,764,672
Suspicion	1,975
Curfew and loitering law violations	112,593
Runaways	93,434

Source: Federal Bureau of Investigation. (2010). *Crime in the United States, 2009.* Washington, DC: U.S. Government Printing Office.

Justice sought to create a national crime data collection effort that enhanced the quantity, quality, and timeliness of crime data and generally improved upon the methodology of the UCR. The result was the National Incident-Based Reporting System (NIBRS), which was introduced in 1989.

NIBRS has several advantages over the UCR Program. First, NIBRS contains incident- and victim-level analysis disaggregated to local jurisdictions and aggregated to intermediate levels of analysis. By comparison, the UCR was a summary-based system. Second, incident details the analysis of ancillary offenses and crime situations. By comparison, the UCR hierarchy rule counts only the most serious offenses. Third, NIBRS data permit separable individual, household, commercial, and business victimizations. Fourth, NIBRS offers data on incidents involving victims under age 12 (the NCVS only targets victims twelve and older). Fifth, NIBRS offers a broader range of offense categories. Sixth, NIBRS contains victimization information beyond which the NCVS provides. Seventh, NIBRS yields individual-level information about offenders from arrests records and victim reports and thus provides residual information on victims and offenders.[10]

As shown in Box 2-2, NIBRS contains 46 incidents in 22 categories for all incidents and eleven additional crimes for incidents that produce arrests. Although there is considerable overlap between the two crime data collection programs, NIBRS offers more information and, specifically, more contextual information about criminal events, as shown in Box 2-3. Since its modest beginning in 1989, more agencies are participating in the NIBRS program. For example, in 1991, 269 agencies participated in NIBRS covering a population of 4.1 million. By 1996, NIBRS participation increased to 1,082 agencies and covered about 15 million people. To date, 25 states participate in the NIBRS program with many other states in various stages of planning and development. This includes 5,271 law enforcement agencies and coverage of about 65 million people.[11]

Despite concerns about the quality of UCR data and the differences between the two programs, NIBRS and UCR data tend to paint the same picture about the incidence of crime in the United States. Ramona Rantala, a statistician with the Bureau of Justice Statistics, and Thomas Edwards, an FBI systems analyst, recently examined the effects of NIBRS on crime statistics. Overall, Rantala and Edwards found that when comparing data from the same year for the jurisdictions in this study, NIBRS rates differed only slightly from Summary UCR rates. Murder rates were the same. Rape, robbery, and aggravated assault rates were about 1% higher in NIBRS than UCR. The NIBRS burglary rate was a mere 0.5% lower than the UCR rate. Differences in theft were just 3.4% and motor vehicle thefts were just 4.5%. The convergence of NIBRS and UCR data suggests that both programs are worthwhile estimates of crime in the nation.[12]

National Crime Victimization Survey (NCVS)

Perhaps the most damaging criticism of official measures of crime, such as the UCR and NIBRS, is that they omit crimes not reported to or discovered by the police. During the mid-1960s, criminologists such as Albert Biderman and Albert Reiss began to write about the "dark figure of crime," a term that describes the actual amount of crime that

BOX 2-2

NIBRS OFFENSE CATEGORIES

GROUP A OFFENSES (REPORTED FOR ALL INCIDENTS)

1. Arson
2. Assault offenses (aggravated assault, simple assault, intimidation)
3. Bribery
4. Burglary
5. Counterfeiting/forgery
6. Vandalism
7. Drug/narcotics offenses (drug/narcotics violations, drug equipment violations)
8. Embezzlement
9. Extortion/blackmail
10. Fraud offenses (false pretenses/con game, credit card/ATM fraud, impersonation, welfare fraud, wire fraud)
11. Gambling offenses (illegal betting, operating illegal gambling, gambling equipment violations, sports tampering)
12. Homicide offenses (murder and non-negligent manslaughter, negligent manslaughter, justifiable homicide)
13. Kidnapping/abduction
14. Larceny/theft offenses (pocket-picking, purse-snatching, shoplifting, theft from building, theft from coin-op machine, theft from motor vehicle, theft of vehicle parts/accessories, all other larceny)
15. Motor vehicle theft
16. Pornography/obscene material
17. Prostitution (prostitution, assisting/promoting prostitution)
18. Robbery
19. Forcible sex offenses (forcible rape, forcible sodomy, sexual assault with object, forcible fondling)
20. Non-forcible sex offense (incest, statutory rape)
21. Stolen property offense
22. Weapons law violations

GROUP B OFFENSES (REPORTED FOR INCIDENTS PRODUCING ARRESTS)

1. Bad checks
2. Curfew/loitering violations
3. Disorderly conduct
4. Driving under influence
5. Drunkenness
6. Family offenses, nonviolent
7. Liquor law violations
8. Peeping tom
9. Runaway
10. Trespass
11. All other offenses

Source: Rantala, R. R., & Edwards, T. J. (2000). *Effects of NIBRS on crime statistics, Special Report.* Washington, DC: U. S. Department of Justice, Office of Justice Programs, Bureau of Justice Statistics.

> **BOX 2-3**
>
> ## INFORMATION THAT NIBRS RECORDS ON EACH CRIME INCIDENT
>
> **ADMINISTRATIVE SEGMENT**
> ORI number
> Incident number
> Incident date/hour
> Exceptional clearance indicator
> Exceptional clearance date
>
> **OFFENSE SEGMENT**
> UCR offense code
> Attempted/completed code
> Alcohol/drug use by offender
> Type of location
> Number of premises entered
> Method of entry
> Type of criminal activity
> Type of weapon/force used
> Bias crime code
>
> **PROPERTY SEGMENT**
> Type of property loss
> Property description
> Property value
> Recovery date
> Number of stolen motor vehicles
> Number of recovered motor vehicles
> Suspected drug type
> Estimated drug quantity
> Drug measurement unit
>
> **OFFENDER SEGMENT**
> Offender number
> Age of offender
> Sex of offender
> Race of offender
>
> **ARRESTEE SEGMENT**
> Arrestee number
> Transaction number
> Arrest date
> Type of arrest
> Multiple clearance indicator
> UCR arrest offense code
> Arrestee armed indicator
> Age of arrestee
> Sex of arrestee
> Race of arrestee
> Ethnicity of arrestee
> Resident status of arrestee
> Disposition of arrestee under 18
>
> **VICTIM SEGMENT**
> Victim number
> Victim UCR offense code
> Type of victim
> Age of victim
> Sex of victim
> Race of victim
> Ethnicity of victim
> Resident status of victim
> Homicide/assault circumstances
> Justifiable homicide circumstances
> Type of injury
> Related offender number
> Relationship of victim to offender
>
> Source: Rantala, R. R., & Edwards, T. J. (2000). *Effects of NIBRS on crime statistics, Special Report.* Washington, DC: U.S. Department of Justice, Office of Justice Programs, Bureau of Justice Statistics.

takes place but is impossible to detect because most crimes are neither reported to the police, nor result in arrest.[13] As part of President Lyndon Johnson's war on crime, The President's Commission of Law Enforcement and Administration of Justice conducted a pilot study of 10,000 households to assess the incidence of criminal victimization. The findings indicated that there was much more crime than the estimates produced by official data indicated. Inspired by these findings, the U. S. Bureau of the Census and the Bureau of Justice Statistics agency of the U. S. Department of Justice initiated the National Crime Survey (NCS) in 1972–1973. Now known as the National Crime Victimization Survey (NCVS), it is the victim's perspective on measuring crime.

The NCVS is a survey that obtains information about criminal victimizations and incidents from an ongoing, nationally representative sample of households in the United States. In 2009, 38,728 households and 68,665 people age 12 or older were interviewed. Nearly 92% of the eligible households participated in the NCVS.[14] The crimes measured by the NCVS are rape/sexual assault, robbery, aggravated assault, simple assault, and personal theft and constitute violent crimes. Murder is not included in the NCVS because it is impossible to interview murder victims, of course. Household burglary, theft, and motor vehicle theft constitute property crimes.

Of course, like any form of data, the NCVS has its limitations. By its very design, the NCVS does not measure the criminal victimization of persons younger than 12. Similarly, the NCVS is a survey, not a census, and thus is susceptible to sampling error. Finally, victims can inadvertently or intentionally report inaccurate information for a variety of reasons, such as embarrassment about being a crime victim, shame in hiding their own criminal activity, or simple misunderstanding of the definitions of various crimes.[15]

The Bureau of Justice Statistics has produced numerous reports based on NCVS data. In sum, the NCVS sheds further light on the quantity of crime and victimization occurring annually. Some of the highlights from these reports appear below.

- More than 20 million crimes occurred among U.S. residents age 12 and older.
- The violent crime rate was 17.1 victimizations per 1,000 persons age 12 or older; for property crimes it was 127.4 per 1,000 households.
- Males experienced 18.4 violent victimizations and females experienced 15.8 violent victimizations per 1,000 persons age 12 or older.
- African Americans experienced higher rates of violence (26.8 violent victimizations per 1,000 persons age 12 or older) than whites (15.8 violent victimizations per 1,000 persons age 12 or older).
- Strangers commit 55% of victimizations of males and 30% of victimizations of females.
- About 22% of all violent crime incidents involved an armed offender.

- Overall, 49% of violent and 40% of property victimizations were reported to police.[16]

- College students were the victims of nearly one half million violent crimes annually.

- Overall, college students have lower victimization rates than similarly aged non-students.[17]

- African Americans are six times more likely than Whites to be murdered and about eight times more likely to be murdered than other racial groups.[18]

- With a rate of 8.4 per 1,000 African Americans age 12 or older, blacks have a firearm victimization rate that is 40 percent higher than Hispanics and 200 percent greater than Whites.[19]

Do Official and Victimization Data Match?

Official measures of crime, such as the UCR and NIBRS, and victimization surveys, such as the NCVS, are most important in understanding the incidence of crime. To what degree do official and victimization data paint the same picture about the extent of crime in the United States? This is an important question. If official and victimization reports conflict widely, then we should have little confidence in our understanding about the true magnitude of crime. Moreover, there would be all the more reason to believe methodological criticisms of these methods. If official and victimization data converge, then we are likely measuring the crime problem with confidence, validity, and reliability.

Fortunately, official and victimization data match. For example, criminologists Janet Lauritsen and Robin Schaum recently compared UCR and NCVS data for robbery, burglary, and aggravated assault in Chicago, Los Angeles, and New York from 1980 to 1998. As the three largest cities in the country, this sampling method represents the bulk of crime that is committed in the United States. They found that for burglary and robbery, UCR crime rates were generally similar to NCVS estimates over the 18-year period. Police and victim survey data were more likely to show discrepancies in levels and trends of aggravated assault perhaps because of its susceptibility to domestic violence polices. Lauritsen and Schaum also found that even when UCR and NCVS data were different, the differences were not statistically significant.[20] Substantively, the UCR and NCVS tell the same story about the magnitude of these three serious crimes in the nation's three biggest metropolitan areas. In fact, criminologists have examined the concurrent validity of official and victimization (and even self-reported) data for decades. With a few minor exceptions, researchers have found that official estimates like the UCR and victimization data like the NCVS are indeed measuring the same thing: the actual incidence or existence of crime.[21]

◆ Criminal Justice Structure and the Magnitude of the Crime Problem

First, there is a staggering amount of crime that occurs in the United States. If you were to boil the incidence of crime down to regular time intervals it would occur with frightening regularity. Indeed, as the Crime Clock shows, one violent crime occurs every 24 seconds and one property crime occurs every 3 seconds. Think of it this way: Your university criminal justice course lasts approximately one hour, which is 3,600 seconds. In the span of each and every one-hour criminal justice course that you take, 150 violent crimes and 1,200 property crimes occur!

Second, the criminal justice system has often been referred to as a funnel because cases are subjected to increasing levels of legal scrutiny as they pass from the possession of police to courts to corrections. As the UCR, NIBRS, and NCVS show, most crimes do not result in arrest because they never come to the attention of the police. The "dark figure" of crime is immense; the capacity of the criminal justice system is significantly more limited. Even if a crime is cleared by arrest, it does not mean that it will result in criminal punishment. There are many ways that a case can be ejected from the criminal justice system resulting in very few cases at the end of the criminal justice funnel. The next sections provide evidence for the sheer magnitude of the crime problem and the structural limitations and inabilities of the criminal justice system to address it.[22]

Federal Justice Statistics

Criminal justice often refers to local and state entities that combat crime across the country. Importantly, the United States has its own criminal justice system comprised of numerous federal agencies, such as the Federal Bureau of Investigation, the U.S. Marshals Service, the Drug Enforcement Administration, the Executive Office for the U.S. Attorneys, the Administrative Office of the U.S. Courts, the U.S. Sentencing Commission, and the Federal Bureau of Prisons. In one year, the federal criminal justice system investigated 124,335 persons for violations of federal law in which 124,074 were ultimately arrested. Of those arrested, 87,727 persons were actually prosecuted. In other words, U.S. Attorneys declined to prosecute more than one in four (27%) federal arrestees. Among those prosecuted, 71,798 were convicted and 53,682 were sentenced to prison. Of those originally investigated for federal violations, only 43 percent end in prison.[26] Although these data might seem unnerving, it is important to recognize that the federal criminal justice system is *tougher* than the various state-level criminal justice systems. As you will see, non-federal criminal justice is characterized by even more slack and leniency.

State Justice Statistics

Overall, similar funnel-like processes characterize state criminal justice systems. Thomas Cohen and Tracey Kyckelhahn, statisticians with the Bureau of Justice Statistics, examined the course of felony defendants in the 75 largest urban counties in the United States in a one-month period. Total arrests exceeded 58,100 of which 23% were violent felonies. Among the felony defendants, 60% are released on bond prior to their case reaching its ultimate disposition. Among the violent felonies, the conviction rate was a meager 50%. The conviction rate for misdemeanors and non-violent felonies was 68%. Almost all of these convictions are secured via guilty pleas. Among the serious violent felonies that result in conviction, 55% are sentenced to prison, 326% are sentenced to jail, and 18% are sentenced to probation.

The funnel-like nature of criminal justice becomes even clearer when you reduce these cases in scale. For instance, of 1,000 serious crimes, 500 go unreported and 500 are reported to the police. Of the remaining 500 cases, 400 are unsolved and 100 result in arrest. From the 100 remaining cases, 65 are adult cases in which 25 are dropped. Of the 35 cases that go to juvenile court, 30 of these result in summary probation or are dismissed. Only five juvenile cases will ultimately result in incarceration. Among the criminal cases (with an adult defendant), 30 go to trial and 10 defendants abscond on bail. Of the 30, 27 plead guilty, two are found guilty, and one is acquitted. Of the 29 guilty, 20 are ultimately incarcerated and nine are placed on probation.[24]

The volume of crime that goes unpunished can also be observed by simply analyzing data from successive stages of the criminal justice system. For example, recall that the FBI collects data on the percent of crimes cleared by arrest. Overall, these data tend to show that most crimes are not solved. The percent cleared by arrest for the Index crimes are relatively low: murder (61%), forcible rape (41%), robbery (25%), aggravated assault (54%), burglary (13%), motor vehicle theft (13%), larceny (17%), and arson (17%).[25] Moreover, the probability of being convicted and sentenced to incarceration, provided that a criminal is actually arrested, is similarly low. Just over 70% of murders, about 30% of rapes, 35% of robberies, 15% of assaults, and about 27% of burglaries result in imprisonment.[26] However, even imprisonment is adulterated or watered down. For example, the average sentence for violent convictions is 89 months of which only 43 months or 48 percent of the sentence is actually served. On average, murderers serve a meager 71 months of a 149-month sentence. Rapists serve 65 months of a 117-month sentence. Kidnappers serve 52 months of a 104-month sentence, and robbers serve 44 months of a 95-month sentence.[27]

CSI and the Iceberg of Unsolved Cases

The most popular show on television is *CSI: Crime Scene Investigation*. The show and its two spin-offs, *CSI: Miami* and *CSI: New York,* document the investigative role that forensic scientists and crime labs play in solving crimes. In addition to crime scene investigation, criminalists and crime laboratories perform a variety of important analytical responsibilities including ballistics, toolmark and footwear analysis, trace analysis, latent print analysis, fire debris, conventional serology, toxicology, and blood alcohol analysis. There are 389 publicly funded forensic crime labs in the United States that employ about 12,000 full-time employees. The typical lab has two managers, two secretaries, 12 analysts, two technicians, and a median budget of $1.3 million. On average, a crime lab begins the year with a backlog of 390 requests. Overall, labs outsource nearly 240,000 requests for forensic services to private laboratories. Criminologists Joseph Peterson and Matthew Hickman estimated that 1,900 additional full-time employees costing more than $70 million would be needed to achieve a 30-day turnaround for all forensic requests. Moreover, about 75% of the labs indicated that additional technological and equipment resources with estimated costs of $500 million would be needed to achieve the 30-day turnaround.[28]

However, unlike the television programs which operate with exceptional speed and finality (quintessential crime-control characteristics), real criminal justice forensics move much slower. For example, at the beginning of 2001, 81% of DNA crime laboratories had backlogs totaling 16,081 subject cases and 265,329 convicted offender samples. To complete DNA case and convicted offender sample analyses, 45% of crime labs contracted with private laboratories which in turn had a backlog of 918 subject cases and 100,706 convicted offender samples.[29]

The backlog of unsolved cases presents a host of problems that compromise criminal justice. For example, the National Institute of Justice appropriated funds to the Miami-Dade Police Department, Palm Beach County Sheriff's Office, and New York City Police Department to analyze DNA evidence from property crimes. They have found that using DNA evidence to solve seemingly minor property crimes often nets arrests for more serious violent crimes. In New York, DNA from murder crime scenes often matches DNA from non-related burglary scenes. The state's first 1,000 checks of DNA records showed that the vast majority of defendants were linked to other crimes. Indeed, 82 percent of persons involved in murder or rape were already in the Combined DNA Index System (CODIS) for property crimes like burglary. In Miami-Dade, 526 no-suspect DNA profiles produced 271 hits and in Palm Beach 229 profiles produced 91 hits. Of the 362 Florida CODIS hits, 56 percent came from evidence collected at burglary scenes.[30]

Fortunately, the national backlog of unsolved cases and the potential of forensic technology to solve crimes are increasingly being noticed by the criminological research community. Criminologists at Washington State University recently conducted a nationally representative survey of law enforcement agencies to examine the number of unsolved cases and barriers associated with case processing. They produced four major findings. First, the backlog of unsolved homicides, rapes, and burglaries with possible biological evidence is massive, about 700,000 cases. Second, nearly 25% of law enforcement agencies do not send DNA evidence to labs because they do not have a suspect. These are exactly the kinds of scenarios where the existing offender

DNA database (CODIS) is most useful. Third, crime laboratories are overworked, understaffed, and insufficiently funded. This contributes to their inefficiency and law enforcement's reluctance to explore forensic angles to solving crimes. Pratt and his colleagues' corroborate the conclusions of the Bureau of Justice Statistics reports, which also found that crime labs are overburdened and saddled with case backlogs. Finally, the major policy implication from their study is that the federal government could play a larger role in reducing the national backlog of cases.[31]

Summary: Balancing Crime Control and Due Process

- The volume of crime far exceeds the capacity of the criminal justice system.
- Most crimes go undetected, unsolved, and without notice of the criminal justice system.
- The UCR Program is the most venerable and validated source of crime data and provides the most coverage.
- The NIBRS program provides more contextual information about crimes and encompasses more offenses than the UCR.
- The NCVS is a nationally representative sample of 76,000 households of crime victims 12 and older and includes much information about crimes, criminal offenders, and crime victims.
- All sources of crime data, official, victimization, and self-report, have various strengths and weaknesses relating to coverage, validity, and reliability.
- According to all sources of data, youths, males, and non-whites disproportionately commit crime.
- Throughout the criminal justice process, cases exit the system for a variety of reasons. For this reason, criminal justice has been likened to a funnel.
- Most crimes are not cleared by arrest, for example nearly 40 percent of murders are not cleared or solved.
- Federal and state criminal justice systems ultimately punish a fraction of those initially investigated and arrested.
- Hundreds of thousands of serious unsolved crimes are backlogged annually.

◆ Web Links

Association of State Uniform Crime Reporting Programs
(www.asucrp.org)

Bureau of Justice Statistics
(www.ojp.usdoj.gov/bjs)

Combined DNA Index System
(www.fbi.gov/hq/lab/codis/index1.htm)

FBI Uniform Crime Reports
(www.fbi.gov/ucr.htm)

Justice Information Center
(www.ncjrs.org)

National Crime Victimization Survey
(www.ojp.usdoj.gov/bjs/cvict.htm)

National Incident-Based Reporting System
(www.ojp.usdoj.gov/bjs/nibrs.htm)

National Institute of Corrections
(www.nicic.org)

NIBRS Frequently Asked Questions
(www.fbi.gov/ucr/nibrs/faqs.htm)

Office for the Victims of Crime
(www.ovc.gov)

Office of Community Oriented Policing Services
(www.cops.usdoj.gov)

Office of Juvenile Justice and Delinquency Prevention
(www.ojjdp.ncjrs.org)

President's DNA Initiative
(www.dna.gov)

Questions

1. Part One crimes comprise of:

    a. Theft, car jacking, rape, murder, arson, non-negligent manslaughter and robbery
    b. Murder, non-negligent manslaughter, rape, robbery, burglary, larceny-theft and motor vehicle theft
    c. Murder, non-negligent manslaughter, rape, robbery, burglary, larceny-theft, motor vehicle theft and arson
    d. Murder, non-negligent manslaughter, rape, robbery, burglary, larceny-theft, motor vehicle theft and car jacking

2. Participation in the UCR is voluntary.

    a. True
    b. False

3. The volume of crime far exceeds the capacity of the criminal justice system.

    a. True
    b. False

4. Most crimes go undetected, unsolved and without notice by the criminal justice system.

    a. True
    b. False

5. The NCVS is a nationally representative sample of 76,000 households of crime victims aged 12 and older.

    a. True
    b. False

6. According to all sources of data, youths, females and whites disproportionately commit crime.

    a. True
    b. False

7. Throughout the criminal justice process, cases exit the system for a variety of reasons. Therefore, criminal justice has been likened to a _____.

    a. Syphon
    b. Funnel
    c. Inverted cone
    d. Shutter

8. Most crimes are not cleared by arrest; for example, nearly _____ percent of murders are not cleared or solved.

    a. 20
    b. 60
    c. 80
    d. 40

9. The UCR Program is the most venerable and validated source of crime data and provides the most coverage.

    a. True
    b. False

10. The NIBRS program provides more contextual information about crimes and encompasses more offenses than the UCR.

    a. True
    b. False

Endnotes

1. Federal Bureau of Investigation. (2010). *Crime in the United States, 2009.* Washington, DC: U.S. Department of Justice, Government Printing Office.
2. Vandiver, M., & Giacopassi, D. (1997). One million and counting: Students' estimates of the annual number of homicides in the U. S. *Journal of Criminal Justice Education, 8,* 135–144.
3. Federal Bureau of Investigation. (2010). *Crime in the United States, 2009.* Washington, DC: U. S. Department of Justice, Government Printing Office; Federal Bureau of Investigation. (2005). *Uniform Crime Reporting Handbook, 2004.* Washington, DC: U. S. Department of Justice, Government Printing Office.
4. Federal Bureau of Investigation. (2005). *Uniform Crime Reporting Handbook, 2004.* Washington, DC: U. S. Department of Justice, Government Printing Office.
5. Federal Bureau of Investigation, note 4.
6. Uniform Crime Reporting (UCR) Summary Reporting: Frequently Asked Questions, Retrieved February 24, 2011, from http://www.fbi.gov/ucr/ucrquest/htm.
7. Federal Bureau of Investigation, note 4.
8. Federal Bureau of Investigation. (2005). *Uniform Crime Reporting Handbook, 2004.* Washington, DC: U.S. Department of Justice, Government Printing Office. Definitions and other information about Part II offenses can be found in the UCR Handbook from pages 139 to 147.
9. http://www.fbi.gov/ucr/ucrquest.htm, Retrieved February 24, 2011.
10. For more summary information on NIBRS, readers can consult the following. Maxfield, M. G. (1999). The National Incident-Based Reporting System: Research and policy applications. *Journal of Quantitative Criminology, 15,* 119–149; Rantala, R. R., & Edwards, T. J. (2000). *Effects of NIBRS on crime statistics, Special Report.* Washington, DC: U.S. Department of Justice, Office of Justice Programs, Bureau of Justice Statistics.
11. Hirschel, D. (2009). *Expanding police ability to report crime: The National Incident-Based Reporting System.* Washington, DC: U.S. Department of Justice, National Institute of Justice.
12. Rantala & Edwards, note 13.
13. Biderman, A. D., & Reiss, A. J. (1967). On exploring the 'dark figure' of crime. *The Annals of the American Academy of Political and Social Science, 374,* 1–15.
14. Truman, J. L., & Rand, M. R. (2010). *Criminal victimization, 2009.* Washington, DC: U.S. Department of Justice, Office of Justice Programs, Bureau of Justice Statistics.
15. For investigations of the strengths and weaknesses of victimization data, see Bachman, R. (1998). Factors related to rape reporting behavior and arrest: New evidence from the NCVS. *Criminal Justice and Behavior, 25,* 8–29; Bachman, R. (2000). A comparison of annual incidence rates and contextual characteristics of intimate-partner violence against women from the National Crime Victimization Survey (NCVS) and National Violence Against Women Survey (NVAWS). *Violence Against Women, 6,* 839–867; Gottfredson, M. R., & Hindelang, M. J. (1977). A consideration of telescoping and memory decay biases in victimization surveys. *Journal of Criminal Justice, 5,* 205–216; Lauritsen, J. L. (2001). The social ecology of violent victimization: Individual and contextual effects in the NCVS. *Journal of Quantitative Criminology, 17,* 3–32; Maltz, M. D., & Zawitz, M. W.

(1996). *Displaying violent crime trends using estimates from the NCVS.* Washington, DC: U.S. Department of Justice, Office of Justice Programs, Bureau of Justice Statistics.

16. Truman & Rand, note 17.
17. Baum, K., & Klaus, P. (2005). Violent victimization of college students, 1995–2002. Washington, DC: U.S. Department of Justice, Office of Justice Programs, Bureau of Justice Statistics.
18. Rennison, C. (2001). *Violent victimization and race, 1993–1998.* Washington, DC: U. S. Department of Justice, Office of Justice Programs, Bureau of Justice Statistics.
19. Perkins, C. (2003). *Weapon use and violent crime, National Crime Victimization Survey, 1993–2001.* Washington, DC: U.S. Department of Justice, Office of Justice Programs, Bureau of Justice Statistics.
20. Lauritsen, J. L. & Schaum, R. J. (2005). *Crime and victimization in the three largest metropolitan areas, 1980–1998.* Washington, DC: U.S. Department of Justice, Office of Justice Programs, Bureau of Justice Statistics.
21. For studies that dispute the UCR-NCS or NCVS overlap, see, Menard, S. (1987). Short-term trends in crime and delinquency: A comparison of UCR, NCS, and self-report data. *Justice Quarterly,* 4, 455–474; Menard, S., & Covey, H. C. (1988). UCR and NCS: Comparisons over space and time. *Journal of Criminal Justice,* 16, 371–384. For studies that affirmed the overlap, see, Blumstein, A., Cohen, J., & Rosenfeld, R. (1991). Trend and deviation in crime rates: A comparison of UCR and NCS data for burglary and robbery. *Criminology,* 29, 237–264; Hindelang, M. J. (1974). The uniform crime reports revisited. *Journal of Criminal Justice,* 2, 1–17; MacDowall, D., & Loftin, C. (1992). Comparing the UCR and NCS over time. *Criminology,* 30, 125–132; Messner, S. F. (1984). The 'dark figure' and composite indexes of crime: Some empirical explorations of alternative data sources. *Journal of Criminal Justice,* 12, 435–444; O'Brien, R. M. (1991). Detrended UCR and NCS crime rates: Their utility and meaning. *Journal of Criminal Justice,* 19, 569–574.
22. Although it is commonly understood that there is more crime than the criminal justice system can handle, few criminologists have explicitly commented on this. Indeed, there are scores of books and articles lamenting the size of the American criminal justice system, but none of these make the obvious point that criminal justice would be even more pronounced if more crimes were processed. An exception is a study by economist Richard Freeman who found that about 2% of the American GDP is allotted to crime control activities. Depending on your perspective, crime control or due process, this is part of the overhead of running a modern society or is pure waste. See, Freeman, R. B. (1996). Why do some many young American men commit crimes and what might we do about it? *Journal of Economic Perspectives,* 10, 25–42.
23. Smith, S. K., & Motivans, M. (2005). *Federal criminal case processing, 2002: With trends 1982–2002.* Washington, DC: U.S. Department of Justice, Office of Justice Programs, Bureau of Justice Statistics.
24. Cohen, T. H., & Kyckelhahn, T. (2010). *Felony defendants in large urban counties, 2006.* Washington, DC: U.S. Department of Justice, Office of Justice Programs, Bureau of Justice Statistics; Cohen, T. H., & Reaves, B. A. (2006). *Felony defendants in large urban counties, 2002.* Washington, DC: U.S. Department of Justice, Office of Justice Programs, Bureau of Justice Statistics.
25. Federal Bureau of Investigation, note 4.

CHAPTER 3
ORIGINS OF MODERN POLICING

Providing or requiring a body of citizens to take responsibility for protecting each other and their property is recorded in the earliest records of human activities. That is not to say or suggest that in history there were police forces, as we understand them today. In most instances, policing was fragmentary and comprised of local men often unwillingly conscripted into a role that they performed under duress. Those in power often created the position of bodyguard to make sure they were personally protected. Today we usually consider this a paid position, but it was certainly not the case for those providing protection to ancient kings, pharaohs and Caesars. Additionally, many males were employed or forced into door keeping roles to protect valuables, not just the leader or temples, but also food and supplies for the citizenry.

Night watchmen and guards were often military personnel or, in remote rural communities, men and boys from the village who took turns watching the perimeters of the village to ensure that others in the community could sleep safely at night.

There are ancient Egyptian records of an organized force of men providing security to tombs and living souls, and these men appeared to receive a salary for their work from the pharaoh's treasury. Exactly when in history this transformed into 'policing' is not clear.

The word police has origins in the Greek 'politia', but this encompassed many job tasks not undertaken today by modern police forces. However, as we shall see, in many continental

From *Crime and Policing Crime* by Peter Johnstone. Copyright © 2013 by Kendall Hunt Publishing Company. Reprinted by permission.

European countries the police still undertake a considerably larger number of civic activities than seen in the Common Law countries, such as Canada, the US, the UK, India and Australia.

It is important to recognize that many of the police forces of the world today owe their origins to either the Greek and Romano based Civil Law policing systems or to the Common Law derivation. They are fundamentally different. Those nations that adhere to Civil Law principles tend towards a military or quasi-military form of policing with armed officers who look and feel like military personnel. These police are normally highly centralized and may answer to a ministry of the interior or to the Ministry of Defense. Frequently the officers live in barracks and have a rigid, hierarchical rank structure.

Police officers under the Common Law model tend to be local and de-centralized; they may or may not carry a weapon and they are answerable to a combination of local interests and a minister. They rarely if ever live in barracks. The value of this model is believed to be that the people serving are part of the community they serve.

It is important to recognize these differences from the outset as there is no one model of policing and what it means to be a police officer can, and does, vary greatly in different jurisdictions.

There is a widely held view that is authored in a number of US criminal justice textbooks that the overwhelmingly major influence upon policing in America has been Robert Peel and the Metropolitan Police Act of 1829. In this chapter, I will explore this position and suggest that the influence of Peel is important but represents only one part of a far more complex policing history for the US—one drawn that draws in part from 17th century Paris and evolved in England around 1720 with adoption of the word 'police', more by accident than by choice. Over the course of the following 100 years, and frequently to the chagrin of the British political elite, England subsumed a number of European policing models alongside uniquely English creations that resulted in a uniformed police force known as the Metropolitan Police. Some of these characteristics came to America, resulting in a 21st century policing model that is the product of a complex and multi-faceted policing history influenced by an English metropolitan police, a French gendarmerie, a Roman vigilante, a contemporary 12th century Norman tax collector (who acted as a part-time peace officer) and private detectives from French prisons.

◆ Early Days: Sheriffs, Constables and Night Watchmen

Influences upon policing in the US are as diverse[1] as the pattern of policing within the country. It was perhaps inevitable that given the swaying power of Britain upon the early development of the USA there would be an adoption of established criminal justice practices from Britain, especially those from England and the Common Law.

In America, the English criminal justice lexicon—sheriff, constable, 'Hue and Cry', magistrates, justices of the peace, circuit judges and a concept of what it means to 'police'—are all largely, but not exclusively, informed by England. However, a closer inspection of the informing factors reveals that much of what occurred in policing in England throughout the Middle Ages and into the 18th century was not exclusively a domestic creation. Subsequently, what transferred to the US as an English system was in fact concomitant with Anglo-Saxon[2] and Nordic customs, with influence from France in the 11th century and then again, significantly, in the 18th century.

> "The office of sheriff is the one secular dignity generally known in English-speaking lands which for more than nine centuries has maintained a continuous existence and preserved its distinguishing features."[3]

Over time the responsibilities of the shire-reeve, the sheriff, increased and his role developed into, *inter alia,* that of tax collector, jailer and court administrator.[4] The task of securing felons and then holding them until the arrival of a court was a responsibility assigned to the sheriff from the period of Alfred the Great.[5]

William the Conqueror and first Norman king of England significantly increased the responsibilities of the sheriff. Within the first few years of his reign, he appointed numerous fellow countrymen to the county shire-reeves position to ensure that there was a close watch upon the fiscal as well as local feudal responsibilities.[6] Importantly though, local and new French sheriffs did not lose any of the previous responsibilities of the office. "Among these may be named his powers connected with peace and with police."[7] Whereas in the pre-Norman period the sheriff had authority to preside over a hundred court hearings, to uphold the king's peace and to apprehend suspected criminals, under William these functions were formalized and positively encouraged.

The office of constable also existed prior to the arrival of the conqueror. At the time of the invasion, sheriffs were ordered by Harold of England to "... appoint constables in the hundreds, townships and neighborhoods. All were to obey the head constable of the shire in matters."[8]

Aside from his famous dispute with Thomas Beckett, Henry II was responsible for many legal innovations. The Assize of Clarendon, 1166, has frequent references to the sheriff[9] in their policing and custodial roles:

> "And when a robber or murderer or thief, or harbourers of them, shall be taken on the aforesaid oath, if the Justices shall not be about to come quickly enough into that county where they have been taken, the sheriffs shall send word to the nearest justice through some intelligent man, that they have taken such men; and the Justices shall send back word to the sheriffs where they wish those men to be brought before them: and the sheriffs shall bring them before the Justices."[10]

King John reluctantly signed the Magna Carta in 1215, one year before his death. This famous document contains 63 clauses, 27 of which relate to the role and functions of the sheriff. Clause 47 states that "We will not make men justices, constables, sheriffs, or bailiffs, unless they are such as know the law of the realm, and are minded to observe it rightly."[11]

By the time of Henry III,[12] roving felons were a significant problem and constables were regularly assisting sheriffs in providing patrols within villages and across the countryside to ensure safe passage between villages and to market towns.[13] Henry III also increased the remit of his peace officers to take responsibility for patrolling the English coastline and vulnerable fortifications.[14]

Towards the end of Henry's reign, the sheriffs and their assistants, the constables, had accumulated significant powers, including the provision of protection to inland castles. To counteract this encroachment upon their 'bailiwick',[15] the barons collaborated and managed to reaffirm themselves as the primary custodians of the shire.

By the close of the 13th century, the 'shire keepers" role had developed into a regional responsibility,[16] which in some respects had the effect of restoring the primary policing function within the bailiwick back with the sheriffs[17] and constables. The elevated office of shire keeper remained and gained in stature to become the primary administrative functionary of a county. It still exists in England today as the, largely ceremonial, Lord Lieutenant[18] who is served by his assistant the High Sheriff.[19] The first person to hold the office of sheriff in America was William Stone in 1634 in the County of Accomack, Virginia.[20]

One visible policing aspect of being sheriff was the ability to require that local citizens assist in the apprehension of offenders. This right to demand help existed in medieval England as well as in colonial America. The formation of a posse[21] gained greater actual, as well as fictional, notoriety during westward expansion in the US. It has also been attributed to the development of vigilantism and private policing during the 18th and 19th centuries.[22] In terms of policing models, the sheriff is one of the only examples of centralized policing ever to occur in England. Its transposition to the US alongside decentralized city forces gives the US uniqueness lost to England centuries ago.

In England, the night watchmen, beadle and constable limped through protecting citizens and apprehending criminals for the next 500 years, whereas in France the king had created a policing presence, the *Maréchaussée,* as far back as the early 1100s. This was followed by a larger military police response from 1337[23] onwards.

Between 1536 and 1544, King Francis I implemented a range of measures to formalize policing across the nation.

The 'Sun King' Louis XIV reigned in France from 1643 to 1715. He was renowned for his work on legal reform largely instituted and executed by his minister Jean Baptiste Colbert.[24] In October 1666, Louis ordered Colbert to design a plan for a Paris police force. By March of the following year, Louis authorized the creation of the office of Prefect of Police for Paris,[25] followed in 1699 by a royal decree that authorized the establishment of Prefecture of Police for each major city in France.[26]

Over the period of the next 150 years, the role and function of the city police of France expanded. This occurred particularly with the Prefecture of Police and his officers, who assumed judicial responsibilities unfamiliar to sheriffs and constables in England. In one instance, the 'police court' at *Le Châtelet,* Paris, heard 200 cases in a three-hour period. Forty-five women and 16 men were sentenced that day, May 25, 1759.[27] The sentencing powers of the police court were also extensive. Benjamin Dechauflour was tried for sodomy on May 24, 1726. He was convicted the same day and sentenced to death by burning. The punishment was carried out the following morning.[28]

As the pending revolution gained momentum in France, so too did the anxiety of the monarchy, and Paris slid into a period of sinister policing where spying became the main thrust of police work within the capital. Often quoted but never verified, Gabriel de Sartines, Lieutenant-General of Police from 1759 to 1774, reportedly told the king that wherever three persons speak to one another on the street, one of them would be one of his police spies.[29] Undoubtedly, the pre-Revolution Paris police[30] represent a well-organized body of law enforcement personnel that had specialist skills and responsibilities far beyond those represented in England during the same period. The cities of France had a formal civilian police presence and the smaller towns and villages had the protections provided by a military police. By 1788, there was one police officer for every 193 residents of Paris.[31]

After the tumultuous events of the revolution, the Maréchaussée managed to remain in form but were renamed the *Gendarmerie Nationale*.[32] Drawn from the ranks of serving military personnel, the *Gendarmerie Nationale* consisted of well trained, well resourced, well paid military men who lived in barracks[33] and provided police services to the citizens and the highways of rural France.

As 'the man who would restore order to a society plagued by crime, violence and uncertainty',[34] Napoléon created a military police force that was copied throughout continental Europe. His less famous civilian police continued to employ dubious spying methods under the directorship of Joseph Fouché;[35] but combined, the military country police and the civilian city police provided a comprehensive and effective policing response for France that was superior to every other nation state in the world at the time.

Introducing the Word 'Police'

In 18th century England, the word police was virtually unknown.[36] When the word was introduced "... it was regarded with the utmost suspicion as a portent of the sinister force which held France in its grip."[37] As Edward Burt wrote in 1720, "... Soon after his arrival in London, he had observed a good deal of Dirt and disorder in the Streets, and asking about the *Police,* but finding none that understood the Term, he cried out, Good lord! How can one expect Order among these people, who have not such heard a Word as *Police* in their Language."[38]

London was reeling under a crime wave and the local watch and beadle system was woefully incapable of dealing with the organized serial felon.

The constable system was still a reflection of medieval England and the night watchmen were old, inept and frequently asleep or drunk on duty.[39]

In 1792, the Middlesex Justices Act created the establishment of a police office within London.

In reality, much had been achieved before passage of this legislation and a recognizable police force had been in existence in a number of manifestations for the City of Westminster and the River Thames for many years. "In fact, there were a number of police offices, all rather similar to the Bow Street police office which had been functioning for 30 years."[40]

In the early years of the 18th century, Thomas de Veil was appointed as magistrate to the City of Westminster. Over the course of the next 17 years he established his Bow Street office as one of the most efficient within the metropolis.

In 1748, the novelist Henry Fielding and his half-brother John Fielding succeeded De Veil.[41] Henry soon authored *An Enquiry into the Cause of the Late Increase of Robbers* and, to the surprise of some of his contemporaries, Fielding immersed himself into writing about[42] and practicing the establishment of a police force for the City of Westminster and Middlesex County from the Bow Street residence.

Over time, the mixed bag of assistants that Fielding managed to employ proved themselves to be reliable thief catchers with an in-depth knowledge of the criminals within the immediate vicinity of Bow Street.[43]

His associates were soon nicknamed the Bow Street Runners,[44] and their official title was Principal Officer of Bow Street.[45]

The combined efforts of De Veil, the Fieldings and Patrick Colquhoun all amount to a significant influence upon policing London. Armed officers patrolled the main streets of London during the nighttime,[46] the highways into and out of the metropolis were 'policed' by 68 patrols[47] and on the eve of the 1829 Act uniformed officers patrolled the central streets during daylight hours.[48]

In 1792, a Scottish born merchant who had spent a number of years in Virginia was one of the first appointees under the new legislation that created stipendiary magistrates.[49] Patrick Colquhoun[50] immediately took up the issue of providing London with a regular, paid, full-time police force.

He anonymously published *A Treatise on the Police of the Metropolis* in 1795 in which he estimated that the indigent population of London was so great that there was in existence a class of habitual criminals, 50,000 in number, who had no alternative but to engage in crime.[51] He even suggested that the French police[52] were a suitable model[53] for adoption in England.[54]

Needless to say, these views won him no friends in the British parliament and his strenuous attempts to bring about the adoption of legislation that would establish a London police force were repeatedly defeated.[55] Undaunted by the intransigence of the British ruling elite, Colquhoun persisted and he can certainly be credited with playing a significant role in the establishment of a full time police force for the River Thames.[56]

In June 1798, the merchants of London established a Marine Police Establishment[57] with a permanent staff of 80[58] and a reserve of more than one thousand. By the end of the year, *The Times* reported that, "It is astonishing the effects the institution has already achieved in the preventing of piracies and robberies...."[59]

In 1800, the British government endorsed the private policing enterprise and a Police Bill[60] was passed to formalize and make public policing of the River Thames. The main proponents of the bill[61] were John Harriot,[62] Patrick Colquhoun[63] and Jeremy Bentham.[64]

There can be no doubt that London now had a permanent, uniformed police force that operated as a "public institution, regulated by statute and designed to safeguard commercial and other property on the river."[65]

Views about the impact of the Fielding's and Colquhoun are varied.

Sir Robert Peel

Opposition against a fulltime land force for London was still strong in the early years of the 19th century. Britain was at war with France and the populous, the press and the parliament repeatedly rejected anything that had the slightest resemblance to a *Gendarmerie*.[66] "The necessities of time, emphasized by the crime wave and frequent riots, created the stage for London police reform; however, little could have been accomplished without the political skills of Sir Robert Peel."[67]

Peel[68] was promoted to Chief Secretary for Ireland in September 1812. His responsibilities included the maintenance of law and order in the country, and to this effect he was responsible for the Peace Preservation Act 1814,[69] which established the Irish Peace Preservation Force,[70] a forerunner to the Royal Irish Constabulary of 1822.[71] Public disturbances had become a regular feature of life throughout Ireland and the government frequently faced the task of quelling public disorder.

Peel was much impressed by Napoléon's *Gendarmerie;* he approved of the military rigor and the utilization of a barrack system to house members of the force. And whereas he might not have been as enamored as Colquhoun, who had referred to the French police as having "The greatest degree of professionalism,"[72] he certainly recognized the value of having a countrywide paramilitary policing response that was answerable to a central authority.

Peel retired from his post as Chief Secretary for Ireland in 1817 and returned to England. His departure from Ireland was lamented in many quarters,[73] and it has been said, perhaps generously, that he may have intentionally created the Peace Preservation Force to help alleviate the "pitiable condition of Ireland"[74] by providing a source of employment.

Peel left Ireland with the blueprint for a Common Law Gendarmerie that was to be exported around the globe to almost every former British colony. It was considered by some as, "Being without parallel in its semi-military organisation, with exception, perhaps, of the French gendarmerie. . . ."[75]

In 1822, Peel was elevated to the position of Home Secretary where he would now have the opportunity to grapple with the police issue back in England.[76]

Peel had become an astute and cautious politician. He recognized that to move forward he would need to advocate a moderate approach that emphasized preventative measures and crime detection provided for by a uniformed but distinctly civilian force.[77] A compromise was inevitable.

One significant factor for Peel was the strong opposition voiced by the financial 'City of London'.[78] He decided not to attempt to bring the 'Square Mile' into his new plans,[79] and on Tuesday September 29, 1829,[80] the first uniformed officers of the London Metropolitan Police commenced evening patrol across the metropolis, save the City.[81]

Their uniforms were carefully chosen to reflect civilian fashion of the day, top hat and blue tunic tails,[82] and they carried no more than a truncheon to protect themselves against the criminal underworld of the metropolis.

Within eight months the initial intake of one thousand men[83] had risen to more than three thousand.[84]

The new police force was led by two commissioners, both of Irish descent, one a lawyer, Richard Mayne,[85] and the other a former military officer, Lt. Colonel Charles Rowan.[86]

Despite initial criticism of Peel and his influential supporter the Duke of Wellington, London's 'Raw Lobsters'[87] slowly turned the hearts and minds of its skeptics and the more endearing terms 'Peelers' and 'Bobby'[88] began to enter the 'new policing' language.

Every recruit to the new London Metropolitan Police was issued a handbook of *General Instructions* compiled by Sir Robert Peel.

It stated: "It should be understood at the outset that the object to be attained is the prevention of crime . . . The absence of crime will be considered the best proof of the complete efficiency of the police."[89] These words have endured and are still viewed as the fundamental basis for policing in many parts of the world today. By 1856, the County and Borough Police Act required every county and borough in England and Wales to establish a police force.[90]

One of the dilemmas Peel faced was whether to establish a uniformed or a plain clothed police force. Either way he was likely to be criticized.[91]

If uniformed, they would be a *Gendarmerie* and if plain clothed, they would be Paris police 'spies'.[92] As we know, he opted for uniforms.

A detective unit was not established in London until 1842.

During the interim period, Principal Officers[93] from the disbanded Bow Street Police Office served as a detective agency available for hire to individuals as well as to the Metropolitan Police.

French Detectives

In France, a significant detective police department, much maligned by the English as 'sinister', had been operational for more than one hundred years. Then under Fouche, this unit gained greater notoriety and the name *brigade de sûreté*. But it was not until the arrival of a former criminal, Eugène Vidocq, in 1812 that the *Sûreté* became synonymous with sleuths and undercover work associated with contemporary police detection.[94] Vidocq was variously described as, "A lower type of man, yet still a great name in the history of French police . . . who began his career as a thief"[95] and "From unpromising origins as a two-bit thief, army deserter, grafter and convict, he rose in fame to become the celebrated chief of the Paris Sûreté police and an internationally renowned private detective."[96]

The 'poacher turned gamekeeper,'[97] Vidocq was apparently a larger-than-life character who captured the friendship and imagination of Dumas and Balzac.

He was "Known to embellish his tales, and historians have difficulty separating fact from fiction in his accounts."[98]

Regardless of the criticism and colorful nature of his character, Vidocq was a pioneer in detective techniques. Not only did he utilize handwriting, paper, and ink analyses to solve cases, but he also foresaw the day when fingerprints would be used to identify suspects.[99]

After his departure, the *Sûreté* continued to rise in stature as the preeminent detective police agency until the arrival of 'Scotland Yard'.

Notwithstanding the rise of the 'Yard', Vidocq's impact traversed the Atlantic and Vidocq is credited with inspiring Allan Pinkerton[100] and J. Edgar Hoover.[101]

The quality and effectiveness of the *Sûreté* did not go unnoticed in London either, and a number of years after Vidocq's[102] resignation, a London Metropolitan Police officer implemented a version of his model.

There are two dates associated with the introduction of plain clothed detectives in London, 1842 and then 1878.[103]

The first attempts to run an effective detective unit were plagued by allegations of corruption and scandal[104] culminating in the "Trial of the Detectives" in 1877.[105] The following year Charles Howard Vincent,[106] a lawyer, police officer and politician was given the opportunity to re-organize the detective branch and form the modern C.I.D.

Over time, Scotland Yard detectives became synonymous with criminal investigation excellence[107] and surpassed the *Sûreté* in stature.

Colonial Policing in America

Between 1605 and 1905 policing in America was influenced by a multitude of European forces.

There is a collective agreement among a number of authors[108] that early policing methods were drawn from the established roles of the sheriffs, constables,[109] Hue and Cry, night watchmen, vigilantes, and 'watch and ward' along with the wide and varied assortment of criminal justice law enforcement officials that had developed over the previous sixteen hundred years, mostly from England.[110]

Attractive as this simplistic and often very brief approach may be, these accounts rarely, if ever, pay any attention to the role of France and the influences that were made upon English policing by the French.

In reality, much of the old world systems were either irrelevant or rejected by the new settlers and the utilization of an established system of policing was adopted due to familiarity until a better system was created that would be uniquely American.

For the time that colonies were forced to operate under the English crown, adoption of English law, and its policing style, was inevitable. But once the opportunity arose to forge a new body of policing and laws the colonists moved forward swiftly, modifying the familiar and substituting the irrelevant.[111]

Although few formal policing systems were in place in 17th century America,[112] informal ancient and familiar vestiges of a manorial system were prevalent, especially in the Northern states.

In England, bringing a prosecution for a criminal matter was still an individual affair. The private citizen bore the entire cost of the prosecution until legislation partially relieved this burden in 1752. In an effort to encourage the participation of the public in curbing the 18th century crime wave, the crown offered increasingly large rewards[113] to those who gave evidence against felons.[114] Due to the high cost of taking a case before the courts, it became common practice for merchants, farmers and civic groups to form associations to help defray the cost of bringing a criminal prosecution.[115]

A version of the English 'associations' manifested as a more forceful 'crime-control vigilantism'[116] in America, where a relationship between the sheriff and the posse, of which a number grew into vigilantes, was not an uncommon feature of the American frontier.[117]

A crucial distinction should be drawn, however. The English societies never operated outside of the law, whereas the American development into vigilante groups[118] frequently did.[119]

Nevertheless, the similarities are clear; both developments were in response to inadequacies in established policing provision and failures of the criminal justice system to protect the interests of the individual. The corollary between the extra-legal methods employed by the American frontier vigilantes and the emergence of private policing groups that used strong-arm tactics on behalf of railroad and mining companies should not be understated.[120]

By the close of the 18t century, much as England was struggling to make sense of its own crime problems, especially those in the capitol, America too needed to apply a diversity[121] of police responses to the wide variety of challenges facing Southern business entrepreneurs, Northern biblical refugees and Westward bound migrants.

Critics of this view may seek to take refuge in terminology and explain the history of individual entities such as sheriffs as being distinctly different from those of the police. Yet we have seen that the term police was unfamiliar in England during much of the colonial years and once adopted had a broad and varied application.

Narrowing the parameters of the word to Peel's application may indeed have been for the English a way of circumventing something overtly French, but the early role of the police constable in America carried a very broad portfolio of responsibilities far more closely resembling a *sergeant de ville* than a 'Bobby'.

As Inciardi reminds us, "But while the powers of the English sheriff diminished over time, those of the American sheriff expanded to include not only the apprehension of criminals, but also the conducting of elections, the collection of taxes, and the custody of public funds."[122]

◆ Private Policing and the Emergence of State Troopers

Alongside appointed local and municipal law enforcement officials, America also adopted private policing.[123] This was due in part to the slow development of city and statewide policing responses as well as due to the expansion of railroads, industry and commerce that sought to protect its own interests often in the face of worker unrest and labor disputes. Familiar names like Wells Fargo,[124] Brinks,[125] The Pinkerton Agency[126] and The Burns Detective Agency[127] identified a lacuna in the protection of goods and property that public entities were unable to fill. At the same time, population growth, industrialization and the development of cities drew much of American society closer to contemporary European standards. Consequently, the policing needs of the burgeoning East Coast cities were very different from the needs of the rural communities and the pioneers. Social unrest, unemployment and vagrancy needed a policing response in accord with contemporary European models.

By the end of the 19th century, Alan Pinkerton, "The Vidocq of the West,"[128] and other private police agencies found it opportune to transition from personal protection to property protection.

By the close of the 19th century, unemployment was at 20 percent in America's declining employment market, 600 banks had closed and unions had become a significant force in US employment,[129] which meant that American industry increasingly needed to have a body of 'Cossacks'[130] or hoodlums to break strikes.[131]

In 1902, the Great Anthracite Coal Strike devastated Pennsylvania. Coal prices soared[132] and the national and state governments were at a loss as to how to deal with the private labor dispute.

Municipal police officers were either incapable or unprepared to arrest striking miners, and the private police responses provided by the Coal and Iron Police[133] under the supervision of Pinkerton's Detective Agency were heavy handed and frequently accused of brutality by the miners.[134]

It was clear to many observers that these groups "... owed a duty to no one but their employers, and these in turn hired for their private police force the most irresponsible toughs and rough-necks obtainable."[135]

In 1905, the Pennsylvania state governor, Samuel Pennypacker, signed Senate Bill 278 into law. This legislation created the first statewide police agency in America, The Pennsylvania State Constabulary.

Captain John Groome,[136] formerly of the Philadelphia City Cavalry, was tasked with creating and supervising a working statewide police force.

During a subsequent Congressional investigation[137] into alleged reprisals against striking miners by the new force, Major Groome stated, "Of course there were no rules, no regulations, and nothing to go by; and these men were divided into four troops.[138] They were sent to barracks. I designed the uniforms, decided how they should be armed, and decided that it would be necessary for each man to be mounted; and purchased the horses and drilled men and gave them as much instruction."[139]

When questioned about the inspiration for the force, he replied, "... I got the Italians, the Germans and Royal Northwestern police, and the Irish police; and from going over their reports I came to the conclusion that the conditions in Ireland were more similar to those in Pennsylvania, so far as the industrial and agricultural conditions and the character of the population were concerned."[140]

Major Groome then reported to the Committee that he had paid a three week visit to the R.I.C. to fully investigate its organization and operations.[141] Advocates and opponents of the Pennsylvania State Police[142] are agreed; the statewide force copied the Royal Irish Constabulary.[143]

◆ City Policing in America

By 1845, New York had abandoned its previous system of watchmen and adopted a London-style municipal police force.

It was the first outside of the British Empire.[144]

The new force appeared very different from the London model. Officers did not wear a uniform,[145] simply a copper badge, and very soon they exchanged truncheons for firearms.[146]

But it was not the external appearance of the officers that denoted fundamental differences; it was the exercise of power.[147]

The London force had been created to be politically neutral and institutionally controlled.[148] The New York officer's authority was limited by the ballot box.[149]

Interestingly, in New York there was a general concern that the London 'Bobby' was too centralized and accountable to the government and yet the London force was considered within England de-centralized and independent. By 1857,[150] the municipal force was abolished and a metropolitan force was created that would be commanded by state-appointed commissioners.[151]

◆ Summary

The New York police,[152] although allegedly modeled on the English police, were soon undertaking a range of tasks far closer in practice to the Paris police than to their London brothers. For example, New York officers provided babysitting services at the police station, helped people find employment, fought fires, fed the homeless and provided basic medical care.[153] They "... returned lost children by the thousands, shot stray dogs, enforced sanitation laws, inspected boilers, took annual censuses, and performed myriad other small tasks."[154] "Arrests were of little importance, the primary mission of the police was to provide services to citizens and garner votes for politicians."[155]

Not only was there a remarkably different political and social setting for policing New York, there was a remarkably different job specification.[156]

In reality, adapting the London police model to New York meant discarding political neutrality and increasing individual discretion.[157]

This looks very much like a different force altogether, one that more closely resembles the French police who, like America, were born out of political instability resulting in a broad palate of responsibilities.

As Monkkonen noted, "At best, one could say that the creation of the police force reflected a growing intolerance for riots and disorder, rather than a response to an increase in crime".[158] It was not until after the impact of initial formation settled that the city forces of America became practitioners of the narrow term police[159] and 'urban reformers took over the welfare functions of the police."[160]

Sheriffs from Anglo-Saxon England whose powers were enhanced by a Frenchman, Hue and Cry vigilantes[161] in "rural areas and small towns across the nation,"[162] uniformed officers patrolling Paris in the 17th century and military police, policing civilians in rural France and Ireland,[163] a convict turned sleuth who inspired the establishment of private policing in America and city police officers responsible for political policing and the provision of welfare services—all were part of the development of American policing. We have credited Robert Peel with being the 'father' of American policing. But perhaps it is time to adopt a contemporary view of this and consider him more of a 'Significant Other' rather than the exclusive patriarch.

◆ Questions

1. Over time, the responsibilities of the shire-reeve increased and his role developed into, inter alia, those of:

   a. Tax collector, jailer and court administrator
   b. Police officer, issuer of licenses for gaming and court bailiff
   c. Tax inspector, jailer and coroner
   d. All of the above

2. The first person to hold the office of sheriff in America was William Stone in 1634 in:

   a. The County of Accomack, Virginia
   b. The County of Middlesex, Plymouth, MA
   c. Boston, Massachusetts
   d. The County of Potomac, Virginia

3. In October 1666, Louis XIV ordered _____ to design a plan for a Paris police force.

   a. Bonaparte
   b. Baptiste
   c. Colbert
   d. Clouseau

4. By 1788 there was one police officer for every 193 residents of Paris.

   a. True
   b. False

5. In 1892, the Middlesex Justices Act created the establishment of a police office within London.

   a. True
   b. False

6. The official title of the Bow Street Runners was:

   a. Principal Officer of Bow Street
   b. Police Officer of Bow Street
   c. Fielding Officer of Bow Street
   d. There was no official title

7. On Tuesday September 29, 1829, the first uniformed officers of the London Metropolitan Police commenced evening patrol across the metropolis except for:

   a. The County of Middlesex
   b. The City of London (The Square Mile)
   c. The City of Westminster
   d. None of the above

8. "A lower type of man, yet still a great name in the history of French police . . . who began his career as a thief." This statement describes the detective

   a. Jack Clouseau
   b. Eugene Vidocq
   c. James Pinkerton
   d. Sherlock Holmes

9. "We will not make men justices, constables, sheriffs, or bailiffs, unless they are such as know the law of the realm, and are minded to observe it rightly." This statement is taken from:

   a. The English Bill of Rights
   b. The Assize of Clarendon
   c. The 4th Lateran Council
   d. The Magna Carta

10. Military police have existed in France since:

    a. 1337
    b. 1667
    c. 1537
    d. 1369

Endnotes

1. It is believed that there are in the region of 20,000 assorted law enforcement agencies in the US. Many of these are very small in size and comprise of as few as five or six sworn officers. For the purposes of this paper my discussion will focus upon the development of state and local forces. Each of the large number of federal agencies in the US has produced a version of its history that can be viewed on the agency website. Also c.f. the following article that discusses the history of the reorganization of federal agencies: Grafton, C. 1979. The reorganization of federal agencies. *Administration & Society,* February, 10, pp. 437–464, doi:10.1177/009539977901000403
2. Comprehensive coverage of the entire period is contained within the influential works of, inter alia, William Maitland's History of the English law, William Holdsworth's *History of English law* and, more recently, Leon Radzinowicz's *A history of the English criminal law.* These works are voluminous and remarkable reading.
3. Morris, W. 1916. The office of sheriff in the Anglo-Saxon period. *The English Historical Review,* Jan., 31(121), pp. 20–40 at p. 20.
4. During the later part of the Anglo-Saxon period, the alderman was the chief judicial officer within the shire and the sheriff served as the second.
5. Alfred the Great reigned from 849 to 899. He was responsible for the division of lands into boroughs and a number of boroughs together were designated as a shire. Consequently, many cities in Britain are named as boroughs, such as Edinburgh, Peterborough and Wellingborough, and numerous counties are shires, e.g. Cambridgeshire, Worcestershire, Leicestershire. In the late 880s or perhaps early 890s, Alfred issued his legal codes known as the *domboc.*
6. William also retained the services of a number of Englishmen sheriffs, such as Marloswein, Freeman, Robert fitz Wymarc, Round, Touid, Davis, Edric, Edwin and Elfwine. Source: Morris, supra. p. 26 note 52
7. Morris, supra. p. 30
8. Harding, A. 1960. The origins and early history of the kepper of the peace. *Transaction of the Royal Historical Society* (Fifth Series), 10, pp. 85–109 at p. 87. "... for the preservation of the peace of the kingdom and against foreign invaders or others acting against the peace of the realm."
9. Clause 1. Referring to the harboring of robbers, murderers and thieves, "And the Justices shall make this inquest by themselves, and the sheriffs by themselves." Cited in Ernest Henderson, 1896, *Select historical documents of the Middle Ages.* London: George Bell and Sons, p. 16 (taken from Stubbs, Charters, p. 142).
10. Ibid. p. 17
11. Op. cit. Henderson. P. 147
12. Henry III of England, 1207–1272
13. Harding, supra, cites an example from the Public Record Office J.I. 1/734 where in Shropshire 1256 there were ... one hundred and eighty six cases of homicide presented, but only nineteen felons executed ... Crime after crime was presented as committed by *malefactores ignoti* [persons unknown]. The system was incapable of dealing with the hardened criminal who wandered from shire to shire." At p. 86
14. Harding, supra. p. 89

15. Bailiwick is an interesting term that is a combination of French and English, *balli* a French administrative official and wick an Anglo-Saxon village. *The Oxford English Dictionary* 2nd ed. apparently implies that the term originates from the 15th century. Harding, supra, p. 92 has sourced this term to the 13th century with his specific reference p. 92, note 5 to C.P.R. 1258–66 at p. 283. C.f. http://www.wordorigins.org/index.php/bailiwick/
16. Perhaps an early example of auxiliary policing, to support the local police in cases of civil disobedience, is found within the Harding, supra, p. 99 where "Edmund of Cornwall was appointed general 'keeper of the peace' in the English counties with power to appoint deputies to deal with improper assemblies beyond the sheriffs' control" citing Calendar of Chancery Rolls, various, pp. 271–218. Footnote 5.
17. E.g. In 1236 we see the sheriff continuing to have responsibility for forming a jury. C.P.R. 1232-47, p. 65 cited in Harding, supra p. 103 at note 9. This function remained with the sheriff until 1857. (In 1856 all policing functions were transferred to local police constabularies, and in 1857 all prison functions were transferred to the prison service.) The other previous primary role, tax collection, had already been handed to the Exchequer under Henry I. For further discussion see: Carpenter, D.A. 1976. The decline of the curial sheriff in England 1194–1258. *The English Historical Review,* Jan., 91(358), pp. 1–32.
18. The Lord Lieutenant is the monarch's personal representative in a county.
19. The High Sheriff is the sovereign's judicial representative in a county.
20. See: Buffardi, H C. 1998. *The history of the office of sheriff, Schenedachy County Sheriff.* Not paginated. The appointment was soon followed by numerous other counties and states across colonial America and the sheriff became the de facto ranking police officer and chief tax collector for many counties. In 1679 the sheriff of Middlesex County appointed a jailer to run the county prison. Ibid. Accomac [sic] County Records 1640–1645, p. 150 in Karracker, C.H. 1930. *The seventeenth century sheriff.* Chapel Hill: University of North Carolina Press.
21. *Posse comitatus* meaning "the power of the county" was the legal basis for sheriffs to recruit assistance from any male over the age of 15 years to assist in the pursuit and capture of felons.
22. Infra
23. This *connetablie,* or military unit, was directed by a Constable of France.
24. In association with his legal colleague Guillame de Lamoigen, Colbert drafted more than 150 pieces of legislation, including the 1670 Ordinance on Criminal Law and Criminal Procedure.
25. The office was first held by Nicholas Gabriel de la Reynie.
26. Jones, M. and Johnstone, P. 2011. *History of criminal justice.* 5th ed. Boston: Anderson, pp. 220–221.
27. Jones, supra. p. 220
28. Ibid.
29. Ibid.
30. By 1716 the police wore a blue uniform, walked a defined beta and were the only citizens of Paris permitted to carry a firearm. Jones, supra. p. 221
31. Ibid.
32. Germinal 28, Year VI of the French Revolution. April 17, 1798
33. Typically in brigades of six to ten men. Preference was for single men but married men were permitted to serve. It was intentional that the officers were recruited from an area

different from where they would be policing. However, the Gendarmerie was eventually close to the people and held in higher regard than the despised Administrative Police of Fouche. Notwithstanding this, the period between 1789 and 1799 placed France under enormous internal conflict and upheaval and the Gendarmerie was often interpreted as a pro-revolutionary faction that was caught between supporters of the old regime and those who were forging a new. C.f. Broers, supra. p. 28

34. Broers, M. 1999. The Napoleonic police and their legacy. *History Today,* 49(5), pp. 27–33, p. 27.
35. Minister of Police 1799–1810 and 1815–1816
36. C.f. Emsley, C. 2009. *The great British bobby: A history of British policing from the 18th century to the present century.* London: Quercus. Radzinowicz refers to the influence of Henry Fielding in bringing the term 'policing' into popular use. He cites Maitland's definition as "such part of social organisation as is concerned immediately with the maintenance of good order, or the prevention or detection of offences." Radzinowicz, supra. p. 4 and footnote 18
37. Radzinowicz, L. 1956. *A history of the English criminal law.* Vol. 3. London: Stevens, p. 1.
38. Cited by Radzinowicz, supra. p. 1
39. Jones, supra Chapter 10
40. Supra. p. 227
41. Blinded at the age of 19 years, Sir John Fielding could recognize criminals by their voices. It is reputed he knew 3,000 London criminals by their voices alone.
42. Henry Fielding was well known for his work of fiction, *A History of Tom Jones.* He also authored 15 plays and a novel based upon the life of London criminal Jonathan Wild. He wrote the weekly law digest the *Covent Garden Journal,* as well as the *Police Gazette* (which remains in publication today as a source of information for serving police officers).
43. Contrary to some incorrect reports (a 'Google' search of this term shows five incorrect entries on the first page), this group did not wear uniforms and was never referred to as "Robin Redbreasts." They did, however, carry a truncheon as a weapon and this instrument frequently bore a crown or other insignia denoting authority. Francis Dodsworth. 2004. 'Civic' police and the condition of liberty: The rationality of governance in eighteenth century England. *Social History,* May, 29(2), pp. 199–216 at p. 212.
44. For a full account of the establishment of the Bow Street Runners see: Cox, D. 2010. *A certain share of low cunning: An analysis of the work of Bow Street Principal Officers 1792–1839.* London: Whillan. The somewhat disparaging term "Runners" may have been first used during a criminal trial at The Old Bailey in 1755. Cited by Emsley, supra, in Cox at pp. 2–3
45. Six were initially appointed. This grew to eight by the early 19th century. All were 'sworn constables' of the City of Westminster.
46. In 1792, policing for London was divided into seven districts.
47. Emsley, supra. p. 22
48. This later group wore blue trousers and red waistcoats. They were soon dubbed the "Robin Redbreasts" C.f. The police of London. *London Quarterly Review,* July 1870, 129, p. 50.
49. The Middlesex Justices Act 1972
50. He established himself at Worship Street and then moved to Queen Square where he remained until 1818. Source Radzinowicz, supra. p. 212

51. Jones, supra. p. 229
52. "In his opinion the French police were worthy of careful and impartial consideration." Radzinowicz, supra. p. 249
53. For further discussion about the impact of Colquhoun see: Barrie, D. and Colquhoun, P. 2008. The Scottish Enlightenment and police reform in Glasgow in the late eighteenth century. *Crime History and Society,* 12(2), pp. 57–79.
54. His *Treatise* appeared in French in 1807. Radzinowicz, supra. p. 221 note 3
55. He was alone in attempting to introduce legislation. William Pitt introduced a Police Bill in 1785 and four Police Bills were introduced in 1799. All were defeated.
56. Colquhoun was closely associated with the Thames Marine Police and at one time held an official position with the office as its Receiver.
57. Located at No. 259 Wapping New Stairs. Source Radzinowicz, supra. Vol. 2, p. 363 and Patterson, supra, p. 4
58. The force had written "General Instructions" pertaining to roles, responsibilities, conduct, rates of pay and the entire range of standing orders that are associated with a police force. Radzinowicz, supra, Vol. 2. P. 365. In addition to the 80 permanent staff a further 1120 were available and utilized as needed on a part-time basis. Radzinowicz, supra. Vol. 2, p. 372
59. Quoted in Patterson, supra. p. 5
60. It was also in 1800 that Colquhoun authored *Treatise on the commerce and police of the River Thames London, Baldwin, 1800,* a work that included specific costs associated with the level of crime being committed on the river estimated by Colquhoun to be at least £232,000 in 1798.
61. The final version was significantly different from the previous draft supplied by Colquhoun and Bentham. The bill passed into law on July 28, 1800. 39 & 40 Geo 3. C. 87
62. Master mariner and friend of Colquhoun's who later served with Colquhoun in the Wapping Police Office. John Harroit was himself a Justice of the Peace and is credited with being the author of the first written plan for the river police. "I have lost no time in transmitting your very sensible paper to Mr. Dundas, which contains a very excellent plan for the protection of shipping in the River Thames . . ." cited in Radzinowicz, supra. Vol. 2, p. 373 and note 65. Reprinted in Harriot's memoirs *Struggles through life, exemplified in the various travels and adventures in Europe, Asia and America, etc.* 3rd ed. 1815. 3 vols. Vol. 3, pp. 112–113. Radzinowicz also supplies evidence of Harriot having first submitted his plan to the Duke of Portland in 1797. Radzinowicz, supra. Vol. 2, p. 373 and at footnote 66
63. By this time Colquhoun was already deeply involved with the Marine Police Establishment as noted in the *Lloyd's Evening Post and British Chronicle.* June 27–29, 1978. "A new Office sitting at Wapping New Stairs, to be under the direction of Patrick Colquhoun, Esq . . ." cited in Radzinowicz, supra. Vol. 2, p. 371–372
64. In an earlier version of the attempts to gain support for the establishment of a government funded river police, Colquhoun, May 1, 1799, refers to assistance from ". . . a friend of great legal knowledge." This legal friend was Jeremy Bentham. Radzinowicz, supra. p. 385 and note 19. Bentham later reports on this involvement in his own memoirs *Works* "*Memoirs . . . including Autobiographical Conversations and Correspondence.*" Bowring's ed. 1843. Vol. 10, pp. 330–333. Ibid.
65. Radzinowicz, supra. Vol. 2, p. 389

66. For example, the MacDonald Bill had failed in 1785 for these reasons and little had changed as the fervor of war and jingoism increased at the end of this century. See: Neocleous, supra. p. 209
67. Jones, supra, p. 230
68. Robert Peel served as British Prime Minister from December 10, 1834 to April 8, 1835 and again from August 30, 1841 to June 29, 1846. He went to Harrow boys' school and then read classics, physics and mathematics at Christ's College Oxford where he took a double first. He trained as a lawyer, Lincoln's Inn, and then entered politics in 1809. He made his maiden speech in the Commons in January 1810. Throughout his career Peel was supported by the Duke of Wellington.
69. Act, 54 George III, c.131, July 25, 1814. "To provide for the better execution of the Laws in Ireland, by appointing Superintending magistrates and additional Constables in Counties in certain cases." Herlihy, infra, p. 29. This act created a permanent police force for rural Ireland. It did not include policing for the city of Dublin that had established a city force under the Dublin Police Act 1786 comprising 10 officers, a chief constable and a night watch. The force wore a uniform dress and carried muskets. Herlihy, J. 1997. *The Royal Irish Constabulary: A short history and genealogical guide.* Dublin: Four Courts Press. P. 27. The force was short-lived. It was abolished in 1795. Dublin maintained a separate force until merger in 1836 when one combined constabulary was established for all of Ireland.
70. John Brewer, Max Weber and the Royal Irish Constabulary: A note on class and status. *The British Journal of Sociology*, Mar. 1989, 40(1), pp. 82–96 at p. 82.
71. Bestowment of the title 'Royal' upon a police force was unique at the time. ". . . a circumstance unparalleled and unprecedented in any police force in the world." Brophy, M. 1886. *Sketches of the Royal Irish Constabulary.* London: Burns and Oates, p. 17.
72. Barrie, supra. p. 5 citing Critchley, T.A. 1967. *A history of police in England and Wales 900–1966.* London: Constable.
73. Fifty-seven Irish Protestants in the House of Commons signed a petition requesting he not leave.
74. Brophy, supra. p. 3. "One could almost believe that Sir Robert Peel, inspired by Mr. Drummond, seeing the pitiable condition of Ireland, and feeling that the powerful sister-country had a hand in bringing that condition about, determined on making some small restitution by creating employment of some useful kind, one branch of which assumed the shape of a police force twelve thousand strong." Ibid. There is some degree of support for this if consideration is given to the number of Irish aristocracy who joined the R.I.C. "Serving in the ranks are to be found the sons and heirs of the embarrassed or utterly ruined landed gentry." Ibid.
75. Brophy, supra. p. 14
76. For comprehensive discussion see: Reynolds, E. 1998. *Before the bobbies: The night watch and police reform in Metropolitan London 1720–1830.* London: Macmillan.
77. The Royal Irish Constabulary required all officers to wear uniforms but have available a suit of civilian clothing to perform duties that required a civilian presence. Brophy, supra. p. 18. This was likely to be interpreted as far too similar to the Paris police 'spies' in London and therefore the metropolis did not have a detective plain clothes presence until 1842. Jones, supra. p. 232. Initial detective work was provided for by the Bow Street Principal Officers. Cox, supra.

78. "Even had the City authorities been anxious to co-operate with the metropolitan force, either in action or in the exchange of information, their very multiplicity would have made it impracticable." Radzinowicz, supra. Vol. 4, p. 171

79. The 'Square Mile' established its own police force under the City of London Police Act 1839. Daniel Whittle Harvey was the first Commissioner of a force of 500 men. The City of London Police continue to operate today across the 'Square Mile'. There are currently 850 officers and 450 support staff of London Police were formed. For further comprehensive discussion see: Andrew Harris. 1968. *Policing the city: Crime and legal authority in London, 1780–1840.* Columbus. Ohio: The Ohio State University Press.

80. Ten years later, the 1839 Metropolitan Police Act extended the initial 10-mile zone from Charing Cross to 15 miles. This Act also increased the force size to 4,300 officers.

81. Officers were required to walk a beat at a regular and steady pace. Initially set at three miles per hour, this was soon reduced to two and a half miles per hour. Infra, Emsley

82. For those opposed to a full-time police presence even the uniform was criticized. "The chief offence of the new police in the eyes of these patriots was the similarity of their dress to that of French gendarmes. Any coats would have been forgiven but blue coats." Hayden, B.R. 1897. *Correspondence and table-talk.* 2 Volumes. Vol. 2. London: Chatto and Windus, p. 340.

83. Eight Superintendents, 20 Inspectors, 88 Sergeants and nearly 900 constables. Radzinowicz, L. 1968. *A history of the English criminal law "grappling for control."* Vol. 4. London: Stevens, p. 161.

84. Emsley, C. 2009. *The great British bobby: A history of British policing from the 18th century to the present.* London: Quercus, p. 39.

85. Mayne was born in Dublin and after attending Trinity College was called to the bar at Lincoln's Inn. He served as the first joint commissioner and then second joint commissioner after the retirement of Colonel Rowan. Mayne finally became the first sole Commissioner of the force in 1855 and remained in this post until his death in 1868. He served a total of 39 years with the London Metropolitan Police and remains the longest serving commissioner to date.

86. One source of criticism even suggested that, "The appointment of a military officer, Colonel Rowan, of the Irish Constabulary, betrayed the intention of creating a 'veritable gendarmerie'." Griffiths, Major A. 1899. *Mysteries of police and crime: A general survey of wrongdoing and its pursuit.* Vol. 1. London: Casell and Co., p. 85. Charles Rowan served in the British army and then as a magistrate in Ireland, his country of birth, before accepting the position as Commissioner of the London Metropolitan Police in 1829. Rowan was not Peel's first choice, which was Col. James Shaw, but he refused and Rowan was offered the position.

87. Ibid.

88. Numerous sources trace the introduction of the term 'Peeler' to describe a 'new' police officer. It is specifically mentioned in the press: "The 'Peelers' withstand riots in London." *The Guardian,* Friday, 12 November 1830.

89. Reith, Charles. 1948. *A short history of the British police.* Vol. 4. London: Oxford University Press, p. 62. Also cited by Radzinowicz, supra. p. 163. There are a number of variations upon the actual number of "Principles" that Peel developed. Some sources cite nine; others 12. E.g. Reith, ibid. and Jones, supra

90. This Act established the system of HM Inspectors of Constabulary who conducted inspections of each force annually. Every force needed to achieve an 'efficient' grade if they were to receive one quarter of their budget from the treasury.
91. Radzinowicz makes numerous references to the obstacles facing Peel, especially, supra Vol. 3. His treatment of the subject is discussed by Emsley in *Ideology, crime and criminal justice,* supra. There is also discussion of these matters in Philip Stead *The police of Britain,* New York: Macmillan, 1985, and Eric Monkkonen. 1981. *Police in urban America, 1860–1920.* New York: Cambridge University Press. An overview of these contributions is available in Wilbur R. Miller's Police and the state: A comparative perspective (review essay). *American Bar Foundation Research Journal,* Spring, 1986, 11(2), pp. 339–348 at p. 343.
92. A discussion about the concern over police spies and the Popay affair, infra, is found in Emsley, supra, *The great British bobby,* pp. 56–64.
93. The Principal Officer was disbanded in 1839 after 90 years of service. It was replaced by the Metropolitan Police Detective Branch in 1842. Jones, supra. pp. 232–233
94. For a colorful description of policing from the eyes of an early 20th century magazine see: Kemp, R. 1910. The evolution of the police. *Munsey's Magazine,* April to September, XLIII(4), at July, pp. 439–450.
95. Kemp, supra. p. 446
96. Walz, R. 2003. "Vidocq, Rogue Cop" in Francois Eugene Vidocq *Memoirs of Vidocq: Master of crime.* London: AK Press, p. xi.
97. Emsley, supra. p. 89
98. Jones, supra. p. 223
99. Ibid.
100. See also: Morris and Vila, supra. pp. 40–42
101. Vidocq *Memoirs,* supra. p. ix
102. 1829. He opened a paper mill, lost all his assets and returned to working for the police, but after a scandal involving theft he was dismissed. Francois Eugene Vidocq died in Brussels in 1857. As was stated about him, "He has two valid claims for inclusion in the rolls of fame—as the Legendary Detective and as The Father of the Detective Story." Translator's notes from the 1935 original edition of Vidocq, supra, 1935 ed. translated by Edwin Gile Rich, p. 367.
103. Another plausible reason for the delay in establishing the detective unit is that Richard Mayne 'distrusted' the existing detective police and therefore was not motivated to increase the size or sphere of its responsibility. Miller, supra. p. 92
104. The Sergeant Popay affair of 1833, the Mazzini mail scandal of 1844, both cited by Emsley, supra. p. 90
105. Also known as the Turf Fraud Scandal was prosecuted at The Central Criminal Court (The Old Bailey), 22 October 1877. R v Clarke and Others. The case involved a horse racing fraud perpetrated by a number of senior Metropolitan Police detectives; Inspector Meiklejohn and Chief Inspectors Clarke, Druscovich and Palmer all stood trial for corruption. D.C.I. Clarke was acquitted; the other three were convicted and given two year terms of imprisonment.
106. He was placed in an unusual situation in this role in that he reported not to the Commissioner of the Metropolitan Police but directly to the Home Secretary. His rank was equivalent to assistant Commissioner, but he never held the formal title. His familiarity

with the French Surete came about during his time studying law at the *Faculte de Droit*, Paris (now Pantheon-Assas II). He resigned from the force to enter politics in 1884. His title in the police was Director of the Criminal Investigation Department, C.I.D.

107. "The detective branch of the (French) civil police, aided by broad powers in investigation and evidence gathering arising from the state's concern for security developed a reputation for being the best in the world during the nineteenth century." Miller, supra. p. 344

108. E.g. Fuller, J. 2006. *Criminal justice: Mainstream and cross currents*. New Jersey: Pearson, pp. 146–152; Bohm, R. and Haley, K. 2008. *Introduction to criminal justice*. 5th ed. Boston: McGraw-Hill, pp. 139–142; Inciardi, J. 1996. *Criminal justice*. 5th ed. New York: Harcourt Brace, pp. 163–167; Roberg, R. et al. 2012. *Police & society*. 5th ed. New York: Oxford University Press, pp. 30–36; Scaramella, G. et al. 2011. *Introduction to policing*. Los Angeles: Sage, pp. 6–7; Peak, K. 2012. *Policing America: Challenges and best practices*. 7th ed. Boston: Prentice Hall, pp. 4–18.

109. Also referred to as 'Schouts' in the Dutch settlements. See: Vila, B. and Morris, C. 1999. *The role of police in American society: A documentary history*. Westport, CT: Greenwood Press, p. 8.

110. E.g. Fuller, Bohm and Haley etc., supra. "Every cunstable . . . hath, by virtue of his office, full powr to make, signe, & put forth pursuits, or hues and cries, after murthrers, man-slayrs, peace breaks . . ." Taken from Massachusetts statute 1646 reprinted in Inciardi, supra. p. 167

111. Jones, supra. pp. 112–132

112. Boston introduced paid night watchmen in 1648 and the Dutch copied this model for New York in 1663, but the expense of running these systems proved too great and both were disbanded due to cost. Jones, supra. p. 233. See also "The Boston Night Watch," Vila and Morris, supra. pp. 6–8.

113. Of course the reward concept has never left either the UK or the US where it operates nationally and internationally today. One manifestation of the 'reward' that is enshrined in legendary views is that of the reward for the capture of a frontier outlaw. See further: "One feature of the early police system in England that was generally accepted and profoundly affected American law enforcement practices in the eighteenth and nineteenth century was the offer of a reward for the return of stolen property and the arrest and conviction of criminals." Traub, S.H. 1988. Bounty hunting, and criminal justice in the West: 1865–1900. *The Western Historical Quarterly,* Aug., 19(3), pp. 287–301 at p. 288.

114. E.g. 5 Anne, c. 31 (1706) that created a reward of £40 for prosecuting burglars. For a comprehensive discussion see; Beattie, J.M. 2004. *Policing and punishment in London 1660–1750*. Oxford: Oxford University Press; and also McLynn, F. 1989. *Crime and punishment in eighteenth century England*. London: Routledge.

115. "Emerging evidence suggest that 'associations' found in this region (Halifax, Yorkshire) are very similar to the numerous others that spread throughout the rest of the country during this period." Little, C.B. and Sheffield, C. 1983. Frontiers and criminal justice: English private prosecution societies and American vigilantism in the eighteenth and nineteenth centuries. *American Sociological Review,* Dec., 48(6), pp. 796–808 at p. 798. At least 450 associations were formed between 1744 and 1846. Ibid.

116. Ibid.

117. As Little and Sheffield comment though, "It would be wrong to infer that vigilantism arose on the American frontier solely in response to a tidal wave of lawlessness. To the

contrary, in many cases the lack (original emphasis) of crime posed no need of a regular, full-time system of law enforcement..." supra. p. 804 note 18

118. See further: Rister, C.C. 1933. Outlaws and vigilantes of the Southern Plains, 1865–1885. *The Mississippi Valley Historical Review,* Mar., 9(4), pp. 537–554; Smurr, J.W. 1958. Afterthoughts on the vigilantes. *The Magazine of Western History,* Spring, 8(2), pp. 8–20. Published by the Montana Historical Society.

119. A limited number of English style societies did exist in America, in particular anti-horse theft societies, some of which were incorporated into state law and achieved constabulary powers. Ibid.

120. "The big 'establishment' security companies, Pinkerton and Burns, abandoned labor espionage and union-busting services completely by the 1930s in favor of the burgeoning areas of industrial espionage and counterespionage, corporate embezzlement and fraud, and residential and commercial security policing." Weiss, R.P. 2007–2008. From cowboy detectives to soldiers of fortune: Private security contracting and its contradictions on the new frontiers of capitalist expansion. *Social Justice,* 34(3–4), pp. 1–19 at p. 6.

121. Boston had a 'warden' as early as 1749 and day watches were prevalent in most major cities by the middle of the century: Philadelphia 1833, Boston 1838, New York 1844, San Francisco 1850, Los Angeles 1851. By the end of the decade these cities had combined the day constables with the night watch to provide comprehensive municipal police cover.

122. Inciardi, supra. p. 168. In some states the sheriff had authority to direct and control the police and in some cases order the call out of the state constabulary. Milton, C. 1921. Legislative notes and reviews edited by W. F. Wood. *The American Political Science Review,* Feb., 15(1), pp. 82–93.

123. England was very familiar with private policing as this had been the model within the City of London for 700 years. The Bow Street Runners, though publically funded, also provided private policing services and the Principal Officers of the Bow Street Police Office hired out their services to private and public entities. Supra.

124. Established in Buffalo, New York, March 18, 1852, by Henry Wells and William G. Fargo.

125. Established as a parcel company by Washington Perry Brink in Chicago, 1859.

126. Famous for allegedly providing personal security to President Abraham Lincoln, the agency was started by a Scotsman, Allan Pinkerton, and a Chicago lawyer, Edward Rucker. Originally named the North-Western Police Agency, they changed the name to The Pinkerton National Detective Agency in part to secure federal contracts. By 1871, the newly formed Department of Justice had hired Pinkerton's to detect and prosecute those committing federal crimes. The relationship lasted until enactment of the Anti-Pinkerton Act of 1893, which no longer allowed private agencies to be employed by the government.

127. This agency was established by William J. Burns in 1909. Prior to starting the William J. Burns National Detective Agency, he had worked as a Secret Service agent. He returned to federal employment in 1921 to become head of the Justice Department Bureau of Investigation, which upon retirement he handed over to J. Edgar Hoover as Director of the FBI.

128. Jones, supra. p. 245

129. Ibid.

130. Ray, G.W. 1995. From Cossack to trooper: Manliness, police reform, and the state. *Journal of Social History,* Spring, 28(3), pp. 565–586. Weiss, R.P. 1986. Private detective

agencies and labour discipline in the United States 1855–1946. *The Historical Journal,* March 1, 29(1), pp. 87–107.

131. The replies to Representative Maurer's questions reveal distressing conditions in nearly every locality where the Cossacks were located. Madison (Darrah P.O.), PA, Feb. 22, 1911. Hon. James H. Maurer, House of Representatives, Harrisburg, PA. 1911. It appears that the terms 'Cossacks', 'Yellow Dogs' and 'Hoodlums' were in use against the Coal and Iron Police, as well as the Pennsylvania State Constabulary.

132. $20 per ton. The equivalent of paying $12 per gallon for gasoline today.

133. "It was a grime joke. The Coal and Iron Police were actually the mercenaries of the great industries." Van de Water, supra. p. 24

134. E.g. The Lattimer Massacre that occurred near Hazelton, PA. 10 September 1897

135. *A history of the Michigan State Constabulary.* Detroit, Michigan: State Constabulary Association, 1919. Chapter 2, p. 31.

136. Captain Groome was apparently promoted to the rank of major once he took responsibility for the Pennsylvania State Constabulary. There are also a number of later references to Groome as Superintendent, as well as to Commander Groome. The congressional hearing, supra, consistently refers to him as Major Groome.

137. May 6, 1915. The Commission on Industrial Relations created by the act of Congress on August 23, 1912, held at the Shoreham Hotel, Washington D.C.

138. Groome took responsibility for a broad range of functions associated with the new force, including setting standards for recruits. During the Industrial Relations Committee Hearings, James Maurer, President of the Pennsylvania State Federation of Labor, was asked, "From what forces are the State constabulary recruited" to which he replied, "The men are recruited from the ranks of ex-United States soldiers, and again many of them are recruited from the ranks or from the degenerate descendants of the middle classes, young men who are educated, but never amount to anything and no good for anything and generally hunt a job in the State police force." *Final Report and Testimony Submitted to Congress by the Commission on Industrial Relations.* May 6, 1915. Vol. XI. Document No. 415. P. 10932.

139. Williams, D. 1921. State police and the Irish "Black and Tans." *The Bridgemen's Magazine,* January, XXI(1), p. 77.

140. Ibid.

141. An interesting lack of geographical knowledge is displayed by Chairman Walsh who at one point asked, "Does the constabulary in Ireland have authority in the large cities like Glasgow and Dublin?" Williams, supra. p. 78. A more pertinent question followed: "You spent, you say, three weeks at the barracks?" Major Groome. "Yes, and got their ideas and their rules and regulations." Ibid.

142. It is variously described as the Pennsylvania State Police and the Pennsylvania State Constabulary. Williams, supra, *Munsey's Magazine,* supra, Van de Water, supra.

143. Describing the officers employed by the new constabulary, Major Groome stated, "My instruction to each trooper leaves a great deal to his discretion. If he starts out to get his man, he must get him, even if he has to butt into the middle of a mob to find him. The troopers are advised not to use their guns unless they have to." *Munsey's Magazine,* supra. p. 448. This makes an interesting contrast with Peel's policing principles.

144. Jones, supra. p. 234

145. When introduced, the police were mocked. See Monkkonen, supra. p. 551

146. See further: Vila and Morris, supra. pp. 36–39
147. Miller, supra. pp. 345, 346, 347
148. Miller, W.R. 1975. Police authority in London and New York City 1830–1870. *Journal of Social History,* Winter, 8(2), pp. 81–101. Miller posits that the fundamental difference between the two jobs is that the authority each officer possessed was different. The London "Bobby' had impersonal authority and the New York 'Cop' had far greater discretion. He cites the example of carrying firearms and how the American officer took to taking a firearm to work and as such became a more powerful presence than his London colleague.
149. "Throughout most of the 19th and into the 20th centuries, the basic qualification for becoming a police officer was a political connection, rather than demonstrated ability." Scaramella, supra. p. 9
150. This relationship lasted until 1870 when a second municipal force was created. Although Boston rejected a London police model in 1832, in 1857 the city decided to move forward with the creation of an amalgamation of night watch and day police to form a full-time police force.
151. Jones, supra, pp. 234–235
152. See: Vila and Morris, supra. pp. 35–37
153. Scaramella, supra. p. 9
154. Monkkonen, supra. p. 554
155. Ibid.
156. It can be further suggested that the London police were a centralized force due to the sole reporting line directly to the Home Secretary. This is true also of the Paris police, but not so the New York police whom the Municipal Police Act decentralized. It is recognized that local town policing in England became de-centralized by the formation of country-wide forces in the 1856 Act, supra.
157. Monkkonen, supra, notes four important innovative features of the new police in the US. The second of these is that the US police were located under the executive rather than the judicial branch. This differed from London where the police ran courts for many years. "This shift also sent the American police down a different developmental path from the English police, who long remained much more active and involved in preparing and prosecuting criminal cases than did their American counterparts." p. 550
158. Monkkonen, supra. p. 553
159. By the early 1900s, most major cities in America had established police forces that prioritized crime fighting as a primary role. The issue of political influence remained prevalent, however, until the 1920s. Commentary on this and the impact of August Volmer as a voice in establishing policing priorities supra. note 134
160. Miller, supra. p. 347
161. C.f. Roberg et al, pp. 36–37 and Jones, supra. pp. 242–243
162. Fuller, supra. pp. 151–152
163. Brophy, supra, relates a fascinating event when two R.I.C. officers were on vacation in Paris at a military parade. They both wore their green R.I.C. uniforms at the time. Apparently Napoléon III saw the officers and questioned their origins. He then invited them to join in the parade and later referred to them as *"Officers de la gendarmerie Irlandaise,"* pp. 22–23

CHAPTER 4

POLICE RECRUITMENT

Why we need to have the police in contemporary society will have a different response depending upon where we are when you we the question.

Some countries prioritize the social service aspects of policing so that in many ways the police appear more closely aligned to social workers than to crime fighters and the emphasis is often placed upon community response policing and human rights.

In other countries, such as the US, the primary task of the police is to prevent crime.

Now there are probably a number of academics who will immediately disagree with this statement and cite the emphasis that was placed upon community policing in the 1990s and the huge amounts of money the federal government made available to support Community Oriented Policing (COPS).

In my view, this is no longer an accurate portrayal of policing in America today, as I believe that we have moved progressively towards a quasi-military style of policing with increased emphasis on security and then a focus upon preventing and detecting crime.

Many serving police officers are very happy with this shift, as they have always held the view that policing is about fighting battles,[1] either terrorists or crime (thief taking). Some members of the public are less enthusiastic as they feel that community priorities have been traded out for 'hot spot' crime targeting or a military looking officer (and vehicles) that provide 'enhanced security'.

From *Crime and Policing Crime* by Peter Johnstone. Copyright © 2013 by Kendall Hunt Publishing Company. Reprinted by permission.

What is really needed, and sometimes achieved, is a balance.

How we achieve that balance depends upon a large number of factors and whatever is deemed the right balance for one country will not be the same balance for another due to the make-up of each individual country.

At this point, you might want to question for yourself how it is that for so many developed countries that have similar GDP's and quality and standards of living that we can invest such completely different amounts of money and training on the police—three years training and a degree or five weeks. And yet we call the product the same thing, a police officer.

In the United States, the current emphasis is on 'less is more'.

It spends less time training new recruits than many other countries, and it focuses more on the practical aspects of training and far less on the academic training than other similarly placed nation states.

If it is true to say that the police perform a multitude of tasks within society, then why would it be the case that so little time is spent on academic achievement and relationships with the community in lieu of driver training, firearm training and self-defense?

After all, if the main thrust of police work is crime prevention and crime detection, then surely these issues would be the most important aspect of new recruit training.

But it is not—general patrol is the area most covered, the argument being that this is what most officers do most of the time. This may be accurate, but it depends upon what you call 'general patrol' and whether or not this includes identifiable crime prevention and detection.

So, before we get too much further into the chapter you may want to pause and consider: Is policing about 'Protect and Serve' or 'Prevent and Serve'?

It should be remembered that with around 19,000 different law enforcement agencies in the US there are naturally large differences in terms of policing priorities, recruitment and training.

On this note, it is time to look at how people are recruited into the police in the US and what basic training they undertake.

The New London, Connecticut, Police Department gained notoriety in 1999 for preventing Robert Jordan from joining the department on the basis that he was too intelligent.

Jordan subsequently sued the department after he had scored 33 out of 50 on the initial screening test. His score of 33 was considered to be 6 points *above* the level sought for police recruits and therefore he was not invited for interview. Deputy Police Chief William C. Gavitt stated that "Bob Jordan is exactly the type of guy we would want to screen out ... Police work is mundane. We don't deal in gunfights every night. There's a personality that can take that."[2] Robert Jordan was subsequently interviewed by CNN, and he stated that in a conversation he had with the personnel department at the New London PD he was told, "Listen, Mr. Jordan, we don't like to hire people with too high an IQ to be a cop in this town."[3]

Jordan was unsuccessful in his suit at the District Court and at the U.S. Court of Appeals where both held that his constitutional rights had not been abrogated by the New London hiring policy as its policy was rational and designed to prevent high job turnover.[$] The US Appeals Court stated that "New London's use of an 'upper-cut' did not violate the equal protection clause" and it upheld the judgment of the district court.[5]

Most would agree this is a low point in the discussion about what the requirements are for entry into the police service in the USA, but it does demonstrate a sharp difference between the view taken by some countries that you need to hold at a minimum a baccalaureate degree to be an effective police officer and in some instances in the USA where an above average IQ is a bar to appointment due to the likelihood that bright people will get bored by the mundane nature of police work.

Clearly there is some significant discrepancy between the view of what police work entails is in some parts of the US and in a number of countries in Europe.

This should be borne in mind as more and more criminal investigations involve transnational crime groups and necessitate police forces from a number of countries to liaise and work together despite any linguistic or academic abilities individual officers may have to have.

◆ Basic Requirements

As a general statement police recruits must be physically fit, not have a criminal record and be at least 21 years of age.

Some forces have an upper age limit, but this is liable to challenges of age discrimination (the Washington State Police Academy graduated a student of 52 years of age).[6]

In 2003, more than 50% of US police forces did not have an aptitude test.[7] Twenty-five percent held a polygraph test and just 1% required second language ability. Only 67% of forces required psychological evaluation.[8]

Candidates must be US citizens. Whether or not the recruits need to be local, city or state residents or from out of state varies with each hiring department. State and local law enforcement employ more than 1.33 million full-time personnel of which 765,000 are sworn officers.[9] Forty-nine percent of all agencies employ fewer than 10 full-time sworn officers and 64% are employed in agencies of fewer than 100 officers.[10] One in 8 new recruits is female. And 1 in 10 is Latino.[11]

There are more than 650 state and local law enforcement academies across the nation that provide basic entry level training to new recruits into police departments.

On average, 86% of new recruits successfully complete basic training.[12] Ninety percent of basic training academies now provide terrorism training to new entrants.[13]

According to the US Bureau of Labor Statistics, police applicants "need to meet the minimum educational requirements, which usually include a high school diploma or its equivalent and many law enforcement agencies require some level of college-level courses to be completed before attending a police academy."

The key skills for police listed on the Bureau of Labor Statistics website[14] are: ability to multi-task, communication skills, empathetic personality, good judgment, leadership skills, perceptiveness and strength and stamina.[15]

Arlington, Texas

Many police departments have their own training academies. For example, Arlington, Texas has a 26-week academy with classes in law, procedure, patrol and investigations, as well as driving and fitness training. Classes are based on a 5-day week. In keeping with many forces across the nation, attendance is daily and non-residential.[16]

Following successful completion of the initial academy, officers are assigned to patrol under the direction of a Field Training Officer (FTO) for a further 14 weeks.[17]

As a Texas police force, Arlington is required to adhere to the Texas Commission on Law Enforcement, Officer Standards and Education, TCLEOSE. There are currently 2,644 agencies, 105 training academies and 174 contract training providers in the state of Texas.[18]

After initial training, Texas police officers are required to hold a basic Police Officer Certificate, which is obtained after one year in service. It is possible for citizens who are not employed by a police department to participate in basic training and then to approach a department for employment opportunities. One example of this is the academy run at the Central Texas College 'Basic Peace Officer Academy', a part-time class run during days or evenings that prepares candidates for the Texas Police Officer Licensing Examination. TCEOSE requires a minimum of 618 hours of training before candidates are eligible to sit the licensing examination.[19] College based training programs are eligible for college credit that may count towards a degree later. Typically completion of the Licensing Exam will attract in the neighborhood of 22 hours of potential associate degree credit. Participation in basic training is not precluded due to a candidate having a criminal conviction and this is true with regard to many police departments across the nation. The issue is: What is the conviction for? Felons are excluded from employment as police officers, but conviction for a Class B misdemeanor within the past 10 years would not necessarily prohibit appointment.[20]

Four-Year Degree Requirement

The Tulsa PD application information states that, "All applicants will undergo a police background check before being hired. Any person with a felony conviction or a conviction for a crime of moral turpitude is ineligible for employment with the Tulsa Police Department."[21] Arlington PD[22] and Tulsa PD are two of 36 police departments nationwide that now require all applicants to hold a four-year degree from an accredited university.[23] As a comparison, it is of note that only 11% of police training academies require their instructors to hold a four-year college degree and 8% require a two-year associate degree.[24] Overall, 98% of all hiring departments conduct personal interviews with candidates; 73% conduct a drugs test; and 43% have a written aptitude test.[25] In forces with fewer than 2,500 personnel, sworn and unsworn combined, 31% required a physical agility test, 20% required a written aptitude test, 11% had a polygraph test and 63% required a drug test.[26] Overall, 1% of US police forces require applicants to hold a four-year university degree.[27] This figure equates to the 36 departments that now require a bachelor degree, but the type of degree or the major is rarely specified or perhaps even important.[28] Nine percent of forces require a two-year degree.[29] Thirty-two percent of recruiting departments offer incentives to candidates who hold higher education qualifications.[30] This figure rises to 75% in those large city departments serving populations of greater than 1 million citizens.[31]

Ultimately, no matter how a person is recruited into the police force once he has passed the interview procedures and been offered a position at an academy, he will undertake an average of 19 weeks of basic training that will involve the following: law, weapons, self-defense, human rights and investigations training to equip him with the minimum level of preparedness necessary to then undertake street patrol under the supervision of an experienced officer.

During the first few years of employment, they will have to undertake a number of specialist training courses and then throughout the career mandatory yearly training. Those academies that have a more academic and stress-free philosophy appear to achieve better overall retention and passing rates (89%) than the academies that are more militaristic in approach and paramilitary in shape and form (80%)[32] where the 'shock' of initial military style training is a major deterrent to some applicants and in some instances has led to a significant withdrawal from the program in the first two weeks.[33] Notwithstanding this observation, overall 43% of state academies report their training programs are stress-based; 89% of county police academies are stress-based and 66% of municipal police academies are stress-based.[34]

The controversy over whether or not all police recruits should hold a college degree has been taking place for the past 40 years. Generally the move has gone towards requiring degrees, but this has to be considered in the light of recruitment shortages, officers being called up for military service and regrettable incidents of police corruption that tarnish the image of the police across the entire nation and often result in a lull in applicants. The Police Association for College Education (PACE)[35] is a non-profit organization that encourages and facilitates a minimum education level of a four-year degree for all police officers, and it has worked closely over the past decade to encourage PDs and advisory bodies to promote police degree requirements. The Commission on Accreditation for Law Enforcement Agencies (CALEA) issued the following standard in July 2011: *"A written directive establishes the agency's commitment to higher education through one or more of the following: a. a requirement of all candidates for full-time sworn positions to possess at a minimum a bachelor's degree; . . . ."*[36]

As the author of the report stated, "In summary, an educated workforce is more empowered, diverse in thought, and prepared. Hiring college-degreed candidates into the law enforcement profession does not guarantee they will be good officers. However, better educated officers will have a greater likelihood of creating sound solutions to today's public safety issues."[37]

I started this chapter commenting on the growth of military style policing particularly since 2001. It is not uncommon today for local police departments to undertake paramilitary training with other agencies and to receive specific training from military personnel. That is not to say that many of the skills learned by the military to release hostages for example, are not of enormous value to civilian police operations; but in case you remain unconvinced of the influence that causes some commentators concern, it is worth looking at the Tampa Police Tactical Response Team[38] website and view the array of vehicles they have. If you had any doubts whatsoever as to whether civilian police forces are equipped to deal with a war this site will convince you otherwise. Not only does this force have an "amphibious tank type vehicle that can reach speeds up to 60 mph,"[39] it also boasts ownership of a 12-ton Armored Personnel Carrier that is, "bullet resistant, can hold 13 passengers and is virtually unstoppable . . . this one of a kind APC was purchased from the military. . . ."[40]

Deputy Sheriffs

Sheriffs' departments play a major role in policing across the US, particularly at the county level. Additionally, they provide the corrections element of criminal justice in running county jails. Just like municipal forces, sheriffs' departments may be small and consist of a few sworn officers or very large, such as the Los Angeles County Sheriff's Department.

LACSD, sometimes also known as the Los Angeles Sheriff's Office (LASO) is the fourth largest local police agency in the US and the largest sheriff's department in the world.[41]

Since its creation in 1849, LASO now employs more than 18,000 personnel of which more than 10,000 are sworn officers.

The Court Services Division is responsible for security, providing bailiffs and local custody provision inside the courts to 48 courthouses within the county. The LA County jail system is the largest in the US, and the sheriff's department is responsible for correctional services provision to more than 200,000 inmates each year. The Inmate Reception Center (IRC) is the main intake point for the 18,000 prisoners being held in the county jail system at any point in time. From the IRC prisoners are then allocated to a county facility such as 'Twin Towers', a downtown location spread across 10 acres consisting of more than 1.5 million square feet of prison facility.[42] The IRC central intake point employs 800 people, 450 of which are deputy sheriffs. The Court

Services Division employs 1,100 sworn officers and more than 500 civilians. In addition to court security and judicial protection services, recall that sheriffs also serve criminal and civil process.[43]

Patrol is part of Field Operations and is divided up into three regions that together operate 176 sheriff stations across the county. Detective investigations are conducted through the Detective Division, which has six bureaus: Homicide, Major Crimes, Commercial Crimes, Special Victims, Narcotics and the Taskforce for Regional Autotheft. In 2002, the LASO created the Homeland Security Division with this task: "Our mission is to prevent, intervene, disrupt, mitigate, and provide specialized response capabilities to acts of terrorism and Homeland Security threats, whether[44] natural or caused by man."

In addition to the above, the LASO is the second largest transit police agency in the nation. It provides a police response to the entire Metropolitan Transit Authority system of Los Angeles.

Due to the size of the force, it runs its own basic training academy for deputy sheriffs and custody assistants. Applicants who hold an associate degree are offered an enhanced monthly salary, and those holding a four-year degree are paid an increase above this.[45] Initial deputy sheriff recruits follow an 18-week training program. Deputy sheriffs must be 20 years of age and participate in a written examination and pre-employment physical. Applicants who fail the written test three times may not re-apply for six months. Once selected, the academy operates five days per week and is non-residential. Many aspects of the work of a deputy sheriff are the same as those of a patrol officer in a police department[46] where they differ is in the provision of custodial and protective services. As stated by the LASO, "The Los Angeles County Sheriff's Department differs from other police agencies in several ways. The most significant is that the Sheriff's department provides staffing for 8 custody facilities and security for 48 courthouses throughout the County. The Sheriff's department also provides patrol and investigative services to 40 contract cities and unincorporated areas of Los Angeles County. This difference creates more assignment diversity than any other police agency in the Southern California basin."[47]

State Police

Every state in the US has some form of statewide police provision—state troopers, a constabulary, a state bureau, a highway patrol or a department of public safety. The Pennsylvania State Police were the first statewide police response in the US. Hawaii is the only state without a designated force in name, but it operates a Department of Public Safety,[48] and under this body the sheriff's office provides statewide policing.

The Maine State Police, motto *Semper Aequus*,[49] also operates under the Department of Public Safety; and it consists of 341 sworn trooper officers under the command of a colonel. It is a 'full-service' state police force that patrols all the state's highways and provides police services across the state. These include criminal investigation and forensic services. The original 1921 requirement that all troopers be proficient horsemen has now been dropped, but wearing a military style uniform remains. New recruits undertake a basic 18-week training program including Basic Law Enforcement Training (BLET) that all law enforcement personnel in the state of Maine must undertake. In addition to the usual requirements of honesty, not being a felon and being fit, applicants must be at least 21 years of age unless they possess an associate degree in which case they may enter at the age of 20 years. Total curriculum hours at basic training amounts to 720. The largest single most hours are spent teaching 'Testing and Critiques', while second is 'Lifetime Fitness'.[50] Upon completion of the academy, troopers are assigned to patrol. At this point they are now referred to as Field Troops. "The Troopers who work in the field troops patrol all municipalities in the state of Maine who do not have their own police departments. They enforce criminal and traffic laws through investigation and patrol work. Filed Troopers investigate traffic accidents and respond to a wide variety of criminal complaints including domestic violence, burglary and assault."[51] The state troopers under the responsibility of the Special Services Division conduct a large number of special operations. These include an air wing, a bomb team, criminal investigation and forensics and a tactical team. The investigation unit provides a nationally accredited forensic science laboratory service to all law enforcement agencies in the state of Maine. Members of the tactical team provide support to federal agencies for homeland security issues and they work closely with a number of state and local agencies. The titles and ranks of officers serving with the Maine State Police are military and their dress uniform is styled on an original military uniform. The 23 members of the tactical unit continue this tradition by wearing army combat uniforms and not civilian police attire. Currently 42 of 50 state police agencies have a specialized SWAT provision.[52] In common with most state enforcement agencies the Maine State Police provide protective services to the governor of the state and his family.[53]

Summary

The multitude of law enforcement agencies in the US means that effective collaboration between them is crucial to the successful investigation of a broad range of crimes. Most people who join a law enforcement agency do so at the local or state level. Few of these agencies currently require a four-year degree. Their training programs are ordinarily around 12 weeks in duration and once in the field, officers are monitored and trained for varying periods of time by a more experienced colleague. In the US, entry level policing is very much like an apprenticeship where new recruits cover basic material together and then learn the job by practice under the tutelage of a more senior practitioner. If contrasted with a number of police training programs outside of the US, it is clear that there is a wide discrepancy in some instances and great similarity in others. Compare for example three years of academic and practical training in the Scandinavian countries with three months of training in the US and the UK. Compare flat level entry for the US and the UK, Canada and Australia with multiple entry levels into the police service in France, depending upon how much higher education you have received, or officer entry for university graduates in South Korea.

Policing is a complex job that entails periods of extremely mundane work occasionally spiked by extreme danger and tension. Many people are not comfortable with the pressure of long periods of employment that are self-directed and have a strong social welfare ingredient. They believe police work will be about high action whereas it is mostly about being methodical and can be painstakingly repetitive. Contrary to what popular television and film portrays, most police officers never draw a weapon and few ever catch a criminal in the act of committing a crime. Consequently, there is a miss-match between the job reality and the job expectation and this is reflected in the high turnover of new recruits. Whether or not recruiting better-informed officers who hold four year degrees would result in more employment stability is at the moment unknown in the USA. What is clear is that there are considerable differences in terms of the background, educational achievement and life experiences recruits bring to the job. The US does not have, and is unlikely to ever adopt, a national police force model and therefore it is likely that for the foreseeable future the differences that exist will continue and America will be serviced by police officers from a very broad range of educational achievement levels.

Questions

1. The US Appeals Court stated that in the Robert Jordan case "New London's use of an 'upper-cut' did not violate the equal protection clause."

   a. True
   b. False

2. As a general statement, police recruits must be physically fit, not have a criminal record and be at least _____ years of age.

   a. 18
   b. 20
   c. 22
   d. 21

3. In 2003, more than _____ of US police forces did not have an aptitude test.

   a. 65%
   b. 50%
   c. 40%
   d. 35%

4. Ninety percent of basic training academies now provide terrorism training to new entrants.

   a. True
   b. False

5. On average, 66% of new recruits successfully complete basic training.

   a. True
   b. False

6. Typically, completion of the Police Licensing Exam will attract in the region of 22 hours of potential associate degree credit.

   a. True
   b. False

7. Conviction for a Class B misdemeanor within the past 10 years would prohibit appointment as a police officer.

   a. True
   b. False

8. Overall, _____ of US police forces require applicants to hold a four-year university degree.

   a. 5%
   b. 1%
   c. 10%
   d. 4%

9. Deputy sheriffs must be 20 years of age, participate in a written examination and successfully complete an 18 week training program.

   a. True
   b. False

10. The _____ were the first statewide police response in the US. (1905)

    a. Texas Rangers
    b. Massachusetts State troopers
    c. Pennsylvania State Police
    d. Delaware Troopers

Endnotes

1. Gaines, L. and Keppler, V. 2008. *Policing in America*. 6th ed. Newark, NJ: LexisNexis, infra, cite the findings of Manning 2006 stating that many police officers view themselves as crime-fighters or crook-catchers. p. 16
2. Allen, M. 1999. Ideas and trends; Help wanted invoking the not-too-high-IQ test. Sept. 19. www.expertlaw.com
3. Transcript of interview with Robert Jordan, September 12, 2000 at www.postroad.com
4. Ibid.
5. Robert Jordan v City of New London No. 99-9188. 2000 U.S. App. Lexis 22195. Decided August 23, 2000
6. Source: Recommendations for the North Carolina Highway Patrol produced by Ervin, A., Flores-Macias, G., Lee, H. and Taylor, B. May 2002 for the Terry Sanford Institute of Public Policy, Duke University, NC. Chapter II. Available at www.sanford.duke.edu
7. *Local Police Departments 2003*. Law Enforcement Management and Administrative Statistics. US Department of Justice report prepared by Mathew J. Hickman, Ph.D. and Brian A. Reaves, Ph.D. May 2006 NCJ 210118 at p. 8.
8. Ibid.
9. Bureau of Justice Statistics. This is 2008 data. The information is supplied every four years and 2012 figures are not yet available. www.bjs.usdoj.gov
10. Ibid.
11. Reaves, B.A. 2007. *Local Police Departments*. December 2010. NCJ 231174 at www.bjs.ojp.usdoj.gov
12. www.bjs.ojp.usdoj.gov
13. Ibid.
14. www.bls.gov
15. Ibid.
16. Many municipal forces now participate in Regional Training Academies, such as the North Central Texas Council of Governments Regional Police academy in Arlington, TX.
17. Further information at www.arlingtonpd.org
18. www.tcleose.state.tx.us
19. The total number of course hours varies between colleges; for example, El Paso Community College offers 704 contact hours of training.
20. In Texas, a class b typically incurs a fine not exceeding $2,000 and up to 180 days in jail. Examples include: shoplifting, prostitution, criminal trespass, minor drug possession and first offence DWI.
21. www.tulsapolice.org
22. Three Texas forces require a four-year degree: Arlington, Sugarland PD and Deer Park PD. The largest forces in the state, Houston and Dallas PD, do not have such a requirement.
23. "Applicants must have completed a bachelor's degree with a C+ average or better at an accredited college. No military hours or credits are accepted unless they are received from or converted through an accredited college." www.tulsapolice.org
24. Reaves, B.A. 2009. State and local law enforcement training academies. 2006 (Revised 4/14/09). February 2009 NCJ 222987 at p. 3. www.bjs.ojp.usdoj.gov
25. *Local police departments 2003* op. cit., p. 7.

26. Ibid.
27. *Local police departments 2003* op.cit., p. 9.
28. For further discussion see: Bruns, D. Reflections from the one-percent of local police departments with mandatory four-year degree requirements for new hires: Are they diamonds in the rough? Bacone College. bruns@bacone.edu
29. Ibid.
30. Ibid.
31. Ibid.
32. Source: Reaves, B.A. 2009. State and local law enforcement training academies, 2006 (Revised 4/14/09). February 2009 NCJ 222987 at www.bjs.ojp.usdoj.gov This was confirmed in Recommendations for the North Carolina Highway Patrol produced by Ervin, A., Flores-Macias, G., Lee, H., and Taylor, B. May 2002 for the Terry Sanford Institute of public policy, Duke University, NC. Available at www.sanford.duke.edu
33. Ibid.
34. Reaves, B.A. 2009. State and local law enforcement training academies, 2006 (Revised 4/14/09). February 2009 NCJ 222987 at www.bjs.ojp.usdoj.gov
35. www.police-association.org
36. Is policing a job or profession? The case for a four-year degree. CALEA Update Magazine, Issue 108. The author of the article is the Chief of Arlington PD, Texas, Theron L. Bowman, Ph.D. Available at www.calea.org
37. Ibid.
38. www.tampagov.net/dept_Police
39. Ibid.
40. Ibid.
41. NYPD is the largest, then Chicago PD and Los Angeles PD is third.
42. Other facilities are: Pitchless East, Pitchless North, North County Correctional facility, Mira Loma and Men's Central.
43. Civil process includes matters such as a writ of possession, summons and complaints, and restraining orders. For a complete list, see the LASO website. www.civil.lasd.org/CivilProcess
44. www.lasdhq.org/divisions/homeland
45. Basic monthly pay is $4,702.45, which rises to $464.73 for those with a two-year degree and $5,242.00 for those applicants holding a four-year degree. Source www.lasdhq.org/recruitment
46. For a comparative perspective, see Peak, K. (2012) *Policing America: Challenges and best practices.* 7th ed. Upper Saddle River, NJ: Pearson, pp. 82–86.
47. www.la-sheriff.org
48. State of Hawaii Public Safety Sheriff. This is one of two law enforcement divisions within the Department of Public Safety.
49. Always Just
50. 68 and 57 hours respectively. Source: www.maine.gov/dps/mcja/training
51. www.maine.gov/dps/msp/field_troops
52. Source: Peak, K. Op. cit. p. 62
53. And anybody else designated for protective services by the governor's office

CHAPTER 5: FEDERAL AGENCIES

Many law enforcement applicants are attracted to working for a federal agency. There are the kudos, the opportunity for travel and the attention paid to federal agencies by the film industry—they are usually heroes—and the repute of the agency at home and abroad. And there is the pay.

Federal agencies typically pay far more than local and state agencies. According to Kenneth Peak, the three-year salary range offered by the US Department of Homeland Security is between $100,502 and $118,589 if you hold a master's degree.[1] But since most applicants will not know this, it is probably not the salary that attracts them; it is the variety and caliber of the work.

Federal law enforcement agencies have grown in number significantly over the past one hundred years and their focus has also moved towards a general embracement of more national law provision across the US. Federal agencies have seen their sphere of responsibilities progressively increase and the sense of 'protection' from a federal agency has been manicured successively in the latter part of the last and early years of the current century.

National law enforcement and national prison systems are a growth industry.

Many agencies have been reformatted or merged into 'superagencies' since 9/11, so that today there are 73 agencies with federal arrest authority that are authorized to carry firearms while on duty.[2]

From *Crime and Policing Crime* by Peter Johnstone. Copyright © 2013 by Kendall Hunt Publishing Company. Reprinted by permission.

The Big Four

The four largest agencies of the total 120,000 sworn personnel—Customs and Border Protection, US Immigration and Customs Enforcement, the Federal Bureau of Prisons and the Federal Bureau of Investigation—account for the employment of four of every five federal officers.[3] Customs and Border Protection and US Immigration and Customs Enforcement (ICE) are part of the Department of Homeland Security, which employs 55,000 officers (46% of the total number of federal officers). Between 2002 and 2008, the US Customs and Border Protection service grew 33.1% in size, and during the same period the US Postal Inspection Service decreased in size 23.1%.[4] However, it was the Pentagon Force Protection Agency that grew the most over the period. It expanded its personnel strength by 50.4%.[5] The other large federal law enforcement employer is the Department of Justice (DOJ); the FBI and federal prisons come under this department. The Bureau of Prisons (BOP) is the larger of the two and employs nearly 17,000 correctional officers. There are currently in the region of 165,000 BOP inmates.[6] The FBI employs 12,760 full-time weapons carrying sworn agents, 500 more than in 2004 when the last census was conducted. Also within the DOJ is the Drug Enforcement Administration (DEA) (down 2%), the Marshals Service (up 2%) and ATF (Alcohol, Tobacco, Firearms and Explosives) (up 7%).[7] Other large increases in personnel between 2004 and 2008 happened in the Bureau of Diplomatic Service, which now employs 1,049, an increase of 27%, and the Veterans Affairs law enforcement and protection provision that saw an increase of 29% in officer numbers. There are 16 federal agencies that employ fewer than 250 personnel with arrest powers. The smallest is the Bureau of Reclamation with 21 special agents. The largest employer of federal agents outside of the executive is the Administrative Offices of the US. Courts. It employs 4,696 probation officers with arrest and firearm powers. This unit grew by 14% between 2004 and 2008.[8] The US Capitol Police also grew 7% in size to 1,637 sworn police officers. Offices of the Inspector General employ 3,501 officers with arrest and firearm authority, which is 12% more than in 2004. IG officers investigate cases of fraud, bribery, waste and abuse related to federal programs. Five IG offices employ more than 250 arrest and firearm officers. Despite the labor cuts the US Postal Service is still the largest of the IG agencies with 508 special agents.[9] Currently one-sixth of all federal special agents are women.[10] The largest single percentage of arrest and firearm female special agents is with the Administrative Offices of the US Courts, 46.2%. Of the officers employed by the Pentagon Force Protection Agency, 51.2% are members of a racial or ethnic minority.[11] The highest number of assaults upon federal officers happened against the Bureau of Indian Affairs police where 37.9% of officers were assaulted between 2004 and 2008. The least, with 0.0%, were the special agents of the US. Postal Service. Perhaps not surprisingly one of the largest concentrations of federal agents is in Washington DC—10,222 agents and police. The largest total number of federal agents, arrest and non-arrest power, working in any one state is

Texas where there are 18,322 special agents deployed. The highest concentration of arrest and firearm special agents per 100,000 population is in Washington DC, by a considerable margin, at 1,732. The state with the highest ratio of agents per 100,000 population is New Mexico at 130. The overall average number of federal arrest and firearm officers per 100,000 population is 40. Overall, the number of federal officers employed in the US grew by 14% between 2004 and 2008. Twenty-three percent of all federal officers are involved in some form of police patrol, 15% perform immigration and customs functions and 14% are employed in prisons and detention services.[12]

Department of Homeland Security

The Department of Homeland Security (DHS) was established under the Homeland Security Act 2002 in response to the terrorist attacks upon the US in 2001. DHS brought 22 existing agencies into one new entity.[13] Two of the numerous functions the agency undertakes are passenger and cargo screening at airports and the air marshal's service. The passenger screening program of the Aviation Security Unit employs 50,000 officers to screen more than 1.7 million airline passengers every day and more than 700 million each year.[14] Federal Air Marshals are armed agents who are deployed on national and international flights to protect passengers and crew in the event of a hostile attack on board a flight. Applicants to the agency must be between the ages of 21 and 37 and successfully complete a 30-week training program broken down into two 15-week segments. Part one is basic law enforcement training (BLET). Phase two[15] is specific to the marshal's role and includes training in international law, arrest procedures pertinent to the aircraft industry and on board flights, international communication and advanced firearm tactics. Air marshals have the most stringent pistol firearms qualification score requirement of any police agency in the US. This was shown in action when in 2005 a passenger who claimed he had a bomb was shot and killed by air marshals as he attempted to board a plane in Miami. The 44-year-old US citizen, Rigoberto Alpizar, was on route to Medellin, Colombia, when he claimed to have a bomb in his backpack. When air marshals attempted to engage Alpizar in conversation, he reached into his backpack, at which point he was shot dead.[16] Starting pay is in the region of $40,000 per annum depending upon entry level and previous employment qualifications. Federal air marshals ordinarily work in teams of two on flights.

ATF

The Bureau of Alcohol, Tobacco, Firearms and Explosives is one of the agencies that were reconfigured after 9/11. On January 24, 2003, the ATF was transferred from the Treasury to the Department of Justice—well, some of it was. The law enforcement part of ATF is now under the DOJ, and the tax and trade side of ATF is still with the Department of the Treasury but has been renamed the Alcohol and Tobacco Tax and Trade Bureau. ATF describes itself as "The Violent Crime Bureau," which is an interesting title and you have to ask how closely this would mesh with the idea the general public has of the agency and what it does. Also, I doubt whether many agencies from outside of the US think of ATF when they think of the primary US domestic agency tasked to deal with violent crime. I suspect the response would be the FBI. Perhaps there is a study in here for a student? ATF is "A unique law enforcement agency in the United States Department of Justice that protects our communities from violent criminals, criminal organizations, the illegal use and trafficking of firearms, the illegal use and storage of explosives, acts of arson and bombings, acts of terrorism, and the illegal diversion of alcohol and tobacco products. . . ."[17] The rhetoric gets even more dynamic and emotive: "A dedicated team securing America's future by accomplishing a critical mission today'. 'Combating violent crime is our specialty, our niche." "The profession of special agent is exciting and rewarding. Special agents must be tough-both physically and mentally. They must be able to handle rigorous training, personal risks, irregular hours, and extensive travel. . . ."[18] In order to be considered for employment as a special agent in ATF, applicants must be US citizens, a minimum of 21 and a maximum of 36 years of age and hold a four-year degree.[19] Basic pay for a new entrant is $33,829 plus 25% law enforcement ability pay (LEAP) and locality pay.[20] Applicants that hold a master's degree enter at a salary point of $42,948, plus the enhancements applicable to all entrants. Applicants who have proficiency in a foreign language are eligible for cash awards. Having successfully passed the entrance examination and interview stages of recruitment new recruits enter the academy. There are two stages to initial training. Part one is held at the Federal Law Enforcement Training Center (FLETC), Department of Homeland Security, Glynco, Georgia. This stage includes firearms training, driving, making arrests, basic crime investigations, surveillance techniques and federal court procedures. This is a 12 week class. The second stage of training is Special Agent Basic Training (SABT). This is a 15-week course geared specifically towards the needs of federal agents and includes such issues as field operations, undercover work, report writing and ATF investigation issues.

The nexus between drug trafficking and terrorism has now been clearly established,[21] and these crime organizations use a multitude of criminal operations to create a diverse source of illegal incomes. The idea that cigarette smuggling is not a major crime and that it may only entail a limited amount of tax avoidance is fiction. Cigarette smuggling continues to be a significant criminal enterprise for numerous international crime organizations and much of the wealth produced is then siphoned off into paying for violent criminal attacks upon citizens across the globe—terrorism. According to the ATF, at one time the Real IRA were generating $100 million of terrorist funds through illicit cigarette smuggling every year.[22] On March 31, 2010, President Obama signed into law the Prevent All Cigarette Trafficking Act, a law that amends the Jenkins Act[23] beyond the collection of taxes and illegal trafficking in cigarettes to now impose additional requirements for registration, reporting and record keeping as well as prohibiting the sale of cigarettes through the mail.[24] Violation of PACT is punishable with up to three years imprisonment and a fine, both criminal and civil.[25] It is important to recognize that although cigarette smuggling may not appear to be a significant problem and it does not immediately attract the level of media attention that a bombing or a major firearms incident will, the impact of this type of crime is widespread and does undoubtedly provide a significant revenue stream for a number of diverse crime groups across the globe. More sensational, however, are such investigations as "Operation Anything For a Buck." A joint operation between the ATF, the Escambia Sheriff's Department and the Pensacola Florida Police Department, the case resulted in the indictment of 22 defendants with federal firearms charges and an additional 53 defendants with state offences. In the federal matters, the defendants had sold undercover agents 270 assorted firearms and engaged in more than 100 drug deals for marijuana, cocaine, heroin, Xanax and Oxycodone.[26] As seen by this operation, a major part of ATF work involves checking on the sale and possession of firearms;[27] there are more than 2.4 million handguns in the US and more than 3 million rifles and shotguns.[28] Compliance with the laws, sales licenses, purchasing and ownership are the responsibility of ATF; so too is enforcement of the laws relating to the use of firearms and the elimination of illegal firearms trafficking in the US. There were also 7,367 applications to import firearms into the US in 2010.[29] The unfortunate events surrounding operation "Fast and Furious"[30] have adversely tarnished the image of ATF for now; but in the long term history, the agency that started with just three detectives back in 1863 will recover and continue to make a meaningful and valuable contribution to the prevention and detection of criminal offences involving alcohol, tobacco, firearms and explosives.

The Secret Service

The United States Secret Service was formed in 1865 and today comprises more than 150 offices across the US and worldwide, as well as its headquarters in Washington DC. The Secret Service has two responsibilities: the protection of designated national and international leaders and criminal investigations. The service was originally established to prevent the counterfeiting of US currency. It still undertakes this responsibility today by safeguarding the "financial infrastructure and payment systems to preserve the integrity of the economy. . . ."[31] During the American Civil War, it was estimated that up to one-half of all the currency in circulation was counterfeit. The Secret Service was established to counteract this problem and it continued with this sole responsibility until the attack upon President William McKinley's life in Buffalo, New York in 1901. Since that time a protection service for the President,[32] and then later for designated dignitaries, has been a major function of the service.[33] Since 1965, former presidents and their spouses[34] became eligible for lifetime protective services, but they may decline. In 1997, this was reduced to 10 years of protection upon leaving office unless they were in office before January 1, 1997. President George W. Bush will be the first president to have protection for a maximum of ten years upon leaving office. So if we now return to the two responsibilities—protection and criminal investigations—these are achieved through the protection of designated persons and the investigation of threats against the protected and the investigation of financial crimes. Approximately 3,200 officers are employed in the Secret Service, of which 1,300 are uniformed[35] and the remainder are Special Agents. Established as the White House Police Force in 1922,[36] today the "Secret Service Uniformed Division Officers provide protection for the White House complex, the Vice President's residence, the main Treasury Building and Annex, and foreign diplomatic missions and embassies in the Washington, D.C., area. Additionally, Uniformed Division officers travel in support of presidential, vice presidential and foreign head of state government missions."[37]

Due to the nature of the work, all Secret Service positions require a comprehensive background check and security clearance. Applicants must be a minimum of 21 years of age. Secret Service Uniformed Officers, the uniformed branch, are initially sent to Glynco, Georgia, to complete Federal Law Enforcement Training. Upon completion of this 12-week course they are sent to the James J. Rowley Training Center for completion of law enforcement training. This lasts 14 weeks. Special Agents employed in the criminal investigations side of the secret service attend the Criminal Investigator Training Program (CITP) at Glynco and upon successful graduation attend an 18-week Special Agent Training Course at James J. Rowley. Although most agents are employed within the US, there are offices in 15 countries, as well as at INTERPOL in Lyon, France. On March 16, 2012, the US Department of Homeland Security issued a press release titled "US Secret Service's Operation Open Market Nets 19 Arrests." The operation was a case of cybercrime fraud and identity theft involving the purchase and sale of financial information by international organized crime group members. The operation was conducted by the Secret Service's Electronic Crimes Task Force in association with members of ICE. The 19 suspects have been charged with racketeering, conspiracy, production and trafficking in false identification documents and access device cards. In total 50 people have been charged and further arrests are expected. The investigation established a network of criminal enterprises exchanging financial information and identities to buy and sell money laundering services, fraudulent debit and credit cards and stolen PayPal account information. It has yet to be established exactly how many identities have been compromised, but if a previous investigation, Operation Firewall, is indicative of the numbers, then this operation will amount to millions. Firewall was successfully concluded in 2004 after the Secret Service arrested 28 individuals from six countries for trafficking 1.7 million stolen credit card numbers and false identification documents under websites named "Shadocrew," 'Carderplanet" and "Darkprofits."[38]

US Marshals

The oldest federal agency in the United States is the US Marshals Service. It was formed by President George Washington on September 24, 1789, when he appointed 13 marshals. One of the many tasks this agency undertook was to perform the execution of federal convicts sentenced to death; another was to investigate matters of counterfeiting until the creation of the Secret Service. There are 94 marshals, each representing one federal court district. They are all appointed personally by the President. The marshals are assisted by 3,950 deputy marshals in protection of and the enforcement work of the federal judicial system. Their principal roles are protection services to judges, federal DAs, jurors, members of the public[39] using the courts and defendants. The service also houses and transports federal prisoners, operates the Witness Security Program,[40] apprehends federal fugitives, seizes and distributes property taken under the Department of Justice Asset Forfeiture Program[41] and it assists other federal, state and local law enforcement agencies in fugitive operations. The Service also provides protection to the 'Drug Czar', the Director of the Office on National Drug Control Policy, when he travels, as well as to Supreme Court Justices when they travel, and protection to foreign officials when the United Nations assembly is in session. In 2010, the US Marshal Service (USMS) apprehended 36,100 federal fugitives and assisted local agencies in the arrest of 81,900 state and local fugitives and in the execution of 108,200 state and local warrants. The Service also coordinated 805 extraditions and deportations from 67 countries.[42] The USMS has field offices in Colombia, the Dominican Republic, Jamaica and Mexico. The USMS is responsible for the safe conduct of all federal prisoners from the point of entry until acquittal or conviction. Upon conviction, the agency is responsible for the delivery of prisoners to a federal penitentiary. In 2010, the service received 225,329 prisoners. It has more than 53,000 detainees in custody every day.[43] The Service operates a Special Operations Group for use in high-risk or sensitive enforcement situations or for deployment to assist in national emergencies. Appointment to the USMS requires US citizenship, being aged between 21 and 36 years, a four-year degree and a personal profile assessment. Upon acceptance into the Service, candidates must complete the initial 17.5-week USMS training course at Glynco, Georgia.

Operation Falcon was a nationwide fugitive apprehension operation coordinated by the USMS that involved dozens[44] of other agencies across the US. The first phase was completed in 2005 and since then there have been a number of continuing operations. It is now so famous that there are TV documentaries about the various stages of the operations. Phase 1 took place between April 4 and 10, 2005; Phase II was in April 2006 and Phase III was in October 2006. Phase I resulted in the largest total number of arrests made during one operation when 10,340 fugitives were apprehended over seven days. Operation Falcon[45] continued into 2009 as a national fugitive arrest program with regular statewide arrests[46] being made of large numbers of wanted persons.

To date more than 91,000 arrests and 117,000 warrants have been executed since Falcon commenced in 2005. The last year of reported operations, 2009, resulted in the arrest of 35,190 fugitives and the execution of 47,418 warrants. This last reported operation involved 42 federal agencies, 209 state agencies and 1,973 local sheriff and police departments.[47] The USMS has not operated Falcon since 2009. Instead, in 2010, the USMS Investigative Operations Division focused on a joint initiative with state agencies to implement a gang participation reduction program, "Statistically, the gang surge numbers show great success. The Gang Surge realized a 288% increase in gang member arrests compared to the previous three month average."[48] The USMS is unique in that it has federal and state powers; this means that when the Service is operating within any state, marshals have exactly the same powers as a sheriff of that state in addition to the federal powers they hold.

FBI Special Units

The nature of serious crime is such that it often requires local and state agencies to request assistance from federal units. This is not to say that all murders, assaults, thefts and drug trafficking are of such a scale that additional resources are always needed, but federal agencies are well placed to provide support, resources and expert services for the more complex and organized nature of these crimes, as well as for their impact, locally and nationally and sometimes internationally. In response to this growing need, the Federal Bureau of Investigations (FBI) has created a number of specialist units—Behavior Analysis Units (BAU)—that focus on some aspects of these crimes, for example: serial killings, mass killings, killings and attempted killings of particular persons. The mission of these units is to provide operational and specialist support to state and local agencies for specific and often sensitive crime investigations. Members of BAU are specialists in observing and interpreting offender behavior patterns and the factors behind specialty crimes, such as motive and frequency. All members of BAU hold advanced degrees and are drawn from the supervisory ranks of the FBI, or they are previously serving police officers with a considerable degree of experience in the specialist field. Criminologists and clinical psychologists also serve as members of BAU, as do research and crime analysts.

As the FBI website states, "Spies. Terrorists. Hackers. Pedophiles. Mobsters.[49] Gang leaders and serial killers. We investigate them all, and many more besides." Authority to investigate federal crimes is through a number of statutes, the primary being US Title 18. Assisting and investigating state crimes is at the request of the state, so that the state will make a formal request in such cases as a felony murder of a state law enforcement officer, violent crimes against interstate travelers or serial killers, but the authority to investigate is vested in the FBI through federal legislation.[50] The FBI will take over the investigation in instances of kidnapping or a 'missing child' under the age of 12 years. In other instances of abduction and kidnapping, the FBI will provide support and assistance and monitor the crime developments.

There are four BAUs: Counterterrorism and Threat Assessment, Crimes against Adults, Crimes against Children and Unit 4, ViCAP, Violent Criminal Apprehension Program. Behavioral Analysis Unit 2 (crimes against adults) works on cases of serial killing, spree killings, mass murders, other murders that are particularly complex or sensitive, sexual assaults, kidnappings, missing adults and any other cases of violent crime that involve adult victims. Unit 3 covers the same range of offending that targets children as the victims. Unit 4, ViCAP, focuses on specific murder cases that have involved an abduction or are of a sexual nature or appear to be random or motiveless or stranger killings. They also investigate human remains where cause of death is unknown and this Unit holds the national database for unsolved cases within the above criteria. ViCAP is also the Unit that provides support to state agencies that are investigating violent crimes committed on major highways and it is the repository of all information held about homicides, missing persons and sexual assault victims associated with highways across the nation. Contrary to much television and cinema portrayal, the FBI very rarely takes over a local investigation. What this agency does is supply expert assistance and resources as well as research, analysis and experience to a range of crimes that often test the physical resources and experience base of smaller local and state agencies. In some instances, there will be concurrent jurisdiction, for example, in a case of drug trafficking that involves local, state and federal violations; but unless the offence is one of the few crimes designated exclusively as a federal crime, such as murder of a federal agent or murder committed on federal property, in most cases the local law enforcement response will take lead responsibility for the investigation.

Summary

Over time, local US police officers may develop a portfolio of experience and academic achievement so that they are well placed to apply for employment as federal agents. Once accepted, they will embark upon extended periods of training, field supervised development and continuing education. Most of the federal agencies now require applicants to hold a four-year degree and enhanced pay is available for those with a masters and/or foreign language proficiency. Federal law enforcement work will be more specific and agents have the chance to work in highly specialized fields, nationally and internationally. Whether or not learning the craft of policing at a local level, so that hands-on experience is gained in dealing with dozens of minor theft allegations, assaults, low level drug dealing and missing persons reports, is *sine qua non*[51] for investigating complex major crimes, is, and perhaps always will be, debatable. For those specialist agencies that recruit directly, apparently street experience is not a relevant criterion, although a number of agencies make specific reference to applicants who are currently employed by a local law enforcement agency. For those countries that require their police officers to attend university as part of basic training, very few have federal agencies that supplement the work of the police. Typically, the police in these countries investigate the complex national and international crimes as well as the routine. But there is movement; the UK is creating a super-agency, vigorously claimed by politicians not to be a UK FBI but a National Crime Agency. Member states of Europe have moved beyond a Euro-wide drug unit to a Euro-wide police force, and its sphere of responsibility is growing. The military gendarmes of Europe are following closely behind. Australia already has federal police and the RCMP; well, it is truly unique as it provides national, state and local police, as well as federal style specialist services and support to smaller forces. The UN has a police force too.

One thing is clear—contemporary policing responds to levels of interstate and inter-country criminality on an unprecedented scale. And although minor assaults, thefts and drug deals may be the 'bread and butter' of policing, they are no longer the only carbohydrates on the table. However technology assists or shapes the way forward, it will most definitely have a role in every aspect of policing at every level. Even the most routine theft investigation is now driven by technology; so too are reports of missing persons, the pattern of drug dealing in small cities and the frequency of assaults. Even 'bread and butter' policing cannot survive without some technology input any longer. Global policing arrived the day the first cybercrime was committed. There really never was 'business as usual' for policing; it has always been dynamic; we just added virtual and global policing to that mix.

Questions

1. Many agencies have been reformatted or merged into 'superagencies' since 9/11 so that today there are _____ agencies with federal arrest authority that are authorized to carry firearms while on duty.

   a. 45
   b. 60
   c. 58
   d. 73

2. US Immigration and Customs enforcement is part of the Department of Homeland Security.

   a. True
   b. False

3. The federal agency that grew the most between 2002 and 2008 was:

   a. US Postal Inspection Service
   b. Pentagon Force Protection Agency
   c. Capitol Police
   d. The Federal Bureau of Prisons

4. There are 20 federal agencies that employ fewer than 250 personnel with arrest powers.

   a. True
   b. False

5. Offices of the Inspector General, IG, investigate cases of:

   a. Fraud, bribery, waste and abuse related to federal programs
   b. Fraud, bribery, waste and abuse related to state programs
   c. Both (a) and (b)
   d. Neither (a) nor (b)

6. "A unique law enforcement agency in the United States Department of Justice that protects our communities from violent criminals, criminal organizations, the illegal use and trafficking of firearms, the illegal use and storage of explosives, acts of arson and bombings, acts of terrorism, . . ."

   This statement describes which agency?

   a. FBI
   b. DEA
   c. ATF
   d. Secret Service

7. This service was originally established to prevent counterfeiting of US currency.

   a. US Marshalls
   b. FBI
   c. Secret Service
   d. Capitol Police

8. The oldest federal agency in the United States:

   a. Secret Service
   b. US Marshals Service
   c. Texas Rangers
   d. ATF

9. The mission of these FBI units, _____, is to provide operational and specialist support to state and local agencies for specific and often sensitive crime investigations.

   a. Behavioral Analysis Units
   b. Special Investigations Units
   c. Serial Killing and Mass Murder Units
   d. Criminal Behavior Identification Units

10. Most countries that require their police officers to attend university as part of basic training have federal agencies that supplement the work of the police.

   a. True
   b. False

Endnotes

1. I have not been able to verify these figures. His source is cited in Peak op. cit., p. 65.
2. Source: Census of federal law enforcement officers 2008 produced by Brian Reaves Ph.D. June 26, 2012. NCJ 238250. This census does not contain details of the CIA or TSA (air marshals), as it is 'classified information'. Available at www.bjs.ojp.usdoj.gov
3. Op. cit. Census 2008
4. Ibid.
5. Ibid.
6. Ibid.
7. Ibid.
8. Seven federal courts do not permit their probation officers to carry firearms.
9. The others are: Dept. of Health and Human Services, Dept. of Defense, Dept. of the Treasury and the Social Security Administration.
10. Op. cit., Census 2008
11. Ibid.
12. Ibid.
13. For a list of the 22, see: www.dhs.gov/xabout/history
14. www.dhs.gov
15. Conducted at one of the FAMS training centers in New Jersey or New Mexico
16. Man killed after bomb claim at airport. December 7, 2005. www.cnn.com/2005/us/airplane.gunshot
17. www.atf.gov/careers
18. Ibid.
19. Applicants who do not hold a four-year degree may apply if they have three years of work experience and an associate degree or are currently serving in a law enforcement agency or are currently serving as an investigator in another federal agency. Applicants with a four-year degree who achieved a grade point average of 2.95 or above are eligible for enhanced entry and pay.
20. Locality pay varies between 14.16% and 35.15%.
21. See Johnstone, P. 2012. *Drugs and drug trafficking*. Dubuque, IA: Kendall Hunt. Chapter 5.
22. Ibid.
23. 15 USC Chapter 10A
24. Cigarettes and non-smoking tobacco products. Cigars are exempt.
25. Under title 18 USC
26. See: 75 defendants charged on firearm, drug distribution, or related offenses following 8-month undercover investigation. Available at www.atf.gov/press/releases/2011
27. The state with the highest number of registered guns is California with 242,766; the second highest is Texas with 224,200 license holders. Source: ATF 2011 infra.
28. www.atf.gov/publications/firearms/121611-firearms-commerce-2011
29. Ibid. Sixty-three percent of imported firearms are handguns; 19% are rifles and 18% are shotguns.
30. There was massive media coverage of this incident. See for example, The truth about the Fast and Furious scandal. June 27, 2012. Fortune Magazine. Available at www.fortune.cnn.com

Exclusive: Fast and Furious IG slams ATF Phoenix personnel by Sharyl Attkisson. August 27, 2012. Available at www.cbsnews.com

31. www.secretservice.gov
32. There have been seven direct assaults upon the President since 1950—one resulting in death, President Kennedy. Only one President has been assaulted twice, Gerald R. Ford, two times in September 1975. Source: The US Secret Service: An examination and analysis of its evolving mission: Shawn Reese. December 16, 2009. *Congressional Research Service*. Available at www.crs.gov RL 34603
33. By law, the Secret Service protects the President, the family of the President, the Vice President, the President elect and the VP elect; former Presidents and their spouses; children of former Presidents until they are 16 years of age; other individuals next in line to be President, e.g. the Speaker of the House, the House Minority Whip, and major presidential candidates (within 120 days of a general election; this was extended to six months for the Presidential candidate Barack Obama, the first time in history that there was such an extension for a candidate); visiting heads of state and their spouses travelling in the US; as well as individuals designated by an Executive Presidential Order and national special security events when designated by the Secretary of the Department of Homeland Security, such as a State of the Union Address, a Presidential inaugural celebration or even the SuperBowl.
34. Jacqueline Kennedy and her children were provided with two years of protection after the assassination of President John F. Kennedy. This has not happened since and ordinarily the widow of a former President is not provided with protective services upon becoming a widow.
35. Previously known as the White House police, they were renamed The Executive Protective Service in 1970 and then in November 1977 received the current name: The Secret Service Uniformed Division.
36. October 1, 1922 at the instigation of President Harding. It became part of the Secret Service in 1930.
37. www.secretservice.gov/careers
38. See: US Department of Homeland Security press release, US Secret Service's Operation Firewall nets 28 Arrests. October 28, 2004. The role of the Secret Service in investigating cybercrime was expanded under the Patriot Act (107-56), which included the establishment of a nationwide electronic crimes taskforce. This unit grew again in 2006 from 15 to 24 nationwide 'taskforces'. Since 2003, the Secret Service has made more than 29,000 arrests for cybercrime, counterfeiting and financial crime offences. Source: www.secretservice.gov/history
39. There are in the neighborhood of 1,400 threats against the judiciary every year. Source: www.usmarshals.gov/duties/factsheets
40. More than 8,300 witnesses and 9,800 family members have participated in the program since its inception in 1971.
41. Currently 18,000 assets valued at $3.9 billion. Source. www.usmarshals.gov
42. www.usmarshals.gov/duties
43. The USMS rents local jail space from other prisons and jails around the country to provide daily facilities for federal prisoners.

44. 25 federal agencies, 206 state agencies, 302 county sheriffs' departments and 366 police departments. Source: www.doj.gov
45. Federal And Local Cops Organized Nationally: FALCON
46. E.g., 86 arrests were made under FALCON in Madison, WI on July 9, 2009. www.doj.state.wi.us
47. www.usmarshals.gov/falcon
48. USMS FY 2012 Performance Budget President's Budget. February 2011. Department of Justice publication. Page 34 available at www.justice.gov/jmd/2012justification
49. www.fbi.gov/about-us/invetsigate
50. 28 USC 540, 540A and 540B
51. Meaning an indispensable action or requirement. Often something that is required in advance.

CHAPTER 6
POLICE AND THE RULE OF LAW

◆ Introduction

The moment that the police come into contact with a citizen to investigate the reporting of a crime, the powers of the state and the individual collide. Moreover, the crime control and due process doctrines are poised for battle. The Framers of the United States Constitution were aware of this. For example:

The Fourth Amendment

The right of the people to be secure in their persons, houses, papers, and effects, against unreasonable searches and seizures, shall not be violated, and no Warrants shall issue, but upon probable cause, supported by Oath or affirmation, and particularly describing the place to be searched, and the persons or things to be seized.

The Fifth Amendment

No person shall be held to answer for a capital, or otherwise infamous crime, unless on a presentment or indictment of a Grand Jury, except in cases arising in the land or naval forces, or in the Militia, when in actual service in time of War or public danger; nor shall any person be subject for the same offense to be twice put in jeopardy of life or limb; nor shall be compelled in any criminal case to be a witness against himself, nor

From *Criminal Justice: Balancing Crime Control and Due Process*, 3/e, by Matt Delisi. Copyright © 2011 by Kendall Hunt Publishing Company. Reprinted by permission.

be deprived of life, liberty, or property, without due process of law; nor shall private property be taken for public use, without just compensation.

The Sixth Amendment

In all criminal prosecutions, the accused shall enjoy the right to a speedy and public trial, by an impartial jury of the State and district wherein the crime shall have been committed, which district shall have been previously ascertained by law, and to be informed of the nature and cause of the accusation; to be confronted with the witnesses against him; to have compulsory process for obtaining witnesses in his favor, and to have the Assistance of Counsel for his defense.

The Fourth, Fifth, and Sixth Amendments encompass the interaction between the police and members of the community, the requirement of a warrant and circumstances where warrants are not needed, the scope and limits of police powers when dealing with persons in an investigative manner, and the transition from investigating a suspect to charging the accused. In short, the Fourth, Fifth, and Sixth Amendments cover the "passing of the Constitutional baton" between the police and the courts.

Warrants

Warrants are an important example of due process at work because they involve the interchange between the police and local judges. Warrants are writs or orders by judicial officers, such as a judge or magistrate that direct law enforcement officers to perform specified acts and afford them protection from damage during the course of executing their duties. A warrant can only be executed by the officer to whom it is directed either by name or by description of his or her office. It cannot confer authority to execute it on one officer where a statute provides for its execution by another. The warrant cannot be executed outside the jurisdiction of the issuing court. Finally, the execution of a warrant necessitates that the warrant be in the officer's possession during the search and returned after the search or arrest.

As stated in the Fourth Amendment, probable cause is the evidentiary criterion and due process standard required for the issuance of warrants (and indeed making any arrest). Probable cause is a set of facts and circumstances that would induce a reasonably intelligent and prudent person to believe that a particular person had committed a specific crime. Essentially, probable cause is the reasonable grounds to initiate a criminal investigation. Particularity is the other vital term from the Fourth Amendment. The particularity requirement means that warrants must specify precisely the places to be searched and the items to be seized. This prohibits the police from having unrestricted discretion to search for evidence.

The information that constitutes a warrant arrives from several sources. Frequently, victims, witnesses, or third parties report information of a crime to a police officer. These parties typically have first-hand knowledge that a specific person committed a specific crime (or number of crimes). Police officers conduct interviews, engage in other investigative activities, and produce a written document or affidavit that contains probable cause and the particular circumstances that an individual committed a crime. The report is then presented to a local judicial officer who then determines whether to issue a search warrant. In the field, these are commonly referred to as affidavit warrants.

The information that culminates in a warrant can also come from another interesting party, criminals or informants. Because criminal offenders are disproportionately likely to associate with other criminal offenders, they can often serve as a wealth of information to law enforcement officials who are investigating crimes. Of course, the validity and reliability of information produced by informants can be problematic. For example, informants could simply lie to police to deflect attention from their own criminal activity. Moreover, their testimony could be complete hearsay, and unable to be substantiated. Because of these concerns, the courts have addressed the use of informant information and "anonymous" tips. In *Aguilar v. Texas* (1964) the Supreme Court ruled that magistrates that issue warrants must be advised of (1) the underlying circumstances from which the affiant concluded that probable cause existed and (2) of the underlying circumstances from which the affiant concluded that the anonymous informant was credible or reliable. These two conditions constituted the Aguilar two-prong test for the issuance of warrants.[1]

McCray v. Illinois (1967) held that a reliable informant's identity generally did not need to be disclosed during court proceedings. This was an important preservation of the anonymity of police informants.[2] *Spinelli v. United States* (1969) applied the Aguilar two-pronged test to cases where the informant had not previously been proven reliable. However, it was asserted that some information was so highly specific that it must be accurate, even if its source was not revealed.[3] However, it was the case of *Illinois v. Gates* (1983) that expanded on the Aguilar case. *Illinois v. Gates* (1983) held that the reliability of an informant in search warrant cases should be based on the "totality of circumstances" instead of the rigid two-pronged test of Aguilar. Moreover, Gates established that prior reliability does not have to be established if the information is sufficiently detailed and has indications of credibility.[4]

◆ The Exclusionary Rule

The heart of the Fourth Amendment and by extension, warrants, is the lawfulness of the evidence that the authorities can marshal against a criminal defendant. The protection against unlawfully seized evidence is known as the exclusionary rule. The exclusionary rule is the principle that prohibits the use of illegally obtained evidence in criminal trials. This is an important due process restriction placed on the police. Even if they obtain information or evidence that incontrovertibly suggests guilt, the evidence cannot be used in court if it was obtained in violation of the Fourth Amendment.

The exclusionary rule was established at the federal level nearly 50 years before the state level. *Weeks v. U.S.* (1914) established that the Fourth Amendment barred the use of evidence secured through an illegal search and seizure by federal law enforcement officials.[5] The landmark case *Mapp. v. Ohio* (1961) held that the exclusionary rule was applicable to the states through the due process clause of the Fourth Amendment. Mapp overruled *Wolf v. Colorado* (1949), which applied the Fourth Amendment to the states but did not enforce the proscription of using illegally seized evidence at trial.[6]

A bastion of due process, the exclusionary rule is a judicial mandate designed primarily to further professionalize police behavior, not necessarily to serve as a guarantee of constitutional safeguards. It's a rather harsh rule, the reasoning being that it is better to let some of the guilty go free so that the majority of people would benefit from more thorough and professional police work. A related concept is the fruit of the poisonous tree doctrine, which established that evidence illegally seized is not only inadmissible, but also any evidence or testimony obtained later as a result of the illegally seized evidence is inadmissible. Established in *Silverthorne Lumber Company v. U.S.* (1920), the metaphor paints evidence as poisonous because of the illegalities of the underlying police search and seizure.[7]

In the decades since *Silverthorne,* the Supreme Court has generally softened the fruit of the poisonous tree doctrine. For example, in *Wong Sun v. U.S.* (1963) the Court held that defendant's statements were admissible in court because the connection between an illegal arrest and the statements had "become so attenuated as to dissipate the taint."[8] *Michigan v. Tucker* (1974) established that a witness's testimony against a criminal defendant can be admissible in court even though the initial statements made by the accused were without Miranda advisement and led the police to the witness.[9] The Court nearly reversed itself a year later. *Brown v. Illinois* (1975) held that the Miranda advisement does not reduce the taint of a defendant's illegal arrest and render admissible statements given after the arrest. In other words, the Miranda advisement is not a catch-all formality that covers for improper police behavior.[10] *United States v. Crews* (1980) and *United States v. Havens* (1980) further attenuated the poisonous tree doctrine. Crews held that in-court identification of a suspect was not made inadmissible solely because the defendant's original arrest was illegal. Havens held that illegally seized evidence could be used to impeach the defendant's statements made on direct examination during a criminal trial.[11] Two final cases linked the poisonous tree doctrine to confessions. *Taylor v. Alabama* (1982) held that a confession obtained through custodial interrogation, after an illegal arrest, should be inadmissible unless the confession is sufficiently an act of free will to purge the taint of illegal arrest.[12] *Lanier v. South Carolina* (1985) held that a finding that a confession was voluntary is merely a threshold requirement of Fourth Amendment analysis of confessions made after an illegal arrest. That Miranda warnings have been given is not enough, in and of themselves to purge the taint of illegal arrest.[13]

As this list of case law suggests, the nuances of the exclusionary rule are many. Although the exclusionary rule is a crucially important provision of due process, the majority of Supreme Court decisions since Silverthorne have tended to increase police powers in dealing with criminal suspects. Indeed, there are many situations where the police are neither required to have a warrant nor bound by the exclusionary rule. These exceptions are reviewed next.

◆ Exceptions to the Exclusionary Rule and Warrantless Searches and Seizures

There are a variety of circumstances where it is not reasonable to expect the police to require a warrant, wait on a warrant, or wait to conduct lawful searches during the course of their duties. Broadly speaking, these exceptions are known as exigent circumstances. Exigent circumstances are dangerous or emergency situations where it simply would not be prudent to force the police to wait on a warrant while exercising their professional duties. Situations where public safety is at risk, where evidence could be destroyed, and where the police are in "hot pursuit" are examples of exigent circumstances.[14] The courts have established a variety of exceptions to the exclusionary rule and circumstances where searches and seizures, without a warrant, are permitted. These exceptions with commensurate case law are reviewed next.

Good Faith

The good faith exception to the exclusionary rule is the principle that evidence that was collected via a faulty, erroneous, or technically illegal warrant may be used in court provided the police were acting in good faith. In other words, it does not penalize proper police behavior for the court's mistake. *United States v. Leon* (1984) established the good faith exception.[15] *Illinois v. Krull* (1987) further held that the good faith exception to the exclusionary rule applies to searches conducted by police officers acting in objectively reasonable reliance upon a statute authorizing warrantless administrative searches even though the statute was later found to violate the Fourth Amendment.[16] *Arizona v. Evans* (1995) held that the good faith exception applied to evidence seized incident to an arrest resulting from an inaccurate computer record indicating that there was an outstanding arrest warrant for the suspect. The exception applied regardless of whether police or court personnel were responsible for the erroneous record's continued presence in the police computer.[17] Given the proliferation of computers in society and criminal justice, *Arizona v. Evans* (1995) is sometimes referred to as the "computer errors exception" to the exclusionary rule. At minimum, it is an extension of the good faith exception.

The good faith exception is listed first here for an important reason. A recurrent theme in American case law is the consistent finding that as long as the police are acting in a lawful, reasonable, well-intentioned manner at the outset of their interaction with citizens, the courts are willing to grant them considerable legal discretion. This does not mean that the police have carte blanche to make mistakes and violate due process. Instead, it means that appellate courts favorably view crime control practices achieved via the tenets of due process. Acting in good faith matters.

Incident to Arrest

The most frequent type of warrantless search is one that occurs incident to or while the police are making an arrest. Of course, the arrest must be lawful and based on probable cause. The arrest must be custodial, that is the suspect is not free to leave. Also, the search must occur while the officer is making the arrest. Officers may search the defendant and the immediate physical area within the defendant's reach. The rationales for searching a suspect incident to arrest are to protect the officers (e.g., make sure the suspect does not have a weapon), prevent evidence from being destroyed, and prevent the defendant from escaping. The landmark case for the incident to arrest doctrine, sometimes also referred to as the "arm's length rule," is *Chimel v. California* (1969).[18] Since then, the incident to arrest doctrine has been further refined by the Supreme Court. For example, *Gustafson v. Florida* (1973) held that a full search may be made incident to a custodial arrest even though the officer had no fear for his or her safety and the offense was one for which there was no physical evidence that could be revealed by the search.[19] *United States v. Robinson* (1973) upheld that searches incident to full custodial arrests in which arrests had been made on traffic violations are valid regardless whether the search would produce a weapon, evidence of the crime, or contraband.[20] More recently, *Maryland v. Buie* (1990) held that incident to arrest, officers could look in closets and other spaces immediately adjoining the place of arrest from which an attack could be immediately launched. Such a search is precautionary. To go beyond the immediate area, there must be specifiable facts that would make a reasonably prudent officer believe that the area to be swept harbors an individual posing a danger to the arrest scene.[21]

Plain View

The plain view doctrine means that evidence in the plain view of police officers upon contact with a suspect may be seized without a search warrant. Early conditions for the plain view doctrine were that the officers have a legal right to be in the area where evidence was found, the sighting of the evidence needed to be inadvertent, and upon sighting, the officer must recognize the evidence as contraband, evidence, or the fruit of a crime (e.g., stolen property).[22] Over the past two decades, the United States Supreme Court has generally expanded the provisions of what is meant by evidence in plain view. For example, *California v. Ciraolo* (1986) established that warrantless aerial observation of the fenced-in cartilage (grounds or area adjoining a home) from an altitude of 1,000 feet did not violate the Fourth Amendment.[23] Plain view also meant from the air as was also established in *Dow Chemical Company v. United States* (1986).[24] *United States v. Dunn* (1987) held that observations made from open fields did not violate any expectations of privacy and could be used to assess plain view evidence, in this case peering into the front of a barn.[25] *California v. Greenwood* (1988) established that the police may search garbage left outside of a home without a warrant. Importantly, such police action neither violates rights or expectations of privacy nor violates what is described as being in plain view.[26] Finally, *Horton v. California* (1990) held that evidence does not need to be inadvertently discovered in order to meet the plain view doctrine—this overruled the decision *Coolidge v. New Hampshire* (1971).[27]

Thus, the plain view doctrine has been expanded to include open fields. In a way, this has expanded the "jurisdiction" of what is viewable by police and thus encroached or limited the expectations of privacy from citizens. As long as police officers are acting lawfully in the first place, operating on probable cause, and can immediately identify the illegal nature of the seized material, the plain view doctrine is being met.

Automobile Searches

Among the earliest exceptions for the police to search without a warrant is the automobile exception. *Carroll v. United States* (1925) established that officers may search moveable vehicles if they have probable cause to suspect that the vehicle contains contraband or illegal materials. Because vehicles can be quickly moved away, the Court ruled that it was not prudent to expect the police to wait on a warrant before they searched the vehicle. In the eighty years since Carroll, the Supreme Court has largely expanded the scope of the automobile search doctrine. For instance, without warrants, the police may search vehicles that were impounded for the purpose of forfeiture due to transportation of contraband, drugs, alcohol, or unregistered firearms;[28] may search the entire passenger compartment including containers such as glove compartment, console, luggage, and clothing if incident to a lawful, custodial arrest;[29] and search mobile homes.[30] Several cases established that the police can search closed containers, such as backpacks,[31] and that the right to search a vehicle without a warrant was not contingent upon exigent or emergency situations.[32] A summary case is *Chambers v. Maroney* (1970), which established that if officers had probable cause to believe that if a mobile car contained evidence of a crime, it could be searched at the scene of arrest, after being moved to a police station, or after being impounded—all without a warrant.[33]

Inevitable Discovery

Nix v. Williams (1984) held that the body of a murder victim, which was found after the defendant was illegally interrogated, was admissible on the grounds that it would inevitably have been discovered even if no previous constitutional or statutory violation had taken place. The prosecution must show the inevitability of the discovery by the preponderance of evidence and need not show absence of bad faith in originally securing the evidence.[34] The inevitable discovery clause can be viewed as an "end around" the exclusionary rule.

Consent

Police officers will tell you that many of the searches they conduct are the result of citizen consent. Oftentimes, people voluntarily inform and thus empower police officers to search them. The Supreme Court has busily refined the conditions that must be present for a lawful consent search. *Schneckloth v. Bustamonte* (1973) held that advisement of Fourth Amendment rights was unnecessary as a prerequisite to a consent search in a non-custodial situation. The standard for the evaluation of consent is that the suspect consented voluntarily and without coercion.[35] Since 1973, the consent doctrine has been expanded to encompass searches based on the consent of a defendant's common law spouse[36] and an "informed third party" who it was believed had authority over the premises being searched.[37] Provided that the totality of circumstances reflect reasonableness, due process, and probable cause, consent searched can also encompass closed luggage, closed containers inside vehicles, and pertain to people before they are advised by police that they are "free to go."[38]

Stop and Frisk/Reasonable Suspicion

Arguably the most controversial exception to Fourth Amendment provisions was set forth in *Terry v. Ohio* (1968). In the 8-1 decision, the Court held that a person may be detained without probable cause to make an arrest if there is reasonable suspicion that criminal activity is afoot. Reasonable suspicion must be based on specific, articulable facts from which reasonable inferences must be drawn. When a reasonably prudent officer has a reasonable suspicion that he/she or others in the area are in danger, a "frisk" may be justified when its purpose is to discover weapons for assault of the police officer. The "frisk" must be limited in scope to a pat-down of the outer clothing of the suspect.[39]

Suspiciousness is a slippery term and the Supreme Court has arrived at a variety of decisions on the matter. As long as police officers are operating on the idea of reasonable suspicion, they can temporarily detain someone's personal luggage so that a narcotics sniffing dog can examine it, search a vehicle for weapons, and use a "wanted poster" as the basis for believing that crime was afoot.[40] *New Jersey v. T.L.O.* (1985) held that the Fourth Amendment applies to searches by public school officials. These searches are judged on reasonableness under all the circumstances and do not require probable cause if school officials believe that a student is currently violating, or has violated, a school regulation or law.[41] This case expands the notion of reasonable suspicion from the police to other authority figures in other social institutions, namely schools. *Maryland v. Wilson* (1997) held that police officers may routinely order passengers out of vehicles that are legally stopped. No showing of suspicion or probable cause regarding the passengers' activities need be present. However, the Court did not address whether police could then search the individuals.[42]

The *Terry* decision and stop and frisk doctrine is a mighty indication of police power. By most standards, the police and the courts *must* operate from a principle of probable cause that criminal activity occurred. Otherwise, their conduct is not constitutional. That the police may stop and frisk people because of their suspiciousness, even when police suspicion is the outcome of training, experience, and professional expertise, is incredibly dicey. From a strict due process perspective, the reasonable suspicion doctrine is an invitation for police biases.

Police Custody, Interrogation, and *Miranda*

Perhaps the most iconic topic in criminal justice is the Miranda warning, the police advisement that criminal suspects have the "right to remain silent, anything you say can and will be used against you in a court of law, etc." The Miranda warning is a protection accorded criminal defendants once their interaction with police transitions from contact to custody and from mere investigation to bona fide interrogation. Similarly, the Fifth Amendment is the component of the Bill of Rights that marks the transition in criminal justice from the police to the courts. The Fourth Amendment applies strictly to police and the Sixth Amendment applies to court officials. The Fifth Amendment spans that middle ground where the police mobilize their resources to formally enter their arrest into the criminal justice system.

The Legacy of the Third Degree

A recurrent theme in this book is the evolution of criminal justice from harsh, even brutal, and capricious to its impersonal, bureaucratic, professionalized current form. A vestige of that earlier era was the use of heavy-handed police behaviors especially during the interrogation of people accused of crimes. Heavy-handed interrogation techniques, commonly referred to as the third degree, encompassed many forms of reprehensible police tactics, such as physical beatings, torture, extreme mental coercion, and interrogations that lasted dozens of hours. These tactics were disproportionately employed against African American suspects. (Movie fans might recall the scenes from the acclaimed film *LA Confidential,* which although fictional accurately portrayed third degree tactics). It was not until the early to mid Twentieth Century that the United States Supreme Court in cases like *Brown v. Mississippi* (1936), *Chambers v. Florida* (1940), *Ashcraft v. Tennessee* (1944), *Spano v. New York* (1959), and *Haynes v. Washington* (1963), deemed such egregious interrogation practices unconstitutional because the "confessions" they produced were involuntary and coerced.[43]

Although police interrogation practices became inarguably more civilized, their fundamentally coercive nature remained. Legal scholar Richard Leo has argued that police interrogation has simply shifted from coercion to deception as its operating tactic. "Where once custodial interrogation routinely involved physical violence and duress, police questioning now consists of subtle and sophisticated psychological ploys, tricks, stratagems, techniques, and methods that rely on manipulation, persuasion, and deception for their efficacy. Not only do police now openly and strongly condemn the use of physical force during interrogation, they also believe that psychological tactics are far more effective at eliciting confessions."[44]

The Road to Miranda

During the early 1960s, a handful of Supreme Court decisions laid the groundwork for increased suspect rights when taken into police custody and interrogated. *Massiah v. United States* (1964) held that no indicted defendant can be interrogated under any circumstances in the absence of his or her attorney without having his Sixth Amendment right to counsel impaired. The Massiah doctrine was applied to the states under the Fourth Amendment via *McLeod v. Ohio* (1965).[45] Essentially, the Massiah doctrine declared that criminal suspects are entitled to legal representation as soon as the police establish an adversarial relationship with the defendant. *Malloy v. Hogan* (1964) made the self-incrimination privilege of the Fifth Amendment applicable to the states through the due process clause of the Fourth Amendment.[46] *Escobedo v. Illinois* (1964) established the right to have counsel present during police interrogation once the investigation shifts into "accusatory" mode. At this point, the Sixth Amendment rights to counsel are actuated.[47] A landmark case in its own right, Escobedo established that upon interrogation, the entire adversarial system of American justice is initiated. *Griffin v. California* (1965) held that the Fifth Amendment forbids a state prosecutor's comments on failure of a defendant to take the stand and explain evidence and bars an instruction from the court that such silence may be evidence of guilt.[48]

Miranda v. Arizona (1966)

Miranda v. Arizona (1966) is among the most famous cases in American history.[49] In a narrow 5-4 vote, the Supreme Court held that the privilege against self-incrimination is available outside of criminal court proceedings and applied to police interrogations of persons in custody. Prior to custodial interrogation the following warnings must be given: (1) you have the right to remain silent; (2) anything you say can and will be used against you; (3) you have the right to have an attorney with you during the interrogation; and (4) if you are unable to hire an attorney one will be provided for you without cost during questioning. Fundamentally, the Miranda warning or advisement notifies suspects that they are empowered to be quiet in the face of police questioning. Citizens are not required to provide the police with evidentiary ammunition (pun intended) that could be used against them. Moreover, the police may invoke protections against Fifth Amendment self-incrimination at any time. Suspects may begin to answer questions, then change their mind and remain silent. Two conditions "trigger" the requirement of a Miranda advisement: custody and interrogation. These conditions make clear that the police behavior has moved from initial investigation to a custodial arrest that will bring criminal charges.

Many criminal suspects opt to waive their Miranda rights and agree to talk with police investigators about their case. If Miranda rights are waived, the waiver must be voluntary and knowingly waived. To assure this, officers ask a few short questions that the defendant must clearly and affirmatively answer. In other words, the suspect's answer must be "yes." These questions are:

- Do you understand each of these rights that I have explained to you?
- With these rights in mind, do you now wish to answer questions?
- Do you wish to answer questions without a lawyer present?
- If the suspect is a juvenile, an additional question is "Do you wish to answer questions without your parents, guardians, or custodians present?

Post-Miranda Developments

Miranda was viewed as and still is a pinnacle event in American law and is a symbol of due process. It accords criminal defendants with substantial power against police investigations and the coercion inherent in custody and interrogation. Indeed, Miranda provides legal power to David in the face of the Goliath-like state. It should be expected then, that such an impressive due process measure would be challenged and indeed it has been. Myriad cases have revisited Miranda since 1966 and some of these are reviewed next.[50]

Orozco v. Texas (1969) held that if a suspect's freedom has been restrained "in any significant way" be it at his home or at the police station, the police are required to give the suspect the *Miranda* warnings.[51] *Harris v. New York* (1971) decided that confessions obtained without appropriate Miranda warnings could nevertheless by used in court to impeach the credibility of the defendant's testimony when it was inconsistent with the original confession.[52] *Brown v. Illinois* (1975) held that when a suspect is arrested without probable cause, any evidence obtained including confessions (even those obtained after the warnings are given) is inadmissible as evidence.[53] *Michigan v. Mosley* (1975) held that if a suspect asserts his right to remain silent during an interrogation, police officers have to honor that.[54] *Beckwith v. United States* (1976) held that when a person is not in custody, and is being interrogated in a relaxed atmosphere in the comfort of his or her home the full content of the *Miranda* warnings does not need to be given.[55] *Edwards v. Arizona* (1981) established that once a defendant requests counsel all questioning must cease until an attorney is present.[56]

New York v. Quarles (1984) was noteworthy because it established the public safety exception to Miranda. In this case, police officers frisked and handcuffed the defendant after receiving a tip that he was in possession of a firearm. When asked about the location of the gun, Quarles answered and the police seized the gun. Afterward, they read the defendant his Miranda rights. However, because of the exigent risks to public safety posed by the gun, the Court ruled that officers did not have to Mirandize the defendant.[57]

Along the same doctrine as *Orozco* and *Beckwith, Minnesota v. Murphy* (1984) held that interrogations held in "other potentially coercive environments," in this case, a probation office, may not generate the same necessity to give the *Miranda* warnings as when the interrogations are done in a police station.[58] *Berkemer v. McCarty* (1984) held that persons stopped for traffic violations are not in custody, thus, the *Miranda* warnings may not be given. If the motorist is arrested, however, and taken into custody, *Miranda* warnings have to be given before interrogation.[59] *Oregon v. Elstad* (1985) held that a properly obtained confession after a prior illegally obtained one is admissible in Court. However, the Court overruled this with their decision in *Missouri v. Seibert* in 2004.[60] *Minnick v. Mississippi* (1990) established that interrogation cannot resume after the suspect has contacted a lawyer and the lawyer is no longer present.[61] *Arizona v. Fulminante* (1991) held that a confession obtained by a prison informant, under circumstances where there was a credible threat of physical harm by other inmates unless the informant intervened, was coerced and violated due process. Confessions obtained through coercion may not necessarily amount to reversible error and are subject to the harmless error rule.[62] *Davis v. United States* (1994) held that police officers are not bound to stop interrogating suspects who make "uncertain" requests to have an attorney present.[63]

In sum, the case law since Miranda covers the many contingencies that arise when the police interrogate criminal suspects. Many of these cases have centered on what constitutes police custody, what constitutes police interrogation, and what are reasonable exigent exceptions to Miranda. One of the most recent cases is among the most dramatic in preserving the Miranda doctrine. *Dickerson v. United States* (2000) held that Congress may not legislatively overrule Miranda v. Arizona and thus govern the admissibility of statements made during custodial interrogations. Dickerson essentially invalidated a Congressional law passed in 1968 (18 U.S.C. 3501), which had eliminated the presumption that a confession was involuntary unless the Miranda warning was delivered prior to interrogation. In short, U.S.C. 3501 employed a totality of circumstances approach that was less restrictive than Miranda.[64]

The Costs of *Miranda*?

Crimes Lost

If Miranda is a noteworthy achievement in due process, does that also mean that it is a crippling blow to crime control? After the Miranda decision, legal scholars debated whether the rights-laden decision would negatively impact the ability of the police to secure confessions from defendants. Legal scholar Paul Cassell, who is also a United States District Court Judge, has conducted much research on the empirical costs of the Miranda decision and has been a vocal critic of its negative effects. His research has produced some compelling findings. For example, Cassell examined confession rates in major American cities before-and-after Miranda. He found considerable decreases in suspect confessions to police after Miranda. These included:

- Pittsburgh 19%
- New York 35%
- Philadelphia 25%
- New Haven 16%
- Seattle 16%
- New Orleans 12%
- Chicago 27%

Los Angeles was the only major city where confessions increased (10 percent) after the establishment of Miranda. In additional analyses, Cassell estimated that about 3.8% of cases are lost because of Miranda safeguards. Using Uniform Crime Reports data, Cassell estimated that in 1993 28,000 suspects for violent Index crimes were lost due to Miranda. This amounted to:

- 880 killers
- 1,400 rapists
- 6,500 robbers
- 21,000 aggravated assaulters.

Additionally, Cassell found that 79,000 suspects for property Index crimes, burglary, larceny-theft, motor vehicle theft, and arson were also not brought to justice. Moreover, 67,000 pleas to reduced charges in property cases and 24,000 pleas to reduced charges in violence cases were adulterated because of missed confessions.[65]

Cassell's research caused a stir. Stephen Schulhofer reported numerous methodological flaws in Cassell's analyses and estimated that Miranda negatively impacted less than 1 percent of cases. Moreover, Schulhofer argued that rather than inhibiting police behavior, Miranda liberated the police to conduct lawful custodial interrogations and thus has vital symbolic value.[66] Motivated by these critiques, Cassell and Richard Fowles conducted a quantitative analysis of the effects of Miranda and found that without Miranda safeguards the clearance rate for violent crimes would increase between 8 to 20% and property crimes would increase 4 to 16%. Annually, hundreds of thousands of cases would additionally be cleared without the due process powers of Miranda.[67]

Legal scholars disagree sharply about the benefits and costs of Miranda, but what do criminal justice personnel think? Do law enforcement officers, police administrators, prosecutors, judges, and the like think that Miranda is a centerpiece of America's commitment to due process, or an impediment to effective crime control? Victoria Time and Brian Payne surveyed police chiefs in Virginia to assess their perceptions about Miranda. The produced a variety of interesting findings. For example:

- More than 90% reported that officers are sufficiently trained to ensure suspects' Miranda rights.

- About 40% felt that defendants would "get off easy" because of the protections inherent in the Miranda warning.

- Nearly 90% felt that suspects will routinely confess even after they have been Mirandized, that is, been formally been advised of their rights.

- Nearly 60% of police chiefs felt that Miranda should not be overturned; 40% felt that it should be overturned.

- About 60% felt that abolishing Miranda would have little effect on the day-to-day functioning of the police.

- About 90% of police chiefs believed that the public had misguided perceptions about the Miranda warnings (that is, it had to be advised for any police contact).

- About 80% of police chiefs reported little to no experience of seeing cases dismissed for Miranda violations.[68]

Waive or Invoke?

Additional research has provided evidence to buttress the putative costs of lost crimes that Miranda has created. Legal scholar Richard Leo observed actual police interrogations and arrived at a variety of interesting conclusions. First, among 175 police interrogations, suspects invoked their Miranda rights in only 22% of cases. The remaining 78% of cases involved suspects who knowingly and voluntarily waived their Miranda rights and talked with police investigators. Second, a suspect's criminal record appeared to influence whether or not they spoke with police. Persons with no prior criminal history were most likely to waive their Miranda rights and speak with police. Indeed, 92% of those without criminal records waived their rights. On the other hand, less than 70% of persons with prior felony records waived their rights and nearly 30% invoked their Miranda rights. This offers conflicting support of Cassell's thesis. The majority of experienced criminals actually talk with police, but they are nearly four times as likely as first-time arrestees to invoke Miranda.

After the police interrogation, the effects of waiving or invoking Miranda had variable effects on the case processing through the criminal justice system. Suspect's response to Miranda had no statistical effect on the prosecutor's decision to charge or the likelihood of conviction. However, a suspect who waived Miranda was twice as likely to have his or her case resolved via a plea bargain. Yet, waiving or invoking Miranda did not significantly affect sentence severity.[69] Taken together, the effects of Miranda and whether it is waived or invoked do not dramatically alter the progression of a case through the criminal justice system.

Leo's research touched on a tangential but important issue pertaining to who chooses to waive their rights. Compared to experienced criminal offenders whose prior interactions with criminal justice officials accorded them a sense of what to expect during interrogations, first-time, naïve, or novice offenders had no such experience. Yet, persons without criminal record were overwhelmingly likely to waive their Miranda rights and participate in custodial interrogations. Experimental research similarly conveys that factually innocent suspects, persons who presumably should have nothing to share with police because of their lack of involvement in crime, were most likely to waive their rights and talk with police. For example, Saul Kassin and Rebecca Norwick found that 81% of innocent people agreed to talk with police even in the face of a hostile, closed-minded interrogator where there was nothing to be gained by participating in the interrogation.[70]

Thus, whether a defendant waives or invokes Miranda speaks to the double-pronged nature of the Fifth Amendment protection against self-incrimination. For criminals who invoke Miranda, it is a powerful opportunity to shut down police efforts to marshal evidence against them. For innocents who waive Miranda, it places them in an undeniably coercive interaction with police.

Due Process Symbolism

As described earlier, interrogations have evolved from relying on physical coercion to psychological methods of deception. Today, police investigators employ a variety of subtle but powerful techniques when interviewing criminal suspects in an effort to lawfully secure a true confession. The two most common methods are appealing to the suspect's self-interest and confronting the suspect with existing evidence of guilt. When used in concert, these approaches can be quite effective. There are at least ten other tactics used by police during actual interrogations. These include: (1) undermine the suspect's confidence in his or her denial, (2) identify contradictions in the suspect's alibi or story, (3) ask specific "behavioral analysis" interview questions, (4) appeal to the importance of cooperation, (5) offer moral justifications and face-saving excuses, (6) confront the suspect with false evidence of guilt, (7) praise or flatter the suspect, (8) appeal to the detective's expertise and authority, (9) appeal to the suspect's conscience, and (10) minimize the moral seriousness of the offense.[71]

Of course, the criminal justice system must balance the twin goals of crime control and due process. As such, it is unrealistic to expect police custody to be a cozy environment and police interrogations to be a pleasant, facile experience. Fortunately, Miranda has likely facilitated both crime control and due process goals. Legal scholar Richard Leo noted that Miranda has had four profound impacts on American law enforcement. First, it has brought a civilized tone to police interrogations. Second, it has helped transform and professionalize police culture. Third, it interjected constitutional rights into American culture. Fourth, Miranda inspired police to develop more specialized, sophisticated, and seemingly more effective interrogation techniques.[72] In the course of cementing American due process, Miranda helped the police hone their crime fighting skills.

Symbolically, Miranda is perhaps the greatest example of due process in American criminal justice. Its ultimate social costs are a matter of great debate. To some, Miranda is the antithesis of legitimate police power. For example, Judge Rothwax recommended that Miranda be overruled because it placed unnecessary constraints on the police and inappropriately empowered criminal defendants in ways that were beyond the scope of the original intentions of the Fourth Amendment. According to Rothwax, Miranda (1) has sent jurisprudence on a hazardous detour by introducing novel conceptions of the proper relationship between a criminal suspect and police, (2) has accentuated the features in the criminal justice system that manifest the least regard for truth-seeking, such as the view that the process is a game of chance in which the defendant should always have some prospect of victory, (3) was decided at a time when effective alternatives for restraining unlawful police conduct were ripe for implementation but never pursued, and (4) the many exceptions to constitutional constraints on police behavior render Miranda ambiguous.[73] To some, the Miranda doctrine is a doctrine still under development.

◆ Summary: Balancing Crime Control and Due Process

- The Fourth Amendment of the United States Constitution protects citizens from unreasonable searches and seizures and states that warrants based on probable cause are needed to justify police searches.

- The Fifth Amendment of the United States Constitution covers police and court functions especially the right against self-incrimination during police confessions.

- Custody and interrogation are the conditions that trigger the Miranda advisement of rights.

- The exclusionary rule prohibits the use of illegally obtained evidence to be used during prosecution.

- Due to exigent circumstances and other important contingencies, there are several exceptions to the exclusionary rule and situations where warrants are not needed to search suspects.

- *Miranda v. Arizona* is perhaps the most famous criminal case in American history and has great symbolic and applied due process value.

- Miranda has compromised and facilitated crime control depending on the evidence and perspectives of various legal scholars.

- Police interrogation has evolved from one characterized by physical coercion to psychological deception.

- Suspects who waive their Miranda rights can face adversarial police interviews.

- Persons with more extensive criminal history are more likely than innocents or first-time arrestees to invoke their Miranda rights.

- American case law exists in a continual state of development and refinement. Thus legal doctrines are in a state of flux.

◆ Web Links

United States Supreme Court
(www.oyez.org/oyez/frontpage)

Cornell University Law School Legal Information Institute
(www.law.cornell.edu/)

United States Supreme Court (Official Site) (www.supremecourtus.gov/)

Miranda Warning (www.usconstitution.net/miranda.html)

Police Employment (various information) (www.policeemployment.com/)

Questions

1. *The right of the people to be secure in their persons, houses, papers, and effects, against unreasonable searches and seizures, shall not be violated, and no Warrants shall issue, but upon probable cause, supported by Oath or affirmation, and particularly describing the place to be searched, and the persons or things to be seized.* This statement is taken from:

   a. 6th Amendment
   b. 4th Amendment
   c. 5th Amendment
   d. 8th Amendment

2. A warrant cannot confer authority to execute it on one officer where a statute provides for its execution by another.

   a. True
   b. False

3. Probable cause is a set of _____ and _____ that would induce a reasonably intelligent and prudent person to believe that a particular person had committed a specific crime.

   a. Facts and evidence
   b. Evidence and circumstances
   c. Facts and circumstances
   d. Opinion and evidence

4. The particularity requirement means that warrants must specify precisely the places to be searched and the items to be seized. This does not prohibit the police from having unrestricted discretion to search for evidence.

   a. True
   b. False

5. The protection against unlawfully seized evidence is known as _____ rule.

   a. The inclusive rule
   b. The exclusionary rule
   c. The evidentiary rule
   d. The hearsay rule

6. The landmark case _____ held that the exclusionary rule was applicable to the states through the due process clause of the Fourth Amendment.

   a. *Miranda v. Arizona*
   b. *Gideon v. Wainright*
   c. *Furman v. Georgia*
   d. *Mapp v. Ohio*

7. There is a variety of circumstances where it is not reasonable to expect the police to require a warrant, to wait on a warrant or to wait to conduct lawful searches during the course of their duties. Broadly speaking, these exceptions are known as _____.

   a. Exclusionary circumstances
   b. Exclusive circumstances
   c. Exigent circumstances
   d. None of the above

8. In a narrow 5–4 vote, the Supreme Court held in the case of _____ that the privilege against self-incrimination is available outside of criminal court proceedings and applied to police interrogations of persons in custody.

   a. *Miranda v. Arizona*   c. *Escobedo v. Illinois*
   b. *Mapp v. Ohio*   d. *Aguilar v. Texas*

9. Two conditions "trigger" the requirement of a *Miranda* advisement:

   a. Arrest and interview
   b. Custody and interrogation
   c. Investigation and interview
   d. Arrest and interrogation

10. Cassell examined confession rates in major American cities before and after *Miranda*. He found no considerable difference in suspect confessions to police after *Miranda*.

    a. True
    b. False

Endnotes

1. *Aguilar v. Texas*, 378 U.S. 108 (1964).
2. *McCray v. Illinois*, 386 U.S. 300 (1967).
3. *Spinelli v. United States*, 393 U.S. 110 (1969).
4. *Illinois v. Gates*, 462 U.S. 213 (1983).
5. *Weeks v. United States*, 232 U.S. 383 (1914).
6. *Mapp v. Ohio*, 367 U.S. 643 (1961); *Wolf v. Colorado*, 338 U.S. 25 (1949).
7. Silverthorne Lumber Company v. United States, 251 U.S. 385 (1920).
8. *Wong Sun v. United States*, 371 U.S. 471 (1963).
9. *Michigan v. Tucker*, 417 U.S. 433 (1974).
10. *Brown v. Illinois*, 422 U.S. 590 (1975).
11. *United States v. Crews*, 445 U.S. 463 (1980) and *United States v. Havens*, 446 U.S. 620 (1980).
12. *Taylor v. Alabama*, 457 U.S. 687 (1982).
13. *Lanier v. South Carolina*, 474 U.S. 25 (1985).
14. *Schmerber v. California*, 384 U.S. 757 (1966); *Warden v. Hayden*, 387 U.S. 294 (1967); *Skinner v. Railway Labor Executives' Association*, 489 U.S. 602 (1989); *New York v. Quarles*, 467 U.S. 649 (1984); *Michigan Department of State Police v. Sitz*, 496 U.S. 444 (1990).
15. *United States v. Leon*, 468 U.S. 897 (1984). A sister case to *Leon* is *Massachusetts v. Sheppard*, 468 U.S. 981 (1984).
16. *Illinois v. Krull*, 480 U.S. 340 (1987).
17. *Arizona v. Evans*, 514 U.S. 1 (1995).
18. *Chimel v. California*, 395 U.S. 752 (1969).
19. *Gustafson v. Florida* 414 U.S. 260 (1973).
20. *United States v. Robinson*, 414 U.S. 218 (1973).
21. *Maryland v. Buie*, 494 U.S. 325 (1990).
22. See, *Harris v. United States*, 390 U.S. 234 (1968), *Texas v. Brown*, 460 U.S. 730 (1983).
23. *California v. Ciraolo*, 476 U.S. 207 (1986).
24. *Dow Chemical Company v. United States*, 476 U.S. 227 (1986).
25. *United States v. Dunn*, 480 U.S. 294 (1987).
26. *California v. Greenwood*, 486 U.S. 35 (1988).
27. *Horton v. California*, 496 U.S. 128 (1990).
28. *Cooper v. California*, 386 U.S. 58 (1967).
29. *New York v. Belton*, 453 U.S. 454 (1981).
30. *California v. Carney*, 471 U.S. 386 (1985).
31. *Colorado v. Bertine*, 479 U.S. 367 (1987); *Florida v. Wells*, 495 U.S. 1 (1990); *California v. Acevedo*, 500 U.S. 565 (1991).
32. *Pennsylvania v. Labron*, 518 U.S. 938 (1996).
33. *Chambers v. Maroney*, 399 U.S. 42 (1970).
34. *Nix v. Williams*, 467 U.S. 431 (1984).
35. *Schneckloth v. Bustamonte*, 412 U.S. 218 (1973).
36. *United States v. Matlock*, 415 U.S. 164 (1974).

37. *Illinois v. Rodriguez,* 497 U.S. 177 (1990).
38. *Florida v. Jimeno,* 500 U.S. 248 (1991); *Florida v. Bostick,* 501 U.S. 429 (1991); *Ohio v. Robinette,* 519 U.S. 33 (1996).
39. *Terry v. Ohio,* 392 U.S. 1 (1968).
40. *United States v. Place,* 462 U.S. 696 (1983); *Michigan v. Long,* 463 U.S. 1032 (1983); *United States v. Hensley,* 469, U.S. 221 (1985).
41. *New Jersey v. T.L.O.,* 469 U.S. 325 (1985).
42. *Maryland v. Wilson,* 519 U.S. 408 (1997).
43. *Brown v. Mississippi,* 297 U.S. 278 (1936); *Chambers v. Florida,* 309 U.S. 227 (1940); *Ashcraft v. Tennessee,* 322 U.S. 143 (1944); *Spano v. New York,* 360 U.S. 315 (1959); *Haynes v. Washington,* 373 U.S. 503 (1963).
44. Leo, R. A. (1998). From coercion to deception: The changing nature of police interrogation in America. In R. A. Leo & G. C. Thomas (Eds.), *The Miranda debate: Law, justice, and policing,* pp. 65–74. Boston, MA: Northeastern University Press.
45. *Massiah v. United States,* 377 U.S. 201 (1964); *McLeod v. Ohio,* 381 U.S. 356 (1965).
46. *Malloy v. Hogan,* 378 U.S. 1 (1964).
47. *Escobedo v. Illinois,* 378 U.S. 478 (1964).
48. *Griffin v. California,* 380 U.S. 609 (1965).
49. *Miranda v. Arizona,* 384 U.S. 436 (1966). Miranda gets all of the glory, but the decision reached in it also resolved three similar, contemporary cases, *Virginia v. New York; California v. Stewart;* and *Westover v. United States.*
50. For a more complete review, see Oberlander, L. B., & Goldstein, N. E. (2001). A review and update on the practice of evaluating Miranda comprehension. *Behavioral Sciences and the Law,* 19, 453–471.
51. *Orozco v. Texas,* 394 U.S. 324 (1969).
52. *Harris v. New York,* 401 U.S. 222 (1971).
53. *Brown v. Illinois,* 422 U.S. 590 (1975).
54. *Michigan v. Mosley,* 423 U.S. 96 (1975).
55. *Beckwith v. United States,* 425 U.S. 341, 345 (1976).
56. *Edwards v. Arizona,* 451 U.S. 477 (1981).
57. *New York v. Quarles,* 467 U.S. 649 (1984).
58. *Minnesota v. Murphy,* 465 U.S. 420 (1984).
59. *Berkemer v. McCarty,* 468 U.S. 420 (1984).
60. *Oregon v. Elstad,* 470 U.S. 298 (1985). Hoover, L. A. (2005). The Supreme Court brings an end to the 'end run' around Miranda. *FBI Law Enforcement Bulletin,* 74, 26–32.
61. *Minnick v. Mississippi,* 498 U.S. 146 (1990).
62. *Arizona v. Fulminante,* 499 U.S. 279 (1991).
63. *Davis v. United States,* 512 U.S. 452 (1994).
64. *Dickerson v. United States,* 530 U.S. 428 (2000). For a critical assessment of the Dickerson ruling, see Cassell, P., & Litt, R. (2000). Will Miranda survive? *Dickerson v. United States:* The right to remain silent, the Supreme Court, and Congress. *American Criminal Law Review,* 37, 1165–1193.
65. Cassell, P. G. (1996). Miranda's social costs: An empirical assessment. *Northwestern University Law Review,* 90, 487–499.

66. Schulhofer, S. J. (1996). Miranda's practical effect: Substantial benefits and vanishingly small social costs. *Northwestern University Law Review,* 90, 500–551; Schulhofer, S. J. (1987). Reconsidering Miranda. *University of Chicago Law Review,* 54, 435–461.
67. Cassell, P. G., & Fowles, R. (1998). Handcuffing the cops? A thirty-year perspective on Miranda's harmful effects on law enforcement. *Stanford Law Review,* 50, 1055–1145.
68. Time, V. M., & Payne, B. K. (2002). Police chiefs perceptions about Miranda: An analysis of survey data. *Journal of Criminal Justice,* 30, 77–86. Also see, Payne, B. K., & Time, V. M. (2000). Police chiefs and Miranda: An exploratory study. *American Journal of Criminal Justice,* 25, 65–76.
69. Leo, R. A. (1996). The impact of Miranda revisited. *Journal of Criminal Law and Criminology,* 86, 266–303.
70. Kassin, S. M., & Norwick, R. J. (2004). Why people waive their Miranda rights: The power of innocence. *Law and Human Behavior,* 28, 211–221; Madon, S., Guyll, M., Scherr, K. C., Greathouse, S., & Wells, G. L. (2011). Temporal discounting: The differential effect of proximal and distal consequences on confession decisions. *Law and Human Behavior,* doi: 10.1007/s10979-011-9267-3.
71. Leo, R. A. (1996). Inside the interrogation room. *Journal of Criminal Law and Criminology,* 86, 266–303.
72. Leo, note 74.
73. Rothwax, Judge H. J. (1996). *Guilty: The collapse of criminal justice,* p. 86. New York: Warner Books.

BAIL, JAIL, AND THE PRETRIAL PERIOD

◆ Introduction

What happens between a defendant's arrest and his or her first appearance in court is probably the least understood area of the criminal justice system. Criminal defendants and their families often have many questions. Where do arrestees go after they are placed in police cars and driven away? Can they be released? What is bail? What is bond? What are the differences between bail and bond? What does "own recognizance" mean? Do they have to pay money in order to be released? Who has jurisdiction over arrestees once police officers bring them to municipal holding stations or county jails? How much time transpires before arrestees appear in court? Do arrestees receive due process even without appearing in court? The answers to these questions occur during the pretrial period.

Interestingly, the pretrial phase contains the greatest convergence between the three primary agents in the criminal justice system: police, courts, and correction. The police arrest people and initiate the accusatory and investigatory process that will send their case through the criminal justice system. As always, the police have great discretionary power in determining the treatment of a criminal suspect. Police officers can issue a ticket or summons for crimes ranging in seriousness from petty offenses to felonies. They can charge defendants with municipal violations or state charges. Most importantly,

From *Criminal Justice: Balancing Crime Control and Due Process*, 3/e, by Matt Delisi. Copyright © 2011 by Kendall Hunt Publishing Company. Reprinted by permission.

police officers write arrest reports that chronicle the legal reasons for the arrest, such as the bases for probable cause, the charges, a narrative of how the crime transpired, and a list of victims, witnesses, and co-defendants. The arrest report is the foundational legal document of a criminal case.

Once the police officer completes the arrest report and terminates their discussions (if any) with the defendant, judicial personnel assume responsibility for the case. Most large jurisdictions have judicial officers, variously referred to as pretrial service interviewers, pretrial officers, bond commissioners, and the like. Pretrial service officers serve two interrelated purposes. First, they interview criminal defendants and gather information about the offender's social and criminal history. Information on residency, family contacts, employment status, substance abuse, and psychiatric history are included. They do not interview defendants about their current charges as a way to influence guilt or innocence. Once the information is gathered, the judicial officer writes a report that summarizes the social and criminal history for the court and makes a bond recommendation. This is the second purpose of pretrial service personnel. As judicial officers, they decide the type of bond that a defendant should receive and serve as the primary way to alleviate jail crowding.

All of this activity usually transpires at a county jail. Jails are local correctional facilities that house persons who have been convicted of crimes and sentenced to less than two years confinement and those awaiting trial. Operated by the county sheriff's department, jails are a temporary form of incarceration, thus they are much different than prison. Importantly, persons who are unable to post bond or be released on their own recognizance are detained until their case reaches a resolution in court, such as dismissal or conviction. This creates a sort of paradox in American due process. The presumption of innocence ensures that defendants are considered innocent until proven guilty, yet tens of thousands of criminal defendants each day are detained during the pretrial phase. Think of it this way. Imagine you were arrested for drunk driving while vacationing out of state. Because your community ties would be weak, you technically would be transient or "passing through town," and would likely receive a secured bond. Imagine that you cannot pay the bond amount. Two weeks later, you meet with the district attorney and a public defender and they indicate that charges against you are going to be dismissed. You are free to go. You have not been convicted of a crime, yet you were in custody for two weeks!

This chapter explores the pretrial period, the misunderstood location where police, court, and correctional entities meet, and centers on three main areas. First, the historical and contemporary use of bail as a means of pretrial release and detention is explored. Second, the resultant progression of a criminal case from charging to arraignment to dismissal or conviction is reviewed. The various legal and extra-legal factors that are used to determine bond are discussed. Third, the history and function of jail is described as it relates to the pretrial period. As you will see, jail is distinct from prison despite their common usage as similes. Moreover, jail confinement is an interesting example of the use of confinement as a penalty both before and after conviction. As always, the crime control and due process rationales for these criminal justice processes are highlighted.

 Bail/Bond

Definitions

Bail is a form of pretrial release in which a defendant enters a legal agreement or promise that requires his or her appearance in court. The bail amount is statutory which means that legislatures establish monetary bails based on the legal seriousness of the charge. For example, class A or class I felonies may be "no bond" offenses. Magistrates or judges may increase or decrease the statutory bail amount based on aggravating and mitigating factors of the case. Pretrial service officers do not set bail amounts; they simply follow the statutory schedule of bail amounts. Even though defendants are released from jail custody, they are still under the supervision of the courts. If defendants do not comply with the conditions of their bail, such as abstaining from alcohol use or having no contact with the alleged victim in the case, the court can withdraw the defendant's previously granted release. This is known as bail revocation.

Bond is a pledge of money or some other assets offered as bail by an accused person or his or her surety (bail bondsman) to secure temporary release from custody. Bond is forfeited if the conditions of bail are not fulfilled. The best way to understand how the bail/bond process works is with an example. A person is arrested for felony theft and assigned a bail of $1,000. The defendant can pay $1,000 to the court in exchange for release from jail. The $1,000 is essentially collateral to entice the defendant to appear in court. If the defendant misses any court dates, he or she could lose the $1,000. However, if the defendant complies with all court appearances, he or she will receive the money back net any fees or fines that are imposed. What if the defendant cannot afford $1,000? The defendant can utilize the services of a bonding agent or bondsperson. A bondsperson is a social service professional who is contractually responsible for a criminal defendant once they are released from custody. Bondspersons typically charge a 15 percent fee for their services. Thus, the defendant would pay the bondsperson $150 to be released in turn the bondsperson is potentially liable for the entire $1,000 bond if the defendant misses any court dates or absconds. Bondspersons often have close working relationships with the criminal justice system and utilize many of the same criteria that are used to set bond, such as employment, residency, and criminal history. If defendants indeed abscond while on bond, bondspersons sometimes hire a third party, known as a bounty hunter, to find the escapee. Defendants, bondspersons, and bounty agents are bound by financial relationships. Of course, bondspersons and bounty hunters employ quasilaw enforcement tactics to facilitate their financial arrangements with criminal defendants. However, they are not law enforcement agents per se, thus constitutional safeguards that apply to police officers do not apply to them.

Strictly speaking, the term "bail" usually refers to the monetary value needed for release and the term "bond" refers to the type of release that the defendant was awarded. However, once released defendants are synonymously referred to as "being on bond" or "released on bail." Bail and bond are often used interchangeably even by criminal justice professionals. No great distinction is made here either. Whichever term is used, bail/bond attempts to ensure an accused person's appearance in court. Depending on the risks that they pose and the circumstances of the current charges, a promise, property, money, or some other assets are posted for release. If the defendant misses court appearances, the posted security (or liability in the event of a recognizance release) is forfeited.

Types of Bond

The "best" type of bond that a defendant can hope for is to be released on his or her own recognizance. A recognize bond is a written promise to appear in court in which the criminal defendant is released from jail custody without paying or posting cash or property. Variously referred to as personal recognizance (PR), own recognizance (OR), or release on recognizance (ROR), these bonds are reserved for arrestees with minimal or no prior criminal record, strong community ties, such as employment and long-term residency, and relatively non-serious charges. Persons who are released on recognizance bonds are considered to be low risk in terms of re-offending, dangerousness, and failing to appear in court.

Sometimes the defendant does not have the extensive community ties or minimal prior record to justify a recognizance release, but otherwise poses little risk to the community. In these types of cases, defendants are commonly released on cosigned recognizance bond where a family member, close friend, or business associate signs their name on the bond to guarantee the defendant's appearance in court. Other jurisdictions employ a third-party custody bond that works the same way. Sometimes, attorneys are granted third-party custody of their clients to ensure their appearance in court.

Other criminal defendants pose greater risks of missing court appearances and recidivating. Still others are too dangerous to release because they might be actively homicidal or suicidal. For "riskier" defendants, a variety of secured bonds are used. Secured bonds require the payment of cash or other assets to the courts in exchange for release from custody. In the event that the defendant misses court dates or absconds, the cash or other assets are forfeited to the court. Various jurisdictions across the country employ various forms of secured bonds. Cash-only bonds mean that the defendant must post 100% of the bond in cash to be released. Property bonds are houses, real estate, or vehicles that may be cosigned to the court as collateral against pretrial flight. Absconding on a property bond could result in losing your home! Many criminal defendants pay 10 to 15% of their bond to professional bondspersons for release. In these cases, bondspersons act as sureties and are responsible for the total bond if the defendant absconds. Other jurisdictions use a deposit bail system where the court acts as bondsperson and the defendant posts a percentage of their total bond. Court-run deposit bail systems return the bond money to the defendant, net minor administrative fees, unlike bondspersons. Researchers have found that deposit bail systems produce comparable failure to appear rates as commercial bondspersons.[1]

History and Reform

The concept of bail has a long and interesting history. Processes resembling modern day bail practices appeared as early as 2500 B.C.E. and in Roman law as early as 700 B.C.E. For example, the concept known as "hostageship" involved a person who volunteered to be prosecuted and punished in the place of the actual suspect in the event that the suspect failed to appear for court proceedings.[2] In medieval Germany and England, *wergeld* was the assessed value of a person's life and considered their bail value. Trials by compurgation whereby criminal defendants established their innocence by taking an oath and having various witnesses swear or testify to the veracity of their oath also used *wergeld*. Both practices apply the concept of real or human assets to use as collateral for court proceedings.

Under English common law, sheriffs appointed their acquaintances that were often prominent members of the community called sureties. Sureties promised to pay money or land in the event that released defendants absconded. In this way, a surety is a guarantor that defendants will appear in court. Over time, sureties became de facto sheriffs because of their power of revocation. It is because of their financial investment that sureties, and modern-day bondspersons, employ enforcement-like methods to guarantee that defendants appear in court. There is an important distinction. Bondspersons have contractual power, not law enforcement power, thus they are not bound by the same constraints of police officers.

The English common law surety system was difficult to replicate in the burgeoning United States because of its sheer geographic size and the newness of community ties. Instead, pretrial release relied on the use of bondspersons. The concept of bail appears sporadically in colonial America. For example, the Eighth Amendment of the United States Constitution proscribes the requirement of excessive bail. The Judiciary Act of 1789 established bail as an absolute right in detainable criminal charges with the exception of capital offenses, or those potentially punishable by death.[3] The bail business grew with increasing numbers of bondspersons, bail recovery or enforcement agents, and bounty hunters operating at the periphery of American justice.

Due to concern about the constitutionality of pretrial release and supervision and bail enforcement, the courts addressed the issue. In New York State, *Nicolls v. Ingersoll* (1810) established that bounty hunters have the same rights of capture as bonding agents when authorized by those bonding agents.[4] The United States Supreme Court weighed in on *Reese v. United States* (1869), which established that bounty hunters were proxy pretrial officers that had complete control of returning absconders to the court.[5] *Taylor v. Taintor* (1873) clarified that bounty hunter behavior must conform to law, but was not bound by Fourth Amendment as are the police.[6]

The for-profit bondsperson business steamed along throughout the Nineteenth and Twentieth Centuries. Criminal defendants who had the monetary resources to post bail were released. Otherwise, criminal defendants waited in jail until their court appearances. However, many criminal cases are dismissed meaning that many jail detainees are confined for criminal charges for which they are never convicted. Increasingly, the plight of persons detained prior to trial became publicized and a strictly monetary bail system came under attack.

Six decades into the Twentieth Century, criminal defendants who were unable to pay their bail remained in jail custody. For all intents and purposes, ability to pay was the sole criterion for pretrial release from jail. This changed dramatically in 1961 when the Vera Institute of Justice became a driving force in the area of pretrial supervision of criminal defendants. The Vera Institute of Justice initiated the Manhattan Bail Project in New York City. For the project, Vera staff interviewed defendants to ascertain their community ties including their family connections in the city and employment history. After third party verification of the information, the defendants were assigned a numerical score that represented their likelihood of absconding. Persons with weak community ties were considered high risk and persons with strong community ties were considered low risk. Judges were presented with these recommendations and released criminal defendants accordingly. The results were compelling. Releasing defendants on promise to appear in court with attendant strong community ties was more effective than requiring money bail to assure court appearances. In fact, the experimental group that was released merely on their promise to appear had twice the appearance rate of those released on bail. The project saved more than $1 million in correctional costs for defendants who otherwise would have languished behind bars.[7]

In 1965, Ronald Goldfarb published *Ransom,* a scathing critique of the due process problems inherent in the American bail system. Goldfarb argued that defendants who remain in custody face a variety of risks for further criminal punishment compared to arrestees who are released on bond. For example, detained persons are more likely to be indicted, more likely to plead guilty, have greater trial conviction rates, and receive more punitive sentences.[8] Goldfarb's work and the Manhattan Bail Project prompted institutional change in pretrial services across the country and culminated in the Bail Reform Act of 1966. The Bail Reform Act authorized the use of releasing defendants on their own recognizance in non-capital federal cases when appearance in court can be shown to be likely. This effectively ended the de facto discrimination against indigent defendants. The Bail Reform Act of 1984 reinforced community ties clause of 1966 Act, but also provided for the preventive detention of defendants deemed dangerous or likely to abscond.

In 1967, the Vera Institute of Justice launched the Manhattan Bowery Project that aimed to remove alcoholic defendants in jail on nuisance offenses, such as public drunkenness, disorderly conduct, and vagrancy, and place them in detoxification centers. Proactive police patrols identified visibly intoxicated individuals and encouraged them to enter treatment facilities. The Project resulted in an 80 percent decline in the arrests of transient alcoholics, which saved inordinate monies for jail detention and court costs. Since its development, the program is today called Project Renewal and serves more than 20,000 alcoholic and homeless persons annually.[9]

Another innovative Vera project was its Nonprofit Bail Bond Agencies in Bronx, New York, Nassau County, Long Island, and Essex County, New Jersey (Newark) launched in 1987. Vera paid defendants bail if they agreed to submit to supervision and treatment that included a 24-hour observational period, drug testing, curfews, home visits, and employment monitoring. Defendants entered into agreement with Vera that they could be returned to jail for failing to comply with any conditions of their release. Vera encountered severe problems with its Bronx operations because defendants tended to have overlapping problems such as weak community ties and family support and crippling drug addiction. Many released defendants absconded and Vera closed the operation in 1994. The operations in Nassau County and Essex County were far more successful. Defendants were highly compliant with conditions of their release and recidivism and absconding rates were low. Both were incorporated into independent non-profit organization with county contracts at the conclusion of the Vera Project.[10]

The bail reform movement also sparked federal initiatives to modernize American bail practices. In 1978, the United States Department of Justice awarded grants to the National Association of Pretrial Services Agencies (NAPSA) to develop national professional standards and the Pretrial Services Resource Center (PSRC) to assess the status of the pretrial field. The Bureau of Justice Assistance program then conducted national surveys of pretrial services programs in 1979, 1989, and 2001. The results from the most recent survey are discussed later in this chapter.

Bail Recovery/Enforcement and Bounty Hunters

Sensationalistic criminal justice lore, bounty hunters are persons hired by bondspersons to enforce the conditions of bail and to recover the investment asset of the bondsperson. In other words, bounty hunters track down bail absconders and return them to jail. Afterward, bail agents will commonly revoke their bonds and pay the bounty hunter a fee for returning the absconder. Bounty hunters serve a variety of important purposes. They help prevent insurance companies from raising premiums that they charge to insure bonds. They also preserve the bonding agents' reputation, power, and influence as a de facto member of the criminal justice system by keeping absconding rates down. Bounty hunters are often stigmatized because of their direct contact with criminal offenders and the enforcement aspects of their work. To some, bounty hunters are rogues operating on the fringes of due process.

Brian Johnson and Greg Warchol have studied contemporary bounty hunters and found that these bail recovery/enforcement agents strive to mirror the professionalism, education, and experience of the courtroom workgroup. Johnson and Warchol found that bounty hunters have uneven working relationships with local police that have been characterized as (1) accepting and motivated, (2) cautious but accommodating, and (3) cold and rejecting. The working relationships between law enforcement and bounty hunters is influenced by ideological worldviews of the officers, their level of understanding of bounty hunter function, and acknowledgement of the legitimacy of the bounty hunter's role in the criminal justice system.[11]

Ronald Burns, Patrick Kinkade, and Matthew Leone conducted interviews with bounty hunters and examined their backgrounds and demographic characteristics, training and skills, professional motivation, perceptions of the profession, and bail enforcement practices. The modal bounty hunter was a 51-year-old, conservative, white male. Nearly 90% of the bounty hunters they interviewed were male and more than 80% were white. Nearly 30% had bachelor's degrees and nearly 10% had master's or law degrees. In terms of training and skills, bounty hunters frequently had military, private detection, security, and law enforcement backgrounds. About 92% had training in bail law, 63% had a formal bail certification, and 75% had formal bail training. Money and autonomy were the primary motivations for bounty hunter careers and most reported that bounty hunters were underappreciated and misunderstood by the criminal justice system. Bounty hunters use a variety of resources to locate absconders, including informants, paid information, local police, and the Internet. Most bounty hunters carried an array of sub-lethal weapons, such as mace and handcuffs. Less than 20% carried firearms or used weapons to affect an arrest, although the lethal of risk and physical danger was perceived to be high.[12]

Pretrial Services Today

Bureau of Justice Assistance researches John Clark and Alan Henry analyzed data based on the national survey of more than 200 pretrial services programs across the United States. Their report is a comprehensive look at contemporary pretrial services nationwide. Important findings include:

Staffing, Operations, and Authority

The average pretrial service unit is staffed by 18 persons, receives funding from county and state sources, and interviews more than 5,000 defendants annually. About 40 percent of agencies have between two and five staff members. Programs serving large metropolitan areas, about 2% of all programs, interview more than 50,000 defendants annually. More than half of pretrial service programs operate during normal business hours, however some offer 24-hour, 7-day operations.

About 21 percent of programs have delegated release authority. Of those units with release authority, officers can release some felonies and most misdemeanor offenses. The administrative locus of pretrial service units varies greatly. Probation controls 31%, courts operate 29%, sheriff's departments operate 19%, and private, non-profit firms control 8%.[13]

Bond Interviews and Assessments

About 75% of agencies interview arrestees prior to their first appearance in court. They gather an array of information from the defendant on the social and criminal history. Self-reported criminal history is validated using a variety of data sources such as local police records, local judicial records, jail records, and the National Crime Information Center computer, which can access a database with over 25 million criminal histories.

Bond recommendations are based on objective risk scales, more than half of which have been validated, on subjective or expert judgments of pretrial service staff, or on a combination of objective and subjective approaches. About 42% of pretrial service units employ both, 35% use subjective criteria only, and 23% rely exclusively on a risk assessment instrument.

Special Populations and Monitoring

Nearly 75% of pretrial service programs ask questions about mental health and psychiatric history and many of these refer clients with mental health needs to appropriate agencies. About 25% have developed specialized protocols for dealing with clients arrested for domestic violence. Other special programs have been devised to assist homeless arrestees. Nearly 70% of agencies administer drug testing while defendants are on bond and 50% conduct alcohol testing. Often, substance abuse monitoring is done in conjunction with general counseling services. Approximately 54% of pretrial service units are servicing jails that operate at greater than 100% capacity. Given the problem of jail crowding, pretrial service units are viewed as both a valuable service for the courts and correctional systems, but also an important release valve for the jail population.[14]

Pretrial Release of Felony Defendants

How many criminal defendants are released on bond and what happens to them after their release? The National Pretrial Reporting Program is a national initiative sponsored by the Bureau of Justice Statistics. The National Pretrial Reporting Program collects detailed information about the criminal history, pretrial processing, adjudication, and sentencing of felony defendants in state courts in the 75 largest counties in the United States. A sample of more than 13,000 cases was representative of the more than 55,000 felony cases filed in these jurisdictions per month. Importantly, the 75 largest counties in the country accounted for 50% of the total crime occurring in the United States. Based on these data, Bureau of Justice statisticians Brian Reaves and Jacob Perez produced a number of important findings about felony defendants during the pretrial period of the criminal justice system. For example:

- 63% of felony defendants are released from jail prior to the resolution of their case. This includes 24% of murder defendants, 48% of rape defendants, 50% of robbery defendants, and 68% of assault defendants.

- The most common form of release was personal recognizance, which 38% of all felony defendants received.

- 25% of persons released on felony bond fail to appear in court and have warrants issued for their arrest.

- Overall, 33% of felons released on bond are either re-arrested for a new offense, fail to appear in court, or commit some other violation that results in revocation of their bond.

- Among defendants already on pretrial release when arrested for their current felony, 56% were released again, 32% of these were released while on parole and 44% were on probation.

- 52% of all felony releases occurred the day of arrest.

- 55% of persons released from jail on felony charges had no prior convictions, 45% did have prior convictions. Moreover, 53% had prior arrests, 27% had prior felony convictions, and 9% had a prior violent felony conviction.

- Among those who were released and rearrested, about 8% were arrested within 1 week, 37% within 1 month, 71% within 3 months, and 91% within 6 months.[15]

Federal Pretrial Release and Detention

Pretrial services are not just a state function, but also occur in the federal criminal justice system. Recall that the landmark Bail Reform Act of 1966 was the federal initiative that de-emphasized monetary bail and required the courts to release any defendant charged with non-capital crimes on his or her recognizance or an unsecured appearance bond unless the court determined that the defendant posed significant risks to the community. Importantly, pretrial release facilitated due process in three ways. First, it furthered the presumption of innocence by avoiding unjust or undue jail detention. Second, it enabled criminal defendants to better participate in their defense. Third, it reduced the possibility that defendants would be detained longer than otherwise appropriate for the offense committed. In other words, they would not serve weeks or months for trivial charges, such as shoplifting.

The Federal Pretrial Services Act of 1982 established pretrial services for defendants in the United States district courts. Forty-two Federal districts are served by a federal pretrial service agency. United States Probation serves the remaining 52 districts. Federal pretrial services officers conduct investigations and supervise clients released into their custody. Like state pretrial service staff, federal officers conduct extensive criminal history checks and assess community ties. Together this information is used to assess risks of flight, recidivism, and danger.[16]

Like criminal defendants facing state charges, the preponderance of federal defendants are released from custody on some type of bond. John Scalia found that about 53% of the 56,982 defendants charged with a felony offense were released from custody. Nearly 60% of these were released on their own recognizance on an unsecured bond. More than 34% of federal defendants were detained pending adjudication of their charges, including roughly half of persons charged with violent crimes, immigration violations, and drug trafficking. Non-citizen and homeless defendants were also significantly less likely to be released due to their weaker ties to the community.[17]

Compared to state pretrial service units, federal authorities are more stringent in detaining defendants. In accordance with the Bail Reform Act of 1984, federal authorities conduct a detention hearing within three to five days of the defendant's arrest. At the detention hearing, federal authorities must present clear and convincing evidence that detention is the sole way to ensure not only the defendant's appearance in court, but also to reduce the risks of danger and recidivism that he or she posed. Certain conditions, such as if the defendant's current charges involve firearms, they are already on a criminal justice status, or are a violent recidivist automatically mandate pretrial detention.[18]

◆ Bond Decision-Making and Determinants of Release/Detention

Types of Risk

Whether or not a criminal defendant is released from custody constitutes two sides of the same discretionary coin. Essentially, pretrial service personnel assess three basic types of risk when deciding whether to release a defendant from custody and how they should release the defendant, such as via recognizance or a more restrictive secured bond. The three risks for consideration are (1) danger risk, (2) recidivism risk, and (3) flight or failure to appear (FTA) risk.

Danger risk is the level of danger that the defendant poses toward himself or herself, the specific victim in the current case, or society at large. Danger risk is comprised of several factors, such as the level of injury that the current victim sustained, the seriousness of the current charges, whether the victim is actively homicidal, suicidal, or expresses homicidal or suicidal ideation, and the extent of the defendant's criminal history. Defendants that meet a variety of criteria related to the seriousness of their current charges or the magnitude of their criminal record can be statutorily prohibited from recognizance release. In the event that defendants are charged with capital crimes, criminal suspects can be denied bail altogether.

Recidivism risk refers to the likelihood, assessed by diagnostic instrument, pretrial officer expertise, or both, that the criminal defendant, if released, would immediately engage in criminal behavior. Obviously, pretrial staff cannot see the future and predict future behavior. However, one's criminal history is a relatively reliable predictor of one's future conduct. Thus, defendants with lengthy prior records containing numerous arrests, convictions, and previous involvements with the criminal justice system are viewed as high risk for re-offending. Conversely, persons with no prior record or great intervals of time between arrests, for example, a defendant who was arrested once, twenty years ago, are viewed as low risks for recidivism. Another important indicator of recidivism is current legal status. Many criminal defendants are already on parole, probation, bond, or summons for other charges in other or the same jurisdictions. Since these defendants are "already in legal trouble," the current charges, even if minor, are seen as illustrative that the defendant is a recidivist.

Flight risk is assessed primarily by three factors. First, prior history of missing court appearances, bond revocations, and failing to comply with conditions of probation are viewed as indicators that the defendant would likely miss immediate court dates. Since criminal records contain arrests for failing to appear in court (FTA), a defendant's flight risk is a function of their criminal record. Second, in addition to their current charges, criminal defendants are also found to have active warrants for their arrest because of previous incidents of failing to appear in court. Thus, defendants with one or more current FTA warrants are considered high risk for future missed court appearances. Third, flight risk is related to the community ties of a criminal defendant. Persons with long-term residency in the area, homeowners, currently employed, and persons with extensive family and friendship networks are low risks to miss court dates, flee the jurisdiction, or flee. Conversely, persons who are transient, have little to no financial investment in the community, are unemployed, and have little to no social support have little binding them to the community. As such, there is little incentive to "remain in town" and handle legal responsibilities. Those with weak community ties are viewed as high risks to leave the area, or at minimum, miss court.

Protective and Risk Factors

In determining the risks of recidivism, danger, and flight, pretrial service personnel weigh an assortment of characteristics of the defendant. Some of these factors present the defendant in a positive light and indicate that he or she poses little risk to the community. These are known as protective factors. Alternately, risk factors are damaging or aggravating circumstances that indicate that the defendant will pose some risk if released from custody.

For decades, criminologists have studied the protective and risk factors that influence the assignment of bail and the types of release accorded to criminal defendants, especially because of the traditionally discriminatory bail practices in American criminal justice.[19] Fortunately, the balance of research on pretrial decision-making and bail outcomes indicates that legal factors that influence flight, recidivism, and dangerousness risks are the strongest determinants of pretrial release and detention. By and large, pretrial detention and financially punitive bails are applied to defendants with lengthy criminal records, the most serious current charges, and poor community ties. On the other hand, pretrial release, recognizance bonds, and unsecured bonds are the norm for arrestees with little prior record and with strong community ties.[20]

Conceptually, protective and risk factors should inversely predict release on recognizance and mandatory detention. However, this is not always the case. For example, Sheila Royo Maxwell examined the congruence between predictors of release on recognizance (ROR) and failure to appear (FTA) violations. Expectedly, Maxwell found that defendants with lengthier records, prior crimes of violence, and current serious charges were both less likely to receive an ROR release and more likely to FTA. But, certain demographic characteristics also influenced the decision-making of pretrial officers. Women, persons with prior misdemeanor convictions, and property offenders were more likely to be released on recognizance although they had higher rates of missing court. White defendants were more likely than African Americans to be denied ROR even though race was not a significant predictor of absconding.[21] At the federal level, researchers have found that non-legal considerations also influence pretrial release and bail outcomes. Based on data from 5,660 defendants in ten Federal courts, Celesta Albonetti and her colleagues found that those with lengthy prior records, current or past crimes of violence, and weak community ties were less likely to be released before trial. Albonetti and associates also found that offense seriousness and dangerousness risks negatively affected white, not minority, defendants.[22]

That defendant demographic factors influence pretrial decision making is a troubling threat to due process; prior to the Manhattan Bail Project bail was explicitly detrimental to lower-income persons. Unfortunately, criminologists continue to unearth different pretrial treatment for different types of people.[23] Because of real or perceived weaker community ties, Hispanic arrestees are especially likely to receive more punitive bonds and remain in custody. Importantly, there is a silver lining. Even in studies that found significant differences in the types of bond afforded to various racial and ethnic groups, the size of these effects was negligible compared to the influence of legal factors. For example, Stephen Demuth and Darrell Steffensmeier analyzed the pretrial release process of nearly 40,000 felony defendants from the 75 largest counties in the United States and found that African American and Hispanic defendants were more likely to be detained and held on bail net the effect of legal factors. Yet, offense seriousness, for crimes like murder, rape, and robbery, ranged from 200 to 2000% more powerful of a predictor than race/ethnicity. Several criminal history indicators, such as multiple charges, FTA history, active criminal justice status, prior felony convictions, prior jail detention, and prior imprisonment were as important or usually more significant predictors than demographics.[24]

Conditional release on bond does not necessarily ensure that criminal defendants will either appear in court or desist from criminal offending. John Goldkamp and Peter Jones evaluated pretrial drug testing projects in Wisconsin and Maryland in 1983 and 1989. Goldkamp and Jones tested the assumption that intensive monitoring of drug use during pretrial release would reduce FTA and recidivism rates. The results were negative and counterintuitive. Although fewer than 10% of defendants produced positive drug tests, between 50 to 70% of clients recorded more than five violations of the drug program. Moreover, substance abuse monitoring did not improve the rates by which defendants appeared in court or re-offended. In short, they found substantial non-compliance and continued criminal behavior among drug-using defendants released on bond.[25] Subsequent replications of this approach in Florida and Arizona yielded similarly dismal results of continued non-compliance and criminal offending while on bond.[26]

To summarize, a defendant's risks of flight, recidivism, and danger are the primary determinants of whether he or she is released on bond and how punitive or lenient the bail process is. Strong community ties entail long-term residency, stable employment, and strong familial networks. Weak community ties entail transience, unemployment, and little social and personal connection to the local community. Although researchers still find that demographic characteristics, such as gender and race, significantly affect pretrial outcomes, the effects are negligible compared to legal considerations like offense seriousness and criminal record.

◆ The Effects of Pretrial Detention

Administrative Issues

Despite the advances in the bail process in American justice, there remain unresolved issues about the ultimate due process of pretrial detention. John Goldkamp, Michael Gottfredson, Peter Jones, and Doris Weiland conducted a national assessment of the pretrial process. Their observations were based on analyses of three very different approaches to pretrial service. In Dade County Florida, the department of corrections supervised the pretrial staff; however, an individual judge made the preponderance of bond decisions. In Boston, rotating judges determined bail without the assistance of a pretrial staff. In Arizona, a modern pretrial service unit handled the pretrial release duties as officers of the court.

Goldkamp and his colleagues offered this somewhat grim five-point conclusion. First, there is a continued reliance on financial bail as a major emphasis on release decisions. Of course, protective and risk factors influence the assignment of bail, however cold hard cash or other fiscal resources are still needed for release. Similarly, the presence of profiteering bondspersons remains a visible and dubious part of the pretrial process. Second, the judiciary must assume a leadership role in bringing consistency to the organization, administration, and release policies of bail. Third, it is incumbent that pretrial services move to the adoption of guidelines-based decision-making. Fourth, the judiciary must appropriately staff pretrial service units to meet the pressing problems of jail crowding and unfair or unjust pretrial detention. Fifth, pretrial supervision agencies must serve as the gatekeepers of information for the criminal process as well as for pretrial-release and detention.[27]

Procedural Justice Issues

Unquestionably, the masterwork in this area is Malcolm Feeley's aptly titled *The process is the punishment: Handling cases in a lower criminal court.* Based on his observations of the pretrial court processes in New Haven, Connecticut, Feeley argued that the real punishment for many people is the pretrial process itself, which is burdensome, uncomfortable, bewildering, and seemingly based on the subjective judgments of various criminal justice practitioners. For example, upon arrest defendants must interact with police officers, sheriff's officers and booking deputies, detention officers at the police station, pretrial service officers, bonding agents, defense counsel, private counsel, and the like. These interactions must be accomplished while the defendants are detained and without many of the resources that they need. Court appearances are set in accordance with the court schedule, not a defendant's personal calendar. Thus, the contingencies of being arrested and being released on bond can and often do interfere with work and family obligations. By and large, these officials or "supportive figures" have conflicting responsibilities and duties, and their lack of coordination creates logistical problems for defendants.

Upon intake to the criminal justice system, these "supportive figures" define issues and label defendants for all those who subsequently handle them. Although they may possess limited discretion, their decision-making can have significant consequences at later stages of the process. Because the process is so informal and depends so heavily on oral communications, decisions made by the courtroom workgroup are based heavily on the impressions, information, and recommendations passed on by these supportive figures. The sanctions imposed on defendants are heavily influenced by these people's initial impressions.

According to Feeley, due process concerns are subordinated to the profound short-term impressions of arrest and pretrial behavior and demeanor, arrest record (regardless of conviction record), and professional assessments of whether an individual is worthy or prosecution or dismissal, intervention or given a break, entered into the system or thrown back. Crime control is also not achieved because the courts are structured to offer rapid, informal justice that invites carelessness and error. Because the pretrial period is such a disorganized mess, the majority of criminal defendants prefer to accept plea bargains simply to end their involvement in the process. Since the "punishment is in the process," defendants invoke few adversarial options available to them. The defendant's goal is to end the case as quickly as possible. In return, the state produces perfunctory convictions for reduced criminal charges and justifies the troubling practices of the pretrial period.[28]

Substantive Justice Issues

Enduring the pretrial punishment process carries several legal implications. By and large, two classes of criminal defendants emerge at the pretrial period, those who are released from custody and those who remain in custody. The latter group are purported to suffer deleterious legal outcomes as a function of their remaining in jail prior to court. These negative outcomes can include a greater likelihood of imprisonment, longer sentences, and more punitive sentencing recommendations from the prosecution.[29] Unfortunately, some early research did not adequately control for legally relevant factors that explained pretrial detention. As such, the effects of pretrial detention on subsequent legal outcomes were somewhat cloudy.

Recently, Marian Williams conducted a methodologically more sophisticated examination of the effects of pretrial detention on legal outcomes. Using data from 412 Florida cases, Williams explored the effects of detention on likelihood of incarceration and length of sentence while controlling for a host of important variables, such as offense seriousness, number of felony charges, prior felony convictions, whether the defendant had a private attorney, length of disposition, age, race, and gender. Williams found that defendants who were held in jail prior to court were six times more likely than released arrestees to be sentenced to incarceration and for lengthier terms. Importantly, Williams noted that pretrial detention can be viewed as either a legal variable (or proxy for criminal history), or as an extra-legal variable that relates to social class and therefore ability to pay bond.[30] Irrespective of how it is framed, pretrial detention had meaningfully negative impacts on subsequent criminal justice system outcomes.

 Jails

Definition and Purpose

Being detained in jail is the flip side to being released on bond. Jail is a local correctional or confinement facility that is typically administered by a county-level sheriff's department or a municipal-level law enforcement agency. Jails are utilized to control two general populations of offenders, defendants awaiting trial and persons who have already been convicted and sentenced for their crimes. In addition, jails house a multitude of individuals and are frequently used as waiting stations until persons can be transported to a more appropriate venue or social service provider. At any moment, a jail population might contain persons who have absconded from military service; persons wanted by probation or parole; persons awaiting placement in a psychiatric facility; persons awaiting transport to the hospital or some other medical facility; and juveniles who are being held (in isolation from adult inmates) until their age is ascertained for appropriate placement. Jails are also used by law enforcement as a last resort to detain transients, non-citizens or illegal aliens, people who are highly intoxicated on drugs or alcohol, and anyone else who poses risks to their own and public safety.

Jail Population

Nationally, more than 3,300 American jails supervise more than 767,000 persons. Of these, more than 90% are actually detained and the remaining are supervised in alternative programs outside the jail facility. These programs include weekender programs whereby offenders report for detention only when not working, by electronic monitoring, home detention, day reporting, community service, treatment and therapy, and other work release programs. Overall, the jail population constitutes more than one-third of the nation's correctional population. The jail population has increased fairly steadily since 1990 and reflects sharp demographic differences in rate of confinement. According to Bureau of Justice statisticians Paige Harrison and Allen Beck, males comprise nearly 90% of the jail population and men are seven times more likely than women to be detained in jail on a per capita basis. About 45% of the jail population is comprised of Caucasians, 39% African American, 15% Hispanic, and 2% other racial or ethnic identification. Per capita, blacks are five times more likely than whites, nearly three times more likely than Hispanics, and over eight times more likely than other races to have been in jail.[31]

Approximately 60% of the nation's jail inmates were awaiting court action on their current charge. Thus, more than half of the American jail population *had not yet been convicted for what they were currently charged.* The remaining 40% were post-adjudication defendants serving time for various convictions, probation violations, and parole violations pending transfer to a state department of corrections. Jail confinement is usually a temporary experience. When considering pre- and post-adjudication inmates, the average length of stay is a mere three days. Many defendants are detained for less than 24 hours, remaining in custody until they are able to mobilize resources for release. Ninety-four percent of jail capacity is occupied. Jail facilities vary tremendously in their size and capacity. The fifty largest jails in the United States house more than 30% of all jail detainees nationwide. For example, jail complexes in New York and Los Angeles, which are among the largest penal colonies in the world, house 5% of the American jail population.[32]

Social and Criminal Histories of Jail Inmates

Jail and prison are often used interchangeably in the mainstream media; however, there are vital differences between these facilities. Jails are local, administered usually by the sheriff's department, and entail brief lengths of stay. More than half of the jail population has not yet been convicted. Prisons, explored in Section Four of the textbook, are remote, state-administered correctional facilities used to confine convicted felons. Many people who are in jail will never be in prison, such as persons arrested for DWI; however, almost all prisoners have at some point been detained in jail.

Because jails detain both those who will not be convicted and those who already have been convicted, the population is heterogeneous in terms of the social and criminal history of the inmates. To be sure, many jail inmates have chronic criminal careers.[33] Using data from the national Survey of Inmates in Local Jails, Doris James discovered extensive criminality among some jail detainees. About 46% of all jail inmates were already on probation or parole at the time of their most recent arrest. Nearly 40% had served three or more separate commitments to state or federal prison. Seventy percent of jail inmates had some sort of prior criminal record and 41% of jail inmates had a current or past arrest for violent crimes, such as murder, rape, robbery, or aggravated assault.[34]

Nearly 60% of jail inmates were raised in single-parent households and one in nine was raised in a foster home or institution. Forty six percent of jail inmates had an immediate family member who had been incarcerated. More than 50% of female and 10% of male jail inmates reported that they had suffered from past sexual or physical abuse.[35] Sixty-seven percent of jail inmates were actively involved with drug use prior to their admission to jail, and 16% of jail inmates indicated that they committed their most recent crimes for the explicit purpose of obtaining money to purchase drugs.[36]

History, Reform, and Programs

American criminal justice owes an enormous debt to English common law, and the jail tradition is no exception. Unfortunately, jail history in the United States is overwhelmingly negative and these facilities have been referred to as the sewers and ghettos of the criminal justice system. In the colonial era, jails served no correctional function but instead were used to detain persons who were wanted in the interests of justice and debtors who could not meet their financial obligations. In lieu of jail confinement, those convicted of crimes were banished, branded, pilloried, executed, or maimed. Just as today, jails were then used as last-resort holding bins for groups of people considered outside the mainstream society, namely the mentally ill, alcoholics, and the poor. As the United States expanded and became more modernized, jails also increased in number so that nearly every county and/or municipality had one. However, for most of the Twentieth Century, jails were not appreciably different in their fundamental form and function from those of the Eighteenth Century. Indeed, substantive reform of jail and bail practices was not achieved until the 1960s to 1980s. Otherwise, until very recently, American jails were catchall asylums for the poor and disaffected.[37]

Recently, however, there has been progress. As this chapter has detailed, federal legislation and state and federal criminal justice initiatives have tremendously improved the pretrial phase of the criminal justice system. Professional and efficient pretrial service units utilize community ties and criminal history, not just financial resources, as the determinants of pretrial release. Jail facilities themselves have been redesigned in terms of their physical environment and approach to inmate supervision. "New Generation" jails were first instituted in 1974 and featured podular or direct supervision whereby inmates were housed in single-occupancy cells that adjoined a larger communal area. Inmates interacted in the self-contained living unit or pod for most of the day.

Unlike the traditional jail structure that employed linear supervision or simply a corridor of separate cells, direct supervision facilities allowed correctional staff to constantly observe all aspects of the inmate's living space. The living space itself contained modern amenities, such as carpeting and basic features that one might find in a dormitory. New generation jails served two important interrelated purposes. First, they were more humane facilities compared to the traditional jail in which inmates lived in small cells for most of their detention. Since a jail stint is itself very brief, it makes sense to create a correctional atmosphere that promotes rehabilitation and facilities the offender's reintegration into the community. Second, the increased amenities offered jail inmates an incentive to obey jail regulations. Inmates that did not obey could lose their status in podular modules and go back to traditional cells. Thus, serving inmate needs and ensuring inmate and staff safety were symbiotic. New generation jails have produced a variety of positive outcomes, including reduced inmate violence and misconduct, reduced recidivism after inmates were released, longer delay until re-arrest, and increased inmate and staff satisfaction with the jail environment.[38]

Nevertheless, some continue to assert that jails are a glaring example of injustice and impediment to due process. In his provocative work, *The Jail: Managing the Underclass in American Society* (1985), criminologist John Irwin argued that the function and purpose of jails is to confine disreputable persons not because they have committed crimes but because they are offensive and disreputable. Irwin's thesis is that "rabble," various marginalized groups such as transients, drug abusers, alcoholics, and the like, must be controlled by the criminal justice system to justify and perpetuate the stratification system of American society. Irwin's thesis is radical and sparked subsequent research that largely disconfirmed his hypothesis. For instance, John Backstrand, Don Gibbons, and Joseph Jones empirically found no evidence that persons are arrested for their "offensiveness" or degree of disrepute, instead their actual criminal behavior and the seriousness of their charges influenced their status as jail inmate.[39]

Unquestionably, jail confinement is laden with implicit and explicit types of punishment that affect the social and legal standing of jail inmates.[40] Pure jail confinement is reserved primarily for the most serious criminal offenders with the most extensive criminal records. For the remaining majority of criminal defendants, the contemporary jail offers a variety of programs, treatments, and non-incarceration penalties that aim to serve the interests of community safety (crime control), defendants' rights (due process), and a less damaging, more human pretrial period. Some of these programs are reviewed next.

Due to the prevalence of substance abuse, mental illness, and the co-occurrence of these problems among the jail population, some jurisdictions have devised programs to divert drug-using, mentally ill offenders from jails to more appropriate treatment facilities. Some jurisdictions divert clients prior to booking; others place defendants with appropriate agencies after they have been booked into a county jail (but will be released). A variety of positive outcomes have emerged. Persons who participated in the mental health, substance abuse diversion programs tended to gain independent living skills, reduce substance use, and have lower recidivism rates than persons who did not participate in the program and were simply jailed. Moreover, this saved significant jail space and provided more appropriate, problem-specific treatment.[41]

Henry Steadman and Michelle Naples recently evaluated six jail diversion programs (three pre-booking and three post-booking) in Memphis, Tennessee; Montgomery County, Pennsylvania; Multnomah County, Oregon; Phoenix/Tucson, Arizona; Hartford, New Haven, and Bridgeport, Connecticut; and Lane County, Oregon. Defendants who participated in the diversion programs were primarily female offenders with mental health problems, such as schizophrenia or mood disorders with psychotic traits. Across the six sites, diverted offenders experienced lower recidivism, two months more time spent in the community (and thus not in jail), and greater participation in mental health treatment and counseling, and taking prescribed medication. Diverted individuals did incur higher treatment costs, but these were offset by cost-savings in criminal justice, such as jail. Overall, Steadman and Naples concluded that jail diversion programs that reached out to offenders with mental health needs produced positive outcomes for individuals, criminal justice systems, and communities.[42]

Another programming option is to "outsource" the jail function to the defendant's home. Home incarceration programs, also known as house arrest, home detention, or home detention with electronic monitoring, allow criminal defendants to remain in the community so that they can continue working, fulfilling family responsibilities, and participating in treatment. However, court officials limit the movements and freedom of criminal defendants so that defendants can leave their house only for work, treatment, or other court-approved reasons. All other freedoms are restricted. Offenders are monitored with electronic devices (e.g., ankle bracelets), daily reporting to jail authorities, and other methods. Home incarceration programs are used during both pretrial and post-conviction periods and have met with modest success.[43] For instance, Robert Stanz and Richard Tewksbury examined the programs compliance and subsequent recidivism of nearly 2,500 defendants who participated in a house arrest program. They found that 85% of clients successfully completed the program, and that older defendants from "good" neighborhoods who were charged with DUI-related charges were the most likely to successfully complete the program. Home incarceration costs were 13 times less expensive than jail costs. Stanz and Tewksbury also found that recidivism rates were high, unfortunately. Nearly 70% of clients were re-arrested within five years. More than half of the study group was re-arrested within one year and the most common crime was another DUI.[44] Still, the dramatically reduced costs mean that jail programs that include non-detention components will continue to define the modern jail.

Federal Jails

Do federal jails exist? Actually, they do. The Federal Bureau of Prisons spends nearly $170 million to operate seven federal jails that house less than 6,000 inmates. Federal jails combined have a rate capacity of 3,810, thus federal jails operate at 155 percent of their rated capacity. In this way, they are more crowded facilities than local jails. Interestingly, most jail inmates who are under federal jurisdiction do not reside in federal jails. Instead, more than 12,000 persons wanted by federal authorities are held in local jails to await transfer to a federal facility.[45]

◆ Summary: Balancing Crime Control and Due Process

- The pretrial phase is among the least studied but most important periods of the criminal justice system and contains the transition of police to court power.

- Bail/bond traditionally was limited to wealth, thus indigent persons remained in jail custody regardless of the risks they posed to society.

- Risks of recidivism, flight, and danger posed to victims and community are the primary determinants of bond and pretrial outcomes.

- More than half of the jail population awaits resolution in their criminal case. That so many un-convicted persons reside in jail is a troubling feature of American criminal justice.

- Most criminal defendants, even those charged with serious felonies, are released from jail custody prior to trial.

- A substantial segment of the jail population contains habitual and serious criminals.

- Law enforcement, judicial, and correctional agencies control the pretrial services function depending on jurisdiction.

- Pretrial confinement denotes several negative consequences for subsequent criminal justice decisions, such as sentencing.

- To alleviate crowding and deprivations of liberty, New Generation jails offer a multitude of programs, release options, and alternative sanctions.

Web Links

American Jail Association
(http://www.corrections.com/aja/index.shtml)

Bureau of Justice Statistics Pretrial Release of Felony Defendants
(http://www.ojp.usdoj.gov/bjs/pub/pdf/nprp92.pdf)

Los Angeles County Sheriff's Department (Jail Division)
(http://www.lasd.org/divisions/custody/twintowers/index.html)

National Institute of Corrections
(http://www.nicic.org/)

National Institute of Corrections Jails Division
(www.nicic.org/Jails)

New York City Department of Correction
(http://www.ci.nyc.ny.us/html/doc/home.html)

United States Probation and Pretrial Services
(http://www.uscourts.gov/fedprob/introduction.htm)

Vera Institute of Justice
(www.vera.org)

Questions

1. Jails are local correctional facilities that house persons who have been convicted of crimes and sentenced to less than 12 months confinement, as well as those awaiting trial.

    a. True
    b. False

2. The best type of bond that a person can hope for is

    a. Formal
    b. Informal
    c. ROR
    d. Secured

3. A bondsperson must ensure that all the constitutional safeguards applying to police officers are adhered to.

    a. True
    b. False

4. The concept of bail has a long and interesting history. Processes resembling modern day bail practices appeared as early as:

    a. 1000 BCE
    b. 1000 CE
    c. 2500 BCE
    d. 500 BCE

5. The _____ established bail as an absolute right in detainable criminal charges with the exception of capital offenses, or those potentially punishable by death.

    a. Adjudication Act of 1776
    b. Judiciary Act of 1789
    c. Right to Bail Act 1791
    d. Bail Act 1749

6. The _____ initiated the Manhattan Bail Project in New York City.

    a. The Justice Institute
    b. John Jay College
    c. The Vera Institute of Justice
    d. National Institute of Justice

7. Approximately 24% of pretrial service units are servicing jails that operate at greater than 100% capacity.

   a. True
   b. False

8. Overall, 33% of felons released on bond are either re-arrested for a new offense, fail to appear in court or commit some other violation that results in revocation of their bonds.

   a. True
   b. False

9. Defendant flight risk is assessed primarily by three factors:

   a. Recidivism, employment status and prior history of failing to appear
   b. Prior history of failing to appear, active warrants and community ties
   c. Recidivism, active warrants and community ties
   d. Prior history of failing to appear, employment status and community ties

10. Overall, the jail population constitutes more than _____ of the nation's correctional population.

    a. One third
    b. One quarter
    c. One sixth
    d. One half

Endnotes

1. Conklin, J. E., & Meagher, D. (1973). The percentage deposit bail system: An alternative to the professional bondsman. *Journal of Criminal Justice,* 1, 299–317.
2. Johnson, B. R., & Warchol, G. L. (2003). Bail agents and bounty hunters: Adversaries or allies of the justice system. *American Journal of Criminal Justice,* 27, 145–165.
3. Goldfarb, R. L. (1965). *Ransom: A critique of the American bail system.* New York: Harper & Row.
4. *Nicolls v. Ingersoll,* 7 Johns. 145, 154 (N.Y. 1810).
5. *Reese v. United States,* 76 U.S. 13 (1869).
6. *Taylor v. Taintor,* 83 U.S. (16 Wall.) 366 (1873).
7. Vera Institute of Justice. (2003). *A short history of Vera's work on the judicial process.* New York: Vera Institute of Justice.
8. Goldfarb, note 10, pp. 37–42.
9. Goldfarb, note 10, p. 5.
10. Goldfarb, note 10, p. 3.
11. Johnson, B. R., & Warchol, G. L. (2003). Bail agents and bounty hunters: Adversaries or allies of the justice system. *American Journal of Criminal Justice,* 27, 145–165.
12. Burns, R., Kinkade, P., & Leone, M. C. (2005). Bounty hunters: A look behind the hype. *Policing: An International Journal of Police Strategies and Management,* 28, 118–138.
13. Clark, J., & Henry, D. A. (2003). *Pretrial services programming at the start of the 21st Century.* Washington, DC: U. S. Department of Justice, Office of Justice Programs, Bureau of Justice Assistance.
14. Clark & Henry, note 20.
15. Reaves, B. A., & Perez, J. (1994). *Pretrial release of felony defendants, 1992.* Washington, DC: U. S. Department of Justice, Office of Justice Program, Bureau of Justice Statistics. Substantively similar findings were produced in a follow-up report, see Cohen, T. H., & Reaves, B. A. (2007). *Pretrial release of felony defendants in state courts.* Washington, DC: U. S. Department of Justice, Office of Justice Program, Bureau of Justice Statistics.
16. Wolf, T. J. (1997). What United States pretrial services officers do. *Federal Probation,* 61, 19–24.
17. Scalia, J. (1999). *Federal pretrial release and detention, 1996.* Washington, DC: U. S. Department of Justice, Office of Justice Programs, Bureau of Justice Statistics.
18. 18 U.S.C. §§ 3141–3150.
19. Goldkamp, J. S. (1993). Judicial responsibility for pretrial release decision-making and the information role of pretrial services. *Federal Probation,* 57, 28–35.
20. Gottfredson, M. R. (1974). An empirical analysis of pretrial release decisions. *Journal of Criminal Justice,* 2, 287–303; Goldkamp, J. S. (1979). Bail decision-making and pretrial detention: Surfacing judicial policy. *Law and Human Behavior,* 3, 227–249; Gottfredson, M. R., & Gottfredson, D. M. (1980). *Decision-making in criminal justice: Toward the rational exercise of discretion.* Cambridge, MA: Ballinger Publishing Company; Goldkamp, J. S. (1983). Questioning the practice of pretrial detention: Some empirical evidence from Philadelphia. *Journal of Criminal Law and Criminology,* 74, 1556–1588; Holmes, M. D., Hosch, H. M., Daudistel, H. C., Perez, D. A., & Graves, J. B. (1996). Ethnicity, legal

resources, and felony dispositions in two southwestern jurisdictions. *Justice Quarterly,* 13, 11–30; DeLisi, M., & Berg, M. T. (2006). Exploring theoretical linkages between self-control theory and criminal justice system processing. *Journal of Criminal Justice,* 34, 153–163.

21. Maxwell, S. R. (1999). Examining the congruence between predictors or ROR and failures to appear. *Journal of Criminal Justice,* 27, 127–141.
22. Albonetti, C. A., Hauser, R. M., Hagan, J., & Nagel, I. H. (1989). Criminal justice decision-making as a stratification process: The role of race and stratification resources in pretrial release. *Journal of Quantitative Criminology,* 5, 57–82.
23. Demuth, S. (2003). Racial and ethnic differences in pretrial release decisions and outcomes: A comparison of Hispanic, Black, and White felony arrestees. *Criminology,* 41, 873–908; Demuth, S., & Steffensmeier, D. (2004). The impact of gender and race-ethnicity in the pretrial release process. *Social Problems,* 51, 222–242; Katz, C. M., & Spohn, C. C. (1995). The effect of race and gender on bail outcomes: A test of the interactive model. *American Journal of Criminal Justice,* 19, 161–184,
24. Demuth, S. (2003). Racial and ethnic differences in pretrial release decisions and outcomes: A comparison of Hispanic, Black, and White felony arrestees. *Criminology,* 41, 873–908 (p. 894); Demuth & Steffensmeier, note 3, p. 232.
25. Goldkamp, J. S., & Jones, P. R. (1992). Pretrial drug-testing experiments in Milwaukee and Prince George's County: The context of implementation. *Journal of Research in Crime and Delinquency,* 29, 430–465; Jones, P. R., & Goldkamp, J. S. (1993). Implementing pretrial drug-testing programs in two experimental sites: Some deterrence and jail bed implications. *Prison Journal,* 73, 199–219.
26. Goldkamp, J. S., Gottfredson, M. R., & Weiland, D. (1990). Pretrial drug testing and defendant risk. *Journal of Criminal Law and Criminology,* 81, 585–652; Britt, C. L., Gottfredson, M. R., & Goldkamp, J. S. (1992). Drug testing and pretrial misconduct: An experiment on the specific deterrent effects of drug monitoring defendants on pretrial release. *Journal of Research in Crime and Delinquency,* 29, 62–78.
27. Goldkamp et al., note 4, pp. 307–308.
28. Feeley, note 1.
29. For example, see Ares, C., Rankin, A., & Sturz, H. (1963). The Manhattan Bail Project: An interim report on the use of pretrial parole. *New York University Law Review,* 38, 67–92; Eisenstein, J., & Jacob, H. (1977). *Felony justice: An organizational analysis of criminal courts.* Boston: Little, Brown; Holmes, M., Daudistel, H., & Farrell, R. (1987). Determinants of charge reductions and final dispositions in cases of burglary and robbery. *Journal of Research in Crime and Delinquency,* 24, 233–254.
30. Williams, M. R. (2003). The effect of pretrial detention on imprisonment decisions. *Criminal Justice Review,* 28, 299–316.
31. Minton, T. D. (2010). *Jail inmates at midyear 2009.* Washington, DC: U. S. Department of Justice, Office of Justice Programs, Bureau of Justice Statistics.
32. Minton, note 38, pp. 8–9.
33. Garofalo, J., & Clark, R. D. (1985). The inmate subculture in jails. *Criminal Justice and Behavior,* 12, 415–434; Backstrand, J. A., Gibbons, D. C., & Jones, J. F. (1992). Who is in jail? An examination of the rabble hypothesis. *Crime and Delinquency,* 38, 219–229;

DeLisi, M. (2000). Who is more dangerous? Comparing the criminality of homeless and domiciled jail inmates. *International Journal of Offender Therapy and Comparative Criminology, 44,* 59–69.

34. James, D. J. (2004). *Profile of jail inmates, 2002.* Washington, DC: U. S. Department of Justice, Office of Justice Programs, Bureau of Justice Statistics.
35. James, note 41, p. 1.
36. James, D. J. (2000). *Drug use, testing, and treatment in jails.* Washington, DC: U. S. Department of Justice, Office of Justice Programs, Bureau of Justice Statistics.
37. Goldfarb, A. (1976). *Jails: The ultimate ghetto of the criminal justice system.* New York: Doubleday (pp. 1–86). For assorted looks at the history of jails, see Adler, F. (1986). Jails as a repository for former mental patients. *International Journal of Offender Therapy and Comparative Criminology, 30,* 225–236; Irwin, J. (1985). *The jail: Managing the underclass in American society.* Berkeley, CA: University of California Press; Mattick, H., & Aikman, A. (1969). The cloacal region of American corrections: Prospects for jail reform. *Annals of the American Academy of Political and Social Science, 381,* 109–118.
38. Applegate, B. K., Surette, R., & McCarthy, B. J. (1999). Detention and desistance from crime: Evaluating the influence of a new generation jail on recidivism. *Journal of Criminal Justice, 27,* 539–548; Tartaro, C. (2002). Examining implementation issues with new generation jails. *Criminal Justice Policy Review, 13,* 219–237; Williams, J. L., Rodeheaver, D. G., & Huggins, D. W. (1999). A comparative evaluation of a new generation jail. *American Journal of Criminal Justice, 23,* 223–246.
39. Backstrand, J. A., Gibbons, D. C., & Jones, J. F. (1992). Who is in jail? An examination of the rabble hypothesis. *Crime and Delinquency, 38,* 219–229.
40. Pogrebin, M., Dodge, M., & Katsampes, P. (2001). The collateral costs of short-term jail incarceration: The long-term social and economic disruptions. *Corrections Management Quarterly, 5,* 64–69.
41. Hoff, R., Baranosky, M. V., Buchanan, J., Zonana, H., & Rosenheck, R. A. (1999). The effects of a jail diversion program on incarceration: A retrospective cohort study. *Journal of the American Academy of Psychiatry and the Law, 27,* 377–386; Lamb, H., Shaner, R., Elliott, D., DeCuir, W. J., & Foltz, J. T. (1995). Outcomes for psychiatric emergency patients seen by an outreach police–mental health team. *Psychiatric Services, 46,* 1267–1271; Steadman, H. J., Cocozza, J. J., & Veysey, B. M. (1999). Comparing outcomes for diverted and nondiverted jail detainees with mental illness. *Law and Human Behavior, 23,* 615–627.
42. Steadman, H. J., & Naples, M. (2005). Assessing the effectiveness of jail diversion programs for persons with serious mental illness and co-occurring substance use disorders. *Behavioral Sciences and the Law, 23,* 163–170.
43. Baumer, T. L., Maxfield, M. G., & Mendelsohn, R. I. (1993). A comparative analysis of three electronically monitored home detention programs. *Justice Quarterly, 10,* 121–142; Courtright, K. E., Berg, B. L., & Mutchnick, R. J. (1997). The cost effectiveness of using house arrest with electronic monitoring for drunk drivers. *Federal Probation, 61,* 19–22; Lilly, J. R., Ball, R. A., Curry, G. D., & McMullen, J. (1993). Electronic monitoring of the drunk driver: A seven-year study of the home confinement alternative. *Crime and Delinquency, 39,* 462–484; Maxfield, M. G., & Baumer, T. L. (1990). Home detention with electronic monitoring: Comparing pretrial and postconviction programs. *Crime*

and *Delinquency,* 36, 521–536; Maxfield, M. G., & Baumer, T. L. (1992). Pretrial home detention with electronic monitoring: A non-experimental salvage evaluation. *Evaluation Review,* 16, 315–332.

44. Stanz, R., & Tewksbury, R. (2000). Predictors of success and recidivism in a home incarceration program. *Prison Journal,* 80, 326–344.

45. Pekins, C. A., Stephan, J. J., & Beck, A. J. (1995). *Jails and jail inmates, 1993–1994.* Washington, DC: U. S. Department of Justice, Office of Justice Programs, Bureau of Justice Statistics.

CHAPTER 8

TRIALS, PLEA BARGAINS, AND THE PHILOSOPHY OF PUNISHMENT

◆ Introduction

Figure 8-1 illustrates the magnitude of serious violent crime, murder, rape, robbery, and aggravated assault, in the United States. The figure clearly shows the gulfs between (1) the actual amount of crime and victimization that occurs annually, (2) the amount of these crimes that are reported to the police, (3) the amount of crimes that are actually recorded by police, and (4) the crimes that result in arrest. In a different way, the figure graphically represents the funnel-like effect of the criminal justice system that has been a recurrent theme in this book. Simply put: There is too much crime for the criminal justice system to handle.

Nowhere does this fact manifest more prominently than in the criminal courts. It is because there are so many cases that the prosecutor exercises great discretion in choosing which ones to dismiss, *nolle prosequi,* or pursue. Cases that are pursued face two fates: plea-bargain or trial. Between 95 and 100 of cases are disposed of via guilty plea, meaning that fewer than 5% of criminal cases are resolved via trial. In this sense, the somewhat informal practice of plea-bargaining has easily overtaken formalized trial procedures.

From *Criminal Justice: Balancing Crime Control and Due Process,* 3/e, by Matt Delisi. Copyright © 2011 by Kendall Hunt Publishing Company. Reprinted by permission.

Marjorie Zatz and Alan Lizotte offered the following heuristic about pleas and trials:

> The system allows first-time offenders to move quickly under four general conditions. First, if defendants are not seen as 'hardened criminals,' they move quickly through the system.... Second, when cases are seen as typical or 'normal crimes,' they are processed in a routine way and this increases processing speed.... Where they are not 'normal,' they move slowly to conclusion at trial. Third, the less serious the case the more willing the prosecutor is to bargain and the faster the rate of pleading. Fourth, in 'dead-bang' cases which involve hard physical evidence pleading is swift.... Conversely, serious cases move slowly, especially when first-time offenders' rights or society's well-being are of elevated concern.[6]

Finally, resources are conserved for repeat criminals who are processed quickly when possible or slowly to trial if needed. Zatz and Lizotte's characterization of the legal process is accurate and this chapter explores why plea-bargaining figures so prominently in the judicial process in addition to assorted aspects of pleas and trials.

Could the criminal justice system survive without plea-bargaining? No. For example, William Rhodes examined the crime savings and losses that are the result of plea-bargains, trials, and dismissals. Using data from defendants in Washington, DC, Rhodes found that if defendants who pled guilty had gone to trial, 34% of assault defendants, 16% of robbery defendants, 31% of larceny defendants, and 32% of burglary defendants would have been acquitted! Furthermore, Rhodes found that among dismissed cases, 59% of assaults, 78% of robberies, 67% of larcenies, and 64% of burglaries would have resulted in conviction.[7] What is clear is that the judicial process is an imperfect system of evaluating criminal cases. What you will have to decide is whether justice is served by the judicial system and its plea and trial functions. More importantly, does it serve crime control and due process functions?

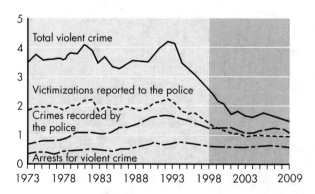

FIGURE 8-1 The Magnitude of Violent Crime in the United States

Source: Rand, M. R., & Truman, J. (2010). *Criminal victimization, 2009*. Washington, DC: U. S. Department of Justice, Office of Justice Programs, Bureau of Justice Statistics.

Court Appearances and Procedures

Recall from Chapter 7 that bail is assigned to most criminal defendants via pretrial court personnel. Local administrative orders preclude the setting of bond for some criminal defendants, such as those charges with serious violent felonies, until the defendant appears formally in court. For defendants who were unable to post bond and remained in custody, they must appear in court within 48 hours of their arrest otherwise they must be released on their own recognizance. This prevents unnecessary delays in due process and guards against prolonged pretrial detention.[8] Importantly, if criminal defendants are not brought to court in time, the judge must release the defendant on his or her recognizance regardless of the underlying charge, even the most serious felonies. Because of this, the courts work swiftly and efficiently to ensure that recently arrested defendants appear in court in due time. For defendants who posted bond and were released, their first appearance occurs within two weeks of their arrest.

Arraignment

The first appearance that a criminal defendant makes in court is known as arraignment. Arraignment is the hearing before a court having original jurisdiction in a criminal case, in which the identity of the defendant is established, the defendant is informed of the charges and penalties potentially faced, the defendant is advised of his or her legal rights, and the defendant is required to enter a plea (if the charges are for misdemeanors). The preponderance of defendants are (1) represented by public defenders or some other publicly assigned counsel and (2) seek to plead guilty to some form of their criminal charges to expedite the case. Often, defendants who wish to talk with an assistant district attorney for plea negotiations will seek a pretrial conference. A pretrial conference is a meeting between the defendant, defense counsel, and the prosecutor to arrange a plea agreement or plea-bargain for misdemeanor, petty, and traffic offenses. (Plea-bargaining is examined extensively in this chapter). Plea negotiations for misdemeanor, petty, and traffic offenses are incredibly brief, provide immediate convictions (favoring the prosecution) for reduced charges (favoring the defense) and result in often-meager penalties. For example, defendants facing non-serious charges often plead guilty to the charges in exchange for a jail sentence equivalent to the time they have already been in custody. "Time served" in the county jail is frequently the sentence for and outcome of plea negotiations for low-level crimes. Finally, nearly all defendants charged with misdemeanor charges admit guilt (guilty plea) or accept guilt without directly admitting it (no contest or *nolo contendere*). For those who plead not guilty, a trial date is set at the arraignment.

For felony cases, the first appearance is more complex to reflect the greater seriousness and penalties implied in felony crimes. As is the case with misdemeanor charges, felony arraignments involve the judge reading the charges and penalties against the defendant, advising the defendant of his or her rights to a preliminary hearing, jury trial, and rights to counsel. The judge can also re-evaluate the setting of bail if requested by defense counsel or the defendant. However, defendants do not enter pleas to felony charges at arraignment. Instead, the matter is set for a preliminary hearing, which is a court appearance to establish if a crime has been committed and if there is probable cause to believe that the defendant committed the offenses alleged in the complaint. At the preliminary hearing, three general outcomes (some jurisdictions refer to products of the preliminary hearing as information) can occur. First, the judge can find that the prosecution lacks probable cause that the suspect committed the crime for which he or she is charged. In this event, the charges are dismissed and the defendant is released. Second, the judge can find that probable cause does exist and the matter is transferred or bound over to district court for trial. Third, criminal defendants frequently waive their right to a preliminary hearing in which the case is automatically bound over to district court. Defendants waive their right for a variety of reasons such as they want to expedite the process or believe that they will plead guilty prior to the initiation of the trial.

Indictment

Some states employ the preliminary hearing to determine the formal filing of charges and whether probable cause exists for trial worthiness. Other states use a grand jury to deliver an indictment (as is explicitly mentioned in the Fifth Amendment). The grand jury is a body of persons who have been selected according to law and sworn to hear the evidence against accused persons and determine whether there is sufficient evidence to bring those persons to trial. Grand juries also investigate criminal activity generally as well as the conduct of public officials and agencies. Grand juries are referred to as investigatory grand juries when they are themselves investigating crimes and charging grand juries when they are deciding to ratify the prosecutor's request for a formal charge. After the grand jury completes an investigation, they prepare a report called a presentment.

The grand jury meets at the request of the prosecution. Unlike preliminary hearings, which are open court proceedings, grand jury hearings are closed and secret. The grand jury hears the testimony of witnesses who had been subpoenaed to testify and evaluates the evidence gathered by the prosecution, a process known as presentment. Unless they need to actually hear testimony from the accused, the defendant is not present at the grand jury hearing. If the grand jury finds that probable cause exists, they issue an indictment, or true bill, which is the formal accusation of charges. If probable cause is not found, the grand jury outcome is a no bill.

The roots of the grand jury extend to 1166 when King Henry II of England required knights and other freemen to file criminal accusations with the criminal court. Historically, the grand jury has served as a counterbalance or buffer between the state (especially the prosecution) and individuals (persons who could be charged with crimes). Trial juries or petit juries have 12 members whereas grand juries have between 12 and 23 members (23 is the conventional number of grand jury members). Although the federal justice system and most states have grand jury systems, most states opt to use the direct filing/preliminary hearing system.

Pleas

The majority of defendants whose case results in conviction plead guilty. According to Bureau of Justice Statistics researchers, 94% of the more than 1.1 million felons sentenced in state courts pleaded guilty. Comparatively, juries found guilt in only 2% of cases and judges found 3% guilty.[9] In pleading guilty, criminal defendants not only acknowledge their guilt and the commensurate punishment, but also waive their constitutional rights implied or expressed in the Fifth and Sixth Amendments. Because of the gravity of these consequences, judges ensure that guilty pleas are made voluntarily, that the defendant understands what he or she is doing, that counsel be provided during plea negotiations, and that the defendant is aware of the maximum punishments for their crimes. Defendants can rescind or withdraw their guilty plea up until sentencing under some circumstances.

A plea of no contest or *nolo contendere* produces the same consequence as a guilty plea, but the defendant does not formally admit guilt. Rather, the defendant has not contested the charges against them. A no contest plea is simply a legal way to secure conviction while the defendant presumably saves face. Similarly, an Alford plea occurs when a defendant does not admit guilt but acknowledges that he or she will be found guilty and thus does not contest the charges. A not guilty plea is entered when a defendant does not accept responsibility for the charges by claiming that he or she did not commit the offense. Defendants that are unresponsive during court proceedings, also technically plead not guilty. Once a not guilty plea is entered, a trial date is set. Although rarely used, defendants can also plead not guilty by reason of insanity in which they assert that they cannot be held legally responsible or accountable for the alleged criminal conduct.

Sentencing Hearing

For defendants who either plead guilty or were found guilty, the adjudication proceeding occurs separately from sentencing. The court appearance where convicted defendants formally receive their punishment or sentence is known as a sentencing hearing, or variously referred to as the sentencing phase or penalty phase. Sometimes, trials are referred to as bifurcated trials with the adjudication and sentencing components held separate.

Pleas have become integral to American justice. Indeed, more than nine of ten cases that result in conviction are achieved via plea bargains, not trials. Plea-bargaining, arguably the most dominant practice in criminal justice is explored next.

Plea-Bargaining

Definition and Purposes

Plea-bargaining, also known as a plea agreement, is the practice involving negotiation between prosecutor, the defendant, and his or her defense attorney that results in the defendant entering a guilty plea in exchange for the state's reduction of charges or the prosecutor's promise to recommend a more lenient sentence than the offender would have ordinarily received.[10] There are three general types of plea-bargains that occur in the criminal courts. First, reduced charge plea bargains are characterized by the reduction of the original charge that automatically reduces the penalty that could be imposed. For example, a youngster arrested for auto theft may agree to plead guilty to unauthorized use of a vehicle, which is usually a misdemeanor. Second, reduced count plea bargains occur when the district attorney dismisses or significantly reduces the number of charges in the complaint to induce the defendant to plead guilty. For instance, an offender charged with four counts of robbery would plead guilty to a single count with the remaining three being dismissed. Third, reduced sentence plea bargains occur when the prosecutor agrees to recommend a reduced sentence in exchange for the guilty plea. For example, although felony convictions denote a prison sentence, prosecutors will commonly recommend that convicted felons receive probation or some other intermediate sanction instead of confinement.

Plea-bargaining produces a legal resolution that satisfies all parties involved. Two truisms explain why plea-bargaining is so frequently used. First, the preponderance of criminal defendants who reach the point of entering a plea is, in fact, guilty! Everyone knows that the defendant is guilty, including the prosecutor, the defense counsel, and the defendant. Recall that the criminal justice system filters cases constantly. Had the defendant not been guilty, he or she would have not only avoided arrest but also had their charges dismissed at arraignment. Second, the power and resources differentials between the prosecution and defense (recall Chapter 8) make it very easy to balance the goals of crime control and due process. In terms of crime control, plea-bargaining guarantees a conviction and some form of punishment albeit in reduced form. Moreover, plea-bargaining permits an inexpensive way to punish criminals because of the time and resource savings of avoiding trials. In terms of due process, plea-bargaining only occurs if there are no procedural errors or violations against the defendant. Moreover, prosecutors are ethically bound to pursue pleas or any prosecution against criminal defendants that they believe are in fact guilty. Finally, the leniency inherent to plea-bargaining gives criminal defendant's a glimpse or mercy that could be viewed as a second chance for the offender to correct his or her behavior. Thus, plea bargains efficiently and expeditiously serve the interests of crime control and due process, prosecution and defense.

The Roles of the Courtroom Workgroup

Legal scholar Albert Alschuler conducted some of the seminal analyses of the roles of court officials in plea-bargaining. Alschuler described the prosecutor as an administrator, advocate, judge, and legislator during plea negotiations. The administrator role pertains to the need to secure convictions in the most efficient and fast way possible. As advocate, the prosecutor is serving the public interest in justice by ensuring that criminal offenders pay a legal price for their crimes. As a judge, the prosecutor uses his or her discretion to mete out the deserved or just plea and sentence for each offender based on the defendant's criminal record, culpability, and other characteristics. As a legislator, the prosecutor can water-down or weaken statutes that appear to be too strict or punitive.[11] On balance, these multiple roles help to serve the multiple agendas of the prosecution. However, it has been argued that the structure of plea-bargaining is calamitous for defense counsel since they are coerced to assist their clients to plead guilty by the court system that almost entirely depends on pleas to operate. Some have asserted that the defense counsel role is so compromised by plea bargains that the practice should be abolished.[12] For more on the controversial aspects of plea-bargaining refer to Box 8-1.

Concerns about the powerlessness of defense attorneys during plea negotiations may have been overstated in early research. Criminologists have found that defense attorneys are an integral part of the plea negotiating process, professionals that are viewed as indispensable colleagues that facilitate court operations. For example, David Lynch and David Evans found that expert defense attorneys tended to be emotionally stable legal experts who exercised charm, creativity, and likeability during plea negotiations. Indeed, the personality characteristics and expertise of defense counsel guarantee that plea-bargaining is conducted professionally and fairly.[13]

Others have also noted the variable roles that the prosecutor, defense attorney, defendant, and judge play in plea-bargaining (see Box 8-2). John Padgett discovered that due to the highly discretionary practice of plea-bargaining, court personnel worked together to arrive at the most appropriate legal resolution. Which legal actor took the lead in plea bargains depending on the character, prior record, and apparent criminality of the defendant and the strength of the prosecutor's criminal case. For example, Padgett described:

- *Implicit plea-bargaining* is when the defendant threw himself to the mercy of the court.

- *Charge reduction plea-bargaining* is where the prosecutor eliminated or reduced charges in exchange for a guilty plea.

BOX 8-1

CRIMINAL JUSTICE AND THE LAW

PLEA-BARGAINING AND THE UNITED STATES SUPREME COURT

***United States v. Ruiz,* 536 U.S. 622 (2002):** the Constitution does not require prosecutors to inform defendants during plea-bargaining negotiations of evidence that would lead to the impeachment of the state's witnesses.

***Godinez v. Moran,* 509 U.S. 389 (1993):** the competency standard for pleading guilty and for waiver of right to counsel is the same as the competency standard for standing trial.

***United States v. Broce,* 488 U.S. 563 (1989):** the entry of a guilty plea foreclosed the defendant's right to challenge those pleas by collateral attack on double jeopardy grounds.

***Ricketts v. Adamson,* 483 U.S. 1 (1987):** double jeopardy was not violated by prosecution of the defendant for first-degree murder following his breach of a plea agreement under which he had pled guilty to a lesser offense, been sentenced, and begun serving a prison term.

***Hill v. Lockhart,* 474 U.S. 52 (1985):** to prove ineffectiveness of defense counsel, a defendant must show a reasonable probability that except for counsel's errors, the defendant would not have pled guilty.

***Mabry v. Johnson,* 467 U.S. 504 (1984):** defendant's acceptance of a proposed plea bargain that the prosecutor erroneously made does not create a constitutional right to have the bargain enforced by the trial court.

***Bordenkircher v. Hayes,* 434 U.S. 357 (1978):** due process was not violated when a prosecutor carried out a threat made during plea-bargaining to re-indict the defendant on more serious charges if the defendant refused to plead guilty to the offense originally charged.

***Corbitt v. New Jersey,* 439 U.S. 212 (1978):** upheld a New Jersey law that made a sentence of life imprisonment mandatory upon jury conviction for first-degree murder, but allowed lesser sentences if the defendant entered a plea of nolo contendere.

***Hutto v. Ross,* 429 U.S. 28 (1976):** a confession was not per se inadmissible in a trial merely because it was made as the result of a plea-bargain agreement.

***Henderson v. Morgan,* 426 U.S. 637 (1976):** defendant's guilty plea was involuntary because he had not received adequate notice of the charges and the elements of the crimes charged.

***Santobello v. New York,* 404 U.S. 257 (1971):** the promise of a prosecutor that rests on a guilty plea must be kept in a plea-bargaining agreement.

***North Carolina v. Alford,* 400 U.S. 25 (1970):** accepting a guilty plea from a defendant who maintains his innocence is valid. The Alford plea means that the defendant does not admit guilt but acknowledges that the state has a strong enough case to convict.

***Brady v. United States,* 397 U.S. 742 (1970):** attempts to avoid a possible death sentence are not grounds to invalidate a guilty plea.

***Boykin v. Alabama,* 395 U.S. 238 (1969):** a defendant must make an affirmative statement that the plea is voluntary before the judge can accept it.

Photo © 2011, Le Loft 1911, Shutterstock, Inc.

> **BOX 8-2**
>
> ## CRIMINAL JUSTICE CONTROVERSY
>
> **PLEA-BARGAINING: NECESSARY EVIL OR SIMPLY EVIL?**
>
> Because the magnitude of crime dwarfs the resources and capabilities of the criminal justice system, the system exerts great discretion in choosing the cases to prosecute. Without the speedy practice of plea-bargaining, the criminal courts would grind to a halt if all defendants actually went to trial. Since the judicial system already costs about $40 billion annually, how expensive would it become if plea-bargaining were discontinued? Due to these concerns, many legal scholars view plea-bargaining as a necessary evil.
>
> For others, plea-bargaining is a dubious practice that accomplishes neither crime control nor due process goals. There are several important criticisms. First, plea-bargains are fundamentally acts of legal leniency since the most serious charges and penalties are reduced. In effect, this excuses and mitigates the actual criminal harm that offenders commit because the system is more interested in resolving the case quickly and inexpensively. A second and related point is that plea-bargains are an affront to crime victims for the reasons stated in point one. For example, a sexual assault arrest that results in a guilty plea to simple assault completed changes the dynamic of the case in the eyes of the victim. Reducing a sexual assault to a minor assault or harassment is legally tantamount to implying that the original crime never occurred. Third, since plea bargains are virtually inevitable, the rights to a criminal trial specifically and judicial due process generally are coerced by the legal system. Fourth, this coercion could result in innocent criminal defendants accepting guilty pleas. Fifth, defendants who insist on taking their cases to trial sometimes receive harsher legal penalties, a phenomenon that has been referred to as the "trial tariff."
>
> Both crime control and due process proponents have important concerns about the practice of plea-bargaining. What do you think?
>
> Sources: Alschuler, A. (1975). The defense attorney's role in plea-bargaining. *Yale Law Journal, 84,* 1179–1313; Barbara, J., Morrison, J., & Cunningham, H. (1976). Plea-bargaining: Bargain justice? *Criminology, 14,* 55–64; McCoy, C. (1993). *Politics and plea-bargaining: Victims' rights in California.* Philadelphia: University of Pennsylvania Press; Schulhofer, S. (1984). Is plea-bargaining inevitable? *Harvard Law Review, 97,* 1037–1107. Photo © *JupiterImages,* Corp.

- *Judicial plea-bargaining* is when the judge, after conferring with the prosecution and defense, offered the defendant a specific guilty plea sentence. Padgett noted that career criminals and other serious offenders were most likely to face judicial pleas, the most severe form of plea-bargaining.

- *Sentence recommendation plea-bargaining* is when the prosecutor, who had already secured a guilty plea, made a sentencing recommendation to the judge who often complied with the recommendation.[14]

Judges have been found to be somewhat passively involved in plea negotiations. When they do exert influence, judges tend to exercise great uniformity in their acceptance of pleas and subsequent sentencing.[15] For instance, Alissa Worden found that judges tend to go along with the sentencing recommendations made by prosecutors and that judicial attitudes are not importantly related to their behavior during plea bargains.[16] Overall, judges rely almost exclusively on legal factors when making assessments of risk to be used in their sentencing decision. For example, Michael Vigorita analyzed more than 1,000 judicial assessments of criminal offenders and found that variables such as, length of criminal careers, prior arrests, convictions, and incarcerations, and whether the defendant had a noted drug problem were the greatest determinants of sentencing.[17]

Criminal defendants actually exert considerable control and discretion when deciding whether to enter a plea agreement. It should be noted that both agreeing to plead guilty and refusing to do so carries various legal costs. Jodi Viljoen, Jessica Klaver, and Ronald Roesch found that young criminal defendants were significantly likely to plead guilty in the first place because they were likely to perceive that the prosecution has a strong case against them. Furthermore, criminal defendants with a poor understanding of their legal rights and court processes were less likely to agree to plea bargains.[18] It is important to recognize that all criminal defendant know with absolute certainty whether they are truly guilty or not. Whether they believe that they should be found guilty or admit their guilt is another matter entirely. Nevertheless, plea-bargaining is so widespread because criminal defendants are able to calculate the degree of justice that is produced with a guilty plea. Oftentimes, this amount of justice is far more palatable than the justice that could be administered upon conviction at trial. It is a gamble that most defendants are not willing to take. Indeed, defendants who opt for trials instead of plea bargains often face more serious legal penalties.[19]

Finally, does the victim play any part in plea-bargaining? Most states provide crime victims with some level of prosecutorial consultation about plea negotiation; however, in no state does the victim have veto power over the plea agreement. The victim can provide input but has no real power.[20] Indeed, one of the most compelling arguments against plea-bargaining is the "bargained" justice that the defendant receives at the expense of the victimization and suffering of the crime victim.

Legal and Extra-Legal Factors

A recurrent theme in American criminal justice is the salience and primacy of legal factors, such as evidence, offense seriousness, prior record, and criminality, compared to extra-legal factors, such as gender, race, and social class, to official discretion, decision-making, and criminal justice outcomes. This is also the case for plea-bargaining.[21] Gary LaFree conducted one of the most authoritative comparative studies of plea-bargaining and trial using data from 3,269 male robbery and burglary defendants in El Paso, Texas; New Orleans, Louisiana; Seattle, Washington; Tucson, Arizona; Norfolk, Virginia; and Delaware County, Pennsylvania. Three of the jurisdictions had few restrictions on plea-bargaining whereas the others had recently attempted to eliminate or greatly reduce the practice. LaFree produced two important findings. First, although defendants who "pushed" for trial received greater penalties than defendants who plead, the effects disappeared when trial acquittals were included. In other words, this contradicts the assertion made by critics of plea-bargaining who maintain that defendants face a "trial tariff" or penalty for exercising their Sixth Amendment rights. Second, legal factors such as criminal record and offense seriousness were the greatest predictors of adjudication for both trials and pleas. Again, this indicates that the legal system relies on legal criteria, not discriminatory variables such as gender.

Reform and Future Prospects

Plea-bargaining has been one of the most controversial legal topics in criminological and legal discourse. For some, it is a disaster that precludes both crime control and due process. To others, plea-bargaining is a perfectly lawful practice that involves legal experts (the prosecutor and defense attorney) conscientiously and appropriately weighing the costs and benefits of the plea and producing justice.[22] Calls to abolish plea-bargaining were mostly academic, but one jurisdiction did just that. The Memphis Tennessee District Attorney's Office implemented a no plea-bargain policy for murder, aggravated rape, and aggravated robbery. Defendants either pleaded guilty to the maximum (non-reduced) charge or faced trial on the charge. In the first year, 164 cases of first-degree murder and nearly 2,000 cases of aggravated robbery were processed. The result was a 90% combined conviction rate. Thus, the most violent criminals were convicted and received longer sentences; moreover, the policy did not result in a predicted backlog of cases. In fact, community support of the criminal justice system increased after the policy's implementation.[23] In the end, plea-bargaining is an imperfect but effective way of efficiently processing the massive volume of cases in the criminal courts. For creative ways that criminal courts have attempted to address specific crimes, see Boxes 8-3 and 8-4.

◆ Trials and Trial Procedures

Trial Initiation

Pursuant to the 1974 Speedy Trial Act, cases must be brought to trial within two months of arrest unless motions have caused delays. Prior to trial initiation, a pretrial conference is held whereby the prosecution, defense, and judge stipulate those things that are agreed upon and thus narrow the scope of the trial to the things that are in dispute. Other activities include the disclosure of required information about witnesses and evidence, making motions, and organizing the presentation of motions, witnesses, and evidence. The process whereby the prosecution presents his or her case to the defense is known as discovery.

> **BOX 8-3**
>
> # CRIMINAL JUSTICE SPOTLIGHT
>
> ## DRUG COURTS
>
> The criminal courts process the broad spectrum of criminal behavior, from traffic violations to felonies, nuisance offenses to violent crimes. However, some criminal behaviors are viewed as specialized problems that may require different types of adjudication than the traditional courts can offer. One example is drug court that combines intensive drug rehabilitation services for addicted offenders with legal requirements to complete treatment. Unlike traditional criminal courts that simply impose a legal punishment for drug violations of the criminal law, drug courts have a different mission. Drug courts provide longer treatment, address overlapping drug and mental health problems, provide intensive supervision and monitoring, and help children with various social services.
>
> Federally funded drug courts have been established in California, Florida, Maryland, Oklahoma, Nevada, Kentucky, Oregon, and Hawaii, mostly as a response to local cocaine or methamphetamine problems. Professionals have identified several key components of effective drug courts.
>
> - Drug courts integrate alcohol and other drug treatment services with justice system case processing.
> - Using a non-adversarial approach, prosecution and defense counsel promote public safety while protecting offender due process rights.
> - Eligible participants are identified early and promptly placed in the drug court program.
> - Drug courts provide access to a continuum of treatment and rehabilitation services.
> - Abstinence is monitored via frequent drug testing.
> - A coordinated strategy governs drug court responses to participant compliance.
> - Ongoing judicial interaction with each drug court participant is essential.
> - Monitoring and evaluation measure the achievement of program goals and assess effectiveness.
> - Continuing interdisciplinary education promotes effective drug court operations.
> - Forging partnerships among drug courts, public agencies, and community-based organizations generates local support and enhances drug court effectiveness.
>
> Drug courts appear to be working. Across several locations, about 15% of drug court participants are re-arrested and retention and graduation rates are high (especially compared to normal recidivism statistics that hover around 70% or higher). Sustained abstinence from drugs also resulted in 40 to 80% reductions in crime. In addition to reductions in recidivism, drug courts also help address some of the collateral problems associated with drugs and crime.
>
> Sources: Goldkamp, J. S. (2003). The impact of drug courts. *Criminology & Public Policy, 2,* 197–206; Gottfredson, D. C., Najaka, S. S., Kearley, B. (2003). Effectiveness of drug treatment courts: Evidence from a randomized trial. *Criminology & Public Policy, 2,* 171–196; Harrell, A. (2003). Judging drug courts: Balancing the evidence. *Criminology & Public Policy, 2,* 207–212; Harrell, A., & Roman, J. (2001). Reducing drug use among offenders: The impact of graduated sanctions. *Journal of Drug Issues, 31,* 207–232; Huddleston, III, C. W. (2005). *Drug courts: An effective strategy for communities facing methamphetamine.* Washington, DC: U. S. Department of Justice, Office of Justice Programs, Bureau of Justice Assistance; Senjo, S. R., & Leip, L. A. (2001). Testing and developing theory in drug court: A four-part logit model to predict program completion. *Criminal Justice Policy Review, 12,* 66–87. Photo © 2011, joingate, Shutterstock, Inc.

BOX 8-4

CRIMINAL JUSTICE SPOTLIGHT

DOMESTIC VIOLENCE COURTS AND BATTERER INTERVENTION PROGRAMS

Another "specialized" criminal problem is domestic violence. The prevalence of domestic violence or spousal violence is relatively high; however, domestic violence, like drunk driving, is also frequently committed by persons who otherwise are not involved in criminal behavior. As such, a number of jurisdictions have devised programs specifically for persons charged with domestic violence. Instead of being sentenced to jail, batterers are sentencing to a domestic violence or batterer education program that contains months of group therapy that seek to reduce not only violent behavior but also antisocial attitudes that the defendant may harbor against women and about domestic violence (the modal offender is the male husband who abused his female spouse). Batterer courts offer the promise of reducing recidivism and the circumstances and attitudes that give rise to domestic violence.

Unfortunately, recent studies indicate that domestic violence courts and batterer intervention programs are ineffective. The National Institute of Justice sponsored two evaluation studies of batterer intervention programs in Broward County, Florida and Brooklyn, New York. The Broward study found no significant difference between the treatment and control groups in attitudes toward women, whether wife beating should be a crime, and whether the state has the right to intervene in domestic violence situations. It also found no differences in whether victims expected their partners to beat them again. Furthermore, no significant differences were found in probation violations or re-arrests except that men who were assigned to the treatment program but did not attend all of the sessions were *more likely* to be re-arrested than the control group. Attending the batterer program had no effect on the incidence of violence. Like Lawrence Sherman found in studies of mandatory arrest for domestic violence, offenders who had a greater stake in conformity (e.g., employed, married, homeowners) were less likely to commit violence.

In Brooklyn, batterers assigned to 26 weeks of treatment were less likely to recidivate than a control group and batterers ordered to eight weeks of treatment. The former group has fewer subsequent criminal complaints but no differences existed in terms of attitudes toward domestic violence.

These early results indicate that specialized courts for the treatment of domestic violence are not overwhelmingly better than traditional courts that sentence batterers to jail or non-conditional probation. Fortunately, criminologists are devising ways to improve batterer intervention programs so that domestic violence courts meet with some of the successes of specialized drug courts.

Sources: Davis, R. C., Taylor, B. G., & Maxwell, C. D. (2000). *Does batterer treatment reduce violence? A randomized experiment in Brooklyn.* Washington, DC: U.S. Department of Justice, Office of Justice Programs, National Institute of Justice; Feder, L., & Forde, D. R. (2000). *A test of the efficacy of court-mandated counseling for domestic violence offenders: The Broward Experiment.* Washington, DC: U.S. Department of Justice, Office of Justice Programs, National Institute of Justice; Jackson, S., Feder, L., Forde, D. R., David, R. C., Maxwell, C. D., & Taylor, B. G. (2003). *Batterer intervention programs: Where do we go from here?* Washington, DC: U.S. Department of Justice, Office of Justice Programs, National Institute of Justice. Photo © 2011, joingate, Shutterstock, Inc.

Jury Selection

Being called for "jury duty" is a part of Americana. The list of potential jurors, called the jury array or venire, is produced from voter registration lists, motor vehicle lists, or property tax assessments. The list of potential jurors is meant to encompass the local citizenry to ultimately produce a jury of peers to decide the legal fate of criminal defendants. A variety of persons are automatically excluded from serving on juries, such as convicted felons (in most states), public officials, attorneys, and the like. Those deemed unqualified or ineligible under state law are removed from the list. Otherwise, the court clerk randomly produces 12 jurors and two alternates. Interestingly, the use of 12 jurors is not mandated in the Constitution, but is more a reflection of common law custom. Indeed, the Supreme Court held in *Williams v. Florida* (1970) that the traditional 12-person jury was the result of "historical accident" and smaller juries are permissible under the Sixth Amendment.[24] Nevertheless, a 12-person jury remains the normal standard at least for felony trials.

Voir Dire

Voir dire, meaning to speak the truth, is the actual process of selecting a jury from the list of potential jurors. Both the prosecution and defense play a role in determining the appropriateness of an individual to sit on the jury in an unbiased and objective manner. The background, work and residency history, interest in, and knowledge of the current case are evaluated. During *voir dire*, potential jurors can be removed from consideration because they are deemed to be potentially biased and subjective. A challenge for cause occurs when either the prosecution or defense removes a juror because specific circumstances imply that the juror would be unable to impartially evaluate the evidence and render a verdict in the case. For example, jurors who are relatives, friends, or acquaintances of the defendant would be removed for cause. Additionally, persons who indicate that they have already arrived at a verdict in the case can be removed for cause. Because the jury must be fair and impartial, the prosecution and defense are not limited in the number of jurors they can challenge for cause, thus *voir dire* can be a prolonged process.

    The United States Supreme Court has evaluated some interesting legal scenarios that have arisen from challenges for cause. For instance, *Witherspoon v. Illinois* (1968) held that a sentence of death cannot be carried out if the jury that imposed or recommended it was chosen by excluding prospective jurors for cause simply because they voice general objections to the death penalty, or expressed conscientious or religious scruples against its infliction.[25] On the other hand, the Court held in *Wainwright v. Witt* (1985) that a juror may be excluded in a death penalty case if his or her personal views on capital punishment would prevent or substantially impair the performance of his or her duties as a juror in accordance with the instructions and his or her oath to serve on the jury.[26] Similarly, *Lockhart v. McCree* (1986) held that the Constitution did not prohibit the removal for cause, prior to the guilt phase of a bifurcated capital trial, of prospective jurors whose opposition to the death penalty was so strong that it would prevent or substantially impair the performance of their duties as jurors at the sentencing phase of the trial.[27] In *Mu' Min v. Virginia* (1991), the Court held that questioning during *voir dire* in a capital murder case, which asked jurors if they had heard something about the case and formed an opinion, but did not ask specifics regarding what prospective jurors had heard did not violate the Sixth and Fourteenth Amendments.[28] As is always the case, the application of the law is open to interpretation especially when attempting to remove prospective jurors for substantive reasons.

More controversial is the peremptory challenge, which is the dismissal of a potential juror by either the prosecution or defense for unexplained, discretionary reasons. With peremptory challenge, attorneys need not provide justification as to why a particular individual should be removed. Given the competing goals of the prosecution and defense, it is east to imagine that the composition of the jury differently meets the needs of counsel. Prosecutors want jurors whose demeanor and responses to questions indicate that they are conservative, tough-on-crime, punitive, and perhaps prone to side with the state. Conversely, defense counsel might want jurors who appear to be more liberal, sympathetic to characteristics of the accused, and more due process oriented. Predictably, court officers often used demographic characteristics like age, race, and gender as proxies for criminal justice orientation or group-based behavior. For instance, the state might prefer a predominantly female jury when prosecuting a male defendant for multiple counts of rape.[29]

The Supreme Court has established a variety of rulings on the use of peremptory challenges as they relate to gender, race, and viewpoints about gender and race. *Ristaino v. Ross* (1976) held that the defendant had the right to have prospective jurors questioned regarding their racial prejudices only if the facts of the case suggested a significant likelihood that racial prejudice might infect the black defendant's trial.[30] *Turner v. Murray* (1986) held that a defendant in a capital case who was accused of an interracial crime was entitled to have prospective jurors informed of the race of the victim and questioned on the issue of racial bias. A defendant could not complain that the trial judge did not question prospective jurors on racial prejudice unless the defendant specifically requested such an inquiry during jury selection.[31]

In *Batson v. Kentucky* (1986), the Court held that the equal protection clause of the Fourteenth Amendment forbid prosecutorial use of peremptory challenges to exclude potential jurors solely on the account of their race or on the assumption that black jurors as a group would be unable to impartially consider the state's case against a black defendant. To establish a case the defendant must show that he or she is a member of a cognizable racial group and that the prosecutor had exercised peremptory challenges to remove members of the defendant's race from the jury. After the defense makes this initial showing the burden shifts to the prosecution to use a neutral explanation for challenging jurors.[32] *Powers v. Ohio* (1991) held that a white defendant had standing to have a conviction reversed due to violation of the equal protection clause of the Fourteenth Amendment if the prosecutor used peremptory challenges to exclude prospective black jurors.[33] This doctrine was affirmed in *Purkett v. Elem* (1995), which held that peremptory challenges could not be used for racially discriminatory reasons.[34] Finally, *J. E. B. ex rel. T. B.* (1994) held that the Fourteenth Amendment equal protection clause prohibited the use of peremptory challenges by state actors on the basis of gender. The case arose from a civil paternity suit filed by the State of Alabama. The equal protection clause prohibited discrimination in jury selection on the basis of gender, or on the assumption that an individual would be biased in a particular case for no reason other than the fact that the person happens to be a woman.[35] This case basically applied the logic of *Batson* to gender.

Opening Statements

Once the jury is officially selected or impaneled, the trial adversaries make their opening statements to the court and jury. Because the prosecution carries the burden of proof beyond a reasonable doubt, they make the initial opening statement. Here, the prosecutor concisely tells a story as to the evidence that the state has assembled that proves that the accused committed the crimes for which they are charged. The opening statement contains an overview of the evidence, witnesses, motives, and expert witnesses that will prove that the accused is guilty. The opening statement is confined to facts and cannot be made in an argumentative fashion. In kind, defense counsel presents their story that the state's case cannot or does not prove that the client is guilty. Since defense counsel has already reviewed the state's case during discovery, the purpose is simply to show how the state cannot prove guilt beyond a reasonable doubt. Opening statements are very important because they provide a summation of the facts of the case to the jury. If the defendant waives his or her right to a jury trial and instead opts for the judge to serve as jury, known as a bench trial, opening statements are often not made.

By this point, it should be clear that the prosecution and state are the offense and the defense is, obviously, the defense. The subsequent stages in the criminal trial, such as presentation of evidence, direct and cross examination of witnesses, and closing statements, are presented first by the prosecution then by the defense. These adversarial positions are the hallmark of American justice and are intended to best meet the twin goals of crime control and due process.

Rules of Evidence

Recall that the Bill of Rights is the procedural rulebook for the police, courts, and correctional systems. The Federal Rules of Evidence are the "rulebook" that governs proceedings in American courts. Although the Federal Rules of Evidence do not apply directly to state courts, the states have modeled their judicial rules of evidence on the federal model. The Federal Rules of Evidence contain eleven articles that encompass 67 judicial rules pertaining to:

- general provisions
- judicial notice
- presumptions in civil actions and proceedings
- evidence relevancy and its limits
- privileges
- witnesses
- opinions and expert testimony
- hearsay
- authentication and identification
- contents of writings, recordings, and photographs, and
- miscellaneous rules.

Whether at the federal or state level, the purpose of the rules of evidence is to secure fairness in judicial administration, the elimination of unjustifiable expense and delay, and the promotion of growth and development of the law of evidence to the end that the truth may be ascertained and proceedings justly determined.[36]

Presentation and Types of Evidence

Evidence is information provided to the courts during trials and includes testimony, documents, and physical objects that are intended to resolve the factual dispute that exists between the prosecution and defense. Several types of evidence may be presented at trial. Direct evidence establishes a fact without the need for inferences or presumptions. The majority of direct evidence that is presented in trials is eyewitness testimony and videotaped documentation. Circumstantial evidence proves facts that may support an inference or presumption of the disputed facts. Prima facie evidence suffices to prove a fact until there is evidence presented that could be used for rebuttal. Real evidence consists of physical material or traces of physical activity, such as fingerprints. Once the trial judge approves the admission of real evidence, it is presented in the form of an exhibit. With real evidence, prosecutors attempt to establish associative evidence defined as the link between the accused and the crime scene by information obtained from physical evidence found at the crime scene and physical evidence found on the accused or in places traceable to the accused. Again, evidence is primarily used as "proof" or data to support the presentation of the prosecution or the defense. The totality of the evidence presented often means the difference between conviction and acquittal.

Direct Examination

The prosecuting attorneys begin the presentation of evidence by calling their witnesses. The questions they ask of the witnesses are direct examination that may produce both direct and circumstantial evidence. Witnesses may testify to matters of fact or be called to identify documents, pictures, or other items that are introduced into evidence. Generally witnesses cannot state opinions or give conclusions unless they are experts or are especially qualified to do so. Witnesses qualified in a particular field as expert witnesses may give their opinion based on the facts in evidence and may give the reason for that opinion. Attorneys generally may not ask leading questions of their own witnesses. Leading questions are questions that suggest the answers desired, in effect prompting the witness. Objections may be made by the opposing counsel for many reasons under the rules of evidence, such as to leading questions, questions that call for an opinion or conclusion by a witness, or questions that require an answer based on hearsay. Most courts require a specific legal reason be given for an objection. Usually, the judge will immediately either sustain or overrule the objection. If the objection is sustained, the lawyer must re-phrase the question in a proper form or ask another question. If the objection is overruled and the witness answers the question, the lawyer who raised the objection may appeal the judge's ruling after the trial is over.

Cross-Examination

Once the prosecution completes direct examination, the defense attorneys may then cross-examine the witness. Cross-examination is generally limited to questioning only on matters that were raised during direct examination; however, leading questions may be asked during cross-examination since the purpose of cross-examination is to test the credibility of statements made during direct examination. Moreover, when a lawyer calls an adverse or hostile witness (one whose testimony is likely to be prejudicial) on direct examination, the lawyer can ask leading questions as on cross-examination. Essentially, defense counsel are attempted to impeach the witness or the evidence in the sense that they want to reduce the credibility of the witness or evidence. For example, witnesses may be asked if they have been convicted of a felony or a crime involving moral turpitude (dishonesty), since this is relevant to their credibility. Opposing counsel may object to certain questions asked on cross-examination if the questions violate the state's laws on evidence or if they relate to matters not discussed during direct examination. In short, cross-examination is the pure arena of adversarial justice.

The same process then occurs with the legal adversaries switching roles. The defense will offer evidence that indicates that their client was not guilty of the charges. In turn, the prosecutor can cross-examine the defense witnesses. However, the defense does not have to present evidence particularly if they are confident that the state/prosecutor did not prove its case. In a criminal case, the witnesses presented by the defense may or may not include the defendant. Because the Fifth Amendment to the U.S. Constitution protects against self-incrimination, the prosecution cannot require the defendant to take the stand and explain what happened, nor can it comment or speculate on the reasons the defendant has chosen not to testify. The jury will be instructed not to take into account the fact that the defendant did not testify. Once the defense has completed its presentation, the prosecution can present rebuttal witnesses or evidence to refute evidence presented by the defendant. This may include only evidence not presented in the case initially or a new witness who contradicts defense witnesses.

Directed Verdict and Closing Arguments

After the presentation of evidence, either the prosecution or defense can move for a direct verdict that, if granted, means that the trial is over. In closing arguments, first the prosecutor, then the defense attorney discuss the evidence and properly drawn inferences in their summation of the case. They cannot discuss issues or evidence that was not presented at trial. Before closing, the judge indicates to the lawyers which instructions he or she intends to give the jury. In turn, in their closing arguments the lawyers can comment on the jury instructions and relate them to the evidence. The closing argument is the opportunity for each side to "tell their story" about why they won, or should win, the case. The defense is not obligated to make a closing argument.

The Judge Instructs the Jury

The judge instructs the jury about the relevant laws that should guide its deliberations. The judge reads the instructions to the jury in what is often referred to as the judge's charge to the jury. In giving the instructions, the judge will state the issues in the case and define any terms that may not be familiar to the jurors. The judge must discuss the standard of proof, which in all criminal cases is beyond a reasonable doubt. Indeed, the Supreme Court held in *Sullivan v. Louisiana* (1993) that failure to give the jury an adequate instruction on "proof beyond a reasonable doubt" violates the defendant's right to a jury trial and is a fundamental error requiring reversal.[37]

Fundamentally, the judge instructs the jury to objectively as possible arrive at a verdict. In doing so, the judge may (1) read sections of applicable laws, (2) advise the jury that it is the sole judge of the facts and of the credibility of witnesses, (3) acknowledge that the jurors are to base their conclusions on the evidence as presented in the trial, and that the opening and closing arguments of the lawyers are not evidence, (4) explain what basic facts are in dispute, and what facts do not matter to the case, (5) note the relevant laws that govern the case and that jurors are required to adhere to these laws in making their decision, regardless of what the jurors believe the law is or ought to be. In short, the jurors determine the facts and reach a verdict within the guidelines of the law as determined by the judge. Many states allow the lawyers to request that certain instructions be given, but the judge makes the final decisions about them. To increase fairness and uniformity, some states created standardized instructions or give the jurors' copies or a recording of the instructions.

Jury Deliberation, Verdict, and Judgment

After receiving the instructions, the jury begins the process of deliberation. The jury elects a presiding juror or foreperson that will lead discussions, handle the voting process, and deliver the verdict to the court. The jury works with the court bailiff who ensures that no one communicates with the jury during deliberations and obtains needed information or exhibits from the court at the request of the jury. If jurors have questions about the evidence or the judge's instructions, they give a note to the bailiff to take to the judge. The judge may respond to the note, or may call the jury back into the courtroom for further instructions or to have portions of the transcript read to them. Of course, any communication between the judge and jury should be in the presence of lawyers for each side or with their knowledge. The court provides the jury with written forms of all possible verdicts so that when a decision is reached, it only has to choose the proper verdict form. In most but not all instances, the verdict in a criminal case must be unanimous (12-0).

Sometimes juries are unable to arrive at a decision or appear to be deadlocked because of one or two obstinate jurors.[38] In this event, the judge will bring the jury to the court and advise them of their duties. Known as an Allen Charge, this judicial warning is a subtle form of judicial coercion to keep the jury on course.[39] Additionally, the jurors may be sequestered where they are housed in a hotel and secluded from all contact with other people and news media. Unless the jury was sequestered because of concerns about their physical safety, jury members are permitted to go home at night but instructed not to consider or discuss the case with anyone outside of the jury room.

When jurors cannot agree on a verdict, the result is a hung jury and mistrial. A variety of factors can increase the likelihood of a hung jury. Case complexity was a major determinant of hung juries, as cases with multiple counts of criminal offenses, complex or sophisticated types of evidence, and complex, difficult-to-interpret legal instructions increased the likelihood of juries being unable to reach a verdict. Other important concerns among hung juries were concerns about a weakly presented case, questions about police credibility, and overall concerns about fairness of the law.[40]

Since the case is not adjudicated or decided, it may be tried again at a later date before a new jury. The prosecution may also decline to pursue the case further.

After reaching a decision, the jury notifies the bailiff, who notifies the judge. All of the participants reconvene in the courtroom and the jury foreperson or court clerk announces the verdict, guilty or not guilty. Sometimes the losing side requests that the jury be polled whereby each juror is asked whether they agree with the decision. Afterward, the decision is read, accepted by the court, the jury is dismissed, and the trial is over. The decision of the jury does not legally take effect until the judge enters a judgment on the decision or files it in the public record.

Sentencing

Upon conviction, the judge sets a separate court proceeding to formally sentence the defendant. Judges rely on a formal report called a pre-sentence investigation (PSI), which is a legal dossier that includes information about the defendant's criminal history, family, work, and residency history, diagnostic information, and other relevant legal information. Depending on the jurisdiction, the PSI is prepared by pretrial services officers, judicial officers, or even probation officers. The PSI guides the judge's decision to determine the appropriate sentence from the range of possible sentences established by the legislature in the state statutes. However, the judge receives input from several sources, including the prosecutor, defense attorney, victims who deliver a victim-impact statement, the defendant, and occasionally family members of the defendant and victim. With the exception of death sentences, only the judge determines the sentence to be imposed.

Although the judge ultimately decides the sentence, his or her discretion is overwhelmingly guided by legislative sentencing guidelines that are primarily a function of two factors, the legal seriousness of the offense and the criminal history of the defendant. Within sentencing guidelines is room for flexibility for the judge to impose a minimum (leniency) or maximum (punitive) sentence. Factors that lead a judge to sentence in a lenient manner are mitigating factors or circumstances or characteristics that seem to reduce the seriousness of the charge. Age can be a mitigating factor since very young and very old defendants are often viewed as less deserving of harsh punishment. Factors that worsen sentences are aggravating factors or circumstances or characteristics that seem to exacerbate the seriousness of the charge. For example, violent crimes that are committed in an especially cruel, depraved, or heinous manner will often result in the most severe sentence.

Finally, implicit in the sentencing of a criminal defendant is a punishment philosophy or rationale. Five general punishment philosophies are utilized in the criminal courts. Retribution implies the payment of a debt to society and the expiation or atonement of one's offense. From this perspective, punishment is deserved and appropriate based on the seriousness and harm of the criminal offense. Criminals must be administered their "just desserts," almost as a form of societal revenge. Deterrence is the idea that swift, certain, and severe punishment will generally discourage or deter future criminal acts. General deterrence refers to the "general message" that is sent to potential criminals that they will be punished for their crimes. Specific deterrence pertains to the individual offender who is being punished. Deterrence rests on the theory that humans are rational actors empowered with free will who choose whether to commit crime. If the legal consequences are grave enough, theoretically people are discouraged from criminal behavior. Incapacitation, the modal punishment rationale in the contemporary United States, is the removal of criminals from society that precludes their ability to commit crimes against the citizenry. Incapacitation is achieved by incarceration. Rehabilitation seeks to restore, repair, or correct an offender's behavior so that he or she can become a non-criminal, productive member of society. The rationale is that punishment shows the offender a needed lesson or provides some type of treatment that can help the offender overcome the inclination or motivation to commit crime. Restoration, the newest of the rationales, seeks to respond to the needs of crime victims by building a coalition of sorts between the offender, victim, and community. The restoration philosophy has spawned a different paradigm of justice known as restorative justice that places exceedingly less emphasis on crime control and more on making efforts to rehabilitate ad reintegrate offenders into the community.[41]

Appeal

An appeal is the legal right of the defendant to contest a material error of law that occurred in his or her trial, such as a procedural violation. A substantive basis for appeal is also known as a potentially reversible error. A trivial error that did not substantively impair the case is known as a harmless error and cannot be appealed. Of course, the defendant cannot appeal merely because they were convicted. The prosecution cannot appeal a case because of the Fifth Amendment prohibition of double jeopardy. A "catchall" tactic for appeal for defendants in state courts is to file a writ of habeas corpus in federal court to show a constitutional rights violation. Importantly, an appeal is *not* a retrial. Instead, appellate courts review the trial's procedure or examine errors in the judge's interpretation of the law.

The appeals process goes as follows. First, the appeal is initiated by the filing of a formal document in the court having appellate (as opposed to original) jurisdiction. Second, a record of the original proceedings of the trial court is obtained from the court reporter's official transcript. Third, the opposing parties file briefs and if there will be oral arguments, a hearing is scheduled and the arguments are heard. Finally, after presentation of briefs and/or oral arguments, the appellate court deliberates by considering the original trial and the arguments made by both sides. The ultimate ruling of the appellate court is referred to as the majority opinion. Appellate judges who agree with the outcome but have a different rationale often write a concurring opinion whereas the minority that disagrees with the majority will write a dissenting opinion. An opinion of the entire appellate court is known as *per curiam.*

◆ Motions

A motion is an oral or written request made to a court at any time before, during, or after court proceedings that asks the court to make a specified finding, decision, order, or ruling. Written motions are referred to as petitions. Both the prosecution and defense can and often do make formal motions before, during, and after criminal trials. The most common trial motions appear below. As you will see, defense counselors are more likely to file motions in an effort to equalize their chances against the prosecution.

Discovery

The motion of discovery is functionally the most important motion. It is filed by the defense and allows the defendant's lawyers to view the prosecution's evidence that will be presented at trial. The defense is provided physical evidence, witness lists, documents, and any other evidence that the state will use against the accused. During discovery, the defense counsel ascertains the strength or weakness of the case that the state is brings against their client.

Bill of Particulars

A motion for a bill of particulars asks the prosecutor to provide detailed information about the charges that are being filed. Defendants facing multiple charges or multiple counts of the same offense commonly make the motion.

Dismissal

The motion to dismiss the charges is the criminal defendant's dream because if the motion is accepted, the case is terminated. A variety of circumstances can result in the dismissal of charges. For example, procedural violations that breach the due process rights of the defendant taint the government's case and must result in dismissal. Other times, cases are dismissed because the prosecutor's case is simply too weak to proceed to trial (let alone result in a conviction). Defendants who agree to testify for the state against co-defendants often have their charges dismissed as part of the agreement. Finally, the motion to dismiss is sometimes prompted by a different motion. For instance, the motion to suppress evidence (discussed below) can greatly weaken the prosecutor's case and necessitate a dismissal.

Suppress Evidence

The motion to suppress evidence occurs when defense counsel moves to exclude evidence that the prosecution obtained unlawfully. Consider this scenario. A defendant is arrested upon suspicion for murder. During a lengthy interrogation, the defendant confesses to the killing. However, not only did the police ignore the defendant's repeated requests for an attorney, but also the police did not advise the defendant of his Miranda rights. Such a scenario is doubly crippling for the prosecution. First, the confession itself is tainted and worthless. Second, if it is the sole evidence of guilt and is suppressed, the prosecution's case dissolves.

Change of Venue

Cases involving famous persons as defendants or victims and cases characterized by extreme violence, such as multiple homicides, generate enormous public interest and media frenzy. Because of this, it may be difficult or nearly impossible to assemble a jury that can objectively deliver a verdict. Often, the defense will file a motion of change of venue to transport a case to another jurisdiction within the state where presumably the pretrial publicity is markedly lower and the likelihood of selecting unbiased jurors is greater.

Severance of Offenses and Severance of Defendants

Frequently, a single criminal episode contains numerous charges and multiple co-defendants. In an effort to save time and money, the prosecution often files a single criminal case that encompasses all of the charges and pertains to the co-defendants. To some, the consolidation of charges gives the appearance of obvious guilt. For example, the prosecutor may present a case against two defendants that includes 80 counts of burglary, 35 counts of felony theft, and 30 counts of receiving and selling stolen property. A motion for severance of offenses requests that defendants be tried separately for the charges. A motion for severance of defendants is requested when the defense believes that one defendant is clearly more responsible than the other (usually the defense counsel's client), and trying the individuals separately might reduce the likelihood of conviction.

Continuance

The motion for a continuance seeks to delay a criminal trial for some substantive reason, such as change in counsel. The judge must walk a fine line when considering motions for continuance. On one hand, the defense must be provided enough time to locate witnesses and adequately defend the accused. On the other hand, frequent delays in a trial tend to favor the defense and could be used as a tactic to prolong and thus weaken the state's case. Even when granted for substantively important reasons, continuances can significantly increase trial length.

Arrest of Judgment

A motion for arrest of judgment is requested after the jury returns a guilty verdict but prior to sentencing whereby the defendant believes there is a legally substantive reason why he or she should not be sentenced at that particular time. Physical illness, mental illness, and insanity are some reasons that may prompt a defendant to request an arrest of judgment.

Present Sanity

Similarly, a motion to determine present sanity occurs when the defense asserts that the defendant has become insane during the course of a trial. Importantly, defendants cannot be tried, sentenced, or punished if they are currently insane. A motion to determine present sanity seeks to delay court proceedings until the defendant can be stabilized. It is different from a plea of non guilty be reason by insanity.

Mistrial and New Trial

A motion for a mistrial is commonly filed when either the prosecution or defense makes highly inflammatory remarks that would seem to irreparably alter the case. Other reasons for a mistrial are the death of a juror or attorney, impropriety in the drawing of the jury that was discovered during trial, a fundamentally prejudicial error against the defendant, jury misconduct, or the inability of the jury to reach a verdict. Such a motion suggests that the current trial is broken and court proceedings must start over. If the defense moves for a mistrial, they cannot subsequently claim that a new trial is a violation of the double jeopardy clause of the 5th Amendment. Upon discovery of important evidence that will incontrovertibly show that their client is not guilty, the defense may file a motion for a new trial that will set aside or invalidate a prior conviction.

◆ Summary: Balancing Crime Control and Due Process

- Although the criminal trial is the symbolic battle of the state versus the individual, virtually all convictions are secured via plea-bargaining.

- Plea-bargaining has its pros and cons in terms of the achievement of crime control and due process goals. However, the judicial system likely would not work with the reliance on guilty pleas.

- The adversarial system of justice is less pronounced with plea-bargaining.

- Legal factors, such as quality and quantity of evidence, number of charges, offense severity, and the defendant's prior criminal history, are the strongest determinants of judicial outcomes.

- Challenges for cause and peremptory challenges are legal maneuvers used by the prosecution and defense to produce a jury that will be most amenable to their version of events.

- Despite public hype, hung juries and jury nullification are rare and caused mostly by case complexity.

- A variety of specialized courts addressing offenders/offenses such as domestic violation and drug violations have been devised to increase the treatment and rehabilitative potential of the criminal justice system.

- Criminal sentences are laden with philosophical rationales for punishing the criminal offenders. These include retribution, deterrence, incapacitation, rehabilitation, and restoration.

◆ Web Links

The Federal Judiciary
(www.uscourts.gov)

Community Justice Initiatives
(www.cjiwr.com)

Federal Judicial Center
(www.fjc.gov)

Federal Rules of Evidence
(www.law.cornell.edu/rules/fre/#article_vii)

United States Code
(www.uscode.house.gov/usc.htm)

National Drug Court Institute
(www.ndci.org/home.htm)

United States Sentencing Commission
(www.ussc.gov)

Questions

1. Ninety-five out of 100 cases are disposed of via guilty plea, meaning that fewer than 5% of criminal cases are resolved via trial.

    a. True
    b. False

2. Defendants who are unable to post bond and remain in custody must appear in court within _____ hours of their arrest, otherwise they must be released on their own recognizance.

    a. 24 hours
    b. 36 hours
    c. 48 hours
    d. 72 hours

3. The first appearance that a criminal defendant makes in court is known as:

    a. Indictment
    b. Arraignment
    c. Nolle prosequi
    d. Summary hearing

4. Grand juries are referred to as investigatory grand juries when they are themselves investigating crimes and _____ when they are deciding to ratify the prosecutor's request for a formal charge.

    a. Charging grand juries
    b. True bill grand juries
    c. Indictment grand juries
    d. None of the above

5. A plea of no contest or *nolo contendere* produces the same consequence as a guilty plea, but the defendant does not formally admit guilt.

   a. True
   b. False

6. More than _____ cases that result in conviction are achieved via plea bargains, not trials.

   a. Five out of ten
   b. Nine out of ten
   c. Seven out of ten
   d. Three out of ten

7. According to Gary LaFree, legal factors such as criminal record and offense seriousness were the smallest predictors of adjunction for both trials and pleas.

   a. True
   b. False

8. A _____ occurs when either the prosecution or the defense removes a juror because specific circumstances imply that the juror would be unable to impartially evaluate the evidence and render a verdict in the case.

   a. Peremptory challenge
   b. Voir dire
   c. Challenge for cause
   d. Discretionary challenge

9. Opening statements are often not made if the defendant waives his or her right to a jury trial and instead opts for the judge to serve as jury, which is known as a _____.

   a. Judge trial
   b. Summary trial
   c. Jury trial
   d. Bench trial

10. Discovery, Bill of Particulars, Dismissal and Severance of Offenses are all examples of

    a. Evidence
    b. Procedure
    c. Motions
    d. Judicial rulings

Endnotes

1. Zatz, M. J., & Lizotte, A. J. (1985). The timing of court processing: Towards linking theory and method. *Criminology,* 23, 313–335, pp. 330–331.
2. Rhodes, W. M. (1978). *Plea-bargaining: Who gains? Who loses?* Washington, DC: Institute for Law and Social Research.
3. *McNabb v. U. S.,* 318 U. S. 332 (1943).
4. Rosenmerkel, S., Durose, M. R., & Farole, Jr., D. (2009). *Felony sentences in state courts, 2006—Statistical tables.* Washington, DC: U. S. Department of Justice, Office of Justice Programs, Bureau of Justice Statistics.
5. Rush, G. E. (2000). *The dictionary of criminal justice* (p. 252), 5th edition. New York: Dushkin/McGraw-Hill.
6. Alschuler, A. (1968). The prosecutor's role in plea-bargaining. *University of Chicago Law Review,* 36, 50–112.
7. Alschuler, A. (1975). The defense attorney's role in plea-bargaining. *Yale Law Journal,* 84, 1179–1313.
8. Lynch, D. R., & Evans, T. D. (2002). Attributes of highly effective criminal defense negotiators. *Journal of Criminal Justice,* 30, 387–396.
9. Padgett, J. F. (1985). The emergent organization of plea-bargaining. *American Journal of Sociology,* 90, 753–802.
10. Meyer, J., & Gray, T. (1997). Drunk drivers in the courts: Legal and extra-legal factors affecting pleas and sentences. *Journal of Criminal Justice,* 25, 155–163. Also see, Alschuler, A. (1976). The trial judge's role in plea-bargaining, part I. *Columbia Law Review,* 76, 1059–1154.
11. Worden, A. P. (1995). The judge's role in plea-bargaining: An analysis of judges' agreement with prosecutor's sentencing recommendations. *Justice Quarterly,* 12, 257–278.
12. Vigorita, M. S. (2003). Judicial risk assessment: The impact of risk, stakes, and jurisdiction. *Criminal Justice Policy Review,* 14, 361–376.
13. Viljoen, J. L., Klaver, J., & Roesch, R. (2005). Legal decisions of preadolescent and adolescent defendants: Predictors of confession, pleas, communication with attorneys, and appeals. *Law and Human Behavior,* 29, 253–277.
14. LaFree, G. D. (1985). Adversarial and non-adversarial justice: A comparison of guilty pleas and trials. *Criminology,* 23, 289–312; Walsh, A. (1990). Standing trial versus copping a plea: Is there a penalty? *Journal of Contemporary Criminal Justice,* 6, 226–237.
15. Gillis, J. W. (2002). *Victim input into plea agreements.* Washington, DC: U. S. Department of Justice, Office of Justice Programs, Office for Victims of Crime.
16. For investigations of legal and extra-legal factors in plea-bargaining, see Champion, D. J. (1989). Private counsels and public defenders: A look at weak cases, prior records, and leniency in plea-bargaining. *Journal of Criminal Justice,* 17, 253–263; Kellough, G., & Wortley, S. (2002). Remand for plea: Bail decisions and plea-bargaining as commensurate decisions. *British Journal of Criminology,* 42, 186–210; LaFree, G. D. (1985). Adversarial and non-adversarial justice: A comparison of guilty pleas and trials. *Criminology,* 23, 289–312; Meyer, J., & Gray, T. (1997). Drunk drivers in the courts: Legal and extra-legal factors affecting pleas and sentences. *Journal of Criminal Justice,* 25, 155–163.

17. For a colorful symposium on plea-bargaining, see Scott, R. E., & Stuntz, W. J. (1992). Plea-bargaining as contract. *Yale Law Journal,* 101, 1909–1968; Easterbrook, F. H. (1992). Plea-bargaining as compromise. *Yale Law Journal,* 101, 1969–1978; Schulhofer, S. J. (1992). Plea-bargaining as disaster. *Yale Law Journal,* 101, 1979–2010; Scott, R. E., & Stuntz, W. J. (1992). Reply: Imperfect bargains, imperfect trials, and innocent defendants. *Yale Law Journal,* 101, 2011–2016.
18. Gibbons, W. L. (1999). Instituting a no plea bargaining policy. *Prosecutor,* 33, 35–40.
19. *Williams v. Florida,* 399 U. S. 78 (1970).
20. *Witherspoon v. Illinois,* 391 U. S. 510 (1968).
21. *Wainwright v. Witt,* 469 U. S. 412 (1985).
22. *Lockhart v. McCree,* 476 U. S. 162 (1986).
23. *Mu' Min v. Virginia,* 500 U. S. 415 (1991).
24. For interesting studies of the criminology of jury selection, consult Fukurai, H. (1996). Race, social class, and jury participation: New dimensions for evaluating discrimination in jury service and jury selection. *Journal of Criminal Justice,* 24, 71–88; Fukurai, H. (1997). A quota jury: Affirmative action in jury selection. *Journal of Criminal Justice,* 25, 477–500.
25. *Ristaino v. Ross,* 424 U. S. 589 (1976).
26. *Turner v. Murray,* 476 U. S. 28 (1986).
27. *Batson v. Kentucky,* 476 U. S. 79 (1986).
28. *Powers v. Ohio,* 499 U. S. 400 (1991); also see *Georgia v. McCollum,* 505 U. S. 42 (1992).
29. *Purkett v. Elem,* 514 U. S. 765 (1995).
30. *J. E. B. ex rel. T. B.,* 511 U. S. 127 (1994).
31. Federal Rules of Evidence. (2011). Retrieved February 25, 2011, from www.law.cornell.edu/rules/fre/rules.htm.
32. *Sullivan v. Louisiana,* 508 U. S. 275 (1993).
33. A related issue is jury nullification defined as the improper insistence on acquittal of a demonstrably guilty defendant because of some pre-existing bias on the part of one or more jurors. If a juror is successful at jury nullification, he or she produces a hung jury and subsequent mistrial. Although jury nullification is a controversial issue, it is exceedingly rare. For studies of jury nullification, see Hannaford, P. L., Hans, V. P., & Munsterman, G. T. (1999). How much justice hangs in the balance? A new look at hung jury rates. *Judicature,* 83, 59–67; Hannaford-Agor, P. L., & Hans, V. P. (2003). Jury nullification at work? A glimpse from the National Center for State Courts Study of Hung Juries. *Chicago-Kent Law Review,* 78, 1249–1277.
34. *Allen v. U. S.,* 164 U. S. 492 (1896).
35. Hannaford-Agor, P., Hans, V. P., Mott, N. L., & Munsterman, G. T. (2002). *Are hung juries a problem?* Washington, DC: U. S. Department of Justice, Office of Justice Programs, National Institute of Justice.
36. The literature of criminal sentencing is simply massive. Some well-known and interesting works on the subject include, Andenaes, J. (1974). *Punishment and deterrence.* Ann Arbor, MI: University of Michigan Press; Blumstein, A., Cohen, J., & Nagin, D. (Eds.). (1978). *Deterrence and incapacitation: Estimating the effects of criminal sanctions on crime rates.* Washington, DC: National Academy of Sciences Press; Tonry, M. (1998). Intermediate

sanctions in sentencing guidelines. *Crime and Justice,* 23, 199–253; Zimring, F. E., & Hawkins, G. J. (1973). *Deterrence: The legal threat in crime control.* Chicago: University of Chicago Press; Zimring, F. E., & Hawkins, G. J. (1995). *Incapacitation: Penal confinement and the restraint of crime.* New York: Oxford University Press.

PRISON

◆ Introduction

With the possible exception of the police, no other area of the criminal justice system has inspired as much public interest, political wrangling, and academic study as prisons. Indeed, prisons and the state of the prisoner population have meaningful implications for both crime control and due process. To crime control advocates, prisons are good because the most serious criminal offenders, or at least persons convicted of the most serious criminal offenses, are removed from conventional society. As such, prisons literally incapacitate the most serious criminals' (unless, of course, the offender escapes) opportunity to victimize others. Moreover, roughly 30% of prisoners seem to "learn their lesson" and do not recidivate after release from custody. Prisoners who are able to reform their behavior tend to reattach and re-commitment themselves to conventional social institutions, such as family, work, church, or military. Many former prisoners receive substantive counseling and treatment for substance abuse problems, mental illness, and other personal problems. Prison treatment amenities facilitate their rehabilitation.

Crime control proponents also have at least three reasons to be dissatisfied with prisons. First and foremost, the recidivism rates among ex-prisoners (discussed later in this chapter) are approximately 70%. Although prisons effectively incapacitate offenders, most do not commit themselves to rehabilitation. In this sense, the crime

From *Criminal Justice: Balancing Crime Control and Due Process,* 3/e, by Matt Delisi. Copyright © 2011 by Kendall Hunt Publishing Company. Reprinted by permission.

control capacity of prison confinement is short-lived. Second, prison is the most expensive form of social control and, as described above, does little to reduce offending patterns among most prisoners.

Third, there is evidence that incarceration and mere exposure to incarceration actually exacerbates inmates' antisocial attitudes and behaviors, which results in higher rates of recidivism after release. Consider the example of Scared Straight programs. Created in 1979 at the Rahway State Prison in New Jersey, Scared Straight programs feature an aggressive presentation of prison life by inmates serving life sentences to at-risk and adjudicated juvenile delinquents. The inmates harangue the youthful offenders, use shocking street language and profanity, and intimidate the youths in hopes that the deterrence program will literally "scare" the youths into renouncing their delinquency and leading productive lives. Scared Straight programs remain very popular among the general public.

Unfortunately, the programs do not work. In fact, instead of controlling crime, they tend to increase it. Anthony Petrosino, Carolyn Turpin-Petrosino, and John Buehler conducted a systematic review of Scared Straight programs and found that youths who went through the program had higher rates of offenders than youths who did not. In their words, "on average these programs result in an increase in criminality in the experimental group when compared to a no-treatment control. According to these experiments, doing nothing would have been better than exposing juveniles to the program."[1]

Due process-oriented persons often have more cause for alarm when considering prisons. However, the majority of this concern does not deal with fundamental due process rights that have been discussed throughout this text. Instead, the due process concern is more an overtly liberal concern about the salience of prisons in American life, particularly as prisons have impacted the poor and racial minorities. As shown in Figure 9-1, there has been a 400% increase in the imprisonment rate since 1980.

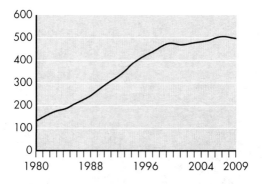

FIGURE 9-1   Imprisonment Rate, 1980–2009

Source: Bureau of Justice Statistics. (2011). Key facts at a glance. Accessed March 1, 2011, from http://bjs.ojp.usdoj.gov/content/glance/incrt.cfm.

To many, the dramatic increase in the use of imprisonment, and the inequalities or disparities of imprisonment by race, suggest a fundamentally unfair American society. To others, disparities in imprison reflect real differences in criminal offending.

Finally, another criminal justice controversy pertains to the *types* of offenders that are subjected to incarceration. A popular viewpoint is that many drug offenders should not be incarcerated because they are benign criminals who require treatment, not punishment, to overcome their substance abuse problem. In the end, crime control and due process advocates can agree about one thing: Prisons are an exciting and controversial subject matter in criminal justice.

History of American Prisons

Overview and Major Themes

Although confinement has existed in Western societies for centuries, prisons as they are understood today are considered an American invention. At their inception, prisons, then symbolically known as penitentiaries, were hailed as an outgrowth of the Enlightenment in which criminal offenders were confined and expected to contemplate their criminal behavior and work toward their rehabilitation and ultimate redemption. Indeed, inmates were expected to be penitent, defined as feeling or expressing remorse for one's misdeeds or sins. As such, the penitentiary was designed as a place for criminals to repent. Throughout American history, prisons have reflected the social conditions of the day. Early prisons reflected the intense religiosity of the colonial era. Modern prisons reflect the pragmatic goals of incapacitation, crime control, and due process. Prisons have always been controversial and, like the history of the police, been marked by periods of reform. This section briefly highlights the social history of American prisons.

The Colonial Era, Pennsylvania System, and Auburn System

The colonial American criminal justice system was rooted in the English common law tradition in which most criminal offenses were punishable by death and corporal punishment, including torture and mutilation, were considered appropriate punishments of criminals. When criminals were detained, they were kept in municipal jails that were characterized by squalor, the inappropriate mixing of men, women, children, and criminals of diverse criminality, and brutal administrative control.[2]

Led by William Penn, the Pennsylvania Quakers were dissatisfied with the abuses of these early forms of confinement and initiated reforms of the colonial approach to correction in which physical punishment would be replaced by isolation. In 1787, Benjamin Franklin and Dr. Benjamin Rush (among other distinguished citizens) organized The Philadelphia Society for Alleviating the Miseries of Public Prisons, which mobilized the Commonwealth of Pennsylvania to set the international standard in prison design. It took decades to convince state leaders of the superiority of such an approach, but would culminate in the Eastern State Penitentiary that opened in 1829.

Eastern State Penitentiary was the most expensive American building of its day (it had running water and central heat before the White House), one of the most famous buildings in the world, and a major tourist attraction. As described earlier, the function of the Penitentiary was not simply to punish, but to move the criminal toward spiritual reflection and change. The Quaker-inspired system involved total isolation from other prisoners, labor in solitary confinement, and strictly enforced silence. The social control was extraordinarily strict, for instance inmates were hooded whenever they were outside their cells. Theoretically, the forced silence and extreme isolation would cause criminals to think about the wrongfulness of their crimes and become genuinely penitent.[3]

As a punishment philosophy, the Pennsylvania System was developed in the Eighteenth Century. However, the Auburn System began in 1816 with the opening of the Auburn Prison in New York—13 years before the opening of Eastern State Penitentiary. Although heavily influenced and similar to the Pennsylvania System, the Auburn System was a congregate system in which inmates ate and worked together during the day and were kept in solitary confinement at night with enforced silence at all times. The Auburn System was viewed as more humanistic in the sense that it replaced the systemic use of solitary confinement. But the Auburn System also employed the lockstep (inmates marching in single file, placing the right hand on the shoulder of the man ahead, and facing toward the guard), the striped suit, two-foot extensions of the walls between cells, and special seating arrangements at meals to insure strict silence. Auburn also introduced the tier system with several floors or wings that have stacked cells over another and classified (and punished) inmates by their level of compliance. By the 1830s, the Auburn System generally replaced the Pennsylvania System, which was discontinued as a prison approach by 1913.

The Reformatory Movement

During the Jacksonian Era spanning the first several decades of the Nineteenth Century, there was dissatisfaction with American prisons that essentially revolved around the perennial goals of crime control and due process. Upon visiting Eastern State Penitentiary in 1842, Charles Dickens wrote, "I hold this slow and daily tampering with the mysteries of the brain to be immeasurably worse than any torture of the body." In other words, the methods of correction inherent in the Pennsylvania and Auburn Systems were viewed as cruel, counterproductive, and flagrantly in violation of basic tenets of human, civil, and due process rights.

There was also the widespread public belief that crime threatened the stability and order of society, and prisons appeared to be doing little to reduce the crime rate. Even in the middle Nineteenth Century, the general public considered prisons as mere holding stations, regardless of how innovative their design, until criminals were released to offend again. Edgardo Rotman described the state of American prisons as follows:

> The elements of the original penitentiary designed, based on regimentation, isolation, religious conversion, and stead labor, had been subverted by a pervasive over-crowding, corruption, and cruelty. Prisoners were often living three and four to a cell designed for one, and prison discipline was medieval-like in character, with bizarre and brutal punishments commonplace in state institutions. Wardens did not so much deny this awful reality as explain it away, attributing most of the blame not to those who administered the system but to those who experienced it. Because the prisons were filled with immigrants who were ostensibly hardened to a life of crime and impervious to American traditions, those in charge had no choice but to rule over inmates with an iron hand.[4]

These concerns did not go unnoticed. The New York Prison Association commissioned Enoch Cobb Wines and Theodore Dwight to conduct a national survey of prisons and correctional methods. Inspired by their report, the National Congress on Penitentiary and Reformatory Discipline met in October 1870 in Cincinnati, Ohio and established principles of modern, humanistic correctional theory and practice. One of the most famous practitioners who placed the reformatory theory into practice was Zebulon Brockway. Brockway, who was warden of the Elmira (New York) Reformatory, infused educational programs, vocational training, an administrative and operating system based on military discipline, and a humanistic orientation to American corrections.[5]

Bureau of Prisons (BOP)

Another important correctional innovation was the development of a formalized federal prison system. In 1930, the Bureau of Prisons was established within the Department of Justice and charged with the management and regulation of all Federal penal and correctional institutions. This responsibility covered the administration of the 11 Federal prisons in operation at the time. At the end of 1930, the agency operated 14 facilities and over 13,000 inmates. By 1940, the BOP had grown to 24 facilities with 24,360 inmates. Except for a few fluctuations, the number of inmates did not change significantly between 1940 and 1980 when the population was 24,252. However, the number of facilities almost doubled (from 24 to 44) as the BOP gradually moved from operating large facilities confining inmates of many security levels to operating smaller facilities that each confined inmates with similar security needs. As a result of Federal law enforcement efforts and new legislation that dramatically altered sentencing in the Federal criminal justice system, the 1980s brought a significant increase in the number of Federal inmates. The Sentencing Reform Act of 1984 established determinate sentencing, abolished parole, and reduced good time; additionally, several mandatory minimum sentencing provisions were enacted in 1986, 1988, and 1990. From 1980 to 1989, the inmate population more than doubled, from just over 24,000 to almost 58,000. During the 1990s, the population more than doubled again. Today, the BOP inmate population is more than 210,000 and the staff population is nearly 40,000.[6]

The Hands-Off Doctrine, Prisonization, and Deprivation

The reforms initiated by Brockway and others proliferated across the country as correctional systems attempted to strike a balance between punishing offenders to assuage concerns about public safety and providing the opportunities for rehabilitation. For many decades, the prison rate was low and remained relatively constant.[7] A "hands-off" doctrine characterized American prisons whereby prison administrators enjoyed unfettered discretion to run their facilities without outside influence or pressure from the government, press, or academics.

By 1940, academic criminologists began to gain entrée into American prisons. What they described was unsettling. Donald Clemmer's *The Prison Community* published in 1940 showed that prisons were wholly separate micro-societies that contained their own language or argot, values, beliefs, and norms, and expectations of behavior. Clemmer developed the idea of prisonization defined as the socialization process whereby inmates embrace the oppositional and antisocial culture of the prisoner. A variety of circumstances made prisonization more likely, such as serving a lengthy sentence, having an unstable personality and associating with similarly disturbed inmates, having few positive relations with those on the outside, readily integrating into prison culture, blindly accepting prison dogma, associating with hardened offenders or career criminals, and continuing to engage in antisocial behavior while imprisoned.[8] Indeed, Norman Hayner and Ellis Ash, two contemporaries of Clemmer, depicted prison conditions in the following way, "a clear realization of the degenerating influence of our present prison system should encourage more experiments aiming to devise a community for offenders that will actually rehabilitate."[9]

In 1958, Gresham Sykes' *The Society of Captives: A Study of a Maximum Security Prison* portrayed the prison as a despotic, punitive, inhumane social organization designed purely for punishment, retribution, and retaliation—not rehabilitation. This became known as the deprivation model of inmate behavior in which guards created a regime or social order that forced inmates to conform. The regime was totalitarian, not because guards felt this was the best way to proceed, but rather because of society's desire to prevent escape and disorder. Sykes highlighted the deficiencies of this approach, including the lack of a sense of duty among those who were held captive, the obvious fallacies of coercion, the pathetic collection of rewards and punishments to induce compliance, and the strong pressures toward the corruption of the guard in the form of friendship, reciprocity, and the transfer of duties into the hands of trusted inmates. The deprivation resulted in five pains of imprisonment: (1) deprivation of liberty, (2) deprivation of goods and services, (3) deprivation of heterosexual relationships, (4) deprivation of autonomy, (5) deprivation of security.

To adjust to this new environment, Sykes developed archetypal inmate roles, such as rats, center men (those who aligned with guards), gorillas, merchants, wolves, punks, real men, toughs, etc.[10] Over time, criminologists have found that the deprivation model of inmate behavior is still relevant to the present day and that correctional facilities characterized by regimes of rigid social control tended to experience more inmate-related problems than facilities with a treatment or less repressive form of administrative control.[11]

Importation and the Crime Boom, Circa 1965–1993

For all of the strengths of the deprivation model as an explanation of inmate behavior, there is a glaring weakness. Prisoners are inarguably among the most violent and lawless of citizens, thus it should be expected that prisons are dangerous, bad places given the concentration of antisocial people. Academic penology ushered in a subtle but important change in our national view of prisons, one that persists today. The point is this. Early critiques of prison centered on the deplorable conditions of confinement and the unjust and unconstitutional treatment of inmates. These were righteous concerns about due process violations. But, academic penologists usually attributed blame for the appalling state of American prisons toward the criminal justice system (e.g., wardens, prison administrators, correctional officers), not the inmates. Indeed, whether one blames the criminal justice system or criminals for various crime-related problems often informs whether one is crime control or due process oriented.

Ironically, it was a former prisoner turned academic named John Irwin who along with Donald Cressey advanced a new explanation of prisoner behavior in 1962.[12] The importation model argued that prisoner behavior and the conditions of prisons were mostly a function of the characteristics, values, beliefs, and behaviors that criminals employed on the outside of prison. In other words, inmates of varying degrees of criminality imported their behavioral repertoire and behaved accordingly. To connect to the earlier point, prison conditions were often horrendous because of the commensurate behavior that offenders brought to the facility. The importation model has received substantial empirical support evidenced by the continuity in criminal behavior among the most hardened offenders.

It was during the late 1960s where the link between prisons and conventional society achieved its greatest synergy since the initial design of the penitentiary in the early Eighteenth Century. The 1960s and 1970s were decades of great turmoil, malaise, and revolution that centered on civil rights, minority rights, women's rights, worker's rights, and overall a broadening liberalization of society. Also occurring between 1965 and 1993 was an unprecedented increase in the crime rate.[13] Rising crime rates, particularly for violent crimes such as murder, rape, and robbery, became a primary concern of the general public and an increasingly important political item. To appear "soft" on crime was to virtually guarantee a loss at election polls. American society generally shifted to the political right during the 1980s and 1990s, and correctional policy followed suit.

The New Penology and Beyond

As shown in Figure 9-1, the imprisonment rate increased approximately 400% since 1980. Imprisonment became the standard method of punishing criminal offenders and incapacitation was the assumed rationale for confinement. Malcolm Feeley and Jonathan Simon dubbed this approach "the new penology," defined as the management of groups or sub-populations of offenders based on their actuarial risk to society. The new penology emphasized control and surveillance of offenders, considered rehabilitation to be largely idealistic, and de-emphasized the likelihood of offender reintegration.[14] For ideological reasons discussed in the introduction of this chapter, the increased reliance on imprisonment was portrayed as unjust and discriminatory. Moreover, many criminologists disliked and were apparently confused by the excessive use of prison during an era of falling crime rates that occurred from about 1993 to the present.

Just as prisons were the policy response to the proliferation of crime during the latter part of the Twentieth Century, the exponential growth in imprisonment was also the chief reason for the rather amazing decline in crime that occurred and continues to occur from approximately 1991 to the present. During this era, two correctional factors contributed to the crime decline. First, the likelihood that criminal offender were sentenced to prison increased. Second, the amount of time served behind bars increased dramatically as most states adopted the 85% federal truth-in-sentencing standard. The impact of these policies and practices was that more active and chronic offenders were being sentenced to prison and they were staying there for longer periods of time. Criminologists have feverishly studied the effects of prison expansion on crime, and the bottom line is that the prison boom explained between 13 to 54% of the recent crime decline.[15] Based on official and victimization data, the violent crime rate dropped between 34 to 50% from 1991 to 2001 and many of the largest American cities experienced reductions in the homicide rates upward of 80%.[16]

Compared to penitentiaries, reformatories, and prisons from any other era in American history, the contemporary prison is the safest, provides the most humane treatment, provides the most treatment and programming, and is the most transparent in terms of its openness to outside scrutiny. Today's correctional systems use scientifically influenced actuarial methods to appropriately classify, supervise, treat, and manage prisoners based on their level of risk. Unfortunately, there are currently and always have been a cadre of criminal offenders who are thoroughly opposed to quitting crime and for whom there is no realistic chance of rehabilitation. Many of the most serious criminals are intractably antisocial and are increasingly punished via an extreme form of solitary confinement.[17] In this sense, the American prison has regressed to the methods of the Pennsylvania System to punish the most non-compliant prisoners.

Statistical Profile of Prisoners and Prisons

Prisoner Population

Overall, the United States imprisoned more than 1.6 million persons as of December 2010, the most recent point of data collection. The rate of imprisonment was 502 per 100,000 residents. When taking into account those who have been imprisoned, more than 5.6 million Americans, or one in every 37 adults, have prison experience. The prisoner population is 93% male and 7% female. Thus, the male imprisonment rate is 14 times higher than the female imprisonment rate. By race and ethnicity, the prisoner population is 38% African American, 34% Caucasian, 21% Hispanic, and 7% multi-racial or other. In the federal Bureau of Prisons (BOP), 30% of inmates were foreign citizens the majority of whom were Mexican Nationals. Blacks have an imprisonment rate that is six times higher than the rate for whites and three times higher than the rate for Hispanics. Differential involvement in criminal activity accounts for these racial and ethnic disparities.[18]

Offense Type

The American prisoner population is increasingly comprised of violent offenders. From 1980 to 2000, the proportion of state prisoners who were confined for a violent crime increased by more than 200%. Today, about 52% of state prisoners were incarcerated for a violent offense. The most common offense types were robbery and murder/manslaughter. Roughly 18% of state prisoners were confined for property offenses, the most common of which was burglary. Drug offenders comprised 18% of offenders and those convicted of public-order crimes comprised 9% of prison admissions. By comparison, drug offenders comprised 51% of the federal inmate population. However, the number of federal offenders incarcerated for violent offenses has increased dramatically. In the past decade and a half, the amount inmates in federal custody increased nearly 150% for homicide and nearly 100% for other serious violent crimes.[19]

Time Served and Truth-in-Sentencing

The criminal justice system goes to rather extraordinary efforts to utilize community corrections before sending felons to prison. In terms of its costs, prison is the last resort. Curiously, once an offender is sentenced to prison, the criminal justice system again goes to great lengths to release him or her from custody. Since the 1970s, many state legislatures have sought to reduce judicial discretion in sentencing and the determination of when the conditions of a sentence have been satisfied. Determinate sentences, mandatory minimum sentences, and guidelines-based sentencing have increased the predictability of release. Today, 90% of state prisoners can estimate their probable release date and more than 95% of inmates will be released from prison (very few are sentenced to death or meaningful life-imprisonment). For these reasons, there tends to be very little truth-in-sentencing, defined as the correspondence between the prison sentence and the time actually served prior to prison release.[20]

Indeed, the statistics on how little time felons actually serve in prison are alarming. Lawrence Greenfeld analyzed the time served in prison for violent offenders in 31 states. These persons had been convicted of murder, kidnapping, rape, sexual assault, robbery, assault, extortion, intimidation, reckless endangerment, hit-and-run driving with injury, or child abuse. Overall, violent offenders were sentenced to 89 months in prison but served just 43 months on average. In other words, the most violent criminals in the United States served about 48 percent of their actual sentences. The average sentence, average time served, and percent of sentence served followed this trend even for the most serious offenses. For example:

- Homicide   149 months   71 months   48%
- Rape   117 months   65 months   56%
- Kidnapping   104 months   52 months   50%
- Robbery   95 months   44 months   46%
- Sexual assault 72 months   35 months   49%
- Assault   61 months   29 months   48%

The Violent Crime Control and Law Enforcement Act of 1994 rectified the truth-in-sentencing problem by assuring that offenders served a larger portion of their sentences. By 1998, incentive grants were awarded to 27 states and the District of Columbia to require that violent offenders serve at least 85% of their sentence. Eleven additional states adopted truth-in-sentencing laws in 1995. Immediately prior to the 1994 legislation, violent offenders were sentenced to 85 months and served 45 months on average. After, the average sentence for a violent offender was 104 months and the average time served was 88 months. Nationally, about 70% of state prison admissions for a violent offense were required to serve at least 85% of their sentence. Nearly one in five inmates (18%) served their entire prison sentence.[21]

State prison systems have been following the lead of the federal system for some time. William Sabol and John McGready of The Urban Institute examined time served in prison by federal offenders between 1986 and 1997. The results were comparable to the trends produced from data from state prisoners. Between 1986 and 1997, federal prison sentences increased from 39 months, on average, to 54 months and the average time served of a BOP inmate increased from 21 months to 47 months. In terms of proportion of time served, this increased from 58 to 87%.

From the mid 1980s to mid 1990s, the number of BOP inmates increased 65%of this increase was attributable to an increase in the time served. During this time frame, the time served until first release nearly doubled from 15 months to 29 months on average. The number of federal inmates serving life sentences increased 872%![22]

Prison Facilities

The Bureau of Justice Statistics has conducted a census of correctional facilities in 1974, 1979, 1984, 1990, 1995, 2000, and 2005 to produce a national snapshot of prison systems in the United States. Based on data from the most recent census, James Stephan found that there were 1,821 federal, state, and private correctional facilities. About 71% are confinement facilities and the remaining 29% are community-based facilities. About 53% of all facilities were rated as minimum-security, 26% as medium-security, and 20% as maximum-security. Commensurately, 40% of inmates were classified as minimum-security, 40% as medium-security, and 20% as maximum-security.[23] Private prisons house slightly more than 5% of the total prisoner population,[24] are generally no more cost-effective than public prisons,[25] and produce equivalent recidivism outcomes as public prisons.[26]

The overall safety of correctional facilities depends on the classification of the inmates and the facility. For instance, assaults on inmates and staff were overwhelmingly concentrated in state prison facilities and significantly less common in federal and private facilities. Moreover, the rate of inmate assaults against staff was dramatically higher in maximum-security facilities compared to medium- and ultimately minimum-security facilities. In state correctional facilities, the rate of assault on staff was *61 times* greater in maximum-security than minimum-security facilities. The respective differences in assault rates were eight times in private facilities and four times in federal facilities.

Correctional facilities serve a variety of functions to address the punishment and treatment needs of the inmates. The primary purpose is general confinement evidenced that nearly all correctional purposes are simply geared toward general confinement or incapacitation. Correctional facilities are also used for boot camp/shock incarceration; reception, diagnosis, and classification; medical treatment or hospitalization; substance abuse treatment; youthful offender placement; and work-release programs. The second most common facility type is described as "other." These facilities house very specific sub-populations of offenders, such as geriatric inmates, sex offenders, inmates in protective custody, inmates with profound psychiatric problems, and condemned offenders.

As a rule, prisons are crowded places with limited capacity to house inmates. The rated capacity is the number of beds or inmates assigned by a rating official to institutions within a jurisdiction. The operational capacity is the number of inmates that can be accommodated based on the facility's staff, programs, and services. The design capacity is the number of inmates that planners intended for the facility. One in five correctional facilities operated under a court order or consent decree to limit its population. The BOP and 24 state prison systems operated above capacity, indeed the BOP operated at nearly 150% of rated capacity. Servicing these facilities is a correctional work staff of 445,000.[27]

Correctional Programs and Treatment

This book has documented the assortment of risk factors and individual-level deficiencies that present so many difficulties for serious criminal offenders. Data on educational attainment by criminal justice status are illustrative. State and federal prisoners were 200 to 300% more likely than the general population to have dropped out of completed high school. The prevalence of college graduation is 1,100% higher among the general population than the state prisoner population. Nearly 50% of prisoners reported that behavioral problems, academic difficulties, disinterest, or criminal activity as the reasons why they dropped out of high school. Depending on the inmate's level of education, the unemployment rate among prisoners was between 400 to 800% higher than the general population. Approximately 30% of prisoners derived their income from illegal sources in the month before their most recent arrest. Finally, the prevalence of homelessness and welfare dependency among prisoners is several times the rate of these social problems among the general population.[28]

To surmount these deficiencies, correctional facilities offer an array of educational and treatment programs to facilitate the rehabilitation of prisoners. Caroline Wolf Harlow of the Bureau of Justice Statistics reviewed educational programs and other treatment amenities among federal, state, and private prisons. Federal prisons have the greatest resources and offer the most educational programs. All facilities within the Bureau of Prisons (BOP) have an education program that provides basic adult education and secondary education, 94% provide vocational training, 60% provide special education, and more than 80% provide college courses. More than 90% of state prisons provide educational programs, 56% provide vocational training, 40%

provide special education, and 27% provide college courses. In private prisons, 88% offer educational programs, 44% provide vocational training, 22% provide special education, and 27% offer college courses. Despite the availability of these programs, inmates only modestly take advantage. About 52% of state prisoners and 57% of federal prisoners have participated in an educational program during their current incarceration. Vocational programs are the most popular among inmates because they are an opportunity to learn a particular trade to use after release.[29]

Prisons also offer an array of work, treatment, and counseling services to inmates. Across federal, state, and private facilities, approximately 97% of confinement facilities and 75% of community-based facilities provide work programs. The most common forms of prisoner work were facility support services and public works programs. About 46% of prisons had prison industries, 29% operated farms or other agricultural activities, and 60% performed road and parks maintenance.

More correctional facilities provided counseling programs than either educational or work programs. Indeed, 97% of state confinement facilities, 93% of state community-based facilities, and 92% of BOP facilities offered counseling or other special programs to inmates. Drug and alcohol dependency counseling or awareness was the most common. Among facilities providing counseling programs, all BOP facilities, 66% of state, and 46% of private facilities offered psychological and psychiatric counseling. Counseling services for employment and job skills, life skills and community adjustment, HIV/AIDS awareness and education, parenting classes, sex offender treatment, and others are also provided.[30]

Correctional treatment is certainly difficult given the multitude of problems (attitudinal, behavioral, mental health, substance abuse, etc.) that the average prisoner has. Moreover, many criminals have absolutely no intentions of reducing their antisocial behavior upon release from custody. Fortunately, there are a variety of correctional programs that seek to rehabilitate criminal offenders. For instance, Moral Reconation Therapy (MRT) increases the moral reasoning ability of offenders. Reasoning and Rehabilitation (RR) programs seek to change antisocial or criminogenic thinking patterns and attitudes. Both MRT and RR are cognitive treatments designed to correct maladaptive/criminal thoughts, beliefs, and attitudes into conventional and pro-social ones. To date, they have produced modestly positive treatment outcomes.[31]

Similarly, evaluations of correctional substance abuse treatment programs and therapeutic communities have shown favorable results particularly when there is continuity in care from prison to the community. Vocational and work programs have been shown to reduce recidivism and improve job readiness skills for ex-offenders. Educational programs do not reduce recidivism but increase the educational achievement scores of offenders. In sum, assorted correctional programming has proven to be helpful in the sense that offenders who participate in treatment programs tend to reintegrate into society better and desist from crime sooner than prisoners who do not.[32]

Collateral Costs of Imprisonment

The American correctional population creates a variety of collateral costs that likely have wide-reaching impact on society. The majority of men and women behind bars are parents meaning that nearly 1.5 million children under the age of 18, more than 2% of the national child population, have one or more parents currently in prison. Approximately 80% of prisoners see their children less than once per month.[33] Due to parental incarceration, these children are shunted into various living conditions with various caregivers, such as grandparents, other relatives, foster homes, and other social service agencies. Given the exceedingly high rates of substance abuse, unemployment, mental illness, and abusive criminal behavior, many children of prisoners are exposed to some of the most deleterious social environments.

The collateral costs of imprisonment also extend to the communities from which prisoners originate. John Hagan and Ronet Dinovitzer identified several ways that incarceration damages communities, social institutions, and prisoners' likelihood of reintegration. For instance, prisoners have lackluster work histories that are further damaged by ex-convict status. Thus, they are less able to contribute to their families and communities. Additionally, many prisoners have no intentions of "going straight" and instead return to their neighborhoods and immediately engage in damaging criminal behavior. To the most impoverished communities, a large increase in paroled offenders can result in a substantial short-term crime wave. In sum, the large correctional population has serious implications for the prosperity and sustainability of social institutions, such as family and work.[34]

◆ Prisoner Criminality

Criminal History

Since prison is the punishment of last resort, the criminality of prisoners is significantly higher than the criminality of offenders who are placed on intermediate sanctions. Generally speaking, one has to earn their way to prison via their pronounced and recurrent antisocial behavior. This applies to the most violent and notorious criminals and even the seemingly non-serious offenders. Matthew Durose and Christopher Mumola of the Bureau of Justice Statistics recently created a profile of nonviolent prisoners released from prisons in 15 states. Nonviolent offenders were defined as persons convicted of drug violations, theft, or burglary. In other words, these were not offenders who were convicted of murder or rape, but instead those convicted of what are commonly considered "garden variety" crimes. The following are highlights of what the average criminal history of a nonviolent (non-serious) prisoner:

- Over 40% had less than a high school education.
- Nearly 70% were using drugs in the month preceding the commitment offense.
- About 40% were using drugs during their commitment offense.
- About 95% had a prior arrest history.
- Over 84% had previously been convicted of a crime.
- The average number of prior arrests was 9.3.
- The average number of prior convictions was 4.1
- Over 50% had three or more prior prison or probation sentences.
- About 64% were on parole, probation, or escape at the time of their commitment offense.
- Over 88% had any "serious offender" indicator on their rap sheet.[35]

Extensive criminal history was also found in an investigation of drug offenders charged in federal district courts. John Scalia examined the offending patterns of nearly 40,000 drug suspects referred to United States attorneys in 1999. Over 65% of those charged had previously been arrested and 505 had previously been convicted of a crime, 33% for a felony. About 44% of federal drug offenders had 5 or more prior arrests, which is the standard criminological measure for career or habitual criminality. One in three federal drug offenders in the sample were already under criminal justice supervision upon their arrest.[36]

This extreme risk profile not only applies to adult prisoners, but also to juvenile delinquents. For example, Brent Benda and Connie Tollett analyzed the criminal histories of 244 adolescents who had been in a serious offender programs operated by the Arkansas Division of Youth Services (DYS). The criminal history of these adolescents indicated an array of serious risk factors. On average, these offenders first committed crime at age 12, first used drugs at age 12, first carried a deadly weapon at age 13, and had previously been confined to a juvenile detention center. Maternal and paternal drug abuse, neglect and abuse, family strife, and other family members who had also been imprisoned characterized their family backgrounds. Benda and Tollett also found that criminal history was itself the greatest predictor of subsequent recidivism and return to confinement. For example, youths who had prior commitments to DYS were nearly 14 times more likely to be returned to confinement than youths without prior incarcerations. Similarly, youths with prior weapons offenses were 335% and gang members 203% more likely to be returned to DYS.[37]

Institutional Misconduct

Given the pronounced criminality of most prisoners and the stressful conditions of prison life, inmate violence and misconduct behind bars are fairly commonplace. In their census of federal and state correctional facilities, James Stephan and Jennifer Karberg found that more than 34,000 inmate-on-inmate assaults occurred annually, an average of 94 per day. Inmates murdered 51 fellow inmates in 2000, an average of nearly one murder per week. Additionally, inmates totaled nearly 18,000 assaults against staff members, an average of nearly 50 per day. In 2000, five of these assaults resulted in the death of prison officials. While in custody, inmates also caused 606 major disturbances defined as incidents involving five or more inmates and resulting in serious injury or significant property damage, set 343 fires, and caused 639 other disturbances.[38] The projected rate of crime per 100,000 persons is much higher in prisons than in American society. For instance, Matt DeLisi found that the prison murder rate was nearly twice the national murder rate and the incidence of male-on-male sexual assault in prison was higher than forcible rape rates in conventional society. Rates for arson, aggravated assault, and theft were dramatically higher behind bars than in conventional society.

Most inmate violence and misconduct can be attributable to the most habitual and recalcitrant criminals. For example, about 30% of inmates are never contacted for prison violations and more than 70% are never contacted for a serious or violent violation. On the other hand, 40% of inmates continued to be chronic criminal offenders even while incarcerated. A small cadre of inmates accounted for 100% of the murders, 75% of the rapes, and 80% of the arson incidents occurring in one state's prison system.[39] Indeed, a variety of studies have found that individual-level characteristics of prisoners, such as their criminal propensity, criminal record, number of prior prison sentences, psychopathology, and antisocial attitudes are the strongest predictors of continued misconduct, non-compliance, and violence behind bars.[40]

Post-Release Recidivism

The staggeringly high recidivism rates among released prisoners are arguably the main reason that many citizens, social commentators, and academics are critical of prisons. Indeed, the norm among parolees or ex-convicts who served their entire prison term to expiration is to rather quickly engage in criminal behavior. Patrick Langan and David Levin of the Bureau of Justice Statistics conducted the most impressive study of recidivism in terms of the scope, magnitude, and representativeness of their sample. Langan and Levin tracked more than 27,000 former inmates for three years after their release from prison in 1994. The study group represented two-thirds of all prisoners released during that year and contained released offenders from Arizona, California, Delaware, Florida, Illinois, Maryland, Michigan, Minnesota, New Jersey, New York,

North Carolina, Ohio, Oregon, Texas, and Virginia. Four measures of recidivism were used: re-arrest, re-conviction, re-sentence to prison, and return to prison with or without a new sentence.[41]

Within three years from their release from prison, the following are highlights from Langan and Levin's study:

- 68% of prisoners were re-arrested for a new offense (almost exclusively a felony or serious misdemeanor).

- 47% were re-convicted for a new crime.

- 25% were re-sentenced to prison for a new crime.

- 52% were back in prison for new crimes or parole violations.

- 30% of the recidivism occurred within 6 months of release and 44% occurred by the end of the first year.

- Prisoners committed an average of four new crimes after release.

- Offenders averaged 18 arrest charges over their criminal career.

- About 6% of prisoners totaled 45 or more career arrests.

- Among prisoners with the lengthiest criminal records, 82% recidivated.

- Prisoners were arrested for homicide at a rate 53 times higher than the homicide arrest rate for the adult population.

- No evidence was found that spending more time in prison raised the recidivism rate. The evidence was mixed regarding whether serving more time reduced recidivism.[42]

The same theme is found using different classifications or types of offenders. Patrick Langan, Erica Schmitt, and Matthew Durose studied nearly 10,000 sex offenders from the same 15-state-sample described before. The sex offender sub-sample contained 3,115 rapists; 6,576 sexual assaulters; 4,295 child molesters, and 443 statutory rapists. The sex offenders comprised less than 4% of all offenders and had an average prison sentence of 8 years of which they served over three years (45 percent of total sentence).

Compared to non-sex offenders, sex offenders were 400% more likely to be re-arrested for a new sex crime. About 40% of the recidivism occurred within one year of release. Sex offenders were 200% more likely than non-sex offenders to be re-arrested for child molestation. Overall, the more prior arrests that a sex offender has, the greater recidivism for all types of crimes. Within three years of release, 43% of sex offenders were re-arrested, 24% were re-convicted, and nearly 40% were returned to prison.

Like other criminals, sex offenders tended to have extensive criminal histories for a multitude of crimes. Nearly 80% had previously been arrested, 58% had prior convictions, 25% had previously been imprisoned, and 14% had prior convictions for a violent sex offense.[43] The average number of prior arrests among sex offenders was nearly five, again the standard threshold for habitual criminality.[44]

◆ Summary: Balancing Crime Control and Due Process

- Prisons are among the most controversial of criminal justice topics and are critiqued from both crime control and due process perspectives.

- The Pennsylvania System viewed prison as an opportunity for the offender to be redeemed through isolation, work, prayer, and strict social control.

- The Auburn System employed the same general philosophy but allowed inmates to congregate for work during the day.

- Solitary confinement was historically not a punishment but the means to be penitent.

- Prisons generally reflect the social conditions of the era, reflecting the degree of public leniency and punitiveness, and can be used to reduce crime.

- Deprivation theorists assert that prison conditions cause inmate behavior; importation theorists assert that inmate characteristics do.

- More than 2.4 million people are held in a variety of correctional facilities in the United States.

- Racial and ethnic minorities, such as African Americans and Hispanics, commit crime and are imprisoned at levels that are disproportionate to their numbers in the general population.

- Because so few offenders served even half of their sentence, the federal and many state correctional systems mandated that the most serious criminals serve at least 85% of their sentence to reflect truth-in-sentencing.

- The average prison provides educational and vocational training as well as several types of treatment.

- Prison creates collateral costs, such as damaging family and work networks in communities from which inmate originate.

- The criminality of prisoners is extremely high based on their criminal histories, institutional misconduct, and post-release recidivism rates.

- The extreme criminality of prisoners lends support to the notion that prison is the punishment of last resort in the corrections continuum.

Web Links

American Correctional Association
(www.aca.org)

Association of State Correctional Administrators
(www.asca.net)

Bureau of Justice Statistics: Corrections Statistics
(www.ojp.usdoj.gov/bjs/correct.htm)

Federal Bureau of Prisons
(www.bop.gov/)

National GAINS Center
(www.gainscenter.samhsa.gov/html/default.asp)

National Institute of Corrections
(www.nicic.org/)

National Law Enforcement and Corrections Technology Center
(www.nlectc.org/)

State Departments of Corrections
(www.corrections.com/links/state.html)

The Center for Community Corrections
(www.communitycorrectionsworks.org)

Questions

1. Inmates harangue the youthful offenders, use shocking street language and profanity, and intimidate the youths in hopes that the youths will renounce their delinquency and lead productive lives. This describes which program?

   a. Boot camp
   b. Scared straight
   c. Juvenile intimidation program
   d. Just say no

2. Although heavily influenced by and similar to the Pennsylvania System, the _____ was a congregate system in which inmates ate and worked together during the day and were kept in solitary confinement at night with enforced silence at all times.

   a. New York system
   b. Carolina system
   c. Auburn system
   d. Franklin system

3. Over time, criminologists have found that the deprivation model of inmate behavior is irrelevant to the present day.

   a. True
   b. False

4. Based on official and victimization data, the violent crime rate dropped between 34 to 50% from 1991 to 2001 and many of the largest American cities experienced reductions in the homicide rates upwards of 80%.

   a. True
   b. False

5. When taking into account those who have been imprisoned, more than 5.6 million Americans, or one in every 37 adults, have prison experience.

   a. True
   b. False

6. According to Lawrence Greenfield, the average time served in prison for homicide was:

   a. 65 months
   b. 71 months
   c. 89 months
   d. 102 months

7. Assaults on inmates and staff are overwhelmingly concentrated in federal prison facilities and significantly less common in state and private facilities.

   a. True
   b. False

8. State and federal prisoners were _____ more likely than the general population to have dropped out of high school.

    a. 200 to 300%
    b. 100 to 200%
    c. 300 to 400%
    d. None of the above

9. The majority of men and women behind bars are parents, which means that nearly 1.5 million children under the age of 18, or more than 2% of the national child population, have one or more parents currently in prison.

    a. True
    b. False

10. According to the Arkansas Division of Youth Services, juveniles, on average, first committed crime at age _____, first used drugs at age 12, first carried a deadly weapon at age _____, and had previously been confined to a juvenile detention center.

    a. 12 and 13
    b. 13 and 15
    c. 11 and 14
    d. 12 and 16

Endnotes

1. Petrosino, A., Turpin-Petrosino, C., & Buehler, J. (2003). Scared Straight and other juvenile awareness programs for preventing juvenile delinquency: A systematic review of the randomized experimental evidence. *Annals of the American Academy of Political and Social Science, 589*, 41–62.
2. Excellent primers on the history of American prisons are Friedman, L. M. (1993). *Crime and punishment in American history.* New York: Bantam Books; Morris, N., & Rothman, D. J. (1998). *The Oxford history of the prison: The practice of punishment in Western society.* New York: Oxford University Press.
3. Retrieved March 1, 2011, from http://www.easternstate.org/history/sixpage.html; A & E. (2002). The big house: Eastern State Penitentiary. A & E VHS Video.
4. Rotman, E. (1998). The failure of reform: United States, 1865–1965. In Morris, N., & Rothman, D. J. (1998). *The Oxford history of the prison: The practice of punishment in Western society* (pp. 151–177). New York: Oxford University Press, p. 152.
5. Brockway, Z. R. (1994). The American reformatory prison system. In J. E. Jacoby (Ed.), *Classics of criminology* (pp. 387–396). Prospect Heights, IL: Waveland Press.
6. Federal Bureau of Prisons. (2006). *A brief history of the Bureau of Prisons.* Washington, DC: U. S. Department of Justice, Retrieved March 1, 2011, from http://www.bop.gov/about/index.jsp; West, H. C., & Sabol, W. J. (2010). *Prisoners in 2009.* Washington, DC: U. S. Department of Justice, Office of Justice Programs, Bureau of Justice Statistics.
7. Blumstein, A., & Cohen, J. (1973). A theory of the stability of punishment. *Journal of Criminal Law and Criminology, 64*, 198–207
8. Clemmer, D. (1940). *The prison community.* New York: Holt, Rinehart, and Winston; Clemmer, D. (1950). Observations on imprisonment as a source of criminality. *Journal of Criminal Law and Criminology, 41*, 311–19.
9. Hayner, N. S., & Ash, E. (1940). The prison as a community. American Sociological Review, 5, 577–583 (p. 583).
10. Sykes, G. M. (1958). *The society of captives: A study of a maximum-security prison.* Princeton, NJ: Princeton University Press.
11. Akers, R., Hayner, N., & Gruninger, W. (1977). Prisonization in five countries: Type of prison and inmate characteristics. *Criminology, 14*, 527–554; Huebner, B. M. (2003). Administrative determinants of inmate violence: A multilevel analysis. *Journal of Criminal Justice, 31*, 107–117; Jiang, S., & Fisher-Giorlando, M. (2002). Inmate misconduct: A test of the deprivation, importation, and situational models. *The Prison Journal, 82*, 335–358; Poole, E. D., & Regoli, R. M. (1983). Violence in juvenile institutions: A comparative study. *Criminology, 21*, 213–232; Reisig, M. D., & Lee, Y. (2000). Prisonization in the Republic of Korea. *Journal of Criminal Justice, 28*, 23–31; Walters, G. D. (2003). Changes in criminal thinking and identity in novice and experienced inmates: Prisonization revisited. *Criminal Justice and Behavior, 30*, 399–421; Wheeler, S. (1961). Socialization in correctional communities. *American Sociological Review, 26*, 697–712.
12. Irwin, J., & Cressey, D. (1962). Thieves, convicts, and the inmate culture. *Social Problems, 10*, 142–155.

13. Jacobs, J. B. (1977). *Stateville: The penitentiary in mass society.* Chicago: University of Chicago Press; Wilson, J. Q. (1983). *Thinking about crime,* revised edition. New York: Vintage Books.
14. Feeley, M. M., & Simon, J. (1992). The new penology: Notes on the emerging strategy of corrections ad its implications. *Criminology,* 30, 449–474.
15. Conklin, J. E. (2003). *Why crime rates fell.* Boston, MA: Allyn & Bacon.
16. Levitt, S. D. (2004). Understanding why crime fell in the 1990s: Four factors that explain the decline and six that do not. *Journal of Economic Perspectives,* 18, 163–190.
17. On the deleterious effects of solitary confinement, see Andersen, H. S., Sestoft, D., Lillebaek, T., Gabrielsen, G., & Hemmingsen, R. (2003). A longitudinal study of prisoners on remand: Repeated measures of psychopathology in the initial phase of solitary versus non-solitary confinement. *International Journal of Law and Psychiatry,* 26, 165–177.
18. West & Sabol, note 13.
19. West & Sabol, note 13.
20. Greenfeld, L. A. (1995). *Prison sentences and time served for violence.* Washington, DC: U. S. Department of Justice, Office of Justice Programs, Bureau of Justice Statistics.
21. Ditton, P. M., & Wilson, D. J. (1999). *Truth in sentencing in state prisons.* Washington, DC: U. S. Department of Justice, Office of Justice Programs, Bureau of Justice Statistics.
22. Sabol, W. J., & McGready, J. (1999). *Time served in prison by federal offenders, 1986–1997.* Washington, DC: U. S. Department of Justice, Office of Justice Programs, Bureau of Justice Statistics.
23. Stephan, J. J. (2008). *Census of state and federal correctional facilities, 2005.* Washington, DC: U. S. Department of Justice, Office of Justice Programs, Bureau of Justice Statistics.
24. Camp, S. D., & Gaes, G. G. (2002). Growth and quality of U.S. private prisons: Evidence from a national survey. *Criminology & Public Policy,* 1, 427–450.
25. Pratt, T. C., & Maahs, J. (1999). Are private prisons more cost-effective than public prisons? A meta-analysis of evaluation research studies. *Crime & Delinquency,* 45, 358–371.
26. Bales, W. D., Bedard, L. E., Quinn, S. T., Ensley, D. T., & Holley, G. P. (2005). Recidivism of public and private state prison inmates in Florida. *Criminology & Public Policy,* 4, 57–82.
27. Stephan, note 30.
28. Harlow, C. W. (2003). *Education and correctional populations.* Washington, DC: U. S. Department of Justice, Office of Justice Programs, Bureau of Justice Statistics.
29. Harlow, note 35.
30. Stephan, note 30.
31. Farrington, D. P., & Welsh, B. C. (2005). Randomized experiments in criminology: What have we learned in the last two decades? *Journal of Experimental Criminology,* 1, 9–38; Allen, L. C., MacKenzie, D. L., & Hickman, L. J. (2001). The effectiveness of cognitive behavioral treatment for adult offenders: A methodological, quality-based review. *International Journal of Offender Therapy and Comparative Criminology,* 45, 498–514.
32. For exhaustive reviews of correctional treatment or evaluations of specific programs, see Seiter, R. P., & Kadela, K. R. (2003). Prisoner reentry: What works, what does not, and what is promising. *Crime & Delinquency,* 49, 360–388; Prendergast, M. L., & Wexler, H. K. (2004). Correctional substance abuse treatment programs in California: A historical perspective. *The Prison Journal,* 84, 8–35; Cullen, F. T. (2005). The 12 people who saved

rehabilitation: How the science of criminology made a difference. *Criminology,* 43, 1–42; Anglin, M. D., & Maugh, T. H. (1992). Ensuring success in interventions with drug-abusing offenders. *Annals of the American Academy of Political and Social Science,* 521, 66–90; Gendreau, P., & Ross, R. (1987). Revivification of rehabilitation: Evidence from the 1980s. *Justice Quarterly,* 4, 349–407; Lipton, D. S. (1998). Therapeutic community treatment programming in corrections. *Psychology, Crime, and Law,* 4, 213–263; Lipsey, M. W., & Wilson, D. B. (1993). The efficacy of psychological, educational, and behavioral treatment: Confirmation from meta-analysis. *American Psychologist,* 48, 1181–1209.

33. Mumola, C. J. (2000). *Incarcerated parents and their children.* Washington, DC: U. S. Department of Justice, Office of Justice Programs, Bureau of Justice Statistics.
34. Hagan, J., & Dinovitzer, R. (1999). Collateral consequences of imprisonment for children, communities, and prisoners. *Crime & Justice,* 26, 121–162.
35. Durose, M. R., & Mumola, C. J. (2004). *Profile of nonviolent offenders existing state prisons.* Washington, DC: U. S. Department of Justice, Office of Justice Programs, Bureau of Justice Statistics.
36. Scalia, J. (2001). *Federal drug offenders, 1999 with trends 1984–1999.* Washington, DC: U. S. Department of Justice, Office of Justice Programs, Bureau of Justice Statistics.
37. Benda, B. B., & Tollett, C. L. (1999). A study of recidivism of serious and persistent offenders among adolescents. *Journal of Criminal Justice,* 27, 111–126.
38. Stephan & Karberg, note 30.
39. DeLisi, note 7.
40. Gendreau, P., Goggin, C. E., & Law, M. A. (1997). Predicting prison misconducts. *Criminal Justice and Behavior,* 24, 414–431; Homant, R. J., & Witkowski, M. J. (2003). Prison deviance as a predictor of general deviance: Some correlational evidence from Project GANGMILL. *Journal of Gang Research,* 10, 65–75; DeLisi, M., Berg, M. T., & Hochstetler, A. (2004). Gang members, career criminals, and prison violence: Further specification of the importation model of inmate behavior. *Criminal Justice Studies,* 17, 369–383; Allender, D. M., & Marcell, F. (2003). Career criminals, security threat groups, and prison gangs: An interrelated threat. *FBI Law Enforcement Bulletin,* 72, 8–12; Hochstetler, A., & DeLisi, M. (2005). Importation, deprivation, and varieties of serving time: An integrated-lifestyle-exposure model of prison offending. *Journal of Criminal Justice,* 33, 257–266; Drury, A. J., & DeLisi, M. (2010). The past is prologue: Prior adjustment to prison and institutional misconduct. *The Prison Journal,* 90, 331–352.
41. Langan, P. A., & Levin, D. J. (2002). *Recidivism of prisoners released in 1994.* Washington, DC: U. S. Department of Justice, Office of Justice Programs.
42. Langan & Levin, note 51.
43. Langan, P. A., Schmitt, E. L., & Durose, M. R. (2003). *Recidivism of sex offenders released from prison in 1994.* Washington, DC: U. S. Department of Justice, Office of Justice Programs, Bureau of Justice Statistics.
44. DeLisi, M. (2005). *Career criminals in society.* Thousand Oaks, CA: Sage.

CHAPTER 10

PROBATION AND PAROLE

◆ Introduction

Probation is the first sanction of choice for the first-time nonviolent offender. In many cases, probation is not punishment at all but a second, or third, or fourth chance for the offender to mend his or her ways and avoid any further involvement with the criminal justice system.

Probation is a conditional release from custody and avoidance of jail or prison for a specified period of time. The conditions vary, such as the simple requirement that the individual not commit any violation of the law for a specified period of time with no other strings attached. That is *informal*, or *summary*, probation.

Other forms of probation carry more conditions and restrictions, such as to refrain from using alcohol or illegal drugs, submitting to search by any peace officer at any time of the day or night, regularly reporting to a probation officer, staying employed or in school, and various other conditions.

At the end of 2007 there were 4,293,163 men and women on probation in the United States.[1] Of that number, 51% had been convicted of a misdemeanor, 47% for a felony, and 3% for other infractions. Women comprised 23% of the probationers; 55% of adults on probation were white, 29% were black, and 13% were Hispanic.

From *Criminal Justice 101: An Introduction to the System* by Thomas A. Adams. Copyright © 2010 by Thomas F. Adams. Reprinted by permission.

Parole is similar to probation in many respects, with the major difference being that parole is a conditional release after serving a substantial period of time in prison with considerably more stringent requirements of good behavior in order to avoid return to prison to serve out the remainder of the sentence.

Another difference between probation and parole is that in most jurisdictions probation agencies and their officers operate under the aegis of the state or county courts, while parole is an extension of the government's department of corrections.

In this chapter we cover the similarities and the dissimilarities of the two processes and their goals and objectives.

Probation

It all started when a shoemaker named John Augustus secured the release of a drunk from jail in Boston by posting bail for him in 1841 and helping him restore his life to a productive one. Eighteen years later when Augustus died, in 1859, he had helped salvage the lives of more than 1,800 men. Thus was the beginning of probation.[2] In 1878 Massachusetts became the first state to adopt juvenile probation, and other states had followed by 1938. By 1956 all states had adult probation.[3]

Advantages of Probation

1. Probation gives the offender a chance to avoid incarceration or postpone it until a later conviction, which can be reinstated if the offender commits another crime.

2. Allows the individual to prove to himself or herself and to the court that the threat of imprisonment and the period of probation were sufficient to keep him or her from repeating any criminal behavior.

3. The probation allows the individual offender to continue his or her gainful employment and employability. Once the offender acquires the label of "jailbird" or "ex-con," many employers will shy away from candidates with criminal histories.

4. Saves money for the government. Once an individual enters the jail or prison, the government must not only pay for room and board, training, medical and psychological services for the inmate but also support spouses and families, who become dependent on the government because the breadwinner is no longer making money to support them.

5. Saves personnel costs of supervision. Many probationers can be supervised while outside prison much cheaper than in prison.

Probation Timeline

1841 John Augustus started probation in Boston.

1848 Massachusetts had probation statewide.

1925 President Calvin Coolidge signed the Probation Act, establishing probation as a federal court sentence, and assigned probation officers.

1940 Federal probation was transferred to the administrative office of the federal courts from the Bureau of Prisons.

1954 All states had juvenile probation.

1956 All states had adult probation.

1973 *Gagnon v. Scarpelli,* 411 U.S. 778. The Supreme Court held that probationers are entitled to hearing before probations are revoked.

1987 *Griffin v. Wisconsin,* 483 U.S. 868. The Court ruled that warrantless searches of probationers' homes are reasonable.

1994 The Violent Crime Control and Law Enforcement Act (VCCLEA) required a drug testing program for federal offenders on probation and toughened laws on address change requirements for probationers.

Qualification for Probation

The nonviolent violator of a property crime with no prior arrest record is usually the best candidate as opposed to the violent repeat offender who apparently did not benefit from previous lenient treatment.

The individual who has a relatively stable family and private life and a steady job with a good attendance record is also a more likely candidate for probation than the unemployed or unemployable person who has a volatile and unstable lifestyle and constant association with others with similar records. The active gang member is more likely to go to jail or prison as a preventative measure in an effort to separate him or her from the negative influences on the street. Of course, the influences and associations in jail or prison are going to be negative, sometimes even more intense and influential. The judge must weigh the alternatives and decide which is best for the public's safety.

Types of Probation

Summary, or Informal, Probation

A common type of probation for the circumstantial or infrequent violator, which may include those convicted of driving under the influence of alcohol or prescription medications, or a first-time nonviolent offender.

When one is placed on informal probation, his or her name is entered into the probation department's database with no conditions except that he or she shall not get arrested again during a specified period of time, such as three years. If there is a rearrest, the judge may revoke the original probation and send the offender to jail for the full term for that offense, in addition to the sentence for the second conviction.

Shock Probation

The shock is affected by a relatively brief imprisonment—perhaps three to six months maximum—as part of a term of probation for three years or more. The objective of shock probation is to shock the offender with the stark reality of being locked up in a caged environment like an animal and totally isolated from every aspect of a normal life. The effect of such a shock is more than enough to cause the offender to fervently hope to avoid such humiliation and deprivation again.

Formal Probation

The probationer is assigned a specific list of conditions and must sign on to them in order to be granted probation. Conditions of a formal probation will include many of following:

- Keep regular hours and constant attendance at work, school, or counseling sessions.
- Stay alcohol and drug free. Submit to random drug and sobriety tests.
- Regular attendance at alcohol and drug abuse rehabilitation meetings.
- Frequent scheduled and unscheduled meetings with a probation officer.
- Anger management counseling.
- Restitution and personal apologies to victims.
- Attend church.
- Carry signs in public admitting guilt, put a sticker on vehicle, or post a sign in front of the residence.

- Perform specific public service tasks, such as cleaning animal cages at the zoo, sweeping streets, making public service announcements on radio or television, or counseling juvenile offenders against the evils of using drugs or alcohol.
- Home confinement and GPS monitoring.
- Change jobs or living conditions only with consent of probation officer or the judge.
- Other conditions imposed by judges with creative ideas.

Community-Based Probation

This is a variation of a formal probation, which involves the community. The probationer may have special talents and be required to participate with nonprofit organizations such as Big Brothers and Sisters, or Child Advocacy for the Department of Child Protective Services. An attorney may be required to perform services for the courts, or a doctor may be required to contribute his or her services to a county health program.

Functions of Probation Officers

The probation officer (PO) has often been called a "change agent" for good reason. Since the objective of probation is for the offender to change behavior and divert his or her activities and proclivities away from criminal ventures, the PO's goal is to facilitate and encourage those changes. Among other activities, the PO's functions include the following:

1. Conduct presentence investigations and make recommendations to the court for sanctions to be imposed on the offenders.
2. Serve as intake officers at juvenile detention facilities to evaluate status and delinquent offenders, and petition them to the court or counsel and release.
3. Administer diagnostic tests, interview, evaluate, and recommend treatment to the courts.
4. Classify offenders and assist corrections personnel in determining offenders' risk levels.
5. Recommend and supervise community treatment probationers.
6. Counsel and supervise probationers.
7. Collect restitution and nonsupport payments.

Restorative Justice

The purpose for this type of probation is to repair relationships of offenders with their families and their victims. This type of probation would include the following:

- Victim—offender mediation.
- Family group counseling; the offender is only one part of the total family unit.
- Intervention in disputes between offender and employer, teacher, or others.

Work and Academic Furlough

While serving time in jail or prison, the inmate may be allowed to go to work or attend school off the premises as part of his or her rehabilitation. Furloughs also reduce the cost of incarceration as well as allow the individual to continue an occupation or profession that will continue after he or she completes the sentence. The inmate will also be able to support his or her dependents and lessen the state's cost of supporting them during the inmate's imprisonment.

Halfway Houses

The halfway house concept can actually work two ways: (1) as a diversion from jail or prison, allowing the individual to continue work and school and avoid association with a more sophisticated and negative influence on the novice; and (2) as a way station after a long term in prison, easing the parolee back into free society. Moving from the caged and severely restricted existence in prison into the free world again can be a traumatic experience. The longer the time in prison, the longer and more difficult the transition back into society.

◆ Origin of Parole

In early colonial days, wealthy landowners in Virginia paid the debts of inmates serving time in debtors' prison in England and brought them to the colonies, where they would work as indentured servants until they worked off their debts. They would then be released and given a small plot of land to start their lives as free men and women in the less fertile fields of West Virginia. This was a form of parole, which followed several years of forced servitude.

The principal reason for the creation of parole was prison overcrowding. In the early 1800s, when the prisons were full to the breaking point, governors were required to commute the sentences of many inmates who had demonstrated good behavior and let them serve the balance of their time in the community to make room for new arrivals. By the 1930s parole programs became more formalized and a regular practice of the courts to prescribe the terms of sentences to include parole following release.

In 1840 in Norfolk Island, Australia, where prisoners were transported from England, Alexander Macanochie, known as the father of parole, introduced the concept of awarding marks to inmates for good behavior and early release. Although he was not allowed to grant such releases, his principles were published in a book he wrote in 1844.[4]

Purpose of Parole

For all practical purposes, parole is an extension of the prison sentence. The parolee serves the balance of his or her sentence in relative freedom, but under close supervision and specific conditions that must be met or be returned to prison for the balance of the sentence. The prisoner's good conduct while in prison allows him or her to build up credits worth time off, with the built-up credits amounting to one half or one third of the sentence to be spent on parole.

The Parole Board

An inmate must serve at least one third to one half of his or her sentence before being eligible to apply for parole. This provision does not apply in states where mandatory release times are set by the judge or legislature. The board invites prosecution and defense attorneys who were involved in the trial of the convicted offender, the victim's family members, and the inmate's friends and relatives.to testify and present their recommendations as to the fate of the applicant.

If they do not appear, all of those invited may send written statement to the board expressing their appeals for the board's action.

The board meets with the petitioner for parole, who may make a personal presentation and plea for the parole. The board takes into consideration all of the following when it votes *yes* or *no* for the parole:

- Nature and circumstances of the crime.
- Aggravating and mitigating circumstances.
- The sentencing court's statements at time of sentencing.
- Nature and seriousness of prior offenses the applicant has committed.
- The inmate's conduct while serving time in the institution.
- The inmate's attitude and general outlook on life.

- Inmate's openness and acceptance of responsibility for his or her crimes.
- Participation in educational rehabilitation programs.
- Plans for employment and place of residence.

Parole Officer

The parole officer has complete authority to supervise the parolee and to ensure that he or she is following the rules. For example, if there is any reasonable cause to believe that the parolee is dealing or in possession of illegal drugs or other contraband, the officer may conduct a search of the individual at his or her place of residence or employment or anywhere on the streets without having to go through the formality of going to a judge and seeking a warrant.

Parole Revocation

The parolee may be brought before a revocation hearing upon petition by the parole officer who presents evidence of technical violations. If the parolee commits a new crime, then that matter is handled through the prosecuting attorneys and the courts as any other criminal prosecution. At the revocation hearing to determine whether the parolee should be returned to prison for technical violations, he or she is given a written notice with the charges specifying the purpose(s) for the revocation and is given a hearing accompanied by an attorney with a provision for pleading that the revocation not take place. The hearing is similar to a criminal trial.

If the parolee commits a criminal offense, there will be a separate indictment and trial, and sentencing will be independent in addition to the revocation hearing. If the parolee gets arrested for a new offense, it is possible that there will be no revocation proceeding. For example, the parolee who has served time for robbery may get caught for a misdemeanor, such as petty theft or assault. He or she may be convicted for that crime and be sent to jail instead of prison, and released without a revocation hearing. It is possible that the parolee will be on probation simultaneous with the parole.

A parolee is a felon and has lost certain privileges of citizenship, such as holding a public office, getting a government job, and voting. These privileges are not restored at the conclusion of parole.

At the end of 2007 there were 824, 385 adult men and women on parole in the US.[5] Over 96% of parolees had been sentenced to one year or more, and the most common type of offense for which they were on parole was a drug offense (37%). Women comprised 12% of the nation's parolees, and 42% of parolees were white, 37% were black, and 19% were Hispanic.

Conditions of Parole

A parolee's contract is more generally restrictive than that of a probationer, principally because of the more serious nature of felony convictions. Following are some parole restrictions:

1. Change residence and living arrangements (roommates, etc.) only with consent of the parole officer.
2. Forbidden to associate with other parolees in any type of social milieu.
3. Forbidden to use nonprescription drugs or alcohol with random tests.
4. Active participation in rehabilitation programs.
5. Cannot operate any motor vehicle.
6. Not allowed to leave the jurisdiction.
7. Strict curfew hours and home confinement in some cases.
8. Regularly scheduled meetings with parole officers.
9. Unannounced visits by parole officers on the job, in school, or at place of residence.
10. Must stay out of bars, nightclubs, and certain types of sporting events.
11. No gambling.
12. Search at any time or place by parole or peace officers.

Executive Privilege

There are three types of intervention by a president or governor known as executive privilege that are sometimes available to the individual who has been convicted and carries the label "criminal" for life. The president, in federal cases, and the governor, in state cases, may forgive the offender and restore his or her good record by commutation, pardon, or amnesty.

Upon petition by an inmate or someone on his or her behalf or the initiative of the chief executive, the governor or president decrees the sentence cut short or canceled at a specific time. With a commuted sentence, the inmate is summarily freed with no further encumbrance of a parole. This sort of clemency may be granted for an individual or a class of people, for example, all inmates on death row in all states had their death sentences commuted to life in prison following the *Furman v. Georgia* decision that the death penalty laws were unconstitutional.[6]

A pardon not only forgives and releases the convicted person but also wipes his or her criminal record completely off the books. A pardon may accompany a commutation, but may also be granted to a perso n long since released from prison but who still carries the felony record. For example, a young man or woman may have been convicted for felony assault in a bar fight twenty-five years ago and served time and parole, followed by a period of nearly twenty years with absolutely no negative contact with the police. Now the individual would like to vote and seek a government job. He or she files an appeal to the governor or president for a pardon accompanied by petitions by friends, relatives, and employers attesting to the subject's clean record. The chief executive signs the pardon and the record is expunged, restoring the petitioner to full citizenship status.

The third form of clemency is amnesty. The chief executive declares the individual free from indictment for past or future crimes. For example, an individual might have been indicted for a federal crime, but the president or governor grants amnesty, ordering all criminal proceedings to be canceled.

Summary

In this chapter we examined the principles and practices of probation and parole, one that precedes or replaces incarceration and the other that follows a long term of imprisonment. The goals of both are to attempt to dissuade the offender from repeating his or her crimes. The probation and parole officers, in their roles as change agents, strive to supervise the offenders and steer them back on course as law-abiding citizens.

We also briefly covered three types of executive clemency by presidents and governors designed to give the reformed offender to resume his or her respected place in society as a law-abiding citizen.

Suggested Semester Project

Create an imaginary criminal offender who went to prison for a serious felony, such as armed robbery with aggravated assault by a habitual drug user. Write a list of conditions for the offender to abide by in acceptance of parole.

◆ Questions

1. Probation started in 1841 when a shoemaker named _____ secured the release of a drunk from jail in Boston by posting bail for him and helping him restore his life to a productive one.

    a. Augustus John
    b. Jeremy Bentham
    c. John Augustus
    d. John Bentham

2. Shock probation is affected by a relatively brief imprisonment—_____—as part of a term of probation for three years or more.

    a. Perhaps three to six months maximum
    b. Perhaps six to 12 months maximum
    c. Perhaps 12 to 24 months maximum
    d. Perhaps one month maximum

3. An attorney may be required to perform services for the courts, or a medical doctor may be required to contribute his or her services to a county health program. This would best describe which type of probation?

    a. Shock probation
    b. Informal probation
    c. Weekend offender probation
    d. Community-Based probation

4. Restorative Justice Probation includes:

    a. Victim—offender mediation
    b. Offender drug prevention counseling
    c. Both (a) and (b)
    d. Neither (a) nor (b)

5. The principal reason for the creation of parole was prison overcrowding.

    a. True
    b. False

6. If the parolee commits a new crime, then that matter is handled through the probation officer as a continuation of parole.

   a. True
   b. False

7. Over 96% of parolees had been sentenced to one year or more, and the most common type of offense for which they were on parole was a _____ offense.

   a. Theft
   b. Assault
   c. Drug
   d. Sexual

8. There are three types of intervention by a president or governor known as Executive Privilege:

   a. Commutation, forgiveness and excuse
   b. Pardon, sanctuary and absolution
   c. Commutation, pardon and amnesty
   d. Pardon, amnesty and presidential decree

9. President Carter _____ the sentence of millionaire terrorist and bank robber Patty Hearst.

   a. Pardoned
   b. Forgave
   c. Commuted
   d. Absolved

10. When a former criminal is given an executive pardon the record is expunged. However, the person is not returned to full citizenship and may not vote.

    a. True
    b. False

Endnotes

1. Bureau of Justice Statistics website. For the most recent statistics, go to this website and others cited throughout this text.
2. J. Petersilia, "Probation in the U.S." *Crime and Justice* 22, 2002, pp. 149–200.
3. Ibid.
4. Wikipedia.
5. Bureau of Justice Statistics website.
6. *Furman v. Georgia* 408 U.S. 238, 92 S. Ct. 2726 (1972).

CHAPTER 11

HOW THE SYSTEM WORKS

◆ Introduction

From the moment a crime is discovered by, or reported to the police, the process begins. Every part of the system is involved and, considering the complexities involved, the system functions rather well. The police, courts, and corrections each plan their part to ensure justice for the accused as well as the victims.

This chapter is designed to take you on a tour through the system, with stops along the way to discuss how each segment of the system functions and fits into the overall scheme of assuring justice for the people of the United States.

The three basic parts are the police, the courts, and corrections. Then there is a separate subsystem known as the juvenile justice system, which spans all three. The police are responsible for investigating criminal acts, identifying and apprehending the offenders, and bringing them to the courts for adjudication. The courts adjudicate and prescribe punishment for the guilty, and corrections houses and attempts to rehabilitate the convicted persons and prepare them for reintegration into society. The juvenile justice system deals with juveniles separately from adults. In this chapter we examine the process from the commission of a crime to arrest, conviction, and eventual parole of the perpetrator to show how the various components of the system work together to accomplish their respective responsibilities.

© 2012 by Sam72. Used under license of Shutterstock, Inc.

From *Criminal Justice 101: An Introduction to the System* by Thomas A. Adams. Copyright © 2010 by Thomas F. Adams. Reprinted by permission.

The Police

The officer may be a local police officer in the city or county of a state or an officer of the state itself. The officer may be an employee of the federal government. All have a primary responsibility to the branch of government that employs them, as employees of any company have a primary responsibility to that company.

The federal officer investigates federal law violations by people who commit crimes against the United States and questions them wherever they may be, and conducts the investigation wherever it may take him or her. For example, a narcotics dealer ships a large quantity of heroin from Palermo, Sicily, to Baltimore, Maryland. The illegal drugs are intercepted as they arrive in Baltimore. The Drug Enforcement Agency will investigate the case both in Sicily and in Maryland and everywhere in between.

A state investigator for the board of medical examiners and an officer from the state attorney general's office investigate a doctor who is prescribing drugs to imaginary patients and a pharmacist who is filling those prescriptions for the doctor, who is using some of the drugs herself and sharing them with some family members who are not sick.

The Crime

The initial step in the process—the crime—may occur three different ways: (1) reported by the victim or witness during or following its commission, (2) discovered by a field officer while on patrol in the field, or (3) initiated by an officer in a sting operation, such as posing to be a "fence" and buying a vehicle from a car thief to build a theft case against him.

The Response

If the perpetrator is present, the officer makes an arrest, searches him or her, and transports the arrestee to jail or a detention center. The officer then initiates the investigation by interviewing victims and witnesses and collecting evidence. If the officer does not make an arrest on the spot, the next step is to prepare the reports and take the evidence to the laboratory for analysis and/or place it in the evidence locker for storage until the trial.

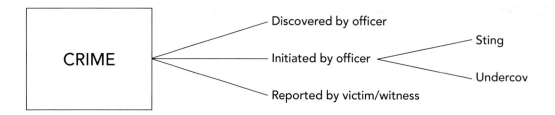

◆ Crime Scene Investigation

Crime scene specialists will take photos and videos and collect evidence at the scene, laboratory technicians will analyze the evidence, and follow-up special investigators (robbery, burglary, crimes against persons) will wrap up the case in preparation for prosecution. These officers are evaluated by their superiors not only on the quality of their work but also on numbers: numbers of arrests, percentage of cases cleared, and numbers of convictions of persons charged with crimes. There is often considerable pressure put on these officers to produce those numbers.

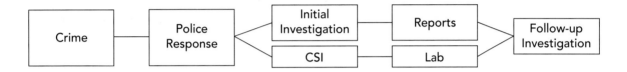

The Reports

To present the case to the prosecutor, the officer completes the crime report and other reports. If he or she made an arrest, that report is included in the package that goes to the prosecuting attorney along with any preliminary reports on results of any laboratory work that has been done.

Follow-Up Investigation

The investigation for the county or city department follows up on the investigation originally conducted by a field officer or deputy. The investigator checks with the lab and verifies that the evidence points to the guilt of the suspect named by the victim and witnesses. He or she then locates the suspect and questions the suspect about the event, asking for his or her side of the story, but may or may not advise him or her of the Miranda rights, depending on whether it is merely an investigatory interview or a custodial interrogation.

Affidavit and Complaint

The officer or a court liaison officer (who may be a civilian employee with special training and education in laws and rules of evidence and procedure) takes the reports to the prosecuting attorney, who will make the decision whether to prosecute the case, depending on the strength of evidence sufficient to prove the crime was committed and the accused is guilty beyond a reasonable doubt. The report's accuracy and thoroughness is critical. It must contain all the information necessary for the prosecutor to ascertain if there is sufficient information and evidence to prove the case beyond all reasonable doubt.

The prosecutor has the officer or complaining witness sign the affidavit attesting to the facts of the case. The signer is doing so based on information concerning the case and belief that it is true. The officer, investigator, or court liaison person may sign the affidavit, but it is most desirable to have the complaining witness (victim) sign it, especially if the offense is a neighborhood-type disturbance of the peace, trespassing, or a "he said–she said–they said" type of event that the officer did not witness and that is lacking physical evidence to support the statements.

Prosecuting Attorney

This individual, sometimes called the district attorney, is an officer of the court who must make decisions on behalf of the court. If the case is federal, the prosecutor is the U.S. attorney. In the case of the state and local violations, the prosecutor is the county attorney or, in some cases, a city attorney. The title varies from one locale to another.

The prosecutor is evaluated on a different set of criteria. Federal prosecutors are appointed by and serve at the pleasure of the president of the United States. County prosecutors are either appointed by the governor during an off-election year or elected, but run for reelection on their record of convictions of offenders every few years (usually four). Their success, and often their tenure, depends on the percentage of convictions they get for the guilty offenders. If they lose too many cases, they will not be reappointed or reelected.

The prosecutor must look at the officers' or agents' work through a different set of eyes and criteria. This is a second opinion, so to speak. It is the prosecutor's responsibility to review the reports and evidence and to make the decision whether to prosecute the suspect named in the reports, for what charge, if at all.

The prosecutor will carefully analyze the case from the standpoint of whether the evidence and statements were gained through constitutional means, anticipate what the defenses will be to the charges, and plan the strategy to ensure conviction. The prosecutor will also look at the case from the defense standpoint and determine if there is a valid and believable defense. The prosecutor may decide to reduce or change the charges, or may decide to decline prosecution.

The prosecutor may see weaknesses in the evidence or the investigation and recommend that the officer reinvestigate and wrap up some loose ends to get answers to questions still unanswered. The officer's judgment is tempered, somewhat, on the basis of knowing that he or she must make no mistakes in collecting evidence and information to convict, but is also under pressure to produce results in the way of numbers of cases cleared and arrests made. Unfortunately, this pressure may tempt an unethical officer to "bend the rules" to build a case against the accused, such as "beach heading," an unconstitutional interrogation technique to avoid the Miranda requirement (discussed in chapter 3).

The Court

The prosecutor, who is an officer of the court, presents the affidavit and complaint to the magistrate, commonly referred to as the judge. All federal cases are brought to a federal magistrate. State cases are brought to a state judge, who could be a municipal or justice court judge.

The Judge

The judge must review the affidavit and complaint and decide to issue the necessary warrants to take the case farther. The judge may choose to discuss the facts with the prosecutor and/or the investigating officer to get more details on the case, but at this point will usually accept the recommendations of the prosecutor, who is an officer of the court and actually a direct representative of the judge at this point in the process. Usually, the police officer does not deal directly with the judge at this preliminary stage but does business through the prosecuting attorney.

Police

With the warrants in hand, the officer locates and arrests the suspect. The *warrant* is directed to any peace officer in the state to arrest the subject of the warrant and to bring him or her to the judge who signed the warrant. In actuality, the officer will take the warrant to the jail where the perpetrator was booked. If he or she has not already been arrested, the officer will locate the suspect and make the arrest and transport him or her to jail for booking.

Booking

The booking process consists of logging the arrest in the files, originally a ledger book (hence the term), photographing, and fingerprinting. In certain types of arrest, such as violent and sex crimes, the booking personnel will also take a tissue swab of the arrestee's mouth to be forwarded to a lab for classification and entry into a central DNA file.

Although a search warrant is not required to search the suspect for weapons, contraband, and means with which to commit the crime charged, it is wise to get the search warrant at the same time. It takes no more time with the judge, and it costs nothing. According to *Chimel*,[1] the search can go no farther than the subject's immediate control (interpreted as being within reach, or "wingspan," of the subject). If the officers have probable cause to believe that they should search the entire premises based on information they gave the judge at the time they secured the arrest warrant, then they should also get the search warrant at the same time. With the warrants in hand, the officers are on firmer ground than if they have to later explain to the judge why they did not bother to get the warrant.

With the arrestee and warrant in hand, the suspect is then taken to either a city detention center or county jail and booked on the charge. If there is any evidence, that is stored in the department's evidence repository, where it is held until it is presented in court, or transferred to the laboratory for analysis, then presented in court during the trial.

Jail

The county sheriff keeps the county jail as part of his or her constitutionally prescribed duties. Since the jail houses people who have been charged but not yet tried and/or convicted for this crimes charged, it is classified as a correctional institution because it also houses convicted misdemeanants serving their time. The suspect, now the arrestee, is "booked" into custody at the jail. BAIL. Once the booking is complete, the suspect may be allowed to post bail and be released until his or her initial appearance in court. The bail bondsperson is not a government employee but an insurance agent. Some people may not be entitled to bail because of the seriousness of the charge(s) or probability of flight from the jurisdiction to avoid prosecution, or because they pose an imminent danger to the public.

ROR

In some cases, the arrestee is allowed to go free pending court appearances and trial without posting bail. Not only depending on the nature of the charges or flight risk, the ROR (release on own recognizance) candidate is established in the community and probably is a longtime resident, has regular employment, has children in school, or has participated in community activities, such as service club membership. Some critics claim that this option discriminates against the poor and the homeless, which is true. Those individuals, once released from jail, would have no incentive to stay around town to be tried and probably convicted. The person granted ROR, however, is most likely in a situation that he or she cannot afford for many reasons to flee to avoid court appearances. Bail schedules are prescribed by the courts, and the principal source of bail is the bail bond office. The courts will accept cash as bail and keep a percentage for costs, but the process most frequently includes the bail bondspeople.

The bondsperson receives a commission from the insurance company. If the client fails to appear when required, then the bail is forfeited and the company pays the court the full amount insured. Some bondspersons decide to bypass the insurance company and keep the entire commission themselves. When they do that and when the client becomes a fugitive, then the bondspersons are more likely to hire bond *recovery* agents (sometimes known as bounty hunters) to capture the fugitives and return them to custody so that the court will reimburse their money that has been forfeited. Insurance companies also hire such agents, who have been glorified on somewhat exaggerated "reality" television programs.

◀▶ The Court

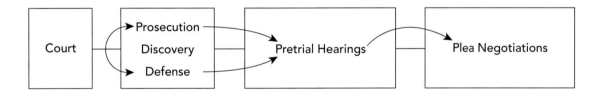

Discovery

According to the laws of discovery, the attorney for the defense must have access to all the reports and evidence as it is accumulated and analyzed by the prosecution. Originally, the process was for the defense to discover through investigation whatever the prosecution had, then go to the court and get a court order for the release of the materials that depended on the vigilance and efficiency of the defense attorney and investigators. As time passed, it is now routine for both sides to exchange whatever data and evidence they have. The exclusion to this rule is that the defense is not required to turn over anything that might be interpreted as being covered by the protection of the Fifth Amendment that would compromise the defendant's right not to be a witness against himself or herself.

Motions to Suppress Evidence

This is a pretrial hearing in court where the defense has raised objections to the manner in which statements or evidence was collected, claiming violations of the Fourth, Fifth, and Sixth Amendments to the Constitution.

In this pretrial hearing the prosecutor must convince the judge through witnesses' testimony, subject to cross-examination by the defense, that the investigating and arresting officers followed all the court-made rules known as judicial decisions, such as *Terry, Mapp, Miranda,* and all the others involved in this case.

If the judge decides that certain evidence or statements will be excluded from the trial, none of it may be used during the trial. Consequently, the prosecutor goes back to prepare the case. At that time, the prosecutor may decide that there is not enough evidence to go ahead with the prosecution. If not, he or she will petition the court to dismiss all or some of the charges against the defendant.

Plea Negotiations

Also known as "let's make a deal," the prosecutor and defense attorneys get together and discuss the case's merits, based on all that the court is going to allow during the trial. As a result of these frank discussions, and some gamesmanship, the defense may agree to talk to his or her client and discuss what options are available. In the bargaining meeting, the prosecution may agree to reduce a felony assault charge to a misdemeanor, or to dismiss three burglaries in exchange for a guilty plea to only one of those burglaries with a sentence somewhat less than what the original charges would have brought.

Once the attorneys agree on a bargain acceptable to both sides, they present it to the judge, who must approve the deal. As both attorneys are officers of the court, this process is usually a "done deal" by the time it gets to the judge. The decisions are usually referred to as "in the interest of justice" and are done to move cases forward, as there are not enough judges, lawyers, or courtrooms to accommodate all cases if every defendant were to plead not guilty and demand a jury trial.

Initial Appearance In Court

At this stage in the process after the defendant has had a chance to confer with counsel and to know what the charges will be, the defendant appears in front of the judge and enters a plea of guilty or not guilty upon formal notification of the criminal charges by the judge. As provided by the Gideon decision,[2] the accused should have an attorney in his or her defense by this time. Many judges will not accept a guilty plea if the accused is not represented by counsel.

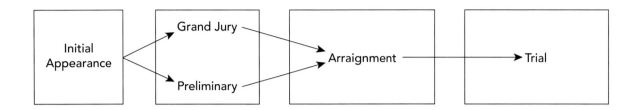

Grand Jury or Lower-Court Hearing

The Fifth Amendment to the Constitution provides that everyone is entitled to his or her case being heard by a grand jury to determine if a crime was committed by having the prosecutor prove the elements of the crime (*corpus delicti*) and sufficient evidence to show that the defendant should be held to answer to the charges. If they render a true bill (*vere dictum*), they will direct the prosecutor to file an indictment in the superior or district court to schedule a trial.

An alternative to the grand jury proceeding is a preliminary hearing before a lower-court judge, who will accept evidence and testimony to prove the crime was committed and the defendant should be held to answer to the charges. At this hearing the judge will direct the prosecutor to file an *information* in the higher court to schedule the trial. The difference between the grand jury hearing and the preliminary is that the preliminary is in open court, while grand jury proceedings are secret while in progress. We discuss these two processes in more detail in the chapter on the courts.

The accused becomes the defendant, and the purpose of the first time in front of the judge is to notify him or her of the charges and to be sure that the accused person has representation by an attorney. The charges may be the same as, or different from, the charges for which the original arrest was made. For example, the arrest may have been for one burglary, but follow-up investigation established that the suspect is now going to be held to answer for a series of eleven burglaries. Conversely, the original arrest was made for a felonious assault, but the victim's visit to the hospital revealed that the injuries were less severe, and now the charge is misdemeanor assault. Another possibility is that the court may have excluded so much evidence in the case the prosecutor decided not to prosecute, so the accused learns that all criminal charges have been dropped.

Misdemeanor Trials

The procedure is similar for felonies and misdemeanors, except that there is no grand jury or lower-court preliminary hearing. After the initial appearance, the misdemeanor defendant goes directly to the trial phase of the process. Misdemeanor trials follow the same rules as felony trials.

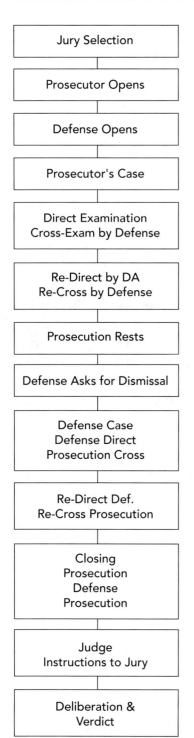

The trial will be either a court trial (no jury) or a jury trial. In the jury trial the jury is the judge of fact, which means that the jurors determine whether to believe the witnesses and the evidence and ultimately whether the accused party is innocent or guilty as charged beyond all reasonable doubt. In the jury trial the judge is the referee who enforces the rules of procedure and laws of evidence. He or she manages the proceedings in both the jury trial and the court trial. In the court (or bench) trial the judge also determines guilt or innocence of the accused based on the evidence and testimony of witnesses.

Felony Trials

Now that all preliminary details have been dealt with, and the case is brought to the superior (or district) court, the trial begins. If there is to be a jury, then the jury selection process begins.

The jury consists of twelve people in most cases, but there is no hard and fast rule that all juries must include twelve. Some may have as few as six, particularly when the judicial district is large and sparsely populated, such as federal court districts. Fewer people are inconvenienced. Sometimes the trial starts with twelve jurors, but someone gets sick or is called away on some family emergency, leaving eleven or ten jurors available to deliberate and arrive at a verdict. In those cases, the judge will ask both prosecutor and defense if they will consent to a "struck" jury of less than the original amount. If both sides and the judge agree to this reduction, it is by stipulation. When the trial is going to last more than a few hours, the judge will choose additional individuals to sit with the jury, but outside the jury "box," as alternates. If, during the trial or during jury deliberations, a juror is called away for some emergency or gets sick, an alternate serves as a replacement. If the jury is intact at the end of the trial when the judge instructs the jurors to go into their room and reach a verdict, the alternates go home unless called back as a replacement during deliberations.

Jurors are chosen at random from a venire (group of prospective jurors), and the judge questions them one at a time, taking them voir dire, which means that the judge is qualifying them as fair and impartial. If, during the questioning, the prospective juror indicates that he or she is biased and has prejudged the verdict, he or she is removed "for cause" and replaced by another candidate. This process is repeated until a fair and impartial jury is seated. Next is a process where the attorneys for both sides may remove jurors (the numbers depend on the type of case) for no cause at all. This is known as a "peremptory challenge." The only time a judge would override such a challenge would be if it were apparent that the attorney for the prosecution or defense were attempting to ethnically or gender cleanse the jury to get rid of all men or women or individuals of a particular ethnic origin.

Once the jury has been seated and sworn in, the trial begins. If there is no jury, then the trial begins with the judge acting as judge and jury.

Opening Statements

Since the prosecution has the burden to prove guilt of the accused beyond all reasonable doubt, the prosecution goes first. This is the opportunity for the attorney to outline in advance how he or she is going to present the evidence and testimony that will prove the defendant guilty. The defense is next, and the attorneys will do whatever they can to begin to sow seeds of doubt about the efficacy of the prosecution's case.

The trial sequence goes like this: First, the prosecution must prove to the judge that a crime has been committed, then through evidence and witness testimony prove the accused person guilty of the crime(s) charged beyond all reasonable doubt. After each witness is examined by the prosecution, the defense cross-examines each witness in turn. Direct examination consists of asking questions that call for yes or no responses and narrative response as to what a person perceived. The purpose of the cross-examination is to challenge the validity of the evidence and truthfulness and accuracy of the witnesses. Therefore their questions may call for explanations and justifications for statements they made during direct examination. It may appear that cross-examination means "cross-up and disqualify the witness," but the objective is to get to the real truth of the matter. Not all witnesses are totally truthful and forthcoming for various reasons.

When the prosecution completes its side of the case, feeling sure of having proven the guilt of the accused, the prosecution rests. The next phase is for the defense to introduce evidence and witnesses to raise doubt about the prosecution's case. Although defense attorneys are not required to prove innocence, they will throw suspicion on other people and attempt to influence the jury that surely someone else committed the crime.

When the defense rests, the judge then instructs the jury. The instruction starts out with the judge instructing the jury as to the elements of the crime(s) charged, what proof is necessary to sustain a conviction, and what options the jury must consider during deliberations. The judge instructs the jury that they should select a foreperson, then deliberate and come up with a verdict of guilty or not guilty, and that the verdict must be unanimous. The jury may also consider lesser but included charges, such as second-degree murder or manslaughter instead of first-degree murder.

The Jury Verdict

When the jury returns with a verdict, its decision of not guilty is irreversible. The defendant is immediately released from custody and can never again be charged with the same crime (the double jeopardy rule of the Fifth Amendment). The verdict of guilty is certified by the judge, but in a rare case the judge may rule that the prosecution did not prove a specific element of the crime charged and reduce the charge, such as from first-degree murder to second degree or manslaughter. There is another option the judge has in overriding the actions of a jury, but only in very rare cases. That is the *directed verdict*. At the conclusion of the prosecution's presentation, the judge, who rules on the evidence, may have determined during that part of the trial that the prosecution's evidence did not support the allegation that a crime was committed and did not sufficiently prove the defendant's guilt, and the judge may either dismiss the charges and declare a mistrial, which would allow the prosecutor to go back and start again, or direct the jury to go into the jury room and declare the defendant not guilty. The latter procedure precludes any subsequent prosecution.

Probation Officer's Report

After the verdict of guilty by the judge or jury, the judge orders the probation officer, who, like the attorneys, is an officer of the court, to conduct an investigation and submit a report on the now convicted person's criminal and personal history and a recommendation as to what the sanctions should be. The probation report includes a summary of any previous criminal record, circumstances surrounding the crime for which he or she was just found guilty, and other crimes for which the prosecution may not have charged. The officer also interviews family members, coworkers, neighbors, and prepares a complete workup on just who this person is and what should be the best punishment not only to fit the crime but to rehabilitate this individual. The probation officer knows the maximum and minimum parameters of sentence for the crime and also the judge's personal philosophy and sentencing practices. The officer will conclude the report with recommended punishment and/or alternative options for this specific individual.

Sentencing Hearing By Judge

At this hearing, the judge invites the victim and family members to confront the defendant and to express their feelings about the crime, including their recommendation as to the punishment. The judge considers all the input from the participants and the probation officer's recommendations, and sentencing guidelines established by law, and prescribes the sentence.

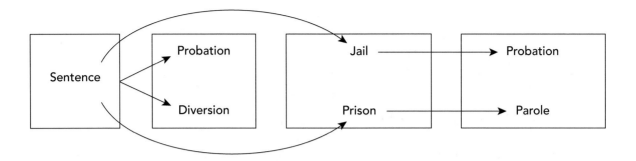

Appeals Courts

Once found guilty and sentenced, an appeal to the state's highest court is automatic only when one is sentenced to death. With all other appeals, it is the prerogative of the court appealed to whether it will agree to hear the appeal. An appeal is made on the basis of a claim by the defense that the trial judge made a procedural error in enforcing the rules or that there is a constitutional issue to be resolved. After the appeals court has reviewed the written arguments and later, if the judges choose to hear the appeal, they hear the arguments by prosecution and defense, and render a decision. The appeals court may affirm the conviction or reverse it. If it is reversed, the prosecution has the discretionary power to decide whether to prosecute again.

Corrections

Once found guilty and sentenced, the defendant is next introduced to the corrections component of the justice system. Actually, the arrest and booking and temporary jailing while awaiting and possibly during the trial involves the accused person in this part of the corrections component, but he or she is still considered innocent until found guilty.

Once convicted and sentenced, the sentence will possibly be for a period of probation with no incarceration, a combination of jail time followed by several months to several years' probation, or state prison for the term prescribed by the judge. If the conviction is in federal court, imprisonment is in federal prison, and probation would be handled by the Federal Bureau of Probation and Parole.

Probation

Probation is one option as an alternative to jail or prison. It is considered a second chance, a form of diversion from the system. One form of probation is summary, or informal, which requires that the individual not repeat the crime or any other violation for a period of time, such as three years. During this type of probation there are no reporting or supervision requirements. The probationer's name is in the computer and that is all. If the individual commits another crime, then he or she has broken the conditions of probation, and the court will be notified. Otherwise, the probation ends, and there is no further involvement of the probation department.

Shock Probation

This is a combination of jail and probation that the judge might impose to shock the convicted person as a deterrent to repeating his or her criminal behavior by getting a taste of what imprisonment is like by spending anywhere from a month to a year in jail plus several years' probation instead of going to prison. Regular probation consists of a specified period of time with a list of requirements for the probationer, such as reporting to the officer weekly or monthly, submitting to random drug tests in the case of drug violations, getting permission from the probation officer to change employment or living conditions, and not violating any laws.

Jail

The county sheriff operates the county jail, but some cities operate their own detention centers to house people who have been sentenced for misdemeanor law violations. As mentioned earlier in this chapter, both felony and misdemeanor violators are incarcerated in jail when first arrested, while awaiting trial, and while in trial for felonies or misdemeanors. Since jail sentences for convicted misdemeanants may be for short periods of time, efforts to rehabilitate and prepare the individual for reintegration back into society are minimal. Local schools and colleges provide brief skills training programs, child care, job searching, and job application procedures.

Prison

Once the individual is sentenced to prison, he or she is prepared for transportation from the local jail to a state prison, where the sentence begins. The first few weeks at the induction center the staff plans assignment of the new inmate. Depending on the seriousness of the crime for which the inmate was convicted and the risk factor, one consideration is whether the assignment will be to a minimum, medium, or maximum security institution, or to a "supermax" prison for the very dangerous and serious flight risks.

The new arrival is evaluated by psychologists, educational staff, and other specialists to attempt to place the person where he or she can learn or practice certain skills and work toward at least a high school diploma or GED certificate. A professional, such as a doctor, dentist, or teacher, will probably be assigned where their services may be used. The doctor or dentist will have lost a license to practice, but may be assigned to work as an orderly in an infirmary or as a dental assistant. The teacher might be assigned as a librarian or to other related work.

The inmate will serve the prescribed sentence, less "good time" and other time rewards and eventually will be released on parole. In the federal system, there is no longer parole. The inmate sentenced to ten years in federal prison, for example, will serve at least eight and a half of the ten years and get a few months off for good behavior. That type of sentence is known as "truth in sentencing," where ten years means ten years.

Parole

The parole officer is an employee of the prison system and is, in essence, a prison guard in plainclothes outside the prison walls. The parole officer enforces the rules of parole, which include restrictions on the parolee's movements and associates, travel restrictions, submission to search and seizure when suspicions warrant it, seeking and maintaining gainful employment, and not getting arresting for any crime. The parolee may be returned to the institution to serve the balance of his or her sentence for technical violations, or will go through the entire arrest and court procedure for any new law violations.

Summary

In this chapter we have shown how all the components of the criminal justice system work side by side to accomplish their respective functions. Despite all the government bureaus and divers collection of individuals involved, the system seems to get the job done remarkably well. In subsequent chapters we cover all of these agencies and departments and their functions in more detail. Consider yourself informally introduced to them for the time being.

Suggested Semester Project

Visit your local courthouse or select a live television production of a criminal trial in progress. Write a journal on the proceedings, commenting on your observations on jury selection, prosecution and defense strategies, and judicial discretion in sentencing, as well as whether you agree or disagree with the pronounced punishment for the crime.

Endnotes

1. *Chimel v. California,* 395 U.S. 752, 898 S. CT. 2034 (1989).
2. *Gideon v. Wainwright,* 372 U.S. 355 83 CT. 792 (1963).

CHAPTER 12
GLOBAL CRIMINAL JUSTICE

How we police crimes varies enormously depending upon the country that we are in when the crimes occur. Although there is a general consensus among all humans that the unjustified killing of another person is a criminal offence or that stealing from one another is wrong, the manner in which we investigate those offences and how we decide to then deal with the offenders is located within a complex set of customs, rules and societal values. Because criminal justice operators across the world view the work undertaken as bonding across national barriers, they recognize similarities of objectives and the effective mechanisms to bring criminals to justice. But the reality is that policing, the courts and the prison systems are not common. Who is recruited into the criminal justice system, how they are trained and what levels of discretion they have once operational can be different within the same country, as well as across countries.

Policing is frequently at the leading edge of investigating and arresting international criminal offenders. The other two limbs of the criminal justice system—the courts and the prisons—are still a domestic construct. We have the International Criminal Court and there are some offenders who are located in jails on behalf of other jurisdictions, but this is rare. International joint policing operations are, however, becoming a normal practice and this final chapter focuses upon the current approach taken towards training and operationalizing police officers who are likely to function across borders during their careers.

Policing is often regarded as being either a military or a quasi-military occupation or a distinctly civilian profession that more closely resembles public service, such as social work, nursing or teaching. But these views are limited by Western interpretation, and in fact there are far more models of policing taking place than these two extremes. For example, in Japan the policing style is strongly geared towards serving the community, with individual officers establishing relationships with citizens within small geographical areas. In China, policing is military and highly centralized, with officers having little discretion. In many countries of the Middle East, religious laws govern policing and officers are charged with upholding civilian and religious laws alongside each other. In Scandinavia, police officers have wide levels of discretion even though many of the forces are centralized. In the USA, there are almost 20,000 law enforcement agencies and collectively they are highly centralized and highly decentralized. Some local small town police forces have as few as two sworn officers who possess considerable latitude in how they apply the law. State policing is typically a very centralized model with officers answerable to the state governor. Large city forces tend to be decentralized and are possibly the closest resemblance to the model espoused by Robert Peel back in the early 19th century in London. Federal forces are fairly unique. They are, *de facto,* centralized, but so too are forces in numerous European nation states; and more countries in Europe are looking at further levels of national centralized policing for the future.

Also, there is the issue of training and qualifications. In some countries entrants into the police must hold a baccalaureate degree; in other countries not even a high school diploma is required. Every country has some degree of initial training for police officers, which again can be local and as little as a few weeks spent with a veteran officer or involve up to two years of initial training conducted in an academy, such as in Sweden where new recruits spend two years in training before individual patrol commences.

Age and gender are also factors in policing. Some countries permit entrants into policing at 18 years of age; in others it is 21 years. Mandatory retirement exists in a number of countries so that once an age or length of service is reached, that police officer must retire. In other countries, it is feasible, even if not realistic, to have patrol officers working the streets until they are 65 years of age. In other countries, there is no legal retirement age whatsoever. Women are now represented in most police forces of the world. Embracement of equality in policing has taken many decades to achieve and there still exist considerable discrepancies between conditions of service, pay and uniforms and training in some police forces.

Uniforms and the carrying of firearms is also a feature of contemporary policing. Some forces require all officers to carry firearms; some forces do not permit any officers to carry firearms. Some forces only permit men to be firearms licensed whereas others supply the same training and weapons to all recruits, male and female. It is interesting that the word uniform means *the same* and yet police uniforms are most definitely not uniform. Some are totally military; some are more like civilian clothing. Some forces permit all officers to wear the same uniform and others have different dress wear for different ranks or different tasks or different genders. Some require headwear; some do not. Some require protective clothing to be worn on all occasions; other forces have no protective body or headgear.

Policing is a multi-variable entity with great discrepancies existing within nation states and between nation states. What it means to become a police officer is not a constant; the recruitment, training and job are not the same across boundaries even if the types of criminality are remarkably similar—murder, theft, abduction and drug offences exist in every country of the world. But how we police those crimes is as variable as the *modus operandi* of the crimes themselves.

In this chapter, I am going to look at policing in a range of countries that represent policing models that differ from those in the USA, or at least that appear to differ at first blush but which may in fact be recognizable in the US with a little probing. The police forces chosen are those of South Korea, Saudi Arabia, Scandinavia (Sweden, Norway and Finland) and the RCMP of Canada. There are currently 196 countries[1] in the world and each one has some form of law enforcement provision. This book is not the venue to discuss all of the police forces on Earth, but a sample of forces that approach recruitment, training and roles and functions in different ways should provide the basis for lucrative discussion and set the scene for a more in depth look at police within the US covered in the following chapter.

◆ South Korea

South Korea is a nation with more than 4,000 years of history. It is a country that has always been a fusion of cultures and peoples, some transient others resident. Due to its geographical location, Korea has been a center point for military as well as for cultural influences. Four hundred years ago, Korea was invaded by Japan. It was occupied by Japan between 1910 and 1945. Later in the 20th century, it was at war again; this time it was a civil war between the Republic of Korea and the Democratic People's Republic of Korea, resulting in the 38th Parallel division between North and South Korea. Seoul is the capital of South Korea and has a population of more than 10 million people. Pusan is the second largest city with a population of more than 4 million inhabitants. At the cessation of the Second World War, the US assisted Korea in establishing a civilian police force. Initially, policing came under the direction of the Ministry of Home Affairs when the military and civilian policing operations for the country were fused together into one paramilitary police force for the entire nation. By 1989, the Korean National Police comprised 105,000 officers that policed 13 metropolitan districts, numerous provincial regions, a Combat Police Unit, the National Maritime

Police, the Anti-terrorist Police and the National Police Training Academy. All of these entities answer to the National Police Headquarters. Individual police officers operate on a strict 'beat system' within major cities so that officers patrol a regulated area with the intention of providing a strong community presence for the citizens. Recruitment into the police has been challenging for South Korea and it has one of the lowest police/citizens ratios of any non-communist major industrialized countries. The Combat Police is an alternative option for males in South Korea who did not wish to participate in compulsory military service. Women are not required to perform military service. All new recruit training is conducted at the National Training Academy in Seoul. Like many Civil Law countries that operate a national police force, South Korea has different levels of entry into the police service so that, for example, a recruit who has a baccalaureate degree may enter the police as an officer at the rank of lieutenant or inspector. By 1991, the KNP was no longer subordinate to the Ministry of Home Affairs, as a police committee was established to create policy, training and development standards for the entire KNP. In 1991, the police became an independent government entity, the National Police Agency, headed by a commissioner general. In 2007, as a result of internal reorganization, the KNP established a Women and Youth Division. The KNP has six broad policies that direct policing efforts across the country. These are: guarantee for safe environment against crimes and accidents, assure social stability to support government administration, realization of police for human rights supporting people's rights and interests, expansion of basis for security services that meets the needs of the people, creation of healthy and active structure culture and security of police competitiveness to respond to the changing security environment.[2]

The Korean National Police University is open to any Korean national who has graduated from high school. It accepts approximately 120 students each year into a four-year officer entry degree program. Ten percent of applicants accepted are women. Married applicants are not permitted. All recruits live in dormitory accommodation on campus for the four years and all recruits wear a police uniform throughout the duration of their studies. The main areas of academic study are law or public administration. Upon graduation the degree-holding participants are assigned to police management duties at the rank of inspector.[3]

Basic training for new police recruits that are not attending the police university is conducted at the central police academy. Training comprises of 8 months of coursework at the academy followed by practical training in the field. The academy syllabus comprises of 3 weeks of close order drill followed by 25 weeks of preliminary education in law, physical education and knowledge and skills based training. During this 25-week period recruits will spend 6 weeks at a police station working alongside police officers. All new recruits live in academy dormitory accommodation and wear uniforms daily. The academy can accommodate up to 4,500 new recruits each year. Admission to the academy is dependent upon age—not less than 18 years and not more than 30 years of age—and possession of a high school diploma. All participants must hold a valid driver's license, have proportionate height and weight and pass a medical and aptitude test. Upon graduation, all students must have achieved 'masters' level competency in martial arts and self-defense alongside the usual array of competencies in the law, search and seizure, firearms training and crime scene investigation. Classes commence at 6 A.M. each day and conclude at 17.30. Rigorous weekly testing is conducted at every level to ensure competency of recruits in all examined areas. An integral part of the curriculum is "culture-based" training, which incorporates "police spirit, understanding human rights, gender equality and health management."[4] A comprehensive range of evening classes is offered to new recruits, including English conversation classes, yoga and advanced level martial arts.

◆ The Kingdom of Saudi Arabia

The Kingdom of Saudi Arabia is the largest nation on the Arabian Peninsula.[5] Saudi Arabia is surrounded by water, but the interior is dry and arid and known as *Rub al-Khali,* the Empty Quarter. The nation has massive natural resources in oil and gas. Saudi Arabia is a country with a large growing population of which 92% are Sunni Muslim and 8% are Shii Muslim. The country has a monarchy founded in 1932 by the victorious tribal chief Abdul Aziz bin Abdul Rahman al Saud. The basic principles of law are that the Kingdom is based upon Islam's Sacred Law, which is based upon the principles of the prophet Muhammad. Islam is the official religion of Saudi Arabia; laws passed by the Saudi state are therefore considered Koranic laws and binding upon all citizens within the country. The state is responsible for ensuring compliance with Koranic values and teachings and disseminating Islamic and Arab values through Islam's sacred law the *sharia*. The king is legally the ultimate source of all state authority and he possesses full executive powers. The judiciary is independent of the monarch though and considered to be answerable solely to *sharia* law. The country is divided into 13 provinces. Each province has a governor that carries the same rank and status as a Minister of State. Policing and security provision within Saudi Arabia are governed entirely by the provisions of *sharia* law. Saudi Arabia is the birthplace of Islam and the home to the two holy cities of Mecca and Medina. What this means in practice is that the primary function of the police is to protect Islam and its values. The police work under the Ministry of the Interior, which is also the body charged with investigating crimes, apprehending suspects and bringing those suspects before a court. Sharia courts then hear cases brought to them by the Ministry of the Interior. There is very limited information about the recruitment and training of police officers within Saudi Arabia. It is a centralized system that appears to be militarized and to operate as part of the internal defense forces. Members of the Saudi Police participate in international police conferences and the Association of International Police Officers and appear to wish to participate in a modernization of policing efforts within the country. Helicopters, cars and radios are now a common feature of policing within

Saudi Arabia, and a centralized Public Security Service now supplies much of the internal security provision. Uniforms for police personnel are very similar to army uniforms. The distinguishing feature is the red beret worn by the police. Officers are armed with pistols, no longer the standard old style single shot rifle. There is a regular, uniform police division and more recently a special investigation division, the General Directorate of Investigation, the *mubahith* or secret police. The Directorate of Intelligence is responsible for the collation and dissemination of all intelligence, police and military. There is also a SWAT, the Special Security Force. Compliance with religious living and practices is the responsibility of the *mutawwiin*, the religious police. The primary role of the *mutawwiin* is to ensure the observance of religious requirements, for example, prayers five times every day, fasting during Ramadan,[6] the ban on consumption of alcohol and the requirement that women dress modestly. The vigor and enthusiasm for application of sharia law by the *mutawwiin* has been subject to much Western criticism over the past 30 years, as well as some internal commentary also. At one time the *mutawwiin* had authority to detain suspects for up to 24 hours before handing them over to the 'regular' police. In some instances there have been allegations of brutality and the infliction of torture and beatings by the *mutawwiiin*. In was estimated that in 1990 there were in the region of 20,000 *mutawwiin* operating within Saudi Arabia. The current number is thought to be significantly fewer. Members of the religious police wear the traditional white *thaub*. In February 2012, an article titled "Saudis split on admitting women into Islamic police"[7] reported that citizens of the kingdom are split over whether or not women should be permitted to join the religious police. Apparently the new director of the Commission for the Promotion of Virtue and prevention of Vice stated that he was considering the recruitment of women into the often feared and secretive *mutawwiin*. Saudi society is clearly divided on the subject, and one commentator stated "No and 1,000 no's . . . The women's society is uncontrollable and admitting them into the Commission will only increase problems and disasters."[8] Another citizen stated "Yes and 1,000 yes's . . . But there must be conditions for this, including that a female recruit must be a university graduate and must be above 35 years of age."[9] The training of regular police officers, members of the Public Security Forces, is conducted through a police academy.[10] The actions of the regular police in Saudi Arabia do not attract the levels of international interest that the religious police achieve, mainly due to the interest that is held for policing methods that are not easily identifiable with Western policing models. There are no religious police units in any countries other than those that follow Islam, and consequently there is some reticence by the Saudi authorities to divulge details of police recruitment, training and operations. The Crime Prevention and Criminal Justice Division of the United Nations Office in Vienna is responsible for compiling information about the criminal justice systems of all nations; and this also involves commentary about police practices and issues, such as compliance with regulations and how matters pertaining to incidents involving police use of force are recorded. In every aspect, Saudi Arabia is compliant with recognized international criteria for the training and conduct of police officers and the manner in which complaints and the use of force are investigated.[11] The 20,000 or so religious police still manage to attract considerable international attention for alleged abuses of fundamental human rights. On February 15, 2012, ABC News reported that the *mutawwiin* had arrested more than 140 people for celebrating Valentine's Day. "In a six page statement, the religious police stated that they were saving women from 'deceiving men', who used the day [Valentines] to give the fake impression that they loved a woman while pretending to be a 'harmless lamb.'"[12] Authorities reported that Muslims who participate in Valentine's Day are "weak, lacking imagination, and far removed from the 'sublime and virtuous' objectives of their religion."[13] In addition to making hundreds of arrests, the religious police also confiscated red roses from florist shops. Dancing, playing music and showing movies in public are also all religious crimes in Saudi Arabia. Mingling between the sexes is discouraged and may be viewed as an offence punishable as a crime, *khulwa*. Women who are arrested for socializing with men who are not relatives or husbands are liable to be charged with prostitution.

Finland

Finland is one of a number of countries that may be referred to as Scandinavia. There is some debate as to whether or not Finland joins Sweden, Norway and Denmark in making up "Scandinavia." The ambiguity extends further as the Faroe Islands and Iceland are also sometimes referred to as Scandinavia. For the purposes of discussing the policing of the northern European region of Scandinavia I am including Finland with Norway and Sweden. It might be easier to talk of the Nordic countries, but this too is problematic as generally this term includes Denmark as well. Linguistically the Swedes, Danes and Norwegians have similarities that do not apply to the Finnish, but the term Nordic Countries appears to be more inclusive than Scandinavia. That said, I am still using the term Scandinavia to include Finland, Norway and Sweden, and I leave you to thrash out the niceties at another time.

Finland shares borders with Sweden, and it was part of that country until 1809 when it became a duchy within the Russian empire until its independence in 1917. It is the eighth largest country in Europe and the least densely populated. Immediate neighbors are The Russian Federation, Sweden, and to the extreme north, Norway. Helsinki is the capital and largest city with a population of around 600,000 inhabitants. Finland operates under the Civil Law judicial system. Both Finnish and Swedish[14] are official languages of the country. Finland has a centralized police model with officers appointed to serve anywhere across the country. The first comprehensive police law came into effect in 1967[15] (as amended) and brought into effect the creation of police advisory units that bring citizens and police officers together to agree upon strategies and policing initiatives. The Ministry of the Interior is ultimately responsible for the police in Finland. The Police Department, the Supreme Police Command, reports to this ministry and has the day-to day-policing responsibility for the nation. Policing is divided up into five main regions and 24 police departments and the Aland Islands. Since Finnish police provision is national, there are national centers for training, a National Bureau of Investigations, Security Police, Mobile Police and a National Technical Center. New recruits are trained at the Police School in Tampere, POLAMK. Until January 1, 2008, entrants trained at the Police College of Finland in Espoo. The two colleges have now merged and are jointly referred to as The Police College of Finland. Typically the Tampere school trains in the region of 300 new recruits every year. All police officer recruits are trained to university level and must achieve the Diploma in Police studies before graduating from the police college. Senior appointments in the police service ordinarily require candidates to hold at least a master's degree and increasingly a doctorate. Previous military service is considered an advantage for entry to the police service and a reduction in the basic training program is possible for military veterans. The Diploma in Police Studies takes 30 months to complete. It consists of practical and academic courses, similar to many aspects of all police academies, but the timeframe is considerably longer than initial training in the USA or the UK for example. Courses are offered in Finnish and Swedish. The national training school accepts approximately 200 to 400 recruits from the 1,600 applications it receives each year. Typically, 25% of applicants to the national police force of Finland are women. There are in the region of 8,000 sworn officers in Finland, which represent one police officer per 681 citizens. The Police Act of Finland requires that "Police discharge their duties in an appropriate and impartial manner and seek to promote a conciliatory spirit. The actions of the police must not cause any more damage or inconvenience than is necessary to carry out the duty at hand. Measures taken must be justifiable in relation to the importance and urgency of the duty and the factors affecting overall assessment of the situation."[16] In the majority of Civil Law jurisdictions, police investigations are divided up into degrees of seriousness so that less serious crimes will be investigated exclusively by the police and more complex crimes will have a judge or Examining Magistrate appointed to help direct the investigation, interview witnesses and suspects and prepare the file for prosecution. In Finland the pre-trial investigation conducted by the police establishes whether or not a crime has been committed and who should take responsibility for further investigations. However in Finland it is extremely rare that any authority other than the police will conduct the entire investigation into a criminal matter, and it is only in instances where a police officer is the suspect that a state prosecutor will take responsibility for the investigation. In Finland, the National Bureau of Investigation (NBI) investigates organized crime, domestic and international. Unlike the FBI in the USA, members of the NBI are sworn police officers rather than federal agents.

In March 2012, police sergeant Marko Forses, 'Fobba', was named Finland's police officer of the year for his pioneering work in crimes against youths committed via social media networks on the Internet. Fobba noticed that many crimes against young people were occurring on the social network IRC-Galleria, a network that typically attracts around 60% of young people who are social networking in Finland. Initially on a part-time basis, and then recently full-time, Sgt. Forses opened a profile to patrol the site online. He found that his profile received in the neighborhood of 5,000 visitors a week and at one point as many as 35,000. On his profile he posted a large number of user questions resulting in the official police page having 46,000 hits in the first 9 months. Eventually, and in part due to a school shooting incident leaked online, the Ministry of the Interior agreed to fund three officers to work permanently on the social networking site. Social network sites are a prime recruitment tool for pedophiles and traditional methods to encourage reporting are generally low in most countries due to the nature of the crime and the age of the victims. Encouraging young people to report offences through the non-visual and indirect medium of the Internet has already paid off for numerous police agencies. Cyber bullying is also increasing significantly and, according to Forses, "It's sometimes enough to give the buller, youth or adult, a virtual warning. Usually that stops the bullying because normal people want to avoid police investigation."[17]

Sweden

Sweden is an immediate neighbor to Finland. It is the fifth largest country in Europe and, like Finland, it too has a small population—9.5 million, of which 85% of the population lives in the southern part of the country. Stockholm is the capital and has a population of around 2 million. Sweden has a constitutional monarchy as well as a democratic parliament. Prior to 1965, policing was municipal and regional. Since then it has become a national force with the National Police Board as the governing body. There are about 17,000 sworn police officers representing a ratio of less than two police officers per 100,000 population.[18] Policing is divided up into counties (districts); there are 21 in total, the largest being Stockholm with 4,500 officers.

Each county typically has operations, criminal investigations, drugs and technical support divisions. The overall responsibility for the police rests with the National Police Commissioner who answers to the Ministry of Justice. In addition to district police responses, there are a number of national level departments, such as the antiterrorist unit, the National Security Service, criminal investigations, the National Criminal Investigations Department and the National Police Academy responsible for initial recruit training and specialized courses. There is also a national forensics laboratory service, the National Laboratory of Forensic Science. The police receive their powers under the Swedish Police Act 1999. Basic training consists of attending a police academy—Stockholm, Umea or Vaxjo. The institution at Solna, Stockholm is exclusively a police academy. The other two police academies are part of universities. Basic training lasts for two years, and after passing university level courses graduates leave with a diploma that permits them to apply for a probationary working position within a police county. This second phase of training lasts six months. Basic training places a strong emphasis on behavioral science and knowledge of the law. Classes are structured around participant discussions that emphasize human rights and the 'science' of policing ethically in a diverse society. Having successfully completed the academic training and the practical training the recruit is now considered a constable/patrol officer. Entry into the national police service is highly competitive. Sweden operates an examining magistrate system so that serious crimes are investigated under the direction of an investigating judge who directs the police in terms of the detention of suspects, what and when charges should be brought and overall responsibility for the preparation of the case prosecution.

Norway

Norway is a country that has the most northern border in Europe and a population spread of just 14 inhabitants per square kilometer. It is one of the least populated countries in Europe. Norway shares borders with Sweden, Finland and Russia. Norway has two official languages—Dano-Norwegian, *Bokmal,* and New Norwegian, *Nynorsk.* Both languages have equal status in the country. There are 19 counties in Norway and one national police force divided into 27 police districts.[19] Each district has a Chief of Police. Overall, the police report to the Ministry of Justice. Legal procedure in Norway is adversarial in nature, rather than inquisitorial, and the courts operate on the principle of binding precedence with decisions of the Supreme Court binding all lower courts. Senior police officers in Norway are part of the Prosecuting Authority and consequently chiefs of police are also qualified lawyers. Norway is a constitutional monarchy like Sweden, and if a chief of police decides to prosecute a senior government official for a criminal offence it is a matter for the king to decide on the appropriateness of proceeding with the matter. Apart from the semi-autonomous 27 police districts, there are centralized training and special services, such as the National Criminal Investigations Service, the National Economic Crime Unit, OKORIM, the Central Mobile Service, the National Police Immigration Service, the National Police Computing and Material Service and the Security Service. Although the origins of policing in Norway are attributable to the French gendarmerie model, today the force is a mixture of relatively independent district forces operating under one chief of police, as well as a centralized system for national services and training. Norway represents a hybrid model of policing that is neither exclusively centralized nor decentralized. Entry into the Norwegian police service requires acceptance into the National Police Academy in Oslo, the Norwegian Police University College. The program is a university level program and all successful graduates are awarded a baccalaureate degree, the bachelor's degree in police education. The three years are divided up into academic and practical training where after the completion of year one, recruits spend 12 months in the field at one of the 27 police districts before returning to complete academic studies and final exams. Law and sociology are required classes in year one. "The purpose of the bachelors program is to educate thoughtful and vigorous police officers who are able to prevent crime, enforce the law, and provide assistance in a manner which attends to the legal protection and safety of the citizens, as well as the interests of society at large."[20] Admittance into the degree program requires Norwegian citizenship, a minimum of 20 years of age, character and background checks, aptitude tests and "required personal maturity and character to serve as a police officer."[21] In 2011, there were 2,760 applicants to the police university college. Of these, 720 were accepted and 36.1% of the accepted applicants were female.[22]

Canada

Canada is the second largest country in the world. It has a population of 34.5 million people.[23] Life expectancy is 80 years on average and education and healthcare are free for all citizens. More than one million of the working population holds a doctorate or a master's degree. Eighty-five percent of all Canadian exports go to the USA. Canada is a federal state as well as a constitutional monarchy headed by Queen Elizabeth II, represented within Canada by a governor general. Canada is a federation comprised of 10 provinces and three territories. Canada has two official languages, French and English. The legal system is the Common Law other than in French speaking Quebec where it is the French Civil Law for civil matters. The Supreme Court of Canada is the ultimate authority for both Common Law and Civil Law matters. There are in the region of 500 different police and criminal justice organizations in Canada,[24] and the largest by far is the Royal Canadian Mounted Police, the *Gendarmerie royal du Canada* (RCMP), who are a national force. Policing provision is provided at the local municipal level, the province and territory level, and at the federal level. Overall, there are in the neighborhood of 185 police officers per 100,000 population. This is less than either the USA or the UK, which both have more than 200 officers per 100,000 population.[25] In 2011, there were a total of 69,438 sworn police officers in Canada,[26] the largest single number being in Ontario with 26,387 sworn personnel.[27] The highest density of officers per 100,000 population is in the Northwest Territories with 451.1 of the province, and the fewest is Prince Edward Island with 167.3.[28] The National Police Services (NPS) is a business arm of the RCMP that provides information and training to all of the various agencies and organizations. Services provided by the NPS include the Centre for Missing and Exploited Children, the Canadian Police College, the Canadian Police Information Centre, the Criminal Intelligence Services Canada and the Forensic Science and Identification Services. The Canadian Police College is not responsible for basic training due to the diversity of police services provided across the nation besides which much is policed locally and at the state level. What the NPC provides is executive level courses for senior officers from the various national, provincial and municipal forces. The RCMP is a world-renowned police force that is unique in that it is a national, federal, provincial and municipal police force. Easily distinguishable by the famous red tunic, known as "The Red Serge," the RCMP has been a feature of Canadian policing since 1873. Today the RCMP policies three territories and eight provinces; it does not provide municipal policing to Ontario or Quebec, 190 municipalities, 184 Aboriginal communities and three international airports. The RCMP is organized under the RCMP Act and reports to the Minister of Public Safety. The current total strength of the RCMP is 29,235.[29] Unlike most other police forces in Canada, the RCMP is not unionized. Training of recruits into the RCMP is conducted at 'Depot', the RCMP Academy in Regina, Saskatchewan. Initial training lasts for 24 weeks. It is called the Cadet Training Program and is geared very much towards adult learning and community policing with problem solving scenarios and discussions. Application to the RCMP requires Canadian citizenship, a minimum age of 19 years, a high school diploma, a current valid Canadian driver's license and proficiency in either French or English. As is the case in the USA and the UK, there is no officer entry into the police service; all recruits join at the constable level regardless of academic qualifications upon entry. Entry requirements also include the statement, "You should possess the following values: integrity, honesty, professionalism, compassion, respect and accountability. Our selection process will determine if your personal history, traits and characteristics are suitable for a career in policing."[30] In addition to the RCMP, there are hundreds of police forces across the country that provide a response to local policing needs. Many of these forces are very small in size and in order to defer training costs they encourage new recruits to obtain the academic stages of training from a community college before being accepted into the force for practical training. Within the more populated provinces, there are also sheriffs in addition to city police forces; for example, the British Columbia Sheriff Service. In addition to supplying police services to the entire province, the sheriff's department also continues to provide services to the courts system of the province in very much the same way as was established back in the Dark Ages in England. As you will recall from Chapter Six, in the UK the office of sheriff is now largely ceremonial. In Canada it is more similar to the USA's model where sheriffs are engaged in every aspect of policing as well as the additional role of protecting Provincial, Supreme and Appeal Courts of BC, judges and Crown Prosecutors. The BC Sheriff's Department also runs the court detention cells (not the city jails) and escorts prisoners. The Vancouver Police Department is one of a number of police forces within the Vancouver metro area. It was the first municipal police force in Canada to appoint a female officer. The VPD started with the appointment of one officer in 1886 and is today a force of 1,700 civilians and sworn officers. In addition to providing police services to the City of Vancouver, the force also has a separate department that employs jail guards for the city jails. Jail guards are not sworn officers though many become sworn police officers after serving in this department. Training to become a jail guard is of one-month duration and takes place during evenings and weekends. The VPD also employs non-union sworn officers as special constables into the Traffic Authority. These officers have limited authority, such as directing traffic at major events. It is a paid, part-time position. Training involves completion of an 85-hour program over evenings and weekends and includes such issues as legal studies, use of force and traffic control. Police officers are selected through an assessment center process where all applicants spend one day at the police academy engaged in role-play scenarios. If successful and all other entry requirements are completed, initial training comprises of attendance at the Justice Institute of British Columbia (JIBC) on Vancouver Island. Training is divided into three blocks: basic training 11 weeks, field training (on patrol under supervision) 13 weeks and then advanced training back at JIBC for a further 11 weeks. There is no officer entry into the VPD.

Two provinces have a statewide police responsibility: the Ontario Provincial Police, OPP, and the *Sûreté du Quebec*. Basic training with the OPP involves completion of a 12-week academy at the Ontario Police College. This is followed by a period of field training and then a further 5 weeks back at the academy. The first 12 months of employment as a sworn officer once all initial training is complete is considered a probationary period. After completion of this probation, a constable officer is confirmed in office and rank. The *Sûreté du Quebec,* referred to in English as the QPP, was formed in 1870 and is responsible for providing police service to the entire province of Quebec. Entry into the QPP requires recruits to obtain a Diploma of Collegial Studies from one of the 12 colleges located within the province and then to have completed the basic Patrol Officer Program at the QPP academy. After successful completion of the first stage, officers must have an offer of employment from the QPP and then attend and complete the 15-week initial training program at the Quebec police academy, the *Ecole Nationale de Police du Quebec*. Upon completion of the second stage of training, ". . . the school issues a report indicating the degree to which the candidate has mastered the competencies learned. This attestation is the result of a continuing formative and summative evaluation process based on instructor supervision as well as the observations of all the contributors encountered by the candidate during his stay at the *Ecole nationale de police du Quebec*. A diploma in police patrolling is awarded in recognition of the successful achievement of the requisite criteria for each of the competencies making up the program."[31] The cost of operating the program per recruit, excluding salary, is $6,615 Canadian dollars for the 15 weeks.[32] The language used at the academy is French and all recruits must pass examinations in French to graduate.

The RCMP

The RCMP was modeled on the Royal Irish Constabulary, which I have argued in Chapter Six is a manifestation of the French gendarmerie disguised as such by Robert Peel. The police of French speaking Quebec are not direct copies of the French gendarmerie though; in fact, they are closer in nature and form to a city force structure that might have originated in London with the Metropolitan Police. Both models are indicative of the diversity of policing seen in Canada. There are national, provincial and municipal forces and there are sheriffs. Additionally, there are Aboriginal police forces that specialize in policing under the First Nations Policing Program.[33] Policing in Canada is truly diverse and complex with a number of apparent police models: centralized, decentralized and hybrids. Together they provide a police response across a massive landmass to a population of numerous multi-cultural origins. There are few countries of the world that have as diverse an arrangement of police provision as Canada. Even in the United States, which has in the region of 20,000 different law enforcement agencies, there is nothing similar to the RCMP; and when you add to that the state, local and sheriff provision, it represents more models of policing encompassed within one nation than any other country.[34]

As seen by the differences above, the recruitment and training of police officers vary greatly between different countries and even within those countries between states and municipalities. What it means to police is a vexing question without one uniform answer. Policing can be centralized and viewed as an arm of the government or decentralized and answerable to a body of elected local citizens. It can be military and serve the whim of a dictator rather than the citizens at all, and it can be religious. In between all these variations there are further layers that have developed over time in response to cultural and societal developments.

One present challenge is that we have a bank of crimes that are international and any country in the world can arrest and prosecute the criminals committing those crimes. Presumably then we would want or need an international police force to conduct those investigations, a police force that is not restricted by national laws or national boundaries and borders.

Perhaps policing international crimes requires an international police agency with powers of arrest and detention anywhere, eventually even into space.

Well, we are certainly not there yet and what international 'police' type agencies we have are restricted in the scope and powers they have. In fact, the majority of global responses are not a police force at all but more of an intelligence collating response that provides support to local forces to effect arrests. As yet we do not have a mobile international police force.

What we do have and the direction we are heading in is the subject of the last part of this chapter: international police responses.

◆ International Police Responses

Today it is not uncommon for a police officer from one country to spend a period of time serving abroad. This might be for the United Nations as part of a UN police keeping mission, working for the D.E.A. in Peru providing assistance and training to the national federal police. It could be on secondment to EUROPOL or working for Interpol gathering evidence to prosecute war criminals before the International Criminal Court in The Hague. Whereas all of these police responses are necessary and undoubtedly attempt to provide a more secure world for us, there are issues about accountability that should be borne in mind. So far we have established that nation states generally write and enforce their own criminal laws. We have also established that some crimes are international. The potential for problems is that if our police forces are locally appointed and locally accountable then who is watching them on the international platform? At the moment most citizens have a pretty good idea of what it means to be policed, locally. But what does it mean to be policed internationally? What laws do and should govern international criminal investigations and what powers do we want police officers to have to effect arrests or to conduct investigations in another sovereign state? Most citizens of the US would be surprised if they were to answer their door and a police officer from Finland started making enquiries of them. This is not to say that we do not have rules and protocols, and we certainly have bi-lateral and multi-lateral agreements that are aimed at providing the appropriate parameters for the powers of international police agencies. The problem though is that the general citizen's awareness of international policing is little if anything, so established limitations on the abuse of power could be compromised with the best of intentions. On the issue of international policing, one question should be who is policing the police? A second issue is whose criminal justice system will dominate, as surely one will? Alternatively, some people will be of the view that these are issues unlikely ever to be a serious problem as a truly international global police force is never likely to happen; but transnational police certainly are a reality and already does exist. One definition of transnational policing is that it is, ". . . any form of order maintenance, law enforcement, peacekeeping, crime investigation, intelligence sharing, or other form of police work that transcends or traverses national boundaries."[35] This is helpful as it causes the reader to look beyond the better-known entities and also consider agencies such as the Financial Action Task Force (IACP)[36] and the UNODC[37] under the framework of international policing responses.

In 1914, the world's first international policing congress was held in Monaco. As a result of this, there was a consensus of agreement to form a police support agency that would act as a conduit to help police forces across the world to share information. INTERPOL is now an organization of 188 countries that collectively contribute to maintain a headquarters in Lyon, France, and seven regional offices (NCBs) around the globe. Each member state has one vote at the annual general assembly. The secretary-general holds office for a renewable four-year term and acts as the chief executive officer. In addition to providing support services to member countries, INTERPOL also tests technology and will assist national agencies in missions. INTERPOL is also the primary agency for circulating wanted persons across the globe; this is achieved through the 'Red Alert' system. As with all information systems, the information is only as good as what is put in; and there have been a few unfortunate instances of innocent civilians[38] being arrested and detained due to faulty or outdated data input. The 'Red Alert' is not a warrant of arrest though. INTERPOL is not a police force and has no powers to arrest or to conduct international crime investigations, but it will send an Incident Response Team (IRT) into a country at the request of that country to provide immediate assistance during a major crisis. IRTs are highly mobile and typically are deployed within 24 hours anywhere across the world. The first use of an IRT was in Bali, Indonesia, in 2002 in response to a request for assistance dealing with a terrorist bombing. INTERPOL assisted in more than 30 police operations in 2011.[39] It is perhaps inevitable that as the nexus of drugs trafficking and organized crime extends across terrorism also, agencies such as INTERPOL will be drawn into a more quasi-operational role where it conducts more and more operations alongside national police forces. Whether this transgresses the concept of national sovereignty in matters of criminal law remains to be seen, but certainly there is a trend towards greater internationalization of policing and INTERPOL is placed to be at the forefront of this discussion. Over the past 10 years, the amount of involvement in drug trafficking operations by INTERPOL has increased significantly, especially in the area of cyber-trafficking in drugs and humans where it can provide expert services without being 'operational'. The issue though is where will the divide fall and at what point is INTERPOL *de facto* an international police agency? In its 2011 annual report, INTERPOL reported that, at the request of SEPCA,[40] INTERPOL designed, implemented and *managed* a project targeted at organized crime groups. Under project BESA, more than 200 arrests were made.[41] It may be a matter of semantics, but when an organization is 'managing' a major police operation to disrupt organized crime and drug trafficking resulting in the arrest of 200 individuals that sounds very much like a police operation.

In 1994, the European Drug Unit was formed. It consisted of police officers drawn from every contributing European Union member state. By 199 this unit had morphed into EUROPOL. The main business of EUROPOL is similar to be that of INTERPOL but exclusively for nation states within the EU. In reality, the scope of its work has grown to be that of an operational police unit that can move across borderless Europe in pursuit of organized criminal enterprises. Additionally, EUROPOL works increasingly with law enforcement agencies outside of the EU and a number of national agencies have law enforcement personnel working with EUROPOL on a secondment basis. Within Europe, there are a number of bi-lateral agreements between nations that share borders so that officers may have a limited level of 'hot pursuit' capability. In 2008, an arrangement between France and Spain was formalized to allow officers on either side of their borders to operate together as one force. This was specifically designed to counter the work of the Spanish separatist organization ETA. Recently ETA announced a cessation of its campaign,[42] but the original anti-terrorist capacity has been formalized into GEAD, a combined dual-nation anti-drug force. Most of the countries of continental Europe have a military gendarmerie as well as a civilian police presence. In January 2006 EUROGENDFOR,[43] EGF, was established as a European gendarme force. It currently has 30 staff and 900 officers that are on detachment from their home countries of France, Spain, Portugal, The Netherlands, Belgium and Romania, to the unit. A challenging question for the future of this police unit is will it have a remit to operate in those countries that do not have a military police force, if perhaps those countries do not want military style policing within their borders.

The United Nations has a number of policing roles, such as the work of the UNODC and UNPOL. UNODC has the mission of "making the world safer from crime, drugs and terrorism."[44] UNODC is not a police unit of the UN. It achieves its mission by working alongside individual countries as well as global agencies, such as INTERPOL, to achieve new levels of crime prevention and criminal justice reform. UNODC has made significant contributions towards opening up dialog between national policing agencies and it is a major voice in encouraging transparency between police forces across the world. UNODC provides expert advice in a number of areas of criminal justice, which is disseminated through its website and also its regional and country programs. UNODC is also responsible for the collation and distribution of crime data and the compilation of annual reports about trends in crime and the ability of nation states to work effectively in preventing human trafficking, drugs trafficking and other crimes against humanity. Scientific and technical support is also offered by UNODC through its Laboratory and Scientific Section. This section provides expert services through manuals, guidelines and publications pertinent to drug analysis, forensic science and the needs of national law enforcement agencies, as well as the UN Commission on Narcotic Drugs and the International Narcotics Control Board.

"The United nations has been deploying police officers for service in peace operations since the 1960's. Traditionally, the mandate of police components in peace operations was limited to monitoring, observing and reporting. Beginning in the early 1990's, advisory, mentoring and training functions were integrated into the monitoring activities in order to offer peace operations the opportunity to act as a corrective mechanism with domestic police and other law enforcement agencies."[45] There are currently more than 17,500 United Nations Police Officers serving across the world. The first UN police unit to be deployed was to the Congo in 1960. By 1994, the number of officers in CIVPOL (the name changed to UNPOL in 2005) had grown to 1,677. A large number were at this time deployed in the former Yugoslavia. The first 'formed police unit' (FPU) was established in 1999. An FPU consists of 140 officers working as a single unit in crowd control and riot situations. There are now more than 600 FPUs employing more than 6,000 officers.[46] By 2009, there were 11,000 UN police officers deployed in more than 100 countries. The number of female officers has steadily increased also and there is now an initiative to get the strength of female officers up to 20% of the force by 2014. Ordinarily, UNPOL officers are sent into a country alongside UN peacekeeping missions and military personnel. Their primary function is to assist local police efforts, in an advisory capacity, with public order, crime fighting and technical advice and training. In some cases throughout the past 50 years, UNPOL has acted as the police force for a nation state while that state rebuilds itself. In these cases, the UNPOL officers have full rights of arrest, search and seizure in the same way as the domestic police. This was the case in Kosovo and is currently happening in the Cote D'Ivoire, the Democratic Republic of the Congo, Haiti and Liberia. Another function of UNPOL is to provide protection to UN personnel within a nation state. Recruitment to UNPOL consists of a Selection and Assessment and Assistance Team (SAAT) interview process that starts in the applicant's home country. Members of UNPOL are all existing police officers in their home nations who serve with UNPOL for an initial six months. Upon acceptance to UNPOL, new recruits undergo UN training before deployment in the field. Entry into an FPU starts in the same way but involves a different training program with the UN that consists of a six-week training program in public order control.

In addition to the various international police responses that are now in existence, many nation states send attaches and liaison officers to work in other countries alongside the domestic police. The UK has more than 180 officers serving overseas; France a similar number.[47] The US has hundreds of CIA, FBI, Federal Marshals Service and DEA personnel serving in a variety of capacities in missions and embassies throughout the world; so too do Canada and Australia.[48] The International Criminal Court in The Hague has no police force of its own to make arrests and secure the attendance of criminals suspected of crimes. The ICC can issue arrest warrants, but without the efforts of other police agencies to make arrests, these actions would be hollow. It is therefore and currently solely reliant upon the resources of member states to provide the local law enforcement services to make arrests. "When the Court's jurisdiction is triggered by the Security Council, the duty to cooperate extends to all UN Member states, regardless of whether or not they are a Party to the Statute. The crimes within the jurisdiction of the Court are the gravest crimes known to humanity and as provided for by article 29 of the Statute they shall not be subject to any statute of limitations. Warrants of arrest are lifetime orders and therefore individuals still at large will sooner or later face the Court."[49]

How the enforcement of arrest warrants develops in the future, as more global criminals are indicted and brought before the international tribunal, will be interesting as there will surely come a time when either UNPOL or another existing, or created, agency will take responsibility for enforcement of ICC warrants. The ICC is currently investigating alleged crimes against humanity[50] in Afghanistan, Colombia, the Republic of Korea, Georgia, Guinea, Honduras, Nigeria and Palestine.[51] There are 108 members of the ICC; the USA has not re-joined the Court since President George

Bush 'unsigned' the joining treaty in May 2002.⁵² Alongside the US China is also a country that has refused to accept the jurisdiction of the ICC over its nationals.

◆ Summary

Policing the world is a huge undertaking—that is, if it should be undertaken at all. The fundamental right of nation states to police themselves is inviolable for many citizens and the idea that a 'superjurisdiction' could or should take responsibility for bringing world criminals to justice is offensive to many citizens (and leaders). But in many ways we are already there. National police forces supply expertise and personnel to a wide range of law enforcements agencies that have supranational reach. Models of policing are shared and copied so that EUROPOL looks like a European DEA. The new National Crime Agency in the UK has already been dubbed the UK's FBI, and France has unified the police of two countries into one force on its southern border with Spain. Gendarmes across Europe have grouped together to provide a military police agency to those that have this policing model (and maybe those who do not). Federal agents from the US, Canada, Australia and many other nations share colleagues across virtual and real borders and the UN has a multi-national police response that now assists in public order matters as well as investigating and assisting in prosecuting terrorism and a wide range of other crimes—the very crimes discussed in previous chapters of this book: murders, abductions, networked thefts and drug trafficking. Our international police responses are no longer restricted to investigating gross human violations as they were 40 years ago. Today we internationally police the entire plethora of the criminality. Perhaps a discussion about what model of policing will 'WorldPol' assume is otiose after all.

In this final chapter we have considered a range of policing models and we have seen that 'becoming a police officer' varies greatly from country to country. It is quite possible that many citizens across the planet have come to view policing as a generalist task that is very similar regardless of where it is taking place. The reality is that policing is not 'one size fits all' and what the police are expected to do is very much a reflection of national and local laws and domestic cultural influences set against a backdrop of increasingly globalized criminal endeavors. Determining how this fits into numerous domestic criminal justice systems rather than one unified global entity is a huge challenge.

In some countries, a person may become a police officer at 18 years of age with little more than a high school diploma; in others, the minimum entry age is 21 and a degree is required. Initial training can be as brief as six weeks⁵³ or as long as three years. Some forces are highly centralized with a government department taking a significant role in how the police are trained and operate; other countries have devolved the policing function to local accountability with considerable local civilian input. In some countries police training is very similar to a military boot camp, whereas in others the emphasis is upon gaining social skills, understanding human rights and group discussion. The police are civilian, military and religious. They are local, municipal, tribal, state, provincial, national and international. And there are also private police agencies and a range of police 'family members' such as: ISD police, parks police, housing police, special jurisdiction police, customs and immigration. We have joint forces, joint operations, formal and informal agreements—lateral, bi-lateral and multi-lateral. We are not constrained by real or virtual borders and the police are not either. If this portrayal is accurate, then the likelihood of a police officer in a rural location managing to complete an entire career without exposure to international crime or criminals is extremely unlikely. It would follow that being aware of 'who' 'what' and 'how' international crime impacts domestic policing would be vital to all sworn officers. The USA has more police officers and police forces than any country on Earth; there are 65 federal agencies, 27 offices of inspector general, 50 state police agencies and more than 19,000 local agencies, some with as few as one sworn officer. [54]

As you the reader may appreciate, crimes often appear local but in reality can transcend county, state, national and international borders. How well prepared our police officers, courts and prison systems are to deal with these challenges is itself a challenge for criminal justice in the 21st century.

Endnotes

1. There are 193 member states that comprise the United Nations. The Vatican City and Kosovo are independent countries and currently not members of the UN. Taiwan meets the UN requirements to be classified as a country but currently does not do so due to its tense political situation with China. Puerto Rico, Bermuda, Palestine, Northern Ireland, Scotland and Wales are frequently referred to as countries. They are not at this time and are not counted as part of the global total of 196.
2. www.police.go.kr
3. See further: www.police.ac.kr
4. www.cpa.go.kr
5. Others include: Yemen, Oman, Bahrain, UAE, Kuwait, Iraq, Jordan, Syria and Lebanon.
6. Interestingly, there was a time when the original police of Paris in the 17th century were required to ensure compliance with the rule not to eat meat on Fridays, once required of all Catholics, and the observance of Lent. Butchers found transgressing the no meat on Friday laws were subject to arrest and financial penalties.
7. www.emirates247.com Nadim Kawach. February 29, 2012
8. Ibid.
9. Ibid.
10. The Royal Saudi Arabian Police Academy, Riyadh.
11. Details available at www.uncjin.org ksuadi.pdf
12. Religious police swoop on Valentine's Day lovers. ABC News, February 15, 2012. www.abc.net.au/news
13. Ibid.
14. Six percent of the population speaks Swedish.
15. No 84/1966
16. General Principles of Operation at www.poliisi.fi
17. Stevens, L. Online patrols: How one Finnish cop tracked youth crime. March 27, 2012. www.policeone.com
18. There is a similar ratio to neighbors in Finland at 1 officer per 681 citizens.
19. The Norwegian Police Directorate was established in 2001 to coordinate central and regional policing efforts.
20. National Police Academy information webpage. Bachelor-Police Studies. www.phs.no
21. Ibid.
22. Ibid.
23. Source World Bank 2011 Public data
24. www.rcmp-grc.gc.ca
25. www.statcan.gc.ca
26. Ibid.
27. Ibid.
28. Ibid.
29. www.rcmp-grc.gc.ca
30. Ibid.
31. www.enpq.qc.ca
32. Ibid.

33. Provides policing services to 408 First Nation and Inuit communities with a total population of 327,430 people by 1,240 officers. Source: www.publicsafety.gc.ca
34. The closest resemblance would be in Australia where there are federal police, state police, municipal police, sheriffs and bailiffs. However, the range of responsibilities assigned to the RCMP is greater in scope and the RCMP, in some instances, provides the only local municipal policing response in remote parts of the country.
35. Bowling, B. and Sheptycki, J. 2012. *Global policing*. Los Angeles: Sage, p. 3.
36. International Association of Chiefs of Police
37. United Nations Office on Drug Control and Crime
38. See for example the incident involving Derek Bond, a UK citizen on vacation in South Africa in 2003, who was detained erroneously for three weeks on a 'red alert'. It was believed Bond was Derek Sykes, alias Bond, wanted in the USA for fraud. The red alert information circulated by the FBI was found to be inaccurate and incomplete.
39. www.interpol.int Annual Report 2011.
40. Southeast Europe Police Chiefs Association
41. Source: 2011 Annual Report. Supra
42. October 2011
43. www.eurogendfor.eu
44. UNODC website home page. www.unodc.org
45. www.un.org/en/peacekeeping/sites/ploice United Nations Policing 'A crucial part of UN peace operations'.
46. Ibid.
47. See Bowling and Sheptycki, supra. pp. 4–6
48. Ibid.
49. www.icc-cpi.int
50. The ICC has jurisdiction over genocide, crimes against humanity and war crimes. It does not currently have jurisdiction over drug trafficking or terrorism cases unless these fall within the previous three even though both of the latter are considered 'global' crimes. Crimes of aggression (invasion, annexation by force, blockades and military occupation) may be included after a planned vote is taken in 2017.
51. www.icc-cpi.int
52. For a thorough discussion of the issue, see: US Policy toward the International Criminal Court: Furthering positive engagement. Report of an Independent Task Force convened by The American Society of International Law. March 2009. Available at www.asil.org The US did eventually sign the Rome Statute in 200, but President George Bush 'unsigned' the US in 2002. And he followed up this removal by threatening military action against the ICC if any US nationals were held at The Hague; see: www.globalissues.org United States and the International Criminal Court and the American Servicemembers Protection Act 2002 (The Hague Invasion Act).
53. In the USA, some 'academies' are of less than six weeks duration. See: www.bjs.ojp.usdoj.gov State and Law Enforcement Training Academies 2006. Published February 2009. NCJ 22987
54. www.discoverpolicing.org

ANSWERS TO CHAPTER QUESTIONS

◆ Chapter One

1. a. True
2. a. True
3. d. Misdemeanors and Felonies
4. b. False
5. a. 2200 BC
6. b. Compurgatory oaths
7. a. Roman
8. b. ratio decendi
9. b. Napoleon Bonaparte
10. a. Vigilante and night watch
11. d. Britain and the Common Law

◆ Chapter Two

1. c. Murder, non-negligent manslaughter, rape, robbery, burglary, larceny-theft, motor vehicle theft and arson
2. a. True
3. a. True
4. a. True
5. a. True
6. b. False
7. b. Funnel
8. d. 40%
9. a. True
10. a. True

Chapter Three

1. a. Tax collector, jailer and court administrator
2. a. The County of Accomack, Virginia
3. c. Colbert
4. a. True
5. b. False
6. a. Principal Officer of Bow Street
7. b. The City of London (The Square Mile)
8. b. Eugene Vidocq
9. d. The Magna Carta
10. a. 1337

Chapter Four

1. a. True
2. d. 21
3. b. 50%
4. a. True
5. b. False
6. a. True
7. b. False
8. b. 1%
9. a. True
10. c. Pennsylvania State Police

Chapter Five

1. d. 73
2. a. True
3. b. Pentagon Force Protection Agency
4. b. False (16)
5. a. Fraud, bribery, waste and abuse related to federal programs
6. c. ATF
7. c. Secret Service
8. b. US Marshals Service
9. a. Behavioral Analysis Units
10. b. False (very few also have federal agencies)

Chapter Six

1. b. 4th Amendment
2. a. True
3. c. Facts and circumstances
4. b. False
5. c. The evidentiary rule
6. d. *Mapp v. Ohio*
7. c. Exigent circumstances
8. a. *Miranda v Arizona*
9. b. Custody and interrogation
10. b. False

Chapter Seven

1. b. False (2 years)
2. c. ROR
3. b. False
4. c. 2500 BCE
5. b. Judiciary Act of 1789
6. c. The Vera Institute of Justice
7. b. False (54%)
8. a. True
9. b. Prior history of failing to appear, active warrants and community ties (p. 138)
10. a. One third

Chapter Eight

1. a. True
2. c. 48 hours
3. b. Arraignment
4. a. Charging grand juries
5. a. True
6. b. Nine out of ten
7. b. False (they were the greatest not smallest, p. 163)
8. c. Challenge for cause
9. d. Bench trial
10. c. Motions

◆ Chapter Nine

1. b. Scared straight
2. c. Auburn system
3. b. False (It is RELEVANT, p. 189)
4. a. True (p. 191)
5. a. True
6. b. 71 months
7. b. False (Most assaults take place in STATE prisons)
8. a. 200 to 300%
9. a. True
10. a. 12 and 13

◆ Chapter Ten

1. c. John Augustus
2. a. Perhaps three to six months maximum
3. d. Community-based probation
4. a. Victim-offender mediation
5. a. True
6. b. False
7. c. Drug
8. c. Commutation, pardon and amnesty
9. c. Commuted
10. b. False

GLOSSARY

Accessory   An individual who gets involved with the postcrime events who did not know or have any connection with a crime or its preparation, but gets involved afterward by helping the perpetrator evade arrest or by providing the perpetrator a place of asylum.

Accidental crime   One that was not planned or premeditated that occurred by happenstance.

Actus reus   The criminal act or omission.

Adjective law   The adjective law prescribes how the police, prosecutors, courts, and others must carry out certain procedures, just as the adjective in English grammar describes a noun. There is no criminal sanction for failure to follow the rules, but the officer may have evidence or a confession excluded if he or she does not follow the adjective laws or court-made rules.

Adjudication   The legal procedure of processing the accused person through the judicial process of initial appearance, preliminary hearing, and trial. This term is often used for processing a juvenile to demonstrate the difference from the adult process.

Administrative law   A law that regulates professional conduct of such professional as doctors, attorneys, or real estate brokers, and violations are punished by suspension or revocation of a license rather than sanctions or imprisonment.

Adversary system   Prosecution and defense present opposing side of the criminal case in the manner of opposing sports teams only with more significant results. Both sides are required to present a vigorous representation of their clients.

Affidavit   A sworn statement that the affiant claims to be true under penalty of perjury.

Alford plea   A plea of guilty to end a period of imprisonment that exceeds the time one would serve if convicted. The accused claims innocence but chooses to plead guilty to get the matter over with instead of more delays with a trial.

Anomie   The situation in a community in transition where there is no spirit of community and everyone is a stranger, living anonymously.

Apparent authority   The individual who answers the door and invites the officer in and appears to be the legal resident. When the officer asks for consent to search, or is invited to search the premises, the authority seems to be apparent. Later, it is ascertained that the person giving consent actually was a former spouse who did not have authority to consent to the search.

From *Criminal Justice 101: An Introduction to the System* by Thomas A. Adams. Copyright © 2010 by Thomas F. Adams. Reprinted by permission.

Appeal The process whereby a person convicted of a crime may petition a higher court to review the rulings of a trial court that the appellant claims made a mistake or that a constitutional issue is at stake.

Area of immediate control This is the space immediately surrounding the arrestee, or the "wingspan." A search incidental to an arrest, since the *Chimel* decision, may cover only the subject's immediate space, not the entire premises. To go beyond one's wingspan requires a search warrant.

Arraignment Usually the first appearance of the accused in court, notifying him or her of the criminal charges that are being brought by the prosecuting attorney. It is not unusual for the officer to arrest a suspect for a felony assault; then, following a medical examination of the victim that finds no broken bones or tissue damage, the prosecution files a lesser charge of misdemeanor assault. On another occasion a suspect may be arrested for a single business burglary, but following forensic analysis of the evidence compared with that from other unsolved crimes, the suspect is notified at the arraignment that he or she is being charged with eight additional burglaries.

Arrest Taking of a person into custody for the purpose of prosecution or interrogation concerning a criminal offense.

Arson Deliberate unlawful burning of one's own property or that of another for unlawful purpose.

Asphyxiate To render a person incapable of breathing, which is likely to cause death. This can be done by choking, smothering, or confining in an enclosed space containing carbon monoxide or that is devoid of oxygen.

Assault A physical assault by one person on another with intent to cause injury.

Atavistic An earlier stage of human development. Cesare Lombroso theorized that born criminals possessed certain physical characteristics resembling humans in earlier stages of development.

Autopsy A complete medical and scientific examination of the deceased to determine the cause and time of death and attendant circumstances. This examination is performed by a medical doctor (with a special designation of pathologist) who is usually assisted by a technician in the facilities of a coroner or a medical examiner in a morgue. Some coroners are medical doctors/pathologists, but many are not. A coroner may be an elected official who also serves as a sheriff or tax collector. This individual then employs pathologists on a full- or part-time basis to perform the autopsy, or postmortem exam.

Bail Insurance to ensure the appearance in court of a person charged with a crime to answer criminal charges.

Bail bond The insurance policy posted instead of cash to ensure the defendant's appearance in court when scheduled.

Battery Completion of the act of actually conflicting physical injury on the victim of an assault. This act is often prosecuted as assault and battery.

Bench warrant An oral direction by the judge to the bailiff to go and arrest the person named by the judge. One purpose for a bench warrant would be for failure to appear in court as a witness or defendant.

Booking The admitting process at the jail immediately following the arrest, consisting of photographing, fingerprinting, and entering the arrestee's name and charges into the jail register. This information was originally entered into the jail's register logbook.

Breaking and entering A common term used for the crime of burglary: entering a building or other enclosure (car, tent, etc.) with the intent to steal or commit certain other crimes.

Camera or recording device in the courtroom The use of media in the courtroom. Attorneys for television and radio broadcasters may petition the court to allow public access to the trial through the media. They will argue the public's right to know what is going on in a public trial. The judge may exclude or restrict the media to avoid making the trial an entertainment event. Reality TV and other media have ongoing presentations because there are a large number of people who watch the trial for entertainment or curiosity.

Case law Decisions made by appellate and supreme courts regarding court and police procedures that have the force and effect of law.

Chemical imbalance A theory that some people commit crime because of chemical ingestion, such as drugs, narcotics, caffeine, or sugar.

Citation A summons issued by a peace officer, ordering the law violator to appear in court to answer to the charges. A traffic citation is a summons.

Civil law Laws of procedure that have sanctions other than fines or imprisonment. Civil laws are known as adjective laws.

Classical theory A crime cause theory originally introduced by Cesare Beccaria, who claimed that criminals weigh the rewards of a crime versus the pain of punishment and make a free choice to commit the crime.

Classification Categorizing an individual or activity in accordance with an established set of criteria, for example, classification of fingerprints involving ridge counts and various other distinctive characteristics.

Commission The act of a person performing a certain behavior that is forbidden by law. He or she is committing a crime of commission.

Common law The early English method of making laws prior to the later legislative procedure of enacting laws and signature by the king. The traveling judge would hear the charge, declare it a law violation, and prescribe the punishment. Other judges would follow the precedent or charge the law and punishment. This process ended during the 11th century.

Community policing Policing that involves all of the community in identifying and seeking methods of addressing problems that adversely affect their quality of life.

Concurrent Sentence   Two jail or prison sentences being served at the same time. A person may be found guilty of two unrelated crimes but sentenced to serve both terms simultaneously.

Conjugal visitation   Some prisons reward married inmates for their good behavior by allowing their spouses to spend a private weekend alone with them in a mobile home or apartment located on a remote part of the prison campus.

Consecutive   One following the other, such as railroad cars passing a stationary spot in sequence. One jail sentence following another is a consecutive sentence.

Consent   To give permission by gesture or vocal statement. If an officer asks a suspect for consent to search his vehicle, for example, the officer must be able to explain in court exactly how the consent was requested and given. It is better to have exact words that can be quoted.

Contempt   An act of disrespect for the court, specifically the judge, either taking place in the courtroom or by refusing to obey a judge's order, such as a subpoena.

Contraband   Something that is unlawfully possessed, such as stolen property in custody of the thief or purchaser who knows (or should reasonably believe) that the property is stolen. Money that a robber takes from a bank is contraband. If the contraband is stolen from the robber by another thief, that is another theft because money is legal property. However, if a drug dealer is in possession of cocaine or peyote, for example, it is contraband that cannot be legally possessed (except, of course, by the police or sheriff's department that is holding it as evidence) and, therefore, cannot be the object of theft. A person who points a gun at a drug dealer and takes a quantity of contraband cocaine is not committing robbery but a lesser crime of pointing a gun in an angry or threatening manner. Of course, you are not likely to get a call from a drug dealer who has been robbed asking for help to recover his or her stolen property.

Controlled substance   Any drug or narcotic that is dangerous to use when not prescribed or when unlawfully used when prescribed in violation of the prescription. If the doctor's directions are to use the pain suppressant once every four hours, substance abuse would be extremely harmful or fatal.

Corporal punishment   Physical punishment, such as spanking or slapping. This practice in prisons in the United States was discontinued in 1948.

Corpus delicti   The body, or elements, of a crime. You must prove each element to establish that the crime was committed. For example, the *corpus delicti* of a theft is the taking, leading, or carrying away of the property of another with the intention to permanently deprive the owner of that property. It would be obvious that the does not intend to return the property if a horse thief were to slaughter the animal and sell the meat to unsuspecting customers. With specific intent crimes such as this, the police must use evidence or testimony to show that the perpetrator had no intention to just borrow the horse to go riding.

Corroboration   Any information or testimony from one source that tends to prove the accuracy or validity of information or testimony from another source. For example, a witness to a robbery sees the event while inside the store and describes the weapon; then another witness sees the robber as he leaves the stores and gets into a 1962 Ford Falcon. The testimony of the two witnesses would corroborate each other.

Criminology   The study of the criminal and sociological implications of crime, causes of crime, and victimology.

Culpable   Directly responsible as the principal perpetrator in a criminal act or omission. The perpetrator will be held to answer to the charges.

Custody   Physical possession of property or legal supervision of an individual, such as a child.

Defamation of character   The slander of a person by speaking falsehoods or libel by printing untruths about another person, knowing that such communications are false and designed to deliberately destroy or damage that person's reputation (or fame). Slander and libel were traditionally unlawful but may still be adjudicated in civil court. In most cases, celebrities and public figures such as politicians and corporate giants are fair game for rumormongers, and little can be done for reparation (except in cases of extremely outlandish and flagrant falsehoods).

Defraud   To cheat, usually by criminal means, such as to present a forged check in exchange for money. A person who sells a used car under the pretense that it is new is defrauding the buyer.

Delinquent act   An act by a child that would be a crime if committed by an adult.

Deposition   The process of a prospective witness being questioned under oath or affirmation to tell the truth, usually conducted in an attorney's office. The witness is subjected to direct questioning and cross-examination as if in court. The purpose of the deposition is to help both sides determine the nature and impact of the testimony in the upcoming trial, which may not be held for months or years in some cases. Sometimes a seriously ill or wounded witness or victim is deposed as to memorialize the testimony for use in the trial in the event that he or she dies or is incapacitated and unable to appear at the trial in person. The deposition may also be used for comparison with statements made during the trial, which may be different than those made at the disposition.

Determinate sentence   The sentence is prescribed by the judge.

Deterrence   A warning or device that discourages a person from committing a crime.

Deviance   Departure from what is normal.

Differential association   A theory by Edwin H. Sutherland that people learn to commit crimes through learning as any other skill.

Diversion   A program that serves as an alternate to jail or prison and diverts the would-be violator away from criminal behavior.

Discovery   The legal process that requires each side in a criminal case to turn over all evidence and data concerning the case.

Discretion   The authority and responsibility to make independent decisions.

Dual sovereignty   A crime that is both a federal and a state law, such as bank robbery, a violation of state robbery laws and the federal bank robbery statute.

Due process   Fair play, according to the rules with respect for the dignity of others.

Duress   Any physical or psychological pressure imposed on a subject under questioning or under arrest to gain a confession or acknowledgment of guilt. Some people are terrified of the police, who present the ultimate moral authority. When an officer even suggests to the subject of a field contact or interrogation that terrible things will happen to him or her for failure to cooperate, all kinds of horrible visions will enter that person's mind. Such an offhand remark as "I guess we'll just have to lock you up until you can cooperate with us" or "Looks like we're going to have to arrest your wife and kids to get to the bottom of this" will work overtime on the imagination of the subject. A statement such as "You help us and we'll help you" or "It will be better for you if you cooperate" will be understood as a promise that the officer will return the favor, while actually the officer has neither the inclination nor authority to do anything but elicit a confession. Positive or negative duress should not be in an officer's repertoire of interviewing or interrogating tactics.

Durham rule   A defense to criminal acts because of a defect of reasoning on the part of the perpetrator.

Entrapment   The inducement by a peace officer or an assigned agent to cause an innocent to commit a crime. If, however, the officer knows a person to be a car thief and sets himself up as a potential buyer to buy a stolen car from the thief, that is operating a sting and is not entrapment.

Evidence   Items or testimony that tends to prove a fact in a criminal case, for example, fingerprints found at the scene of a crime or an eyewitness's identification.

Evidentiary exclusionary rule   The evidence collected by the government (officers, deputies, investigators) in violation of the Constitution that will be excluded and not allowed to be presented during the trial. An otherwise faultless investigation can be totally discredited by an officer's egregious and improper behavior. Consider, for example, what happens when an unreasonable (unconstitutional) search leads to the discovery of a trunk full of illegal narcotics and the officer gets the owner of the car to name his supplier. The original find in the trunk is tainted or poisoned, and the identification of the dealer is "fruit of poisoned tree" and also inadmissible.

Exigent   An exigent circumstance is an unforeseen emergency.

Expectation of privacy   A person's protection from intrusion by the police of one's papers, person, or property ensured by the Fourth Amendment.

Ex post facto   A key phrase meaning "after the fact." For example, a man commits an offensive act—belching in public—in front of someone else, but there is no law on the books that covers such behavior. The offended person goes out and gets several hundred thousand registered voters to sign a petition to get an initiative on the ballot or goes to a legislator who introduces a no-belching bill. It becomes law two months after the offender last belched in public. You cannot get a warrant and arrest the perpetrator for an act he committed when it was not illegal. You have to wait until he belches again and then make the arrest. Changes in laws and procedures are also covered by *ex post facto* provisions. For example, if a person is arrested for a misdemeanor and it is upgraded to a felony by the time she goes to court, the case will still be prosecuted as a misdemeanor. Conversely, if the person is arrested for a felony, which is reduced to a misdemeanor, the case will still be prosecuted as a misdemeanor. As a general rule of thumb, remember that the advantage always goes to the accused.

Extradition   The process by which a person accused of a crime who has fled the state and country where the crime was committed is brought back to the appropriate jurisdiction to answer to the charge and to attend the trial. Although commonly used to describe transportation of the accused back from another state where the accused sought asylum (interstate rendition), the correct application involves a serious felony because of the expense and inconveniences to both countries; the asylum country must have a parallel law. If the suspect is wanted in California for murder and the crime in that state is punishable by death, the asylum country most certainly has homicide laws but may not have the death penalty. There must be an extradition treaty between the United States and the other country that covers the crime. In this case, the California prosecutor would go through the U.S. State Department and demand the asylum country to arrest the fugitive with the assistance of U.S. officers and allow the United States to "extract the accused." If the asylum country has no death penalty, the United States must agree not to ask for or impose the death penalty on the perpetrator when convicted. The court in the asylum country may choose to not allow the extradition, considering the fugitive a welcome guest as long as he or she wishes to stay, or if the accused is a citizen of the asylum country, the government of that country decide to try the accused in court in the asylum country.

Factory survey   A tactic used by immigration officers to visit a workplace and arrest illegal immigrants who are working there.

Fear   An awareness and emotional reaction of anxiety to a situation that causes someone to realize that he or she is in imminent danger of death or injury to self or another person. Fear may be of real or imagined danger, such as fear of the dark or fear of the unknown. In self-defense situations, one must reasonably experience fear of imminent attack in order to respond with the same degree of force anticipated. If one fears that death is an imminent probability, he or she may use deadly force.

Felony   The most serious of the several categories of crimes. The crime of a felony is punishable by death or prison (usually for more than one year) per violation. The sentence imposed may actually not be either death or imprisonment, but it is the maximum allowable.

Fence   A person or establishment that deals in buying and selling stolen property. Some pawnshops and auto repair shops are known to deal in stolen property. Such an auto repair shop might also be known as a "chop shop."

Frisk   A cursory patting down of a subject's outer clothes for weapons and contraband.

Furlough   A temporary release from jail or prison to allow the inmate's sentence for good behavior.

Good faith   Actions by police officers with good intentions, not knowing that the actions are unconstitutional. A good faith exception to a court-made rule may be excused by the court on an individual basis.

Good time   The time an inmate earns and is deducted from an inmate's sentence for good behavior.

Grand jury   A body of citizens who hear testimony and examine evidence to determine whether a person should be charged with a felony.

Habeas corpus   You have the person in your presence, usually following an arrest. The person's attorney is able to locate a judge, who will issue a writ of *habeas corpus,* which commands you to take him or her to court and immediately place formal charges or release the subject without delay and without going through the booking/jailing process. There is no official record of arrest, and fingerprints or photographs are not taken in such a case. In a great many cases, you will arrest people on suspicion that they committed crimes, and you will book and incarcerate them before you have completed your reports and before laboratory analyses have been conducted, much less completed. Back in the "dark ages" of the 1950s and 1960s, officers would sometimes take a suspect in for questioning; when an attorney showed up at the front door of the police station, the officers would take their suspect out the back door and on to another precinct. The service must be at the place where the person is being held, so the attorney would have to go find the location where the person was being held and serve the writ at that location. This was known as holding a suspect incognito. Sometimes, instead of booking an arrestee into the county jail, officers would take the arrestee to the city jail in a nearby city to confuse the press and attorneys. The officers could use this extra time in pre-Miranda days to interrogate and perhaps break the suspect down and get a confession before the attorney could arrive and advise the client to remain silent.

Hate crime   A crime with the additional feature that the motivation included *malice* toward the victim's race, national origin, gender, or sexual orientation.

Immaterial   Of no consequence or importance. Something that does not matter and that has absolutely no probative connection to the case would be immaterial. An example would be that the investigator wore a paisley tie during the investigation. No substance and no material value.

Impaneling the jury   Potential jurors being notified by mail and being required to appear at the court. For each jury trial to be held that day, participants in the pool of summoned person are selected at random and seated in the jury box. After they have all gone through the process known as *voir dire,* the required number of selected jurors make up a panel (usually 12 in some jurisdictions and 6 in others); the judge swears them in and charges them with the duty of hearing the case and eventually agreeing on a verdict. Once they have been impaneled, jeopardy for the defendant attaches.

Impeachment The act of a witness during a trial who admits to or is proven to have a felony record or to lying under oath during previous testimony and claims to be telling the truth now. In this situation, the judge will instruct the jurors that because of the witness being a convicted felon or lying under oath, he or she may or may not be considered by the jury as telling the truth this time (hence the impeachment).

Incapacitation Rending a person incapable of performing a crime in public because he or she is not at liberty to do the act. A burglar is incapacitated while in prison.

Indeterminate sentence The judge sends the guilty person to prison for an indeterminate time, such as 5 to 20 years, then a parole board sets the date when the inmate may be eligible to apply for parole.

Indictment A court process initiated by the prosecuting attorney at the behest of the grand jury that the named suspects should be prosecuted for certain felonies.

Indigent The adjective usually thought of is "poor," but the term applies to all defendants who cannot afford to pay for their legal representation. In the very simple case in which an attorney's service is for only a few hours, many defendants run out of financial resources before their cases have been concluded. At that point, the defense attorney notifies the court that the defendant can no longer pay for his or her own defense and is therefore indigent. The judge then has the option of assigning the case to a public defender, which would probably mean that the whole process would have to start over so that the new attorney could become familiar with the case and provide a competent defense. The judge also has the more acceptable alternative of assigning the current attorney to continue with the defense but at a lower hourly rate of pay. In all complicated cases, all but the wealthy are bound to reach the indigent stage. In a recent California case, two young men were charged with the murder and decapitation of their mother. Their grandmother, the victim's mother, announced to the press she was hiring the best lawyer money could buy, and she did. After a few months (but still long before the trial was to begin), she had used up all of her life savings and had mortgaged her home to the maximum. She then had to declare that she was indigent.

Information A legal document emanating from the lower court directing the prosecutor to take the accused to a superior court for a felony prosecution.

Infraction A minor local or state violation not amounting to a crime that calls for punishment by imprisonment. The penalty is either a line or court expenses with a requirement that a certain action be taken, such as getting a current tax sticker for a vehicle or a business license. Zoning violations (such as a business being operated in a residential area), street vendors without licenses, and other minor problems are solved by issuing a citation for the violation and having the problem rectified.

In loco parentis   In place of parents, for example, a person who has temporary custody with a power of attorney.

Inmate code   The unwritten rules prison or jail inmate must abide by or suffer punishment by other inmates, such as "don't rat on a fellow inmate."

Intake hearings   Hearing at a juvenile intake center to determine whether the juvenile will be required to answer to more formal charges or be released.

Intelligent waiver   The individual understands the wording and implications of the Miranda admonition and freely and voluntarily agrees to talk with the officer.

Intermediate sanctions   Some type of punishment, such as boot camp or counseling, instead of prison or jail.

Interstate rendition   A person wanted for either a felony or a misdemeanor (although this process is used almost exclusively for serious felonies because of the expenses involved) is located in another state where he or she is hiding or seeking asylum, and the agency with jurisdiction where the crime occurred seeks to have the suspect returned for adjudication of the case. The demanding agency must have an outstanding arrest warrant and then go through the governor's office to seek the extradition. If the suspect waives the legal process, the demanding state merely comes and gets him or her, and they return to the court of original jurisdiction. If the accused refuses to return voluntarily, the governor of the demanding state appoints the investigating officer to represent the state. A judge in the asylum state holds a hearing similar to a preliminary hearing, and the officer from the demanding state presents the case. If the asylum state judge determines that the charges are valid, he or she notifies the governor, who authorizes the holding agency to "render up" the accused, and the officer takes him or her back to the demanding state.

Jeopardy   A danger. The Fifth Amendment provides, among other things, "Nor shall any person be subject for the same offense to be twice put in jeopardy of life or limb." When a person has been tried for burglary and found not guilty, he or she can walk out of the courtroom and proclaim, "I committed the perfect crime" without fear of being tried again. If, on the other hand, the jury is "hung," or hopelessly deadlocked, and the judge declares a mistrial, the jeopardy is lifted as though there had been no trial to begin with, and the prosecutor will usually refile charges and repeat the process.

Judicial review   The power of appellate and supreme courts to review the trial courts rulings concerning legal rules or constitutional issues.

Jurisdiction   The legal power and authority to act. There are three types of jurisdiction. (1) Legal authority to enforce federal law is the primary jurisdiction of federal investigative and law enforcement officers. Local city and county officers have secondary legal jurisdiction and can also enforce federal laws. (2) Geographic authority to enforce laws within boundaries, such as city limits or county lines, resides with the resident agency that has primary jurisdiction to enforce local ordinances and state laws. Officers of contiguous agencies may have secondary jurisdiction in other cities or counties in accordance with mutual aid pacts, or agreements. (3) People: An example of jurisdiction over certain people is U.S. government agencies having jurisdiction over U.S. citizens abroad and over U.S. military bases overseas. Another example is that Mexico may prosecute its nationals in Mexican courts for crimes they commit in the United States.

Jury nullification   When the jury agrees on the guilt of the defendant but then agrees to find the defendant not guilty on what they decide to be a matter of fairness. Their decision is final.

Jury of peers   Jurors selected from the same county where the accused is tried in court.

Labeling theory   The theory that if you keep calling a person "bad," he or she will eventually begin living up to the label.

Landmark division   A court ruling that all others in the system use when making their decisions as to how to proceed in investigation, enforcement, prosecution, and rending judgments.

Mala ad prohibitum   An act that is bad because the law makes it so; examples include prostitution, gambling, income tax violations, and other crimes that some people would not consider evil. Some crimes, including certain vice violations, are considered victimless, as well as *mala prohibita*.

Mala in se   An act that is evil in itself, whether or not there is a law forbidding it; examples include rape, robbery, criminal homicide, and embezzlement.

Malicious   To do something with an evil or destructive intent. For example, someone paints graffiti all over a store's newly painted outside wall or punctures the tires or pours sugar in the gas tank of an ex-girlfriend's date. Some crimes require that you prove that the perpetrator performed an act willfully and deliberately rather than by accident. A person may lose control of his or her vehicle because of a mechanical malfunction and run over the neighbor's lawn, destroying the sprinkler system and flower beds. Such an event would not be a malicious act; therefore, it would not be criminally malicious.

Mark system   A system of rewards by Captain Maconochie at the prison colony at Norfolk Island, Australia, in 1840.

Mens rea   An evil mind, such as the mental state one exhibits by deliberately and unlawfully taking another's life without legal justification or provocation. Premeditated murder requires express malice and an evil mind, or mens rea. When one deliberately and maliciously destroys or steals another's property, he or she has criminal intent, or *mens rea.*

Military tribunals   Trials for combatants in Afghanistan currently stationed at Guantánamo Naval Base, Cuba, at the time of this writing.

Misdemeanor   A criminal offense with maximum imprisonment in jail for one year and/or a fine.

Misdemeanor A lesser crime, usually punishable by imprisonment in a city or county jail for one year or less and/or a fine. Although the individual may be jailed for less than a year for each violation, if a person is convicted and sentenced for more than one offense, he or she may serve several years in jail for consecutive misdemeanor sentences.

Mistrial The judge cancels the trial and jeopardy is lifted, which means that the prosecutor may start the process all over again.

Motion A legal offer by a trial participant the particular action be taken, such as a motion for dismissal.

Negligence The failure to take care as an ordinary person would. Every profession or trade has minimum performance standards for every task in its repertoire. If a surgeon performs surgery in a sloppy and careless manner that is obviously below required standards of excellence for the job, the patient may die or suffer a serious injury. In this case, the injury is a result of careless and negligent behavior. If the patient dies, the doctor may be prosecuted for negligent manslaughter, and if he or she has been negligent in the past, the crime may be upgraded to a second-degree murder. The malicious intent and the malice will be implied by the repeated negligent act.

Neoclassical Theories A modern reintroduction of the classical theory of crime with new ideas.

NIBRS Incident-based reporting system. An improvement and expansion of the Uniform Crime Reporting System that is still in the development stage.

Nolle prosequi A decision by the prosecutor that he or she will not go forward with the prosecution.

Nolo contendere A plea of no contest. This has the same effect as a guilty plea, but the person is in effect saying, "I have no defense, so punish me if you will, but I am still not acknowledging guilt." The advantage of using this plea is that if there is a civil case arising out of this criminal action, a guilty plea in a criminal case can be used as evidence against the respondent or defendant in the civil matter, whereas a plea of *nolo contendere* cannot be used in that case as an acknowledgment of responsibility for the act. The person who pleads *nolo contendere* could go to jail for the crime but be exonerated in the civil trial.

Omission The failure to perform a specific act required by law. Examples include not stopping to render aid, not reporting a collision when people are injured, and failing to provide financial support for a wife or child. All these are crimes of omission, or failures to act.

Ordinance A city or county law enacted by a city or town council or county board of supervisors. These laws are of lesser rank than felonies and most misdemeanors and are usually in the infraction category. Ordinances usually involve local matters, such as building and safety codes, business licenses, zoning regulations, and a variety of other matters unique to the local government and the community. For example, the state laws on disturbance of the peace cover the general restrictions against loud noises, but a city may prohibit trash trucks and construction machinery from being operated between the hours of 10 p.m. or 11 p.m. and 6 a.m.

Organized crime Any concerted criminal activity by two or more people to commit crime as a regular activity. Not only is the Mafia classified as organized crime, but so are criminal street gangs, such as the MS-13 Mara Salvatrucha.

Overt act An act in furtherance of a crime. For the overt act of arson, once the conspirators agree on a plan, then one or more of them must go out and buy a gallon of gasoline to start a fire; for robbery, they must acquire a gun with which to commit the act. Mere agreement to commit a crime does not constitute a conspiracy; the agreement must be followed by the overt act.

Parens patrie The principle that juveniles are the ultimate wards of the state as parent if the natural parents do not fulfill their legal obligations. For example, a parent who denies medical cancer treatment for her 13-year-old son will be overridden by a juvenile judge who may declare the child a ward of the court and authorize the treatment.

Parole Conditional release from prison for remainder of a sentence on condition of good behavior.

Perjury An act of willfully giving false testimony in court or presenting sworn statements purported to be true at a deposition or in an affidavit with the intention to lead to a false result. This is also known as lying under oath.

Perpetrator The principal actor in a criminal activity as well as anyone else who participates and whose role significantly affects the outcome. The driver, or "wheelman," and the lookouts who do not actually enter the building to confront the robbery victims are coprincipals, or accomplices, and they are all perpetrators. Once identified and charged, the perpetrator becomes the defendant.

Plain touch Same as plain sight, where the person becomes aware of an object's presence by mere touch, and not as a result of a search.

"Plain view" doctrine The principle that an officer may seize what he or she sees in plain sight without having to get a search warrant.

Plea negotiation Bargaining between defense attorney and the prosecutor to get the best deal possible in exchange for a guilty plea, for example, reduction of sentence for one crime, or punishment for fewer offenses than the number changed, or reduction of the charge from felony to misdemeanor.

Police brutality Abuse of authority by a peace officer by inflicting unnecessary punishment when other means of control are possible.

Posse comitatus The power of the county, which empowers an officer to call on a private person to assist in a police action and giving that person the authority to act with the officer]s authority while under the direct supervision of that officer.

Possession Something you own. For a person to be in possession of stolen property, he or she must have it in close proximity. An employee may be said to be in possession of the employer's property when it is taken in a robbery. For a drug user or dealer to be in possession of contraband, it must be on his or her person or in the immediate proximity, such as in a vehicle or building.

Postmortem exam   An autopsy. A postmortem exam is a medical analysis by a pathologist to determine the nature and cause of someone's death.

Precedent   The preceding case used as authority for making current decisions in arrest, search, and prosecution and for deciding admissibility of evidence. If you have older brothers and/or sisters, haven't your parents made decisions about your dating or other coming-of-age activities based on how they handled the situation previously with your older brothers and/or sisters? Some parents make decisions based on how they were allowed to behave when they were your age.

Preliminary hearing   The court session at which the prosecution presents proof of a felony crime (*corpus delicti*) before a judge and then presents sufficient proof, through witnesses and evidence, to convince the judge (1) that the crime charged was committed and (2) that there is a preponderance of evidence that points to the accused. The judge then directs the prosecutor to proceed to the next step, holding the accused to answer to the charges alleged. The judge directs the prosecutor to file an information in the court with the charges.

Preponderance   The majority (more than half). In a civil case, the plaintiff has to convince the judge or jury that he or she has more than half of the proof to win the case. In a criminal preliminary hearing, the prosecution has to prove conclusively to the satisfaction of the judge that the crime was committed; then it only needs to prove with a preponderance of evidence that the accused should be held to answer to the charges. Later, during the trial, of course, proof of guilt must be beyond a reasonable doubt.

Presentence investigation   Background investigation by a probation officer to aid the judge in prescribing the sentence.

Prima facie   A first sight (what something appears to be when first encountered). An officer may respond to a dead body call, and the deceased is hanging with a necktie around his neck; it appears that the man was murdered, but when the officer investigates further, he or she determines that the death is a suicide, or possibly an accidental death by someone playing the choking game. Or, at an alleged burglary scene, the officer's first impression is that a stranger broke the window to gain entry. On further examination, the officer may find the owner of the establishment, who had lost her keys and had broken the window to get in and recover her keys, inside, or the officer may also discover a body and determine that his or her first impression was correct except that now it's a burglary and a murder.

Principal   The perpetrator of a crime. Principals also include all others who may not play the leading role but who substantially participate in planning, preparation, and counsel; they may advise the others in such a way that it affects the result, or consummation, of the crime. A gang of eight principals may plan a crime (a conspiracy) and decide how the spoils will be divided, who will actually go the scene, who will serve as drivers and lookouts, and how they will make their escape. If three of the eight actually go into the store to rob the clerk and one shoots and kills the clerk, all eight will be equally charged with the robbery/murder.

Privileged communication A private and legally protected confidential communication. The communication can be between attorney and client, clergy and confessor, husband and wife, and doctor or psychiatrist and patient. An exception to the spouse privilege is when the victim of the other or their children are the victims. Also, doctor–patient confidence does not apply in criminal matters, where medical professionals are required by law to report gunshot wounds and violent traumatic injuries.

Probable cause Sufficient basis for an arrest or a search. Usually follows what may have started as a reasonable suspicion.

Probation A second chance, prescribed by the judge as an alternative to jail or prison. A diversion from the system.

Proximate cause The act that leads to the results. For example, a bullet fired at the victim is the proximate cause of the fatal injury. Sometimes you may use the term "but for" when explaining this cause-and-effect relationship between one act and the ultimate result: But for the arsonist setting fire to the building, the occupant would not have burned to death. A rapist may place his hand over his victim's mouth, causing her to drown in her own regurgitation; therefore, but for the rape, the victim would not have thrown up and died. Although the rapist had absolutely no intention or desire that his victim die, he is responsible for her death. In this case he will be prosecuted for murder.

Psychoanalytic theory A theory that some people may commit crimes because of some psychological abnormality. Sigmund Freud opined that a person who has yet to develop a superego is more likely to be tempted to yield to temptation to violate the law.

Racial profile An illegal procedure where suspects for search are singled out exclusively because of their heritage or physical appearance.

Recidivist A repeat criminal. In cases such as the three-time loser, the person is seen in and out of jail as though the jail has a revolving door. No sooner is the subject released at the end of a sentence than he or she is returning, usually for the same crime.

Rehabilitation A program or practice to help the violator to change his or her attitude and behavior and live a crime-free life.

Reintegration A plan or program to introduce the convict back into society following and period of incarceration.

Remand To send back. A judge remands, or send back, the defendant to a psychiatrist to determine whether he or she is competent to stand trial; a juvenile court judge remands a juvenile to adult court when the judge decides that the accused should be tried as an adult. If the accused is found not guilty by reason of insanity, the judge will remand him or her to a mental institution for treatment.

Res gestae   The totality of the event. For example, when a robber leaves the premises and jumps into a waiting car and the police officer arrives on the scene at the same time and follows that car, the chase is still part of the robbery. During the chase, the suspect vehicle collides with another vehicle, and three people die in the collision. The escape and the collision are part of the *res gestae* of the robbery, and the deaths are the direct result of the crime and will be prosecuted as criminal homicide. Statements the suspects make during a robbery, and statements made by the suspect, are not covered by the *Miranda* rule.

Restitution   Payment to the crime victims as reimbursement for their financial loss. Often prescribed as a condition of probation.

Retribution   Getting even with the violator by punishing on behalf of the victim.

Rule of four   Four justices of the U.S. Supreme Court must agree to hear an appeal to that body for review.

Sanctions   Punishments in the form of fines, imprisonment, community service, or removal from public office, and others.

Sequestration   The jury is locked up in a hotel or motel for the duration of a trial when not in court to reduce their opportunities to be influenced by what goes on around them in public, in the paper, television, and radio.

Social disorganization   The theory that if a person cannot live the American dream through legitimate means, the individual may yield to crime to live that dream.

Solicitation   The offer of goods or services, such as an offer to pay another person to commit a crime or to participate in a sex act.

Stare decisis   To use previous cases as an authority for making the current decision. In law, we depend on tradition and stability to a great extent. In court at a pretrial motion, the defense may challenge the constitutionality of some action of a police officer during an investigation. For example, the suspect may spontaneously blurt out statements that are self-incriminatory before questioning has begun and before the officer has had an opportunity to advise the suspect of his Miranda rights against self-incrimination. Attorneys for both sides will argue why the statements are—or are not—admissible. They use examples (precedents of previous cases decided by various appellate courts) to support their point of view. The judge hears all arguments; then, with the assistance of his or her law clerks, the judge will study all cases with similar circumstances, a process known as *stare decisis* (literally, to look at earlier decisions). Sometimes times and circumstances change, and the judge and appellate court will establish their own priorities, which are then used as precedents for future cases.

Status offense   A delinquent act that is not a crime if committed by an adult.

Statutory law   Laws that are written and legal.

Strain theory   A product of social disorganization, the theory is that the strain of failure and being in a downward spiral will tempt the individual to turn to criminal activity for financial success.

Struck jury A jury of fewer than the normal number of jurors. Federal courts and the various state and local courts have established standard sizes for their juries; the number is usually 6 or 12 (but sometimes 8). When a jury is selected for a trial that is expected to last for more than a few hours or days, the court will select a few alternates who will sit through the trial outside the jury box and will be selected at random if one of the seated jurors falls ill or for some other reason has to be excused; rather than the judge declaring a mistrial and starting over, the alternate takes the place of the excused juror. Sometimes there are no alternates left from which to choose a replacement. By stipulation (which means by agreement of the judge and both prosecution and defense), a juror may be released from duty, leaving the jury with less than the standard number of jurors, which results in a struck jury.

Subpoena An order by the court to appear in court to testify as a witness. Although the subpoena is signed by a magistrate and failure to appear is punishable by contempt of court (which is prescribed by the judge in the form of incarceration in jail and/or a monetary fine), the document originates with the attorney for the prosecutor defense. As a police officer, you will usually get your subpoena from the prosecuting attorney because you will be expected to testify for the prosecution and to present evidence in the case. There are times when you may be subpoenaed by the defense because you have uncovered evidence that may be favorable to the defense attorney) that you will hostile to the defense because of your police officer status. Actually, however, your advocacy should be only for the truth and not for one side or the other. The attorneys approach the case as competitors, being on one side or the other, but you should not choose sides.

Substantive law A law that prescribes or proscribes certain behavior and that has punishment attached for the violator. All felonies, misdemeanors, and infractions are substantive laws.

Supermax The ultimately secure maximum security prisons.

Suspended sentence The judge prescribes the sentence, then suspends it and releases the sentenced person on condition to deliver a political or religious message.

Terrorism Criminal activity to terrorize a great number of people to deliver a political or religious message.

True bill (*vere dictum*) An indictment for someone's prosecution. When a grand jury weighs the evidence in a criminal case presented by the prosecuting attorney and votes that the perpetrators should be prosecuted, they render a true bill (the origin of the word "verdict" or *vere dictum*). They direct the prosecutor to file an indictment charging the perpetrator with the crime.

Truth in sentencing When federal courts send a person to prison for a specified period of time that person will serve almost the complete sentence with only a small portion of early release. In other words, "ten years in prison means ten years."

Uniform Crime Reports Collected and disseminated by the FBI, this has been the most reliable source of crime statistics in the United States continuously since 1930.

Venire A panel of several citizens summoned to the court from which a jury will be selected.

Venue The place where the trial is to be held. The venue may correspond with the jurisdiction, but the venue may be changed while the jurisdiction will not be changed. For example, if a crime is committed in Orange County, Florida, the court jurisdiction for the trial will be Orange County. If the defense argues successfully that there should be a change of venue, the trial will be held in another county in Florida, but the jurisdiction will still remain with Orange County, the local office or sheriff, and the Orange County prosecutor and Orange County public defender.

Verdict The declaration of guilty or not guilty by a judge or jury at the conclusion of a criminal trial. You notice that we do not use the term "innocent" but rather "not guilty."

Viable Capable of living. In a case involving an unborn fetus, the question of viability is an issue. At some point, usually during the second trimester between four and six months (about midway through the pregnancy), the unborn child will have developed to the point where he or she would survive as a whole person if given the chance. A premature baby, for example, is viable and developed to the extent that its circulatory and respiratory systems function with the help of the incubator and its accessories. A viable fetus in most states would be the victim of a homicide if his or her life were terminated before birth, but a legal abortion prior to that stage in development when the fetus had not reached the stage of viability would not be an unlawful termination (in legal terms). A woman who is eight months' pregnant, for example, would be the first homicide victim; if the unborn child also dies, he or she becomes the second victim, resulting in a multiple murder. In a case in which the murder victim is two months' pregnant and her unborn fetus also dies, it would a single homicide.

Vigilantes A nonauthorized group of people who choose to distribute justice through riotous and unlawful means, such as a lynch mob.

Voir dire The process whereby the judge and attorneys for the prosecution and defense question prospective jurors to determine their qualifications to serve. A prospective juror could be disqualified by stating "I have already made up my mind because the defendant wouldn't be sitting over there if he wasn't guilty." A person who states that under no circumstances would he or she vote for the death penalty could be disqualified in a capital case in which the jury may have to consider death or life without possibility of parole in the event they find the person guilty. *Voir dire* also applies to qualifications of a witness as an expert, who may express opinions in matters of his or her expertise. A child may be examined by a judge to determine *voir dire* whether there is a question about the child's attention span or knowledge of the difference between right and wrong.

Willfully Doing something deliberately. A willful act is done by a person who is awake and aware of what he or she is doing, and the person is doing whatever it is because of a positive willingness or readiness to perform it. The person has made an independent and willing individual choice to perform the act.